ROCKET
ENGLISH
GRAMMAR

ROCKET ENGLISH GRAMMAR

CARL W. HART

Two Harbors Press
212 3rd Avenue North, Suite 290
Minneapolis, MN 55401
612.455.2293
www.TwoHarborsPress.com

Please visit *rocketenglish.info* to share comments, to ask questions, to learn how to buy an electronic version of this book or to learn more about online courses taught by Carl W. Hart

ISBN-13: 978-1-938690-21-1
LCCN: 2012947234

Distributed by Itasca Books

Printed in the United States of America

CONTENTS

Contents

INTRODUCTION

To the teacher

Rocket English Grammar is not just another English grammar book. It is an affordable, intensive, effective, comprehensive, fast-paced, fun, basic-to-advanced, one-volume English grammar book which is ideal for students at every level—from beginners (and especially false beginners) to advanced students.

A key rationale of *Rocket English Grammar* is that it enable students to make fast progress and reach new heights quickly and affordably—not just beginner and low-intermediate students but also high-intermediate and advanced students who often never reach the advanced grammar taught in the last and highest-level book of a three-book grammar series. And why don't they? Because the books are simply too long and too expensive.

Rocket English Grammar is a condensed and lower-priced alternative to these books, <u>but it is more than that</u>—*Rocket English Grammar* explores essential aspects of English grammar (some frequently overlooked) with innovative, efficient, classroom-tested approaches <u>that work</u>. *Rocket English Grammar*'s inductive methodology and student-friendy format will engage and motivate students.

Rocket English Grammar is a valuable resource for students at every level (including high-intermediate and advanced students). Many aspects of advanced grammar are discussed in <u>greater depth</u> here than they are in other far longer and more expensive English grammar books.

Two of the 20 units in *Rocket English Grammar* focus on aspects of English grammar which are very important yet are often given insufficient attention. One is *have got* (and *have got to*). *Have got* is a highly idiomatic and very common element of the English lexicon. And because it is very common, it is very important to students. I have therefore focused an entire unit on *have got* (and *have got to*) rather than simply include it with other phrasal modals in one of the two modal units.

Another unit focuses on phrasal verbs—also very common and also often highly idiomatic. Most important is that students learn the meanings of phrasal verbs, and there is a very good book for that*, but because the grammar of phrasal verbs is a bit tricky, I have focused one unit entirely on phrasal verbs—how they are sometimes separable, how they can sometimes be used as adjectives and how they can sometimes be used as nouns.

Other aspects of English grammar—very important but often given little attention by other grammar books—are covered thoroughly in *Rocket English Grammar*. Among them are the emphatic *do* and (especially) ellipsis. Several units have an entire section which focuses on ellipsis with many examples and many exercises. Modals are covered in greater depth than in many other grammar books; the special focus on how *should* and *ought to* are used to make predictions based on previous knowledge or experience is a unique feature of *Rocket English Grammar*. Also, the phrasal modal *be to*—very common in formal English but seldom if ever mentioned in grammar books—is discussed. Gerunds and conditional sentences are covered in considerable depth.

Another unique feature of *Rocket English Grammar* is that 16 of the 20 units have a special advanced section. This makes *Rocket English Grammar* a basic-to-advanced book all in one volume. Students and teachers can choose to continue on to the advanced sections or come back to them later. This will allow students and teachers alike to formulate a plan of instruction based on who they are, what they need and how much time they have. Every teacher will have a different opinion regarding what should or should not be in these advanced sections. My decisions were based on two factors—degree of difficulty, of course, but also to what degree I considered the grammar essential.

In many exercises, one or two questions will be deliberately especially challenging. In these cases, and others, advice is given in the Answer Key as to which section to refer to for clarification. Because the focus of *Rocket English Grammar* is grammar, I have limited the difficulty of the vocabulary in the exercises. I do not want a class to come to a halt while time is wasted discussing the meaning of a strange and unimportant word or the pronunciation of a difficult and unimportant name in an exercise. Every teacher has had this happen. I have also avoided what I and many teachers consider to be certain kinds of unproductive and needlessly time-consuming exercises—the kinds of exercises that teachers generally skip because there is no time, they're not worth the effort or because the teacher cannot make any more sense out of them than the student. I want all the exercises in *Rocket English Grammar* to be <u>doable</u>—doable in the classroom and doable at home. I welcome comments and suggestions.

To the student

Rocket English Grammar will teach you English fast and save you money. I want you to make fast progress. That is why I gave this book the name *rocket*. Rockets move very fast from a low level to a high level, and with *Rocket English Grammar* and your hard work, <u>you will too</u>.

There is a lot of grammar in *Rocket English Grammar*—as much as (and sometimes more than) in three grammar books combined—basic, intermediate and advanced—*each* costing more than *Rocket English Grammar*. What is <u>not</u> in *Rocket English Grammar* are things that slow you down: exercises that don't make sense and waste your time, pictures and white space on pages that just make the book longer (and more expensive) but do not teach you anything.

Rocket English Grammar can be used as a classroom text, used with a tutor or used independently. The focus of *Rocket English Grammar* is <u>grammar</u>—not vocabulary, not listening, not writing, not conversation. But don't forget, improving your grammar will help make your English better in <u>every</u> way.

Using *Rocket English Grammar* is like being in my classroom. Each section is organized the way I would teach my class. The examples I give you in **DISCOVER** are what I would write on the board. The questions I ask you in **DISCOVER** are the questions I would ask you in the classroom. These questions are designed to <u>make you think</u>—to help you <u>teach yourself</u>. This way of teaching <u>works</u>. It's also more fun and more interesting. Please do not skip the **DISCOVER** questions. Think about them yourself and discuss them with your classmates. The thinking you do when you try to answer the **DISCOVER** questions will make understanding what is explained in **LEARN** easier.

In **LEARN** I explain grammar the same way I would explain it to you in the classroom. I have tried to keep the language simple, but sometimes that isn't easy to do. But often what you figured out in **DISCOVER** and what you see in the examples in **LEARN** (and there are <u>many</u> examples) will be enough for you to understand.

And what I tell you in **REMEMBER** is what I would tell you in the classroom <u>after</u> the main lesson—reminders of key points that we just talked about in **LEARN**, reminders of important points that we talked about in previous lessons that I don't want you to forget, additional information that is useful and interesting but did not need to be in **LEARN** and <u>most important</u>, answers to questions that I know you often ask (or should ask), help with problems that I know you often have and corrections for the mistakes that I know you often make.

And in **Practice,** lots and lots of exercises. Because I want you to focus on grammar, I have tried to keep the vocabulary in the exercises simple. The exercises usually start out easy but get more difficult. Sometimes there will be more than one possible correct answer. I will tell you when this is true, and I will remind you to be ready to explain your answer. And because good teachers like to make their students laugh once in a while, I have occasionally had a bit of fun in the exercises.

Carl W. Hart
carlwhart@rocketenglish.info

The Ultimate Phrasal Verb Book by Carl W. Hart

Unit 1 ▶ be

1.1 ▶ present affirmative with *be*

DISCOVER

    a   *I **am** happy.*

    b   *You **are**/We **are**/They **are** happy.*

    c   *He **is**/She **is** happy.*

  1   What are the present forms of *be*?

LEARN (See Table 1a and Table 1b.)

▶ There are three forms of *be* in the present: *am*, *are* and *is*.

1a

present forms of *be*	
I	*am*
You/We/They	*are*
He/She/It	*is*

▶ When we combine two words to make one word, we call the one word a *contraction*.

1b

common contractions of present forms of *be*	
contraction with pronouns and *be*	contractions of nouns and *be* (examples)
I am = I'm *you are = you're* *he is = he's* *she is = she's* *it is = it's* *we are = we're* *they are = they're*	*John is = John's* *the car is = the car's* nouns + *are* (It is not common to make contractions with nouns and *are*.)

REMEMBER

▶ It is never necessary to use contractions, but it is necessary to understand them.

▶ *You* is singular <u>and</u> plural. There is no difference.

    ***You** are **a** teacher.*

    ***You** are teacher**s**.*

Practice 1 Complete the sentences with the correct present form of *be*.

  Examples: We _____*are*_____ tired.

             The doctor _____*is*_____ in the lab.

  1   I _____ the boss.

  2   They _____ watching TV.

  3   We _____ helped by our teacher every day.

  4   The book _____ there.

  5   Mary and Sarah _____ at the beach.

  6   My cat _____ fat.

  7   The boys _____ playing.

  8   The children _____ hungry.

  9   Michael and he _____ mechanics.

10   Coffee _____ grown in Brazil.

11   Today _____ Monday.

12   I _____ reading.

Practice 2 Write sentences with contractions.

Examples: We are working.

We're working.

The soup is cold.

The soup's cold.

1   She is angry.

2   I am on the phone.

3   They are watching TV.

4   The door is open.

5   We are here.

6   Her mother is a pilot.

7   Michael is in the library.

8   They are there.

9   Arabic is spoken in Egypt.

10   We are teachers.

Practice 3 Write sentences with the correct present form of *be*. Use <u>common</u> contractions if it is possible. (Review Table 1b.)

Examples: a bird/in the tree

A bird's in the tree.

the men/eating

The men are eating.

1   the children/playing in the park

2   Francesca/doing her homework

3   dinner/served at 7:00

4   I/listening to the radio

5   the students/studying

6   Tom and Jerry/in the kitchen

7   Larry/here

8   the girl/tall

9   the boys/short

10   my children and I/at the beach

1.2 ▶ present negative with *be*

DISCOVER

    a   *I **am not** working.*

    b   *You **are not**/We **are not**/They **are not** working.*

    c   *He **is not**/She **is not** working.*

1   How do we make present negative sentences with *be*?

LEARN (See Table 1c.)

▶ We put *not* after present forms of *be* to make the sentences negative.

  *Lucy **is** at the mall.*

    → *Lucy **is not** at the mall.*

▶ It is possible to make contractions with *is, are* and *not* in two ways.

1c					
contractions of present forms of *be* and *not*					
I am not	=	I'm not			
you are not	=	you're not	=	you aren't	
he is not	=	he's not	=	he isn't	
she is not	=	she's not	=	she isn't	
it is not	=	it's not	=	it isn't	
we are not	=	we're not	=	we aren't	
they are not	=	they're not	=	they aren't	

Practice 4 Write sentences with contractions. Write all possible contractions.

Example:　　She is not watching TV.

　　　　　　She's not watching TV.

　　　　　　She isn't watching TV.

1　They are not outside.

2　The doctor is not at the clinic.

3　You and I are not playing.

4　The windows are not washed every day.

5　She is not listening.

6　He is not an engineer.

7　I am not hungry.

8　She is not from Holland.

9　Tobacco is not sold to people under 18.

Practice 5 Change the sentences to negative. Write all possible contractions.

Example:　　Mary is inside.

　　　　　　Mary's not inside.

　　　　　　Mary isn't inside.

▶ *be*

1   The pencil is on the table.

2   John is a student.

3   We are in front of the supermarket.

4   The men are singing.

5   Michael is here.

6   I'm finished.

7   He's in bed.

8   They're here.

9   It's cold outside.

10 We're next.

Practice 6 Write negative sentences with the correct present form of *be*. Write all possible contractions.

Example: she/a student

She's not a student.

She isn't a student.

1   I/eating breakfast

2   Mark/reading a book

3   the projects/finished

4   she/here

5   the book/under the magazine

6   he and I/mechanics

7   Carlos and Alex/going to school

8   English/spoken in France

9   you/washing the car

10   he and Sofia/married

1.3 ▶ present questions with *be*

DISCOVER

a   ***Am*** *I happy?*
b   ***Are*** *you/**Are** we/**Are** they happy?*
c   ***Is*** *he/**Is** she happy?*

1   How do we make questions with *be* in the present?

LEARN

▶ We put *be* before the subject to make present questions.

   The store is *open.* → ***Is the store*** *open?*
   subject   *be*   *be*   subject

Practice 7 Write answers to the questions with the correct present form of *be*. Use contractions.

Example: Is Alex playing soccer?

   Yes, _____*Alex is playing soccer*_____ .

1   Is the pilot sleeping?

   Yes, _____.

2   Is Ali in the library?

   No, _____.

3   Are the soldiers fighting?

   Yes, _____.

4   Are Toyotas made in Japan?

   Yes, _____.

5   Is her sister here?

   No, _____.

6   Is Sarah an artist?

   Yes, _____.

7   Is Larry tired?

   No, _____.

8   Is the truck driven by Sam?

   No, _____.

9   Are John and Alex hungry?

   Yes, _____.

10   Are the kids in the car?

   No, _____.

Practice 8 Change the sentences to questions.

Example: The car is in the garage.

Is the car in the garage?

1 The cats are under the sofa.

2 Carlos is tired.

3 Tom and his wife are in the gym.

4 You and John are working hard.

5 The house is dirty.

6 They are cheap.

7 Larry is a sailor.

8 The restaurant is near the park.

9 Mark and Sarah are at work.

10 She is correct.

11 The pizza is in the oven.

1.4 ▶ past affirmative with *be*

DISCOVER

a I **was**/He **was**/She **was** angry.

b You **were**/We **were**/They **were** angry.

1 What are the past forms of *be*?

LEARN (See Table 1d.)

▶ There are two forms of *be* in the past: *was* and *were*.

1d
past forms of *be*

I	*was*
He/She/It	*was*
You/We/They	*were*

Practice 9 Complete the sentences with the correct past form of *be*.

Example: Mary _____was_____ here yesterday.

1 The car _____ very expensive.

2 Sofia and her sister _____ doing their homework.

3 That _____ a good movie.

4 They _____ in the lab one hour ago.

5 The book _____ here.

6 My children _____ there yesterday.

7 Rosa _____ playing tennis all day.

8 He _____ at the mall.

9 The book _____ written by me.

10 Sarah _____ here a few minutes ago.

11 Sam and Lucy _____ waiting for the train.

Practice 10 Write sentences with the correct past form of *be*.

Example: Tom and Jerry / at the mall

   Tom and Jerry were at the mall.

1   Noura / dancing

2   the coffee / hot

3   the men / truck drivers

4   the house / sold

5   my parents / there

6   Francesca / drawing a picture

7   they / sick

8   Michael / on the corner

9   your wife / cleaning

10   the people / outside

1.5 ▶ past negative with *be*

DISCOVER

a   *I **was not**/He **was not**/She **was not** angry.*
    = *I **wasn't**/He **wasn't**/She **wasn't** angry.*

b   *You **were not**/We **were not**/They **were not** angry.*
    = *You **weren't**/We **weren't**/They **weren't** angry.*

1   How do we make negative sentences with *be* in the past?

LEARN (See Table 1e.)

▶ We put *not* after past forms of *be* to make negative sentences.
   *Lucy **was** at the mall.*
   → *Lucy **was** **not** at the mall.*

▶ It is possible to make contractions with present forms of *be* and *not*.

1e

contractions of past forms of *be* and *not*		
I was not	=	*I wasn't*
we were not	=	*we weren't*
he was not	=	*he wasn't*
she was not	=	*she wasn't*
it was not	=	*it wasn't*
you were not	=	*you weren't*
they were not	=	*they weren't*

Practice 11 Write sentences with contractions.

Example: They were not swimming.

   They weren't swimming.

1   I was not upstairs.

2   The women were not at the party.

3   She and I were not angry.

4   My house was not clean.

5   Maria was not a secretary.

6   The sick man was not taken to the hospital.

▶ *be*

7   The boys were not playing basketball.

8   We were not shopping.

9   The cat was not behind the sofa.

10 The guy was not there.

11 We were not swimming in the lake.

12 The salad was not eaten.

Practice 12 **Change the sentences to negative. Use contractions.**

Example: Tom was sick.

Tom wasn't sick.

1   John and Mark were in the bank.

2   The keys were in my pocket.

3   I was talking on the telephone.

4   Her car was stolen.

5   Our father was cutting the grass.

6   We were cooking dinner.

7   The book was on the desk.

8   She was a good student.

9   The window was broken.

10 Alex was downstairs.

11 She was with her friends.

Practice 13 **Write negative sentences with the correct past form of *be*. Use contractions.**

Example: the car/in the garage

The car wasn't in the garage.

1   my friends/at the game

2   John/taking a test

3   the letters/sent yesterday

4   I/happy

5   Gary/riding a horse

6   the door/locked

7   the cake/made with flour

8   Carlos/ready

9   I/doing my homework

10 the pens/in the desk

11 the show/over

12 we/done

1.6 ▶ past questions with *be*

DISCOVER

a   ***Was*** I/***Was*** he/***Was*** she angry?

b   **Were** you/**Were** we/**Were** they angry?

1   How do we make questions with *be* in the past?

LEARN

▶ We put *be* before the subject to make past questions:

The children were *sleeping.* → **Were the children** *sleeping?*
   subject   *be*   *be*   subject

Practice 14 **Write answers to the questions with the correct past form of *be*. Use contractions.**

Example: A: Were the boys in the library working?

            B: No, _the boys in the library weren't working_.

1   A: Was the party fun?

   B: Yes, _____.

2   A: Were John and Michael at the meeting?

   B: No, _____.

3   A: Were the students listening to the teacher?

   B: Yes, _____.

4   A: Was the doctor in the clinic?

   B: No, _____.

5   A: Was the movie good?

   B: No, _____.

6   A: Were Mary and her friend playing outside?

   B: Yes, _____.

7   A: Was Linda riding her bicycle?

   B: No, _____.

8   A: Were the women there?

   B: No, _____.

9   A: Was Larry drinking milk?

   B: Yes, _____.

10   A: Were the sandwiches made by you?

   B: Yes, _____.

Practice 15 **Change the sentences to questions.**

Example: The pencils were on the table.

           Were the pencils on the table?

1   Sofia and her sister were sleeping.

2   The calculator was on the table.

3   His father was a police officer.

4   The men were late.

5   The cookies were eaten by the children.

6   They were running.

7   The baby was crying.

▶ ***be***

8   The mechanic was fixing the car.

9   John was speaking Chinese.

10   Ali was reading a book.

11   The criminal was caught by the police.

Practice 16 Change the sentences from present to past.

Example: Are you busy?

Were you busy?

1   Michael is washing the dishes.

2   It's not here.

3   We're angry.

4   Are the girls in the classroom?

5   Is Tom riding his bicycle?

6   They're not there.

7   Sarah isn't in the house.

8   I'm not doing my homework.

9   They aren't eating lunch.

10   Is Noura talking to her friend?

Practice 17 Change the sentences from past to present.

Example: Mary wasn't playing tennis.

Mary isn't playing tennis.

1   Were you at the beach?

2   Maria wasn't in the hospital.

3   Three boys were outside.

4   Was the bird flying?

5   Were Tom and Lucy married?

6   She wasn't reading in the library.

7   Was the boy swimming?

8   The car was parked in the garage.

9   Larry wasn't at work.

10   My classes were boring.

11   She was mopping the floor.

1.7 ▶ short answers

DISCOVER

    a   John: *Is Maria at the bank?*
    b   Lucy: **Yes, Maria is at the bank.**
    c   John: *What did you say?*
    d   Lucy: **Yes, she is.**

1   Look at *b* and *d*. Is their meaning the same?

    e   Tom: *Were the students taking a test?*
    f   Alex: **No, the students weren't taking a test.**

g   Tom: *What?*

h   Alex: **No, they weren't.**

2   Look at *f* and *h*. Is their meaning the same?

LEARN

▶ It is common in conversation to answer questions with short answers which contain a form of *be*.

Sarah: *Were the girls playing in the park?*

John: **No, they weren't.**

Sarah: *Were the boys playing in the park?*

John: **Yes, they were.**

Contractions are used <u>only in negative</u> short answers.

Tom: *Is your mother a teacher?*

Sam: *No,* **she's not.**

Tom: *Is your father a teacher.*

Sam: *Yes,* **he is.**

wrong → Yes, **I'm.**   right → Yes, **I am.**

wrong → Yes, **you're.**   right → Yes, **you are.**

wrong → Yes, **he's.**   right → Yes, **he is.**

wrong → Yes, **she's.**   right → Yes, **she is.**

wrong → Yes, **it's.**   right → Yes, **it is.**

wrong → Yes, **we're.**   right → Yes, **we are.**

wrong → Yes, **they're.**   right → Yes, **they are.**

Practice 18 Answer the questions with short answers in the correct tense. Use contractions only in negative short answers. Use only subject pronouns in the answers (*I, he, she, it, we* and *they*).

Examples: A: Is the girl a good student?

B: Yes, _____ she is _____.

A: Are Mary and Gary married?

B: No, _____ they're not _____.

1   A: Are you hungry?

B: Yes, _____.

2   A: Were Tom and you playing football?

B: No, _____.

3   A: Was the test easy?

B: Yes, _____.

4   A: Was your sister at the supermarket?

B: No, _____.

5   A: Are the boys good students?

B: Yes, _____.

6   A: Is Sarah your sister?

B: No, _____.

7   A: Is the car in the garage?

B: Yes, _____.

8   A: Were Carlos and Alex here?

B: No, _____.

9   A: Are you and your friend from Chicago?

B: No, _____.

10 A: Was Henry eaten by a shark?

B: Yes, _____.

Continue to Unit 1/advanced ↓ or go to Unit 2 →

1.8/a ▶ uses of *be*

DISCOVER

a They **are sick**.
b She **is here**.
c She **is a doctor**.
d He **is in the kitchen**.
e I **am working**.
f French and English **are spoken** in Canada.

1 Look at these ways to use *be*. How are they different?

LEARN

▶ *Be* is used in the following ways. (Continuous is explained in Unit 2. The passive is explained in Unit 15.)

adjectives →	Michael **is tall**.
adverbs →	He **was there**.
nouns →	I **was a pilot**.
prepositional phrases →	The cat **is under the bed**.
continuous →	Larry **is eating**.
passive →	My car **was made** in Germany.

Practice 19/a Match the uses of *be* with the examples.

1 Mary was busy. _a_

2 The book is on the table. _____

3 The man was taken to jail. _____

4 It's a chair. _____

5 Larry wasn't reading a book. _____

6 Dinner is ready. _____

7 The dog was outside. _____

8 My brother is a mechanic. _____

9 The men weren't talking. _____

10 The book was written in 1969. _____

11 It's not here. _____

12 The window was broken by Carlos. _____

13 The window was broken. _____

a	adjective
b	adverb
c	noun
d	prepositional phrase
e	continuous
f	passive

1.9/a ▶ ellipsis examples and practice

DISCOVER

a Alex: Are Mary and Larry here?
Sam: Mary **isn't here**, but Larry **is**.

1 We understand that *Mary isn't here*, but what about Larry? *Larry is? Larry is* what? *Larry is* <u>here</u>, right?

b Joe: Were Sarah and her brother watching TV?
Lucy: Sarah **wasn't watching TV**, but her brother **was**.

2 We understand that *Sarah wasn't watching TV*, but what about her brother? *Her brother was? Her brother was* what? *Her brother was* <u>watching TV</u>, right?

LEARN

▶ A and b are examples of *ellipsis*. Ellipsis is when people do not repeat words in writing and speaking because it is not necessary to repeat them. When we say a word or some words one time, we do not need to repeat them again and again. They are *ellipted* (not repeated). A person reading or listening understands what the writer or speaker means even if the words are not repeated. If my friend asks me *Are you hungry?* and I answer *Yes, I am*, he knows that what I mean is *Yes, I am hungry*. Ellipsis is <u>very common</u> in conversation, but it is also common in writing.

*My father **is angry**, but my mother **isn't**.*

= *My father **is angry**, but my mother **isn't [angry]**.*

*The black cat **wasn't sleeping**, but the white cat **was**.*

= *The black cat **wasn't sleeping**, but the white cat **was [sleeping]**.*

*Sofia **is a teacher**, and Maria **is** too.*

= *Sofia **is a teacher**, and Maria **is [a teacher]** too.*

*Your pen **is on the table**, and your pencil **is** too.*

= *Your pen **is on the table**, and your pencil **is [on the table]** too.*

Practice 20/a Draw a line through the words which can be ellipted.

Examples: My sister was in the living room, but I wasn't ~~in the living room~~.

Alex is watching TV. Is Carlos ~~watching TV~~ too?

1 My house is big, but your house isn't big.

2 John wasn't there, but I was there.

3 Rosa's working hard. Is her sister working hard too?

4 The doctor is in the lab, but the nurse isn't in the lab.

5 The chocolate cake's good. Is the apple pie good too?

6 Mark is a taxi driver, but Linda isn't a taxi driver.

7 My car was stolen, and my motorcycle was stolen too.

8 You were listening to the teacher, but I wasn't listening to the teacher.

9 Alex was home, but I wasn't home.

10 Your car's in the garage, and my car is in the garage too.

11 Sarah is learning to drive, but Sofia isn't learning to drive.

Practice 21/a Write the ellipted words.

Example: I'm tired, but John isn't.

= I'm tired, but John isn't _____ *tired* _____.

1 Alex isn't riding his bicycle, but Carlos is.

= Alex isn't riding his bicycle, but Carlos is _____.

2 I'm not wrong. You are!

= I'm not wrong. You are _____!

3 Ali was in the lab. Were you too?

= Ali was in the lab. Were you _____ too?

4 Mary is done, and Sofia is too.

= Mary is done, and Sofia is _____ too.

5 I'm sick, but Larry isn't.

= I'm sick, but Larry isn't _____.

6   Sarah was studying, but Alex wasn't.

    = Sarah was studying, but Alex wasn't _____.

7   The dish is broken, but the glass isn't.

    = The dish is broken, but the glass isn't _____.

8   Carlos is ready to go, and I am too.

    = Carlos is ready to go, and I am _____ too.

9   We were working hard, but they weren't.

    = We were working hard, but they weren't _____.

10 Linda is married, and her sister is too.

    = Linda is married, and her sister is _____ too.

Practice 22/a Combine the sentences with *but* or *and* as in the examples. Use ellipsis.

Examples: Michael is tall. His sister isn't tall.

       Michael is tall, but his sister isn't.

       Gary was angry. I was angry.

       Gary was angry, and I was too.

1   My house isn't big. Your house is big.

2   John was there. I was there.

3   He's in the basement. Francesca isn't in the basement.

4   The cow is in the field. The horse is in the field.

5   Mexican food is spicy. Swedish food isn't spicy.

6   John is playing football. Michael isn't playing football.

7   Larry is rich. I'm not rich.

8   My mother wasn't home. My father was home.

9   Lucy is on the plane. Her husband isn't on the plane.

10 Henry was eaten by a dinosaur. I wasn't eaten by a dinosaur.

Unit 2 ▶ present continuous and past continuous

2.1 ▶ present continuous affirmative

DISCOVER

    a   *I **am** work**ing**.*

       = *I**'m** work**ing**.*

    b   *You **are**/We **are**/They **are** work**ing**.*

       = *You**'re**/We**'re**/They**'re** work**ing**.*

    c   *He **is**/She **is** work**ing**.*

       = *He**'s**/She**'s** work**ing**.*

1   What do you notice about the verb *work*? How is it spelled?

LEARN

▶ We use the *present continuous* to say that something is happening now. It always follows the pattern *be* + verb + *ing*.

    *I **am reading** a book.*

    *You **are cooking** dinner.*

    *She **is cleaning** her room.*

REMEMBER

▶ Always use *be* and a verb in the *-ing* form (sometimes called the *present participle*). It is <u>never</u> correct to use only one.

    wrong → *The man talk**ing**.*

    right →   *The man **is** talk**ing**.*

    wrong → *They **are** work.*

    right →   *They **are** work**ing**.*

▶ Some books and some teachers say *progressive* instead of *continuous*. They are the same.

Practice 1 Write present continuous sentences with the correct form of *be*. Use contractions.

    Example: she/work

               She's working.

1   the birds/fly

2   I/read a book

3   Michael/dance

4   Tom and Jerry/fight

5   Ali/play cricket

6   the pilot/sleep

7   Mark/use his computer

8   the teachers/talk

2.2 ▶ present continuous negative

DISCOVER

    a   *I **am not** work**ing**.*

       = *I**'m not** work**ing**.*

    b   *You **are not**/We **are not**/They **are not** work**ing**.*

       = *You**'re not**/We**'re not**/They**'re not** work**ing**.*

       = *You **aren't**/We **aren't**/They **aren't** work**ing**.*

    c   *He **is not**/She **is not** work**ing**.*

       = *He**'s not**/She**'s not** work**ing**.*

       = *He **isn't**/She **isn't** work**ing**.*

1   How do we make negative present continuous sentences?

LEARN

▶ We make negative present continuous sentences by putting *not* after the present form of *be*:

Lucy **is** playing tennis.

→ Lucy **is not** playing tennis.

Practice 2 Write negative present continuous sentences with the correct form of *be*. Write all possible contractions.

Example: we / study

We're not studying.

We aren't studying.

1   the printer / work

2   he / do his homework

3   Ali / listen to the radio

4   the children / be bad

5   Mark / help his mother

6   his sister / shop

7   John and his brother / talk to their friends

8   the manager / drive to work

9   I / eat dinner

10   Sofia and Rosa / study

2.3 ▶ present continuous questions

DISCOVER

a   **Am** I work**ing**?

b   **Are** you / **Are** we / **Are** they work**ing**?

c   **Is** he / **Is** she work**ing**?

1   How do we make present continuous questions?

LEARN

▶ We make present continuous questions by putting *be* before the subject:

The airplane **is** landing.

→ **Is** the airplane landing?

Practice 3 Write present continuous questions with the correct form of *be*.

Example: Michael / read

Is Michael reading?

1   the cat/look out the window

2   Noura/talk on the phone

3   the mechanic/fix the truck

4   Gary/swim in the pool

5   Francesca/sit on the sofa

6   Mary and Sarah/play a game

7   the soldier/exercise

8   your father/cook dinner

9   the children/be noisy

10   I/do this the right way

11   the wolf/eat Henry

Practice 4 Correct the mistakes in the sentences. Make all of them present continuous.

1   John not working now.

2   The baby's sleep.

3   Is Mark study?

4   The horse running.

5   Sarah is sleeping now?

6   The doctor is work.

7   I'm no listening to you.

8   He reading.

9   Is you listening?

10   Michael is eat breakfast.

2.4 ▶ past continuous affirmative

DISCOVER
    *a   I **was**/He **was**/She **was** going.*
    *b   You **were**/We **were**/They **were** going.*
1   How is the affirmative past continuous different from the affirmative present continuous?

LEARN
▶ We use the *past continuous* to say that something was happening in the past:
    *I **was sleeping** on the sofa.*
    *You **weren't working**.*
    *She **was talking** to Mark.*

Practice 5 Write past continuous sentences with the correct form of *be*.

Example: they/eat

        They were eating.

1   the nurse/help the doctor

2   I/drive my car

3   Maria/clean the kitchen

4   Alex and I/talk

5   Carlos/read a book

6   they/try to answer the question

7   the students/do their homework

8   my mother/write a letter

9   Linda/download a song

10   the cook/fry a hamburger

11   Lucy/take a test

2.5 ▶ past continuous negative

DISCOVER

    a   *I **was not**/He **was not**/She **was not** going.*

       *= I **wasn't**/He **wasn't**/She **wasn't** going.*

    b   *You **were not**/We **were not**/They **were not** going.*

       *= You **weren't**/We **weren't**/They **weren't** going.*

1   How do we make negative past continuous sentences?

LEARN

  ▶ We make negative past continuous sentences by putting *not* after the past form of *be*.

     *The mechanic **was** fixing the car.*

     → *The mechanic **was not** fixing the car.*

Practice 6 Write negative past continuous sentences with the correct form of *be*. Use contractions.

  Example: Sarah/watch TV

           Sarah wasn't watching TV.

1   Maria and her son/wash the dishes

2   the pilot/talk on the radio

3   I/fly to Poland

4   Tom/make dinner

5   her husband/look for a job

6   the truck drivers/eat lunch

7   Mary and Larry/do their homework

8   the secretary/finish her work

9   Michael/take a shower

10   we/wait for the bus

2.6 ▶ past continuous questions

DISCOVER

    a   ***Was** I/**Was** he/**Was** she going?*

    b   ***Were** you/**Were** we/**Were** they going?*

1   How do we make past continuous questions?

LEARN

  ▶ We make past continuous questions by putting *be* before the subject.

     *Michael **was** washing the dishes.*

     → ***Was** Michael washing the dishes?*

Practice 7 Write past continuous questions with the correct form of *be*.

  Example: John/make a sandwich

           Was John making a sandwich?

1   your children/wait for you

2 John / drink coffee

3 the managers / have a meeting

4 Mary / work in a bank

5 Rosa / plant flowers

6 Alex and his friends / go to the mall

7 Sarah / buy fruit

8 you / lie on the sofa

9 the airplane / land

10 the sun / shine

Practice 8 Correct the mistakes in the sentences. Make all of them past continuous.

1 I was not work.

2 We were go to the beach.

3 Were they do their homework?

4 She was no listening.

5 My sister weren't playing tennis.

6 The bird not singing.

7 They was not working.

8 John wasn't sleep.

9 Was you studying?

10 You were riding a horse?

Continue to Unit 2/advanced ↓ or go to Unit 3 →

Practice 9/a Complete the sentences with the correct form of *be* and the verb in parentheses. Some are present, and some are past. Use contractions if it is possible.

Example: Larry (watch) _____*was watching*_____ TV two hours ago.

1 Sarah (sleep) _____ before, but now she (watch) _____ TV.

2 Look! Those guys (fight) _____.

3 I am very dirty because I (work) _____ in the garden all day.

4 John (not, do) _____ anything now.

5 _____ you (listen) _____ to the teacher in class yesterday?

6 I'm very tired. I was awake all night because our neighbors (make) _____ so much noise.

7 Please be quiet. The baby (sleep) _____.

8 Alex (exercise) _____ a few minutes ago, but he (take) _____ a shower right now.

9 John and I (not, play) _____ soccer yesterday.

10 It's 12:00. Maybe they (eat) _____ lunch.

11 Look at that boy. He (be) _____ bad.

12 We (not, be) _____ noisy in the library last night.

▶ **present continuous and past continuous**

Practice 10/a Choose the correct verb. Then complete the sentences with the correct form of *be*.

be	be	~~cook~~	do	drive	look	play	rain
read	ring	shine	sleep	teach	try	watch	

Example: John is in the kitchen. He _____*is cooking*_____ dinner.

1 Mary was at the library yesterday. She _____ a book.

2 I _____ TV before, but now I _____ my homework.

3 Alex and Carlos are in bed now. They _____.

4 _____ the children _____ football after school yesterday?

5 Sarah _____ fast because she's late for work.

6 I'm angry. I _____ to study, but the children _____ very noisy.

7 It _____ in the morning, but now the sun _____.

8 My math test grade was very bad. Maybe it's because I _____ out the window while the

  teacher _____.

9 Call the police! That car _____ stolen.

10 Listen! The telephone _____.

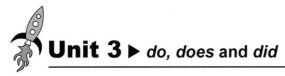 **Unit 3** ▶ *do, does* and *did*

3.1 ▶ present simple affirmative with *do* and *does*

DISCOVER

    a   *She **is speaking** Spanish.*

    b   *She **speaks** Spanish.*

1   Which sentence is about something that is true now? Which sentence is about something that is always true?

    c   *I **work**/You **work**/We **work**/They **work** in a bank.*

    d   *He **works**/She **works** in a bank.*

2   How is the verb *work* different in *d*?

LEARN (See Table 3a.)

▶ We use the present continuous to talk about something that is happening <u>now</u>, but we use the *present simple* when we talk about something that happens <u>sometimes, always, usually or never</u>.

▶ The present simple looks the same as the *infinitive* form (the base form) of the verb (except for *be*). But there is one very important exception—we must add an *-s* to the verb <u>when the subject is *he, she, it*</u> or the name of <u>one person</u> or <u>one thing</u>. (Some verbs have an irregular *-s* form. See the Appendix to learn more about irregular verbs.)

3a	
present affirmative	
<u>subject</u>	<u>verb</u>
I *You* *We* *They*	*work.* *go.* *have.*
He *She* *It*	*works.* *goes.* *has.*

REMEMBER

▶ The verb must be in the *-s* form when the subject is *he, she, it* or the name of one person or one thing.

   wrong → *He **live** in Miami.*   **wrong** → *The teacher **have** a car.*   **wrong** → *Mary **know** the answer.*

   right →   *He **lives** in Miami.*   **right** →   *The teacher **has** a car.*   **right** →   *Mary **knows** the answer.*

Practice 1 Underline the correct form of the verb.

  Examples: Michael (<u>has</u>/is having) three dogs.

              Please be quiet. I (study/<u>am studying</u>).

1   Carlos always (goes/is going) to school at 8:15.

2   Listen to me! I (talk/am talking) to you.

3   Maria likes tea. She never (drinks/is drinking) coffee.

4   I'm fat. I often (eat/am eating) too much.

5   Francesca always (comes/is coming) home from school at 3:00.

6   My father is in the garage now. He (fixes/is fixing) his car.

7   Tom and Mary are pilots. They sometimes (fly/are flying) to Australia.

8   Look! An eagle (flies/is flying) in the sky.

9   I (watch/am watching) TV every night.

10 Help! Henry (is/is being) eaten by a crocodile!

Practice 2 Underline the correct form of the verb.

Example: We (<u>work</u>/works) in a factory.

1   I (speak/speaks) English.

2   She (live/lives) in China.

3   My mother (drink/drinks) apple juice.

4   Ali and his sister (play/plays) tennis everyday.

5   The teacher (eat/eats) lunch at 12:30.

6   The teachers (eat/eats) lunch at 12:30.

7   Michael and his friends (listen/listens) to music.

8   He (want/wants) to eat lunch.

9   We (have/has) a new car.

10 Linda and Lucy (work/works) in an office.

11 Your dog (have/has) a big nose.

3.2 ▶ present simple negative sentences with *do* and *does*

DISCOVER

a   They **do not work** in a bank.
     = They **don't work** in a bank.

b   He **does not work** in a bank.
     = He **doesn't work** in a bank.

1   Is the verb *work* different in *b*? What is different in *b*?

2   How do we use *do* and *does* to make negative sentences in the present simple?

LEARN (See Table 3b.)

▶ We put *do not/don't* or *does not/doesn't* before the verb to make negative present simple sentences. <u>Do not</u> use the -*s* form.

3b		
present negative		
subject		verb
I *You* *We* *They*	*do not/don't*	*work.* *go.* *have.*
He *She* *It*	*does not/doesn't*	*work.* *go.* *have.*

REMEMBER

▶ Use *does not* for negative sentences when the subject is *he, she, it* or the name of one person or thing. Do not use the -*s* form of the verb.

wrong → He **don't** speak English.

right →   He **doesn't** speak English.

wrong → He doesn't **speaks** English.

right →   He doesn't **speak** English.

Practice 3 Change the sentences to negative with *don't* or *doesn't*.

Example: The doctor works on Saturday.

     The doctor doesn't work on Saturday.

1　You have a car.

2　The dog eats potato chips.

3　Sarah has a computer.

4　Our father goes to work at 7:30.

5　My mother likes ice cream.

6　She and I know the answer.

7　Mary gets up at 7:00.

8　I work on Saturdays.

9　He and I work together.

10　Carlos watches TV.

3.3 ▶ present simple questions with *do* and *did*

DISCOVER

　　a　***Do*** they ***work*** *in a bank?*
　　b　***Does*** she ***work*** *in a bank?*

1　Is the verb *work* different in *b*? What is different in *b*?

2　How do we use *do* and *does* to make questions in the present simple?

LEARN (See Table 3c.)

▶ We put *do* or *does* before the subject to make questions in the present simple. <u>Do not</u> use the *-s* form.

3c								
present questions and short answers								
	<u>subject</u>	<u>verb</u>		<u>subject</u>	<u>verb</u>		<u>subject</u>	<u>verb</u>
	I			*I*			*I*	
Do	*you* *we* *they*	*work?*	*Yes,*	*you* *we* *they*	*do.*	*No,*	*you* *we* *they*	*don't.*
Does	*he* *she* *it*	*work?*	*Yes,*	*he* *she* *it*	*does.*	*No,*	*he* *she* *it*	*doesn't.*

REMEMBER

▶ Use *does* for questions when the subject is *he, she, it* or the name of *one* person or thing. Do not use the *-s* form of the verb.

　　wrong → ***Do*** *he have a car?*　　　**wrong** → *Does he **has** a car?*
　　right → ***Does*** *he have a car?*　　　**right** → *Does he **have** a car?*

Practice 4 Change the sentences to questions with the correct form of *do.*

Example:　She studies in the library.

　　　　　　Does she study in the library?

1　Maria swims in the lake.

2　They want to move to Canada.

3　Ali goes to work at 8:00.

4　You and John watch TV.

5　His friends like to dance.

6　Carlos reads a lot.

7   Mary has blue eyes.

8   You live in a big house.

9   Larry sleeps all day.

10 Susan and her sister ride horses on the weekend.

Practice 5 **Read the story and answer the questions with short answers.**

Carl is a teacher. He lives in a hot country. He teaches English, so he doesn't make a lot of money. He works hard, but sometimes his students don't listen to him. They talk and sleep in class. Carl has an old car. He wants to buy a new car. His students have new cars. They make jokes about Carl's old car. Carl doesn't have enough money to buy a new car. Carl works at two jobs to make more money.

Example: Does Carl live in a hot country?

          Yes, he does.

1   Does Carl teach English?

2   Does he make a lot of money?

3   Does he work hard?

4   Do his students listen to him?

5   Do his students sleep in class?

6   Does he have a new car?

7   Do his students have new cars?

8   Do they make jokes about his old car?

9   Does he have enough money to buy a new car?

10 Does he have two jobs?

3.4 ▶ past simple affirmative with *did*

DISCOVER

a   She **works** in a bank every day. I **work** in a clinic every day.
b   She **worked** in a bank yesterday. I **worked** in a clinic yesterday.

1   How is the past form of *work* different from the present form?

c   He **takes** a taxi to work every day. I **take** a bus to work every day.
d   He **took** a taxi to work yesterday. I **took** a bus to work yesterday.

2   Look at *b* and *d*. Do the past form of *take* and the past form of *work* change from the present to the past in the same way?

3   You learned that in the present, all verbs have an *-s* form for *he, she* and *it*. Is this also true in the past?

LEARN (See Table 3d.)

▶ We use the *past simple* when we talk about something that happened in the past. Verbs in English are *regular* or *irregular*. Regular verbs always add *-ed* in the past form. Irregular verbs do not follow a system. (See the Appendix to learn more about irregular verbs.)

3d

regular past examples		irregular past examples	
present form	past form	present form	past form
want	wanted	go	went
talk	talked	see	saw
dance	danced	have	had
clean	cleaned	leave	left
work	worked	break	broke
wash	washed	buy	bought
cooked	cooked	eat	ate

Practice 6 Change the sentences to past simple.

Example: She drinks coffee.

She drank coffee.

1   They live in Spain.

2   We cook dinner.

3   You walk to school.

4   She rides her bicycle.

5   Mary and I drive to California.

6   I see it.

7   You go to the beach.

8   He has a book.

9   John looks at the pictures.

10   Carlos buys chocolate.

3.5 ▶ past simple negative with *did*

DISCOVER
    a   Sarah **cleaned** the kitchen. She **didn't clean** the living room.

    b   He **went** to the library. He **didn't go** to the bank.

1   How do we use *did* to make negative sentences in the past?

2   Do we use the past form of the verb in negative past sentences?

LEARN (See Table 3e.)
▶ We put *did not/didn't* before the <u>present</u> form of the verb to make negative past simple sentences.

3e		
past negative		
<u>subject</u>		<u>verb</u>
I		
You		
He		work.
She	did not/didn't	go.
It		have.
We		
They		

REMEMBER
▶ Do not use the past form in negative past sentences.

    wrong → He didn't **worked** in a bank.

    right →   He didn't **work** in a bank.

    wrong → She didn't **went** to the meeting.

    right →   She didn't **go** to the meeting.

Practice 7 Change the sentences to negative with *did*. Use contractions.

Example: I went to the supermarket.

I didn't go to the supermarket.

1   He worked yesterday.

2   John went to the mall.

3   Michael talked to his sister.

4   We had a red truck.

▶ *do, does* and *did*

5   Your dog ate my dinner.

6   Sarah and her friend took the bus.

7   Alex thought about the answer.

8   Bill flew to Lima.

9   My father called me.

10 Mary put the baby on the bed.

3.6 ▶ past simple questions with *did*

DISCOVER

    a   Mary **talked** to the nurse. **Did** she **talk** to the doctor?

    b   Michael **sold** his car. **Did** he **sell** his truck?

1   How do we use *did* to make questions in the past?

2   Do we use the past form of the verb in questions about the past?

LEARN (See Table 3f.)

▶ We put *did* before the subject to make questions in the past simple. <u>Do not</u> use the *-s* form.

3f									
past questions and short answers									
	<u>subject</u>	<u>verb</u>		<u>subject</u>	<u>verb</u>		<u>subject</u>	<u>verb</u>	
	I			*I*			*I*		
	you			*you*			*you*		
	he			*he*			*he*		
Did	*she*	*work?*	*Yes,*	*she*	*did.*	*No,*	*she*	*didn't.*	
	it			*it*			*it*		
	we			*we*			*we*		
	they			*they*			*they*		

REMEMBER

▶ Do not use the past form in negative past questions.

    wrong → *Did he **worked** in a bank?*

    right →   *Did he **work** in a bank?*

    wrong → *Did she **went** to the meeting?*

    right →   *Did she **go** to the meeting?*

Practice 8 Change the sentences to questions with *did*.

Example: They went to the library.

           Did they go to the library?

1   Ali finished his homework.

2   She flew to Russia.

3   You and John watched TV.

4   Linda saw Larry.

5   He wrote a letter.

6   Carlos slept late.

7   The students read their books.

8   Jack lied to you.

9   He cut the pizza.

10 Sofia knew the answer.

Practice 9 Read the story and answer the questions with short answers.

Larry is from California, but he lives in Florida now. He is a student at the University of Florida. He is studying medicine because he wants to be a doctor. He studies a lot, but on Sundays he likes to relax and go to the beach. His sister was a student at the University of Florida too, but she didn't graduate. Now she works in a big office building in Los Angeles. She is a secretary.

Example: Does Larry live in California now?

No, he doesn't.

1   Is Larry from California?

2   Does he live in Florida now?

3   Is he a teacher?

4   Is he studying law?

5   Does he want to be a doctor?

6   Does he like to relax and go to the beach?

7   Was his sister a student at the University of Florida too?

8   Did she graduate?

9   Does she work in a big office building?

10 Does she work in San Francisco?

11 Is she a doctor?

Continue to Unit 3/advanced ↓ or go to Unit 4 →

Practice 10/a Complete the sentences with *do, don't, does, doesn't, did* or *didn't*.

I _____(1) have a car, so I take the bus to work, but I _____(2) take the bus yesterday because I was sick, and I _____(3) go to work. My boss was angry. She called me at 9:30 yesterday, and she said, "Mary, _____(4) you want to keep your job? If you miss another day, I will fire you."

I think my boss _____(5) like me. She thinks I am lazy. Now I am worried. I _____(6) like my job, but I need it. I _____(7) want to look for another job. My boyfriend _____(8) like his job either. He _____(9) work very hard. He is lazy. He promised to call me yesterday, but he _____(10). I called him, and I said, "Why _____(11) you call me? _____(12) you forget?" He said, "Yes, I _____(13). I'm sorry." Maybe I need a new boyfriend. _____(14) you know anybody?

3.7/a ▶ *do, does* and *did* as main verbs

DISCOVER

    a   They **do** their homework every night.

1   What is the verb in *a*?

    b   They **don't do** their homework every night.

2   Why are there two forms of *do* in *b*?

    c   **Do they do** their homework every night?

3   Why do you see *do* two times in *c*?

LEARN

▶ It is important to understand that *do* is not only an *auxiliary* (or *helping*) verb. *Do* is <u>also</u> a *main verb* (main verbs are verbs like *come, go, walk, eat,* etc.). The different kinds of verbs will be explained in Unit 6. For now, look at these examples. Notice how *do, does* and *did* are used as auxiliary verbs and also as main verbs.

▶ *do, does* and *did*

They **read** their book.   They **don't read** their book.   **Do** they **read** their book?
They **do** their homework.   They **don't do** their homework.   **Do** they **do** their homework?
He **drives** his car.   He **doesn't drive** his car.   **Does** he **drive** his car?
He **does** his job.   He **doesn't do** his job.   **Does** he **do** his job?

Practice 11/a Change the sentence to negative with *don't* or *doesn't*. Use contractions.

Example: We do our homework after dinner.

     We don't do our homework after dinner.

1   I do a lot of work.

2   Lucy does everything well.

3   We do all our shopping on Saturday.

4   I do my homework in the library.

5   She does it carefully.

6   Mark does the dishes after dinner.

7   They do it every day.

8   Carlos and I do our work in the morning.

9   We do the laundry on Sunday.

Practice 12/a Change the sentences to questions with *do* or *does*.

Example: Her brother does his job quickly.

     Does her brother do his job quickly?

1   He does his work slowly.

2   They do the dishes after dinner.

3   They always do it the wrong way.

4   Sarah does her homework at school.

5   They do their exercises before dinner.

6   Michael does his work well.

7   He does his work in his office.

8   Francesca and Alex do the shopping.

9   He does the ironing badly.

Practice 13/a Change the sentences to negative with *did*. Use contractions.

Example: He did his work well.

     He didn't do his work well.

1   She did her work badly.

2   I did it.

3   He did the laundry.

4   He did his homework last night.

5   You did the right thing.

6   Tom did everything wrong.

7   Larry did a lot of work.

8   Maria did her exercises in the afternoon.

Practice 14/a Change the sentences to questions with *did*.

Example: John did a bad job.

Did John do a bad job?

1   Larry did his exercises.

2   You did the laundry this morning.

3   She did the best she could.

4   Carlos did a good job.

5   He did his homework after dinner.

6   They did the wrong thing.

7   He did it yesterday.

8   She did it right.

3.8/a ▶ emphatic *do*

DISCOVER

   a   *My sister **does** have 17 children.*
   b   *I **did** go to the South Pole last year.*

1   What are *do, does* and *did* used for? Negative sentences and questions, right? All students learn that. Now look at *a* and *b*. Are *a* and *b* negative sentences? Are they questions?

   c   Tom: *My sister **has** 17 children.*
   d   Jerry: *I don't believe you.*
   e   Tom: *It's true. My sister **does have** 17 children.*

2   Look at *c* and *e*. Why did Tom change from *has* to *does have*?

   f   Alex: *I **went** to the South Pole last year.*
   g   Mary: *You're lying.*
   h   Alex: *I'm not lying. I **did go** to the South Pole last year.*

3   Look at *f* and *h*. Why did Alex change from *went* to *did go*?

LEARN

   ▶ Sometimes, when we want to make sentences about the past or present stronger, we use *do, does* or *did* and the *infinitive form* of the verb (the base form without any changes—no *-s* or past form). This is called the emphatic *do*. Sentences with the emphatic *do* are <u>not questions</u> and <u>not negative</u>.

   ▶ When native speakers use the emphatic *do* in speaking, they always stress *do, does* or *did.* That means they say the word strongly and raise their voices a little.

   I **do** *believe you.*
   She **does** *have a horse.*
   He **did** *study for the test.*

REMEMBER

   ▶ The emphatic *do* is <u>very common</u> among native speakers, and all students of English should understand it.

Practice 15/a Change the sentences to the emphatic *do*. (Be careful with 10 and 11—remember that *do* is a main verb and an auxiliary verb.)

Example: I drove from New York to Los Angeles in only two days.

I did drive from New York to Los Angeles in only two days.

1   My horse has five legs.

2   I slept for 18 hours.

3   Carlos puts coffee on his cereal.

4   I saw a pink elephant.

5   Alex and Carlos live in a tree house.

▶ *do, does* and *did*   29

6   I went to Mars in a UFO.

7   My dog ate my homework.

8   I believe you.

9   I did my homework yesterday.

10   I do my homework every day.

3.9/a ▶ ellipsis examples and practice (See Section 1.9/a for an explanation of ellipsis.)

DISCOVER

a   *John **speaks** French, and Mary **does** too.*
    = *John **speaks** French, and Mary **[speaks French]** too.*

b   *You **have** a cat, and I **do** too.*
    = *You **have** a cat, and I **[have a cat]** too.*

c   *John **speaks** French, but Larry **doesn't**.*
    = *John **speaks** French, but Larry **doesn't [speak French]**.*

d   *You **have** a cat, but they **don't**.*
    = *You **have** a cat, but they **don't [have a cat]**.*

e   *Larry **doesn't speak** French, but John **does**.*
    = *Larry **doesn't speak** French, but John **[speaks French]**.*

f   *They **don't have** a cat, but I **do**.*
    = *They **don't have** a cat, but I **[have a cat]**.*

g   *Sofia **went** to college, and Alex **did** too.*
    = *Sofia **went** to college, and Alex **[went to college]** too.*

h   *Sofia **went** to college, but Sam **didn't**.*
    = *Sofia **went** to college, but Sam **didn't [go to college]**.*

i   *Sam **didn't go** to college, but Sofia **did**.*
    = *Sam **didn't go** to college, but Sofia **[went to college]**.*

j   *I **don't have** a car. **Do** you?*
    = *I **don't have** a car. **Do** you **[have a car]**?*

k   *Maria **lives** in New York. **Does** her sister too?*
    = *Maria **lives** in New York. **Does** her sister **[live in New York]** too?*

l   *Linda **didn't do** her homework. **Did** you?*
    = *Linda **didn't do** her homework. **Did** you **[do your homework]**?*

Practice 16/a Draw a line through the words which can be ellipted.

Examples: My mother drinks coffee, but my father doesn't ~~drink coffee~~.

              The boys played soccer. Did the girls ~~play soccer~~ too?

1   Mary followed the plan, but Michael didn't follow the plan.

2   I feel sick. Does he feel sick too?

3   My mother likes to eat fish, but my father doesn't like to eat fish.

4   We agree with you, but they don't agree with you.

5   Sarah went to college. Did her brother go to college?

6   He has a job, but she doesn't have a job.

7   My son sent me a birthday card, but my daughter didn't send me a birthday card.

8   Cheese and butter have a lot of calories, but vegetables don't have a lot of calories.

9   One of the students did her homework, but the other one didn't do her homework.

10   We went to the concert last night. Did you go to the concert last night?

Practice 17/a Write the ellipted words.

Example: Maria has a dog, but I don't _____ *have a dog* _____.

1   I like to play pool. Do you _____?

2   Joe went to the library, but I didn't _____.

3   I didn't do it. Did you _____?

4   Sarah wants to eat, but I don't _____.

5   Noura drinks coffee, Does Ali _____?

6   She did it, but I didn't _____.

7   The restaurant stays open late, but the bank doesn't _____.

8   My wife eats breakfast in the morning, but I don't _____.

Practice 18/a Combine the sentences as in the example. Use ellipsis.

Examples: Larry sleeps a lot. Alex sleeps a lot too.

Larry sleeps a lot, and Alex does too.

I went to the baseball game. John went to the baseball game too.

I went to the baseball game, and John did too.

1   The library closes at 8:30. The supermarket closes at 8:30 too.

2   Susan bought a TV last week. I bought a TV last week too.

3   Mary read that book. Michael read that book too.

4   I know how to swim. My brother knows how to swim too.

5   John thinks it's a good idea. Sam thinks it's a good idea too.

6   I like to dance. Linda likes to dance too.

7   Ali passed the test. I passed the test too.

8   I know the answer. You know the answer too.

▶ *do, does* and *did*

Unit 4 ▶ future

4.1 ▶ *will* and *be going to*

DISCOVER

a   The telephone is ringing. I **will** answer it.
b   Brazil **will** win the World Cup.
c   It **is going to** rain tomorrow.
d   I**'m going to** go shopping with my friends tonight.
e   I**'ll** take the book to the library tomorrow.

1   Which sentence(s) is / are about something that the speaker will do but did not already have a plan to do?
2   Which sentence(s) is / are about a *prediction* (something the speaker thinks will happen in the future)?
3   Which sentence(s) is / are about a plan for the future?

LEARN (See Table 4a and Table 4b.)

▶ We use *will* and *be going to* to talk about the future. They are similar but not always the same.

4a	
will and **be going to**	

willness
will
	Will (but not *be going to*) is used to say that we are *willing* to do something. When we are willing to do something, we are talking about how we feel. We are saying that we will do something <u>if</u> there is a need to do it or <u>if</u> somebody asks us to do it.
	    *Your homework looks difficult. I **will** help you if you have a problem.*
	    *Carlos, there are a lot of dirty dishes in the kitchen. **Will** you please wash them?*

predictions
be going to
will
	Both *be going to* and *will* are used to predict the future. *Predict* means to say what we think will happen in the future.
	    *I **am going to** get a 100 on the exam.*
	    *John**'s not going to** be happy when he hears the news.*
	    *He flew to London yesterday. I'm sure he**'ll** have a wonderful vacation.*
	    *Maria **won't** be here when the class begins. She's always late.*

plans
be going to
will
	Both *be going to* and *will* are used to talk about plans (including promises, which are a form of plan).
	    *There is a problem with Jim's car. He**'s going to** take it to a mechanic tomorrow.*
	    *I**'m going to** buy a new computer next week.*
	    *John forgot to call Gary today. He**'ll** call him tomorrow.*
	    *Please stop asking me to cut the grass. I promise I**'ll** do on Saturday.*

▶ There are three ways to make contractions with subject pronouns and *will*. It is not common to make contractions with nouns and *will*.

4b		
contractions of subject pronouns and *will* and *not*		
	more common	less common
I will = I'll	I will not = I won't	I will not = I'll not
you will = you'll	you will not = you won't	you will not = you'll not
he will = he'll	he will not = he won't	he will not = he'll not
she will = she'll	she will not = she won't	she will not = she'll not
it will = it'll	it will not = it won't	it will not = it'll not
we will = we'll	we will not = we won't	we will not = we'll not
they will = they'll	they will not = they won't	they will not = they'll not

REMEMBER

▶ The grammar of *be going to* is present continuous, but we understand future when we use it and hear it.

▶ Never use the *-s* form of a verb after *will*.

    wrong → *He will works tomorrow.*

    right →   *He will work tomorrow.*

▶ Never use *am, is* or *are* after *will*. Use only *be*.

    wrong → *She will is here next week.*

    right →   *She will **be** here next week.*

▶ In informal speech, *going to* is often pronounced *gonna*. Sometimes, in informal writing, people use *gonna*, but remember that *gonna* is never correct in serious, formal writing.

▶ *Shall* is also used to talk about the future, but *will* is more common.

Practice 1 **Change each sentence to future with *will*. Use contractions.**

Example: He works.

     He'll work.

1   I make you a sandwich.

2   They get a good grade.

3   He writes a book.

4   Larry and Carlos go to the mall.

5   He is angry.

6   Sarah goes to the beach.

7   Noura and Ali are at the mall.

8   I'm late.

9   We're at the food court.

10   She's doing her homework.

Practice 2 **Change the sentences to negative. Use contractions.**

Example: Mike will win the game.

     Mike won't win the game.

1   They will help her.

2   I will go.

3   He'll change his mind.

4   Alex will be there.

5   She'll do it.

6   We'll buy it.

7   The engineer will finish the plan.

8   I'll go to the party.

9   She'll be at the museum.

10   We will wait for him.

Practice 3 **Change the sentences to questions.**

Example: You'll meet us for lunch.

     Will you meet us for lunch?

1   They'll come after dinner.

▶ **future**

2   He will lend Mark $1,000.

3   You'll help me.

4   Carlos will be at the party.

5   The girls will draw pictures.

6   She'll do her homework.

7   Mary, Larry, Gary and their parents will be at the graduation.

8   They'll be camping in the desert.

9   The medicine will be given to the sick children.

10 A killer whale will be eating Henry.

Practice 4 Change each sentence to future with *be going to*. Use contractions.

Example: She does her homework.

She's going to do her homework.

1   My mother goes to Alaska.

2   The doctor calls me.

3   John has a pizza.

4   They buy a new car.

5   Larry is late.

6   They're early.

7   She works hard.

8   I go to the supermarket.

9   The class is taught in the fall semester.

10 I'm waiting for you in the lobby.

Practice 5 Change the sentences to negative. Use contractions.

Example: She's going to help me.

She's not going to help me.

1   He's going to be here later.

2   I'm going to do it.

3   We're going to eat in that restaurant again.

4   He's going to read this book.

5   They're going to have dinner after the movie.

6   Larry's going to fly to Iceland.

7   The test is going to be difficult.

8   She's going to look for a new job.

9   You're going to be sorry.

10 I'm going to be there.

Practice 6 Change the sentences to questions.

Example: He's going to play football.

Is he going to play football?

1   Sofia's going to have chicken for dinner.

2   You're going to wash your car.

3   Your friends are going to go to Taiwan.

4   They're going to work in the garden.

5   You and she are going to be here next Sunday.

6   The children are going to go to a movie.

7   Her sister's going to get married.

8   It's going to be cold tomorrow.

9   The team's going to be driven to the stadium.

10 He's going to be studying.

Continue to Unit 4/advanced ↓ or go to Unit 5 →

4.2/a ▶ present continuous used for future plans

DISCOVER

    a   Tom: When **are you flying** to Australia?

    b   Mary: **I'm flying** there **next week**.

1   What is this conversation about? Is it about the future? What grammar do you see? Do you see *will* or *be going to*? If you do not see *will* or *be going to*, how do you know this sentence is about the future?

LEARN

▶ It is <u>very</u> common in English to use the present continuous to talk about future plans. How do we know that people are talking about the future and not about the present? It's easy. We understand from the situation and from words like *soon, in three hours, after dinner, tomorrow, next week, next year,* etc.

    I'm hungry. **Are** we **eating soon**?

    Larry **is moving** to a new apartment **next weekend**.

REMEMBER

▶ It is always correct to use *be going to* and *will* to talk about future plans. There is never a time when you must use present continuous to talk about the future, but you must understand it when you hear and when you read it.

▶ Present continuous for future plans is never used for the verb *be*.

▶ In correct English, we do not say *after three hours*, etc. We say *in three hours*, etc.

    wrong → *We're having a test **after** four days.*

    right →   *We're having a test **in** four days.*

    wrong → *I'll do it **after** a few minutes.*

    right →   *I'll do it **in** a few minutes.*

Practice 7/a Change the sentences so that they use present continuous for future.

Examples: We're going to leave at 2:30.

         We're leaving at 2:30.

         I'm going to go to Germany in a couple of weeks.

         I'm going to Germany in a couple of weeks.

1   Mary is going to call me at 8:00.

2   When are we going to eat dinner?

3   We're going to eat dinner in a few minutes. We're going to have hamburgers.

4   When are you going to do your homework?

5   I'm going to do it in an hour.

6   How many people are going to come to the party?

7   Around 25 people are going to come to the party.

8   Is Carlos going to cook dinner?

9   When are you going to go to Ottawa?

10   Why are you going to go there?

4.3/a ▶ present simple used for future scheduled events

DISCOVER

    a   Mary: When **does** the movie start?
    b   Gary: The movie **starts** at 8:00.

1   What is this conversation about? Is it about the future? What grammar do you see? Do you see *will* or *be going to*? If you do not see *will* or *be going to*, how do you know this sentence is about the future?

LEARN

▶ It is <u>very</u> common in English to use the present simple to talk about future events which are on a schedule, calendar or timetable. How do we know that people are talking about the future and not about the present? You know the answer! It's the same as in Section 4.2/a. We understand from the situation and from words like *soon, in three hours, after dinner, tomorrow, next week, next year,* etc.
    Her birthday **is** in three days.
    My plane **takes off** at 9:40, and it **arrives** in Berlin at 5:30.

▶ The present simple is used to talk about events on a schedule or a timetable. The number of verbs that is used in this way is small. The most common are *be, start, end, begin, finish, open, close, arrive, depart* and *leave*.

REMEMBER

▶ It is always correct to use *be going to* and *will* to talk about future plans. There is never a time when you must use the present simple to talk about the future, but you must understand it when you hear and when you read it.

Practice 8/a Change the sentences so that they use present simple for future.

Examples: My flight is going to leave at 11:14.

    My flight leaves at 11:14.

    When is the wedding going to be?

    When is the wedding?

    Where is this bus going to go?

    Where does this bus go?

1   The show is going to start at 8:00.

2   When is the game going to begin?

3   It's going to begin at 2:00.

4   What time is the store going to open?

5   The store is going to open at 10:00.

6   My English class is going to begin at 8:20.

7   His flight is going arrive at 1840.

8   The meeting is going to be at 10:30.

9   When is the test going to be?

10   The test is going to be next Tuesday.

4.4/a ▶ future time clauses

DISCOVER

    a   After **I go** to the doctor tomorrow, I'm going to go to the library.

1   You can see that *a* has two parts: *After I go to the doctor tomorrow* and *I'm going to go to the library.* Each part

of the sentence is called a clause (a clause is a group of words which contains a subject and a verb). There are two clauses, but they are not the same. One of the clauses could be a good sentence alone. Which is it? The other clause could not be a good sentence alone. Which is it?

2   Which clause in *a* could be a good sentence alone without the other clause? It's the second clause, *I'm going to go to the library*. Because this clause does not need the help of the other clause, it is called an *independent clause*. But the other clause, *After I go to the doctor tomorrow*, does not make sense alone. It must be connected to an independent clause. It is a *dependent clause*.

   b   Before **Mary makes** dinner, she will wash her hands.
   c   I will talk to Sofia when **I see** her.

3   Look at *b* and *c*. Which are the independent clauses? Which are the dependent clauses?
4   Look at *a, b* and *c*. Is the tense in the dependent clauses present or future?
5   Look at *a, b* and *c*. Is the tense in the independent clauses present or future?
6   Look at *c*. How is *c* different from *a* and *b*? Is the independent clause before or after the dependent clause?

LEARN

▶ Future time clauses are dependent clauses which tell you how two things in the future are related in time. They tell you that one will happen <u>before</u> the other one, <u>after</u> the other one or that they will happen <u>at the same time</u>. The future time clause is <u>always</u> in the <u>present simple</u> tense. Many students make the mistake of using *will* or *be going to* in future time clauses.

   wrong → *Before I* **will** *go to bed, I* **will** *call you.*
   right →   *Before I go to bed, I* **will** *call you.*

▶ In sentences with dependent clauses and independent clauses, the clauses can be reversed with the same meaning. Pay attention to where the comma is when the time clause is first. Also pay attention to how names of people are usually in the first clause and pronouns are usually in the second clause. (Future time clauses are a form of adverb clause. See Unit 16 and Unit 17 for more about adverb clauses.)

   After <u>Michael</u> gets home, <u>he</u>*'s going to eat dinner.*
   = <u>Michael</u>*'s going to eat dinner* **after <u>he</u> gets home.**

REMEMBER

▶ Future time clauses must always be in the present tense.

Practice 9/a Reverse the clauses, as in the example. Pay attention to punctuation. Change the names and pronouns when it is necessary.

Example: When Mark gets to work, he will call me.

   Mark will call me when he gets to work.

1   When I see Linda, I will tell her the news.

2   Alex is going to go home after he leaves the gym.

3   Before Carlos does his homework, he's going to eat dinner.

4   We will go to the Vatican when we are in Rome.

5   As soon as Maria arrives in Athens, she will go to her hotel.

6   I'll call you when I get there.

7   After we get home, will you help me with the laundry?

8   John's not going to have time to play golf after he gets married.

9   I'll be happy when she is here.

10   After Bill finishes this book, he'll return it to the library.

Practice 10/a Underline the future time clauses in your answers to Practice 9.

   Example: *Mark will call me <u>when he gets to work</u>.*

Practice 11/a Underline the future time clauses. If the sentence contains an error, correct it.

1   When I will arrive in Madrid, I will call you.

2   She's going to wash the dishes after she is going to eat dinner.

3   Is the teacher going to return our tests after she grades them?

4   Before I go to the beach, I'll stop to buy gas.

5   We won't eat dinner until Daddy will get home from work.

6   Are you going to do your homework after you will get home?

7   As soon as I will get home, I will start to cook dinner.

8   I'll meet you at the gym after I change my clothes.

9   After I will leave my office, I'll get a taxi to the airport.

10   When you get to work, come to my office with the sales report.

11   When you will go to Paris, will you see the Eiffel Tower?

4.5/a ▶ *be about to* used for near future

DISCOVER

    a   *Bill is going to eat lunch in five minutes. He **is about to** eat lunch.*

1   Is Bill eating lunch now, or is he going to eat lunch in the future? Is it far in the future, or is it very soon in the future? What do you think *is about to* means?

    b   *I always leave my job and go home at 4:00. At 3:59 yesterday I **was about to** go home when my boss gave me some work to do. I had to stay until 5:00.*

2   At 3:59 yesterday, was *go home* in the future? Was it far in the future? Was it very soon in the future? What do you think *was about to* means?

LEARN

    ▶ When we want to talk about something that is (or was) going to happen in the near future, we can use *be about to*. *Be* can be in the past or present.
    *Wash your hands. We **are about to** eat dinner.*
    *She **was about to** go to bed when the telephone rang.*

Practice 12/a Answer the questions. Use *be about to* and the words in parentheses.

Example: There is food on the table. Carlos is sitting down at the table.

          (he, eat) He is about to eat.

1   The telephone is ringing. Alex is walking to the telephone.

    (he, answer the phone)

2   Sarah's favorite TV show starts at 8:00. At 7:58 last night she was reaching for the TV remote control.

    (she, turn on the TV)

3   I turned on the shower. I took off my clothes.

    (I, take a shower)

4   John always leaves his job at 5:00. Yesterday, he put on his coat at 4:56, and he walked toward the office door.

    (he, leave)

5   I am cold. The window is open. I am walking to the window.

    (I, close the window)

6   It's windy. There are black clouds in the sky.

    (it, rain)

4.6/a ▶ ellipsis examples and practice (See Section 1.9/a for an explanation of ellipsis.)

DISCOVER

    a   **I'm not going to be here** at 8:00, but **I am going to be** at 9:00.
       = **I'm not going to be here** at 8:00, but **I am going to be [here]** at 9:00.

I'm not going to be here at 8:00, but I **am** at 9:00.
= *I'm not going to be here* at 8:00, but I **am [going to be here]** at 9:00.

c *We're going to study in the library*. Are you **going to**?
= *We're going to study in the library*. Are you **going to [study in the library]**?

d *We're going to study in the library*. Are you?
= *We're going to study in the library*. Are you **[going to study in the library]**?

e Noura **won't help** me, but Carlos **will**.
= Noura **won't help** me, but Carlos **will [help me]**.

f Mary **will be at the meeting**, but I **won't be**.
= Mary **will be at the meeting**, but I **won't be [at the meeting]**.

g Mary **will be at the meeting**, but I **won't**.
= Mary **will be at the meeting**, but I **won't [be at the meeting]**.

h I **haven't done my homework** yet, but I'**m about to**.
= I **haven't done my homework** yet, but I'**m about to [do my homework]**.

Practice 13/a Draw a line through the words which can be ellipted.

Examples: John's going to be late, but Alex isn't going to be ~~late~~.

John's going to be late, but Alex isn't ~~going to be late~~.

I'm going to work in the garden, but she isn't going to ~~work in the garden~~.

I'm going to work in the garden, but she isn't ~~going to work in the garden~~.

1   Rosa isn't going to be here today, but she is going to be here tomorrow.

Rosa isn't going to be here today, but she is going to be here tomorrow.

2   I'm not going to ride my bike before dinner, but I am going to ride my bike after dinner.

I'm not going to ride my bike before dinner, but I am going to ride my bike after dinner.

3   Paul is going to speak at the conference. Is Sam going to speak at the conference?

Paul is going to speak at the conference. Is Sam going to speak at the conference?

4   They're going to go, and I am going to go too.

They're going to go, and I am going to go too.

5   I'm going to leave early today. Are you going to leave early today too?

I'm going to leave early today. Are you going to leave early today too?

Practice 14/a Draw a line through the words which can be ellipted.

Examples: Sam won't be here today, but Alex will be ~~here today~~.

Sam won't be here today, but Alex will ~~be here today~~.

Francesca isn't going to go shopping, but Sofia is going to ~~go shopping~~.

Francesca isn't going to go shopping, but Sofia is ~~going to go shopping~~.

Mark won't help you, but Lucy will ~~help you~~.

I told my son to start his homework, and he was about to ~~start his homework~~, but then his friend called.

1   I didn't say anything, but I was about to say something.

2   We'll get to the meeting around 9:00, but Carlos won't get to the meeting until later.

3   I'm not going to be on time for the meeting, but Gary is going to be on time for the meeting.

I'm not going to be on time for the meeting, but Gary is going to be on time for the meeting.

4   Francesca won't be working when we get there, but Sofia will be working when we get there.

Francesca won't be working when we get there, but Sofia will be working when we get there.

5   I won't be at work tomorrow. Will you be at work tomorrow?

I won't be at work tomorrow. Will you be at work tomorrow?

Practice 15/a Complete the sentences using ellipsis. Use contractions.

Examples: A: Is Sarah going to fly to India?

B1:   I think she _____'s going to_____, but I'm not sure when.

B2:   I think she _____is_____, but I'm not sure when.

A: Are you and Larry going to go to the mall?

B1:   I _____'m not going to_____, but Larry is.

B2:   I _____'m not_____, but Larry is.

A: Are you leaving now?

B: I _____'m about to_____, but I have a little more work to do.

1   A: Are you going to sell your car?

B1:   No, I _____. I'm going to keep it.

B2:   No, I _____. I'm going to keep it.

2   A: Will you help me move my piano to the attic?

B: Yes, I _____, but I don't want to.

3   A: Are you and your brother going to play football?

B1:   My brother _____, but I am.

B2:   My brother _____, but I am.

4   A: Are you going to paint the house this summer?

B1:   Yes, I _____. Please stop asking me.

B2:   Yes, I _____. Please stop asking me.

5   A: You were really angry with your boss today. Did you quit your job?

B: Almost. I _____, but I changed my mind.

6   A: Are we eating dinner now?

B: We _____. Wash your hands.

Unit 4

Unit 5 ▶ nouns and pronouns

5.1 ▶ subject pronouns and object pronouns

DISCOVER

    *a   **Sarah** talked to **John**.*
    *b   **She** talked to **him**.*

    *c   **John** listened to **Sarah**.*
    *d   **He** listened to **her**.*

1   Look at *a* and *b*. Is *Sarah* the same as *she*? Is *John* the same as *him*?
2   Look at *b* and *d*. Why is *she* used in *b* but *her* used in *d*? Why is *him* used in *b* but *he* used in *d*?
3   Look at *a* and *c*. In which sentence is *Sarah* the subject of the sentence? In which sentence is *Sarah* the object?
4   Look at *a* and *c*. In which sentence is *John* the subject of the sentence? In which sentence is *John* the object?

LEARN (See Table 5a.)

▶ In a basic, simple English sentence, the *subject* is the person or thing that is <u>doing</u> the action of the verb. The *object* is the person or thing that is <u>receiving</u> the action of the verb.

    The boy   ate   **the sandwich**.
    subject   object

▶ *Subject pronouns* replace nouns which are subjects. *Object pronouns* replace nouns which are objects.

    He   ate   **it**.
    subject   object
    pronoun   pronoun

5a

subject pronouns		object pronouns	
singular	plural	singular	plural
I	we	me	us
you	you	you	you
he, she, it	they	him, her, it	them

REMEMBER

▶ *You* is singular and plural in English.

Practice 1 Underline the correct pronoun.

Example: (<u>We</u>/Us) saw (she/<u>her</u>).

1   (Me/I) helped (they/them).

2   (Him/He) will call (us/we).

3   (She/Her) loves (I/me).

4   (Them/They) had lunch with (her/she).

5   (We/Us) don't know (he/him).

6   (They/Them) talked to (we/us).

7   (Her/She) is going to visit (we/us).

8   (I/Me) don't like (her/she).

Practice 2 Write one pronoun in each blank to replace the underlined subjects and objects.

Example: <u>Mary</u> talked to <u>her husband</u>.

    _____*She*_____ talked to _____*him*_____.

1   <u>Sam</u> went to the zoo with <u>his wife</u>.

    _____ went to the zoo with _____.

2   <u>John and I</u> work with <u>Sarah and her friend</u>.

    _____ work with _____.

3   <u>The boy</u> told <u>Larry and me</u> a story.

    _____ told _____ a story.

4   <u>Your sisters</u> are going to play with <u>the boys</u>.

    _____ are going to play with _____.

5   <u>Tom and Jerry</u> studied with <u>Mark and me</u>.

    _____ studied with _____.

6   <u>My brother</u> will fix <u>the car</u>.

    _____ will fix _____.

7   <u>You and Alex</u> studied with <u>Mary and Carlos</u>.

    _____ studied with _____.

8   <u>Mary and Carlos</u> studied with <u>you and Alex</u>.

    _____ studied with _____.

5.2 ▶ possessive adjectives and possessive pronouns

DISCOVER

    a   This is **my book**.
    b   This is **mine**.
1   How are a and b different?
    c   **Her office** is on the fourth floor.
    d   **Hers** is on the fourth floor.
2   How are c and d different?

LEARN (See Table 5b.)

▶ *Possessive adjectives* and *possessive pronouns* show *possession*—who or what is the <u>owner</u> of something. A noun must <u>always</u> follow a possessive adjective. A noun must <u>never</u> follow a possessive pronoun.

    *This is **my pen**.*   *Where is **your car**?*
    → *This is **mine**.*   → *Where is **yours**?*

5b

possessive adjectives		possessive pronouns	
<u>singular</u>	<u>plural</u>	<u>singular</u>	<u>plural</u>
my	*our*	*mine*	*ours*
your	*your*	*yours*	*yours*
his, her, its	*their*	*his, hers*	*theirs*

REMEMBER

    wrong → *This is **ours** house.*
    right → *This is **our** house.*
    wrong → *This is **our**.*
    right → *This is **ours**.*

Practice 3 Underline the correct possessive adjectives and possessive pronouns.

Example: (<u>Your</u>/Yours) project is very good.

1   (Our/Ours) TV is bigger than (yours/your).

2   This is not (my/mine). It's (your/yours).

3   This isn't (our/ours). It's (theirs/their).

4   I lost (my/mine) keys.

5   (Mine/My) car is older than (her/hers).

6   (Your/Yours) swimming pool is bigger than (ours/our).

7   I have (my/mine) cell phone. Do you have (your/yours)?

8   Mary took the wrong keys. She didn't take (hers/her). She took (my/mine).

9   This is the wrong room. (Our/Ours) is over there.

10   These books aren't (their/theirs). They're (your/yours).

5.3 ▶ possessive nouns

DISCOVER

a   Tom: *Is that your car?*
b   Jerry: *No, it's not mine. It's **her car**.*
c   Tom: *Who?*
d   Jerry: *Mary. It's **Mary's car**.*
e   Tom: *It's **Mary's**?*
f   Jerry: *Yes, it's **Mary's**.*

1   Look at *b* and *d*. If we are talking about *Mary*, what is another way to say *her car*?
2   Look at *d*, *e* and *f*. If we are talking about *Mary's car*, is it necessary to repeat *car* every time we talk about it?

g   Sam: *Does that pen belong to the **boy**?*
h   Dave: *Yes, it's the **boy's** book.*
i   Sam: *It's the **boy's**?*
j   Dave: *Yes, it's **his**.*
k   Sam: *Do those books belong to the **girls**?*
l   Dave: *Yes, they're the **girls'** books.*

3   Look at *g* and *h*. Is *boy* a singular or plural noun? How does *boy* change to show possession?
4   Look at *k* and *l*. Is *girls* a singular or plural noun? How does *girls* change to show possession?

LEARN

▶ Possessive nouns are nouns which show <u>possession</u>. Singular nouns usually add *'s*. Plural nouns usually add *s'*.

▶ There are some irregular possessive nouns.

children →   children**'s**
men →   men**'s**
women →   women**'s**
people →   people**'s**

Names which end with *s* are written two ways: usually with *'s* (*Marcos's*) but sometimes with only an apostrophe (*Marcos'*).

Practice 4 Complete the conversations using the noun or nouns in parentheses.

Example: A: Who were you talking to on the telephone?

             B: (wife) I was talking to my _____*wife's*_____ brother.

1   A: Is that Sarah's office?

     B: (Sarah) Yes, it's _____ office.

2   A: Do these toys belong to the boys?

     B: (boys/girls) No, they're not the _____ toys. They're the _____.

3   A: Who is that?

     B: (Larry) That's _____ sister.

4   A: What is the name of the company?

     B: (company) The _____ name is ABC Incorporated.

5   A: What are the names of your babies?

     B: (babies) My _____ names are Huey, Dewey and Louie.

6   A: Who were you talking to on the telephone?

     B: (children) I was talking to the principal of my _____ school.

7   A: Excuse me. Are clothes for women on this floor?

     B: (women) No, _____ clothes are on the second floor.

8   A: What are the names of the men you work with?

     B: (men) The _____ names are Sam and Larry.

9   A: What are the names of the parents of your friend?

     B: (friend/parents) My _____ _____ names are John and Mary.

5.4 ▶ articles: *the, a* and *an*

DISCOVER

   a   *I went fishing, and I caught **a fish**. I ate **the fish** for dinner.*

1   Why did <u>a</u> fish change to <u>the</u> fish?

   b   *I picked **an apple** from my apple tree, and I gave **the apple** to my teacher.*

2   Why did <u>an</u> apple change to <u>the</u> apple?

LEARN

▶ *The, a* and *an* are called *articles*. Students sometimes have a problem knowing which article to use—*the* or *a* (or *an*)—but it is really quite easy. First, *a* and *an* have the same meaning. The only difference is that *an* is used before a vowel <u>sound</u>. But how can you know if *a* or *the* is correct? *A* is used when we are talking about one member of a group and all the members of the group are the same. *The* is used when something is unique (not a member of any group) or is different from the group. After somebody <u>changes</u> a member of a group, it is different—it is *the* member of a group that somebody changed. After I catch <u>a</u> fish, it is <u>the</u> fish that I caught. After I pick <u>an</u> apple, it is <u>the</u> apple that I picked.

REMEMBER

▶ *An* is used before the <u>sound</u> of a vowel.
   *I waited for **an hour**. (The h is silent.)*
   *Today is **a holiday**. (The h is not silent.)*
   *I have **an ugly** dog. (The u in ugly is a vowel.)*
   *He joined **a union**. (Union begins with a y sound, and y is a consonant.)*

Practice 5 Choose *a, an* or *the.*

Example: I went to ___*a*___ restaurant and asked ___*a*___ waiter for ___*a*___ cup of coffee. ___*The*___ coffee
            wasn't hot, so I asked ___*the*___ waiter to bring me ___*a*___ different cup of coffee.

1   I took _____(a) book out of _____(b) library next to the high school in my town, but _____(c) book was

   boring, so I returned _____(d) book, and I took out _____(e) different book.

2   _____(a) boy in my class was sick. _____(b) boy's mother took _____(c) boy to _____(d) doctor.

   _____(e) doctor gave medicine to _____(f) boy.

3   Professor Kline is _____(a) English teacher. He had _____(b) sleepy student in his class. Professor Kline

   tried to wake up _____(c) sleepy student again and again because he never lets _____(d) student sleep

   in his class, but _____(e) student could not stay awake. _____(f) sleepy student got _____(g) F on

   _____(h) final exam, and now he must take _____(i) class again.

5.5 ▶ *the* used for generalization

DISCOVER

   a   ***The** cigarettes are bad for your health.*

b **The** cigarettes in this store are cheaper than **the** cigarettes in that store.

1 Which sentence is about <u>all</u> cigarettes? Which sentence is about cigarettes <u>in only one place</u>?

2 One sentence is not correct. Do you know which one is not correct? Why isn't it correct?

    c All people need **the** water to live.

    d **The** water in my swimming pool is cold.

3 Which sentence is about <u>all</u> water? Which sentence is about water <u>in only one place</u>?

4 One sentence is not correct. Do you know which one is not correct? Why isn't it correct?

LEARN

▶ *The* is not used when talking about things in general. It is used only to talk about specific members of a group.

Practice 6 If *the* is necessary, write it in the blank. If *the* is not necessary, write Ø in the blank (Ø = nothing).

Example: Many children don't like to eat _____Ø_____ vegetables.

        _____The_____ vegetables we had for dinner last night were good.

1 _____ sugar is sweet.

2 _____ sugar is in the kitchen.

3 My father taught me that _____ hard work is important.

4 I never drink _____ coffee. It keeps me awake.

5 I never drink _____ coffee in this restaurant. It's very bad.

6 _____ students in my class are lazy.

7 _____ students should study, work hard and listen to their teachers.

8 _____ Mexican food is very spicy.

9 _____ mice like to eat cheese.

5.6 ▶ *any* and *some*

DISCOVER

    a Alex bought **some** sugar.

    b Alex didn't buy **any** sugar.

1 Which word do we use for affirmative sentences (sentences that are not questions and are not negative)? Which word do we use for negative sentences?

    c Did Alex buy **any** sugar?

    d Did Alex buy **some** sugar?

2 Which two words do we use for questions?

LEARN

▶ *Some* is used for affirmative statements. *Any* is used for negative sentences. *Some* and *any* are both used for questions.

Practice 7 Complete the sentences with *some* or *any*. Write all possible answers.

Examples: There isn't _____any____ money in our bank account.

         Does Alex need __any or some_ help?

1 Do you want _____ coffee?

2 I don't have _____ time.

3 There are _____ people in the house.

4 Is there _____ milk in the refrigerator?

5 Please go to the supermarket and buy _____ orange juice.

6 There isn't _____ paper in the printer.

7 We don't have _____ apples, but we have _____ bananas.

8 Do you have _____ time to help me?

▶ **nouns and pronouns**

9   She doesn't have _____ aunts or uncles.

10   Are there _____ tomatoes in the garden?

5.7 ▶ indefinite pronouns

DISCOVER

    a   ***Everyone*** *in my family* ***speak*** *Spanish.*

    b   ***Every one wants*** *to eat Chinese food.*

    c   ***Everyone thinks*** *it is a bad idea.*

1   Two of the sentences are incorrect. Only one sentence is correct. Which sentence is correct? Why are the other two sentences incorrect?

LEARN (See Table 5c.)

▶ We use *indefinite pronouns* to talk about things and people when we cannot say or when we do not want to say exactly what they are or who they are.

5c			
indefinite pronouns			
someone = somebody *something*	*everyone = everybody* *everything*	*anyone = anybody* *anything*	*no one = nobody* *nothing*

REMEMBER

▶ Except for *no one*, <u>all</u> indefinite pronouns are written as <u>one word</u>.

    wrong → ***Every thing*** *is ready.*

    right →   ***Everything*** *is ready.*

▶ You must use the <u>singular</u> form of verbs with indefinite pronouns.

    wrong → *Nobody* ***are*** *here.*

    right →   *Nobody* ***is*** *here.*

    wrong → *Somebody* ***have*** *a problem.*

    right →   *Somebody* ***has*** *a problem.*

  This is true about *every* and *no.*

    wrong → *Every student* ***have*** *a pencil.*

    right →   *Every student* ***has*** *a pencil.*

    wrong → *No man* ***want*** *to lose his hair.*

    right →   *No man* ***wants*** *to lose his hair.*

▶ In English, it is not correct to have two negative words in one sentence.

    wrong → *I* ***didn't*** *do* ***nothing***.

    right →   *I* ***didn't*** *do* ***anything***.

    right →   *I did* ***nothing***.

Practice 8 Correct the mistakes in the sentences.

1   No body went to the meeting.

2   I don't have nothing.

3   Not every man like sports.

4   Are everyone here?

5   Everyone in the office hate the new manager.

6   If everybody are ready, we will start the test.

7   I didn't see nobody.

8   No student understand the homework.

9   Some one took my dictionary.

10 Every cat like to eat meat.

Practice 9 Change the sentences as in the examples. Use contractions.

Examples: I went nowhere.

I didn't go anywhere.

Larry doesn't want anything to eat.

Larry wants nothing to eat.

Talk to no one.

Don't talk to anyone.

1   Michael didn't speak to anybody.

2   She said nothing.

3   Let no one in this room.

4   Don't tell anyone what happened.

5   John doesn't know anything about computers.

6   He doesn't have any money.

7   I have no idea.

8   Mary wants nothing.

9   She didn't go anywhere.

10   Say nothing to nobody.

5.8 ▶ count nouns, noncount nouns and expressions of quantity

DISCOVER
    a   My father gave me **many** good **advices**.
    b   Do you want **rices** with your dinner?
    c   There are **much books** in the library.
1   Look at *a, b* and *c*. All of the sentences are incorrect. Why?

LEARN (See Table 5d.)
▶ Some nouns in English are *countable*. Some are *uncountable*. For example, because *car* is a countable noun, we can talk about *one car* or *two cars* or *many cars* or *a million cars*. But because *rice*, for example, is not countable, we cannot talk about *one rice* or *two rices* or *many rices* or *a million rices*. For count nouns and noncount nouns, we use *expressions of quantity*. Some are for count nouns only, some for noncount nouns only, and some are for both.

REMEMBER
▶ *A lot of = lots of*. There is no difference in meaning.

Practice 10 Some of the sentences contain mistakes. Find the mistakes and use the expressions of quantity in Table 5d to suggest corrections that have the same meaning. There may be more than one good answer.

Example: The teacher taught us many new vocabularies today.

The teacher taught us a lot of new vocabulary today.

1   I bought several food yesterday.

2   Most birds can fly.

3   I have plenty of money.

4   Our teacher gave us many homework today.

5   This book has a lot of interesting informations in it.

6   I was late for work because there was a lot of traffics.

7   We need lots of new furniture for our new house.

8   A great deal of the students failed the test.

▶ **nouns and pronouns**

expressions of quantity used for count and noncount nouns	expressions of quantity used for count nouns	examples of count nouns
		(Most nouns in English are count nouns. These are examples.)
no some/any a lot of/lots of plenty of most all	one, two, etc. each every both a couple of a few several many a number of	banana foot pound cat idea story child kilogram table desk man toy dollar pen woman
	expressions of quantity used for noncount nouns	examples of noncount nouns
		(There are many more noncount nouns, but these nouns are ones that students often make mistakes with.)
	a little much a great deal of	advice history mail traffic bread homework money vocabulary equipment information music water food jewelry permission weather furniture luggage stuff work

9   I need the right equipments to do this job correctly.

10   The histories of my country are very interesting.

11   A couple of men spent a lot of money to buy a lot of stuff.

5.9 ▶ reflexive pronouns

DISCOVER

    a   **I** was very sick, and **he** drove **me** to the hospital.

1   Is the meaning clear?

    b   **He** was very sick, and **he** drove **him** to the hospital.

2   Is the meaning clear? Is this sentence about one man or two men?

    c   **He** was very sick, and **he** drove **himself** to the hospital.

3   Is the meaning clear? Is this sentence about one man or two men?

LEARN (See Table 5e.)

▶ We use *reflexive pronouns* when the object of a sentence is the same as the subject of the sentence.

▶ We use reflexive pronouns to make sentences stronger. For example, if you built your house and nobody helped you, you could say *I built this house,* but to make it clear that <u>nobody helped you</u>, you could say *I built this house myself.*

▶ We also use *by* + reflexive pronouns for the meaning of *alone.* If you ate lunch alone, you could say *I ate by myself.*

reflexive pronouns	
<u>singular</u>	<u>plural</u>
myself	ourselves
yourself	yourselves
himself, herself, itself	themselves

REMEMBER

▶ Reflexive pronouns are <u>always</u> written as <u>one word</u>.

▶ The only correct forms of reflexive pronouns are the ones shown below. No other forms are correct.

    wrong → *hisself*

    right →   *himself*

wrong → *ourself*

right → *ourselves*

wrong → *themself*

right → *themselves*

wrong → *theirself*

right → *themselves*

wrong → *theirselves*

right → *themselves*

▶ Many native speakers make mistakes with reflexive pronouns. They use them when they are not necessary. Below are examples of typical mistakes made by native speakers.

wrong → *Please give your homework to Professor Flagg or **myself**.*

right → *Please give your homework to Professor Flagg or **me**.*

wrong → *Alex and **myself** will attend the conference.*

right → *Alex and **I** will attend the conference.*

▶ *By* + reflexive pronoun = *alone*.

*I live **by myself**. = I live **alone**.*

*Michael sat **by himself** and didn't talk to anyone. = Michael sat **alone** and didn't talk to anyone.*

▶ When we say *help yourself (to something)*, we mean *take anything you want*.

*Welcome to the party. There's a lot of food. **Help yourself.***

Practice 11 Correct the mistakes in the sentences.

1 The hunter shot hisself in the foot.

2 Sam and Dave did the work themself.

3 My wife and myself own a house in Florida.

4 I looked at me in the mirror.

5 We did all the work ourself. Nobody helped us.

6 Larry and myself will meet with you tomorrow at 10:00.

7 Ali lives by him self.

8 The boss asked Sarah and myself to come to her office.

9 The girls did all of the work themself.

10 Myself and Michael will meet with yourself tomorrow.

Practice 12 Complete the sentences with the correct reflexive pronoun.

Example: I need help. I can't do all this work _____*myself*_____.

1 John didn't do all the work _____. I helped him.

2 I cut _____ badly when I was trying to cut my own hair.

3 You and Mark have to do the work _____. Nobody can help you.

4 I know a lot about cars, so when I have a problem with my car, I can usually fix it _____.

5 Francesca was angry, so she sat by _____ and didn't talk to anyone.

6 I never leave my young children at home by _____.

7 I introduced _____ to the new boss.

8 We didn't need any help. We did the job _____.

9 She burned _____ badly when she was cooking.

10 Welcome to the party, Larry. Help _____ to any of this food. Eat as much as you want.

5.10/a ▶ general and specific expressions of quantity

DISCOVER

    a   **All** *students should work hard.*

    b   **All of** *the students in my school work hard.*

1   Which sentence is about students *in general*? Which sentence is about a *specific* group of students?

LEARN (See Table 5f.)

▶ Many expressions of quantity change when we use them to talk about specific members of a group. Sometimes *of* must be used when the expression of quantity is about a specific group.

    Many *people live in California.*

    Many of *the people in California live in Los Angeles.*

▶ Sometimes *of* must be used, but there is no difference between *general* and *specific*.

    A lot of *people live in Egypt.*

    A lot of *the people in Egypt live in Cairo.*

▶ Sometimes *of* is optional and makes no difference in meaning, and there is no difference between *general* and *specific*.

    Half *the children had chocolate ice cream.*

    Half of *the children had chocolate ice cream.*

REMEMBER

▶ *A few/few* and *a little/little* are not the same. With *a few* and *a little*, the focus is on <u>something is more than nothing</u>. With *few* and *little*, the focus is on <u>what is not there</u>—*a little* or *a few* and <u>not</u> *a lot*.

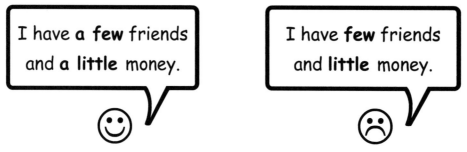

▶ Do not begin a sentence with numerals.

    wrong → *3/4 of the town was destroyed by the fire.*

    right →   *Three-fourths of town was destroyed by the fire.*

Practice 13/a Study Table 5f to better understand how these expressions of quantity are used. Then underline the correct expression of quantity.

1   I'm sure that all of the answers are correct. I checked (each / each of) them.

2   (All / All of) polar bears eat penguins.

3   (Many / Many of) the men in my family have blond hair.

4   I cannot read all of these books because (several / several of) them are in French, and I don't speak French.

5   (Some / Some of) my friends went to Scotland last year.

6   I finished (most / most of) my homework but not all of it.

7   Maria was upset because (a few of / few of) her friends came to her wedding.

8   It was nice that (a few of / few of) my friends visited me in the hospital.

9   I wasn't hungry. I ate (hardly any / hardly any of) the food at the party.

10   Most cheese in the USA comes from Wisconsin, but (some / some of) it comes from California.

11   Alex is a good boy. He gave his sister (a little / little) help with her homework.

12   Jack is not a good father. He spends (a little / little) time with his children.

general and specific expressions of quantity
count nouns

a couple (of)
I was sick for **a couple** days.
I was sick for **a couple of** days.

a couple of
A couple of your answers are wrong.
A couple of them are wrong.

a few (= **some**)
Good news! **A few** people came into our store today.

a few of (= **some**)
Good news! **A few** of the customers bought something.

a number of
A number of people are left-handed.
A number of people in my class are left-handed.
A number of students were absent today.

all
All students should study and do their homework.

all (of)
All the students in my class failed the exam.
All of the students in my class failed the exam.

almost all
Almost all penguins live in Antarctica.

almost all of
Larry ate **almost all of** the cookies in the box.
Larry ate **almost all of** them.

both
Both mothers and fathers want the best for their children.

both (of)
Both the cars in the garage are blue.
Both of the cars in the garage are blue.

each
Each student must pass the final exam in order to go to the next level.

each of
Each of the students in my class failed the exam.
The teacher thinks that **each of** them cheated on the test.

every
Every student should study and work hard.
Every student in my class failed the exam.

every one of
Every one of the students in my class failed the exam.
The boss said that **every one of** us has to be here at 8:30 tomorrow.

few (= **not many**)
Bad news! **Few** people with this disease will live longer than five years.

few of (= **not many**)
Bad news! **Few of** the students understood the teacher.

fractions: one-quarter of, two-thirds of, etc.
Three-quarters of the students in my class are girls.
I finished **2/3 of** the project.

half (of)
>*Half* the students in my class are men.
>*Half of* the students in my class are men.

hardly any
>*Hardly any* people live in North Dakota.

hardly any of
>*Hardly any of* the people I know agree with me.

lots of/a lot of
>*A lot of* people put sugar in their coffee.
>*A lot of* the teachers in this school are crazy.
>*A lot of* them are English teachers.
>*Lots of* boys like to play football.

many
>*Many* people think Casablanca *is the best movie ever made.*

many of
>*Many of* the people in my city work at the Johnson Shoe Factory.
>*Many of* them have worked there for many years.

most
>*Most* Americans speak English.

most of
>*Most of* the books in this library are very old.

no
>*No* boy or girl wants to go to summer school.

none
>*None* has/have red hair.
>*None* is/are ready.

none of
>*None of* the boys has/have red hair.
>*None of* the girls is/are ready.

(Some people believe that singular verbs are correct with *none* and *none of*, but most people use the plural form.)

numerical expressions of quantity (estimated): *dozens of, hundreds of, thousands of,* etc.
>*Hundreds* of the world's top business leaders attended the conference.
>*Millions* of people don't have enough to eat.

numerical expressions of quantity (specific and limited): *one, two,* etc.
>*Three* boys are playing in the park.

numerical expressions of quantity (specific members of a larger group): *one of, two of,* etc.
>*Four of* the boys in my class have the same first name.

percentages: *43% of, 50% of,* etc.
>The company fired *40% of* its workers.
>*Fifteen percent of* the students in my class failed the final exam.

several
>*Several* people were waiting to see the doctor.

several of
>*Several of* my friends went to Stanford University.
>*Several of* them are engineers.

some
>*Some* apples are green.

some of
>*Some of* the apples in the kitchen are green.

the majority of
>*The majority of* people are right-handed.
>*The majority of* the teachers in this school have a master's degree.

noncount nouns

a great deal of
>The teacher gave the students **a great deal of** homework.
>**A great deal of** the information on the internet is incorrect.

a little (= **some**)
>It's good that I have **a little** money. Something is better than nothing.

a little of (= **some**)
>You should save **a little of** this money for the future.

a lot of/lots of
>**A lot of** the fruit that we eat comes from California.
>**A lot of** furniture is made in North Carolina.
>**Lots of** coffee is grown in Brazil.

all
>**All** sugar is sweet.

all (of)
>**All** the information in this book is wrong.
>**All of** the information in this book is wrong.

almost all
>**Almost all** rice is grown in China and India.

almost all of
>**Almost all of** the water in the world is salt water.

fractions: **one-quarter of, two-thirds, etc.**
>Carlos spends **three-fourths** of his time watching TV.

half (of)
>The airline lost **half** my luggage.
>I spent **half of** the cash.

hardly any
>There is **hardly any** food in the house.

hardly any of
>After dinner was finished, **hardly any of** the soup was left.

little (= **not much**)
>It's bad that I have **little** money.

little of (= **not much**)
>I remember **little of** the advice she gave me.

most
>**Most** violence is caused by men.

most of
>I drank **most of** the coffee in the pot.

much
>**Much** money was wasted on unimportant things.

much of
>**Much of** his advice was good.

no
>**No** rice is grown in Alaska.

percentages: **43% of, 50% of, etc.**
>The Middle East has **56% of** the world's oil reserves.

some
>**Some** tea is green.

some of
>**Some of** the tea in the kitchen is green.

5.11/a ▶ problems of pronoun agreement

DISCOVER (See Table 5g.)

    a   *Somebody called me, but **he** didn't leave a message.*
    b   *Somebody called me, but **he or she** didn't leave a message.*
    c   *Somebody called me, but **they** didn't leave a message.*

1 Which is correct—*a, b* or *c*? How many people called? Only one, right? Does the speaker know if the caller was a man or woman?

    d   *If a student has a problem, the teacher will help **him**.*
    e   *If a student has a problem, the teacher will help **him or her**.*
    f   *If a student has a problem, the teacher will help **them**.*

2 Which is correct—*d, e* or *f*? Is *a student* singular or plural? Do we know if the student is a boy or a girl?

    g   *Every car driver should wear **his** seat belt.*
    h   *Every car driver should wear **his or her** seat belt.*
    i   *Every car driver should wear **their** seat belt.*

3 Which is correct—*g, h* or *i*? How many people can drive one car? Only one, right? Is it always a man?

LEARN

▶ What is the answer? An old-fashioned rule of English grammar says that we should always use only masculine pronouns (*he, him* or *his*) when we don't know if a person is a man or woman or if we are talking about an imaginary person who could be a man or a woman. That means *a, d* and *g* are correct. But many native speakers do not follow this rule. Why? Because when a person could be a man <u>or</u> a woman, it sounds strange to use only *he, him* or *his*. Maybe it's correct, but it just sounds wrong. So what is the solution to this problem? There are four possible solutions.

1 Sometimes native speakers use masculine and feminine pronouns together. *he or she, him or her* or *his or her*.
    *Somebody called me, but **he or she** didn't leave a message.*
    *If a student has a problem, the teacher will help **him or her**.*
    *Every car driver should wear **his or her** seat belt.*

    This solution will keep you out of trouble with the grammar police, but this solution is not perfect. Always using both masculine and feminine pronouns together is a lot of work for the mouth.
    *If a student needs help with **his or her** project, **he or she** should ask **his or her** teacher, and then the teacher will try to help **him or her**.*

2 Sometimes native speakers use a *slash*: *he/she, him/her* or *his/her*.
    *Somebody called me, but **he/she** didn't leave a message.*
    *If a student has a problem, the teacher will help **him/her**.*
    *Every car driver should wear **his/her** seat belt.*

    But when native speakers are reading these forms aloud, they usually say "*he or she*", "*him or her*" or "*his or her*," so this solution works only in writing.

3 Sometimes native speakers use the plural to avoid this problem.
    *If **students** have a problem, the teacher will help **them**.*

    This works sometimes, but not always.

4 Solutions 1, 2 and 3 all work sometimes, but the solution most native speakers (even some English teachers) use is to break the rules of grammar. They use *they, them* or *their*.
    *If a student needs help with **their** science project, **they** should ask **their** teacher, and then the teacher will try to help **them**.*

    Using *they, them* or *their* is not the very best English, but it solves a problem. So what should you do? In formal speaking and writing, when you want to use your very best English, use solutions 1, 2 or 3. In informal speaking and writing, do what most native speakers do—use solution 4. (But be careful of the grammar police.)

5g

formal and informal singular pronoun and possessive adjective usage							
subject pronouns		object pronouns		possessive adjectives		reflexive pronouns	
<u>formal</u>	<u>informal</u>	<u>formal</u>	<u>informal</u>	<u>formal</u>	<u>informal</u>	<u>formal</u>	<u>informal</u>
he ☺	*they* ☺	*him* ☺	*them* ☺	*his* ☺	*their* ☺	*himself* ☺	*themselves* ☺
she ☺		*her* ☺		*her* ☺		*herself* ☺	*themself* ☹

Practice 14/a What would you say in these situations? Study Table 5g to better understand how these pronouns and possessive adjectives are used. Then write the words that you think are best for the situation.

1   (You are talking about a football team. All of the players are men.)

Each guy on the team needs to do _____(a) best, try _____(b) hardest and remember

everything that _____(c) coach told _____(d). _____(e) should also study
the game plan carefully.

2   (You are speaking on the telephone to the secretary of the president of a company. You do not know if the president of the company is a man or a woman.)

After I meet with the president of your company and I tell _____(a) about my company's products,

I am sure that _____(b) will want to buy them.

3   (You are watching TV at home. Your sister tells you that you have a telephone call. You do not know who the caller is.)

I don't want to talk on the phone now. Get _____(a) telephone number and tell _____(b)

I will call _____(c) back later.

4   (You are a professor writing instructions for a university laboratory experiment. The students are men and women.)

Each student must first read the instructions that I have given to _____(a) and then carefully record

_____(b) results to be sure that _____(c) findings are accurate. _____(d)

must then submit _____(e) completed report to me on Friday.

5   (You are relaxing and talking to your friends about a party you are planning. You have invited men and women.)

I need to call each person who is coming to the party and tell _____(a) that _____(b) have

to bring _____(c) own towel if _____(d) plan to go swimming.

DISCOVER (See Table 5g.)
   a   *An ambulance came to the high school because a student hurt* **himself** *badly.*
   b   *An ambulance came to the high school because a student hurt* **him- or herself** *badly.*
   c   *An ambulance came to the high school because a student hurt* **themselves** *badly.*
   d   *An ambulance came to the high school because a student hurt* **themself** *badly.*
1   Which is correct—*a, b, c* or *d*? (Boys and girls go to this high school.)
2   Look at *d*. Do you see a problem with *themself*?

LEARN
▶ Many English teachers believe *themself* is a serious crime against English grammar. They are not happy when people use *they, them* or *their* to talk about only one person, but they really hate it when people use *themself*. Why? Because it doesn't make sense (and is not correct) to use the plural *them* with the singular *self*. But many native speakers say *themself* because they don't want to use the plural *themselves* to talk about only one person.

So what is the solution to this problem? As we saw with *they, them* or *their*, there is no perfect solution. The best thing is to remember about <u>formal</u> and <u>informal</u>. When you are speaking or writing informally, relax, but in serious, formal speaking and writing, when you want to use your very best English, use the solutions we talked about before. Try hard not to say *themselves*, and try very hard not to say *themself*.

Unit 6 ▶ asking questions

6.1 ▶ question word order (*yes/no*)

DISCOVER

a   Mary [**was**] sick.

b   [**Was**] Mary sick?

1   Where is *was* in *a*?

2   When *a* is changed to a question, where does *was* move to?

c   John [**will**] **go** to California.

d   [**Will**] John **go** to California?

3   Where is *will* in *c*?

4   When *c* is changed to a question, where does *will* move to?

e   They [   ] **know** the answer.

f   [**Do**] they **know** the answer?

5   Is there a form of *be* in *e*? Is there a modal verb like *will, can, could* or *should* in *e*?

6   If there is no form of *be* or no word like *will, can, could* or *should* in a sentence, how do we change it to a question?

g   Linda [   ] **lives** in Rome.

h   [**Does**] Linda **live** in Rome?

7   Why do you see *does* in the question and not *do*?

8   How did the main verb *lives* change when *g* was changed to a question?

i   Alex [   ] **went** to the mall.

j   [**Did**] Alex **go** to the mall?

9   Why do you see *did* in the question and not *do* or *does*?

10   How did the main verb *went* change when *i* was changed to a question?

LEARN (See Table 6a.)

▶ Students often have problems making questions in English, but it is really quite simple. First, let's focus on verbs. Are all verbs the same? No, they are not. Let's look at three kinds of verbs in English.

6a		
be	*modal verbs*	**examples of main verbs**
is	can	come
are	could	eat
am	may	go
was	might	have
were	must	see
	ought to	sleep
	shall	talk
	should	walk
	will	work
	would	write

▶ Look again at *a* and *b*. You can see that when the verb is a form of *be*, we move the verb to the front of the subject to make a question. Look again at *c* and *d*. You can see that when there is a modal verb before the main verb, we move the modal to the front of the subject to make a question. But what if there is no form of *be*? What if there is no modal? Look again at *f, h* and *j*. You can see the answer. When there is no form of *be* or a modal verb, we must put *do, does* or *did* in front of the subject to make a question.

REMEMBER

▶ Never use the *-s* form, the past form or the *-ing* form of the main verb when *do, does* or *did* are in the sentence.

wrong → *Does she **speaks** Hindi?*   **right** → *Does she **speak** Hindi?*

wrong → *Did he **took** a shower?*   **right** → *Did he **take** a shower?*

wrong → *Do you **studying** in the library?*   **right** → *Do you **study** in the library?*

Practice 1 Change these sentences to *yes/no* questions (questions which can be answered with *yes* or *no*).

Example: He was tired.
                   Was he tired?

1   They are happy.

2   The nurse is in the lab.

3   She's a teacher.

4   His mother was sleeping.

5   It's finished.

6   You're sure.

7   It's written in pencil.

8   It's time to eat.

9   We're leaving soon.

10   Linda's being helped by the police officer.

Practice 2 Change these sentences to *yes/no* questions (questions which can be answered with *yes* or *no*).

Example: He will be here tomorrow.
                   Will he be here tomorrow?

1   She can speak Italian.

2   Noura should take her medicine.

3   The girls will go to the picnic.

4   Carlos can ride a bicycle.

5   You'll help me later.

6   Maria would like to help.

7   We should be going.

8   Alex can change the oil.

9   The books should be returned to the library.

10   We'll be there soon.

Practice 3 Change these sentences to *yes/no* questions (questions which can be answered with *yes* or *no*).

Examples: They work in a factory.
                   Do they work in a factory?
                   He lives in Iceland.
                   Does he live in Iceland?

1   Mary wants to eat.

2   Her sister lives in San Francisco.

3   Her brothers live in Los Angeles.

4   You play basketball.

5   You and he play basketball.

6   The secretary has three children.

7   Sarah goes to work at 5:30.

▶ **asking questions**

8   You go to work at 6:00.

9   Alex runs fast.

10   Our teacher has a big nose.

Practice 4 Change these sentences to *yes/no* questions (questions which can be answered with *yes* or *no*).

1   He's in the lab.

2   They are doctors.

3   Lucy was driving.

4   Mary will go to Japan.

5   Paul should be here.

6   Larry can swim.

7   Sam has three children.

8   Tom went to Ireland.

9   They work in a bank.

10   Sarah takes the 7:30 train every day.

11   Ali had fun at the party.

6.2 ▶ information questions
DISCOVER

a   Tom: ***Who*** *did you talk to?*
b   Jerry: *I talked to **Noura**.*
c   Sam: ***What*** *is that?*
d   Paul: *That is a **zebra**.*
e   Mary: ***When*** *will you help me?*
f   Sarah: *I will help you **tomorrow**.*
g   John: ***Where*** *is the dog?*
h   Mark: *The dog is **outside**.*
i   Alex: ***Why*** *did you close the window?*
j   Lucy: *I closed the window **because I am cold**.*

1   Are these *yes/no* questions? Can they be answered with *yes* or *no*? What information are the question words *who, what, when, where* and *why* asking for?

LEARN

▶ Making information questions is the same as making *yes/no* questions. The only difference is that a question word begins the sentence.

Who is used to ask about people.
  Who *did you go to the dance with?*

What is used to ask about a thing or a piece of information.
  What *did you get for your birthday?*
  What *is the name of your teacher?*

When is used to ask about time.
  When *are you going to play tennis?*

Where is used to ask about a place.
  Where *does Linda live?*

Why is used to ask about a reason.
  Why *are you angry?*

REMEMBER

▶ To make a question, we move a form of *be* or a modal verb from after the subject to before the subject. If there is no form of *be* or a modal verb, then we must put *do* or *does* or *did* before the subject.

wrong → *Who **he is**?*
right → *Who **is he**?*
wrong → *When **he will** come?*
right → *When **will he** come?*
wrong → *Where **he lives**?*
right → *Where **does he** live?*

Practice 5 Write the correct questions to get the underlined information in the answers.

Example: A: Where do you live?

B: I live <u>in Portland</u>.

1 A:

B: John was <u>in the lab</u>.

2 A:

B: Carlos bought <u>a car</u>.

3 A:

B: She will talk to <u>Mark</u>.

4 A:

B: Alex called Sarah <u>yesterday</u>.

5 A:

B: Mary walks to work <u>because she doesn't have a car</u>.

6 A:

B: Jim can play <u>the piano</u>.

7 A:

B: The student is absent <u>because he is sick</u>.

8 A:

B: Tom works with <u>Jerry</u>.

9 A:

B: John is making <u>a cake</u>.

10 A:

B: Ali is going to buy <u>a new keyboard</u>.

6.3 ▶ *what time, what kind of, which, whose*

DISCOVER

a *Paul:* **What time** did you arrive?
b *Mary:* I arrived **at 8:30**.
c *Sarah:* **What kind of** food do you like?
d *John:* I like **Italian** food.
e *Lucy:* **Which** shirt do you like—the red one or the blue one?
f *Mark:* I like the **red** one.
g *Sam:* **Whose** pen is this?
h *Sofia:* It's **my** pen.

1 Look at these pairs of questions and answers. What information are the question words asking for?

LEARN

What time is used to ask about clock time. It is also possible to use *when* for clock time.
  What time does the movie begin?

▶ asking questions

What kind of is used to ask about specific members of a general group or category. *What sort of* and *what type of* have the same meaning. It is also possible to say *which kind of*, *which sort of* and *which type of*.

What kind of *car did your father buy?*

Which is used to ask about a specific member of a group. In informal English, many people say *what*.

Which *finger did you break?*

Sometimes *one* is used with *which*.

Mary: I broke my **finger**.

Sam: *Which* **one** *did you break?* = *Which* **finger** *did you break?*

Whose is used to ask about possession.

Whose *pen is this?*

Practice 6 Write the correct question words in the blanks to get the information in the answers.

Example: _____What time_____ does the game start?   It starts at 8:30.

question   *answer*

1 _____ car is that?   It's his car.

2 _____ music does your brother like?   He likes classical music.

3 There are four cars outside. _____ one is yours?   The blue one is mine.

4 _____ does the movie start?   It starts at 7:45.

5 _____ dog is that?   It's a Yorkshire Terrier.

6 _____ house was the party at?   The party was at Noura's house.

7 _____ shoes are you going to buy?   I'm going to buy the black ones.

8 _____ one do you want?   I want this one.

9 _____ pencil is this?   I don't know. It's not mine.

10 _____ are we going to eat?   At 6:00.

11 _____ did you buy?   I bought the red one.

Practice 7 Write the correct questions to get the underlined information in the answers.

Example: A: *Whose bicycle is it?*

                 B: It's <u>Sofia's</u> bicycle.

1 A:

    B: The class starts <u>at 8.20</u>.

2 A:

    B: I bought <u>the green</u> one.

3 A:

    B: The radio station plays <u>country</u> music.

4 A:

    B: It's not my pen. Maybe <u>it's Tom's</u>.

5 A:

    B: She will come <u>at 1:00</u>.

6 A:

    B: I want <u>that</u> one.

7 A:

    B: That's <u>her</u> dog.

8   A:

    B: I'm going to stay with <u>my brother</u>.

9   A:

    B: He likes <u>history</u> books.

10 A:

    B: Francesca gets home <u>at 3:45</u>.

11 A:

    B: The one <u>with the blue cover</u> is mine.

6.4 ▶ how much, how many, how often, how far

DISCOVER

a   Mary: **How much** salt did you put in the soup?
b   John: I put **a lot of** salt in the soup.
c   Noura: **How many** cars does Paul have?
d   Ali: He has **two** cars.
e   Mark: **How often** do you call your mother?
f   Alex: I call my mother **every day**.
g   Tom: **How far** is it from New York to Los Angeles?
h   Jerry: It is **3,961 kilometers** from New York to Los Angeles.

1   Look at these pairs of questions and answers. What information are the question words asking for?
2   Look at a and c. Why are how much and how many different? Is it possible to count salt? Is it possible to count cars?

LEARN

How much is used to ask about things that we do not count—water, sugar, time, money, etc.
   How much coffee should we buy?

How many is used to ask about things that we count—bottles of water, kilograms of sugar, hours, dollars, people, etc.
   How many children does your sister have?

How often is used to ask about frequency to get answers with words like often, never, hardly ever, every day, etc.
   How often do you eat Mexican food?

How far is used to ask about distance to get answers about inches, meters, miles, kilometers, light years, etc.
   How far is your house from the school?

Practice 8 Write the correct question words in the blanks to get the information in the answers.

Example: ____How far____ is the beach from here?   It's about five miles.

question   answer

1   _____ is it to your house?   It's around a mile and a half.

2   _____ coffee does Carl drink?   He drinks too much coffee.

3   _____ is it from here?   About a hundred kilometers.

4   _____ are you going to do it?   I'm going to do it once a week.

5   _____ pizzas will she buy?   She'll buy five pizzas.

6   _____ time do we have?   Not much, so let's hurry.

7   _____ do you feed your cat?   I feed him twice a day.

8   _____ apples did you buy?   I bought 10.

9   _____ gas is there in the tank?   It's full.

10 _____ windows are there in the room? There are three windows.

11 _____ did you drive?   Around 500 miles.

Practice 9 Write the correct questions to get the underlined information in the answers.

Example: A: *How much time do you have?*

B: I have <u>a lot of</u> time.

1 A: _____

B: It's <u>very far</u> to the park—maybe <u>250 miles</u>.

2 A: _____

B: I go shopping <u>once a week</u>.

3 A: _____

B: She has <u>three</u> children.

4 A: _____

B: There is <u>very little</u> money in my bank account.

5 A: _____

B: It's about <u>15 miles</u> from my house to my job.

6 A: _____

B: I <u>hardly ever</u> go there.

7 A: _____

B: There's <u>a lot of</u> orange juice in the refrigerator.

8 A: _____

B: They didn't eat <u>any</u> cookies.

9 A: _____

B: I <u>almost never</u> eat Japanese food.

10 A: _____

B: It's around <u>three miles</u> to the beach.

6.5 ▶ *how, how* with adverbs, *how* with adjectives, *how long*

DISCOVER

a Larry: **How** *did you get here?*
b Mary: *I* **took a taxi.**
c Tom: **How well** *does Mary sing?*
d Sam: *She sings* **badly**.
e Paul: **How big** *is your apartment?*
f Mark: *It's* **very big**.
g Lucy: **How long** *did you study?*
h Ali: *I studied* **for three hours**.

1 Look at these pairs of questions and answers. What information are the question words asking for?

LEARN

How is used to ask about the way people do things.
> **How** *do you get to work everyday—by car or by bus?*

How is used with adverbs such as *well, fast* and *slowly* to get information about verbs.
> **How** <u>well</u> *do you speak Portuguese?*

How is used with adjectives such as *old, big* and *tall* to get information about nouns.
> **How** <u>tall</u> *are you?*

How long is used to ask about a length of time to get answers with words like *one hour, six years, all day,* etc.
> **How** <u>long</u> *is the movie?*

REMEMBER

▶ *How long* can also be used to ask about the length of an object.
   ***How long** is the Amazon River?*

Practice 10 Write the correct question words in the blanks to get the information in the answers. Choose from the words and phrases below.

How	How	~~How badly~~	How big	How deep	How hard
How long	How old	How soon	How tall	How well	

Example: _____How badly_____ did you do on the exam?   I got a 34.

   question   answer

1 _____ did you fix this?   I did it with a screwdriver.

2 _____ is the pool?   The pool is 10 feet deep.

3 _____ can you get here?   Very soon. In a few minutes.

4 _____ is he?   About six feet.

5 _____ is the book?   It's 434 pages long.

6 _____ will you get there?   I'll take a taxi.

7 _____ is your house?   It's very big.

8 _____ is it?   Not hard at all. It's easy.

9 _____ can you play tennis?   Not very well.

10 _____ is your brother?   He's 35.

6.6 ▶ *how long* + modal verb/a form of *do* + *it take* (someone) *to*

DISCOVER

   a Tom: ***How long does it take to** fly to Dublin?*
   b John: *It takes **about three hours to** fly to Dublin.*
   c Larry: ***How long will it take to** fix your car?*
   d Lucy: *It'll take **around three days**.*
   e Sam: ***How long did it take you to** write your book?*
   f Mark: *It took me **four years to** write my book.*

1 Look at these pairs of questions and answers. What information are the question words asking for?

LEARN

   ***How long** + modal verb/a form of **do** + **it take** (someone) **to** is used to ask about how much time is needed to do something.
   ***How long will it take you to** walk to the bank?*
   ***How long does it take to** fly to Easter Island?*

Practice 11 Write the correct question words in the blanks to get the information in the answers.

Example: A: How long will it take you to paint the house?
            B: It will take me <u>six days</u> to paint the house.

1 A:

   B: It takes around <u>25 minutes</u> to drive to work.

2 A:

   B: It took me <u>three hours</u> to do my homework.

3 A:

   B: It will take us <u>five hours</u> to drive to Toronto.

▶ **asking questions**   **63**

4 A:

   B: It should take about <u>30 minutes</u> to install this program.

5 A:

   B: It took <u>an hour</u> to get there.

6.7 ▶ *what* + a form of *do* used when the answer to a question is a verb

DISCOVER

   a   *John:*   *What is Michael **doing**?*
   b   *Noura:*   *He is **making something**.*
   c   *John:*   *What is Michael **making**?*
   d   *Noura:*   *He is making **a dog house**.*

1   Look at these pairs of questions and answers. Why are the questions different?

LEARN

▶ When a question requires a verb in the answer, we use *what* + a form of *do*.
   Mary: *What are you **doing**?*
   Paul: *I'm **fixing the dishwasher**.*

Practice 12 Write the correct question words in the blanks to get the information in the answers.

   Example: A: *What did he do yesterday?*

                B: He <u>fixed his computer</u>.

1 A:

   B: I <u>watched TV</u> last night.

2 A:

   B: We're <u>studying</u>.

3 A:

   B: He will <u>wash his car</u> on Saturday.

4 A:

   B: She's going to <u>clean her house and go shopping</u> tomorrow morning.

5 A:

   B: Tonight I'm <u>packing my suitcase for my trip to Hawaii</u>.

6.8 ▶ *what* and *who* used when the answer to a question is the subject

DISCOVER

   a   *John:*   ***What** made that noise?*
   b   *Lucy:*   ***A mouse** made that noise.*
   c   *Alex:*   ***Who** stole your car?*
   d   *Sofia:*   ***Jack** stole my car.*

1   Do you remember what you have learned about how to make questions? A form of *be* or a modal verb is moved from after the subject to before the subject, and if there is no form of *be* or a modal verb, then *do, does* or *did* must be put before the subject.

2   Look at *a* and *c*. Do these questions follow the rule about moving a form of *be*, a modal verb or *do, does* or *did* in front of the subject to ask a question? Why not?

LEARN

▶ When the answer to a question is the <u>subject</u> of the answer, we do not put *be*, a modal verb or *do, does* or *did* in front of the subject.
   wrong → *Who **does have** my pen?*   **wrong** → *What **did start** the fire?*
   right →   *Who **has** my pen?*   **right** →   *What **started** the fire?*

Practice 13 Write the correct question words in the blanks to get the information in the answers.

Example: A: *Who went shopping with Larry?*

B: <u>Ali</u> went shopping with Larry.

1 A:

B: Sarah danced with <u>Michael</u>.

2 A:

B: <u>Sarah</u> danced with Michael.

3 A:

B: The car hit <u>the tree</u>.

4 A:

B: <u>The car</u> hit the tree.

Continue to Unit 6/advanced ↓ or go to Unit 7 →

6.9/a ▶ negative questions

DISCOVER

    a   Gary: ***Doesn't*** *your brother live in Montreal?*

    b   Lucy: *Yes, he does.*

    c   Rosa: ***Isn't*** *this cake delicious?*

    d   Ali: *Yes, it is.*

    e   Alex: *I told you to get to work, and you're still watching TV!* ***Didn't*** *you hear me?*

    f   Sofia: *Sorry, I'll get to work now.*

1   Are Gary, Rosa and Alex asking these questions because they really do not know the answers?

2   Which question is asked to confirm (make sure of) information that the speaker already thinks is correct?

3   Which question is asked to show the speaker's attitude or feeling?

4   Which question is asked to start a conversation?

LEARN

▶ We use negative questions to start a conversation (because when you ask people a question, they usually feel that they must answer you),

    Isn't *it a nice day?*

    Doesn't *our teacher look like a giraffe?*

to confirm information that the speaker <u>already</u> thinks is probably correct

    Aren't you *Mary's sister?*

    Didn't *you used to be in my English class?*

and to show the speaker's attitude or feeling.

    I told you ten times already. The answer is no! ***Can't*** *you hear?*

    I've been cleaning the house all day, and you're just lying there on the sofa! ***Aren't*** *you going to help me?*

Negative questions are always *yes/no* questions, and they almost always use contractions.

Practice 14/a Write negative questions that you think are correct for the situation.

Example: You want to start a conversation with the person sitting next to you on an airplane. You think the food on the plane is terrible.

       Isn't the food on this plane terrible?

1   You are talking to your friend, and he is not listening to you.

2   You are a teacher, and you are upset because a student did not do her homework.

3   You left a message for your brother to bring potato chips to your party, and you are not happy that he has just arrived at your party without any potato chips.

▶ **asking questions**

4   You think the test is on Monday, but you are not 100% sure.

5   You want to start a conversation with somebody standing next to you in an art museum. You think that the painting you are looking at is beautiful.

6   You think your friend is asking a lot of dumb questions. He acts like he doesn't know anything.

7   You think my name is John, but you are not 100% sure.

8   You are telling your friend that you got fired, but he acts like he doesn't care.

9   Your son should be studying, but he isn't.

6.10/a ▶ tag questions

DISCOVER

a   Gary: *Your brother **lives** in Oregon, **doesn't** he?*
b   Sarah: *Yes, he does.*
c   Lucy: *This class **is** really boring, **isn't** it?*
d   Rosa: *Yes, it is.*
e   Sofia: *You**'ll** help me, **won't** you?*
f   Tom: *Yes, I will.*
g   Sam: *They **haven't** eaten yet, **have** they?*
h   Ali: *No, they haven't.*

1   Why are Gary, Lucy, Sofia and Sam ending their sentences with questions?

6b

tag questions

be
The form in the base sentence is the same in the tag question.
> *He **wasn't** at the meeting, **was** he?*
> *Mary **is** very intelligent, **isn't** she?*

modals and *don't*, *doesn't* and *didn't*
The modal is repeated.
> *You **won't** forget, **will** you?*
> *He **can** speak Spanish, **can't** he?*
> *She **doesn't** have a car, **does** she?*

When there is no modal, use *don't*, *doesn't* or *didn't*.
> *You live in Atlanta, **don't** you?*
> *He works in a library, **doesn't** he?*
> *Sofia went to Wales, **didn't** she?*

perfect tenses
Have, has and *had* are repeated.
> *You**'ve** eaten, **haven't** you?*
> *He **hadn't** done it yet, **had** he?*

this, that, these, those
Use *it* or *they*.
> *That's** your pen, isn't **it**?*
> *These** aren't John's books, are **they**?*

there is, there are
> *There isn't** a computer in the classroom, **is there**?*
> *There are** five players on a basketball team, **aren't there**?*

everybody, something, etc.
Use *they* or *it*.
> *Everybody came to the conference, didn't **they**?*
> *Nothing is broken, is **it**?*

LEARN (See Table 6b.)

▶ Tag questions are a way to change a sentence that <u>is not</u> a question to a sentence that <u>is</u> a question. Tag questions are similar to negative questions—they are used to start a conversation and to confirm (make sure of) information that the speaker thinks is probably correct, but there is one difference: Sometimes tag questions are used to confirm information that the speaker <u>is not sure of</u>.

▶ If the base sentence is affirmative, the tag question is always negative.
> Today **is** Friday, **isn't** it?
>   +   −

▶ If the base sentence is negative, the tag question is always affirmative.
> Today **isn't** Friday, **is** it?
>   −   +

▶ Tag questions are used to confirm information. When the speaker <u>is almost sure</u> that some information is correct, the voice goes down at the end of the sentence.
> Your test score is very bad. You didn't study, **did you?**

When the speaker <u>is really not sure</u>, the voice goes up.
> I just moved to this town. The library is on Main Street, **isn't it?**

REMEMBER

▶ Many native speaker use the tag question *aren't I?* This is not correct English. It is better to use *am I not?*
> **wrong** → I'm next, **aren't I?**
> **right** →   I'm next, **am I not?**

Practice 15/a Write tag questions.

Example: You don't understand me, _____*do you*_____?

1 We should leave, _____?

2 You went to Russia last year, _____?

3 She hadn't been there before, _____?

4 He told you what happened, _____?

5 There are 30 days in April, _____?

6 He wouldn't do it, _____?

7 Francesca didn't call you, _____?

8 This isn't correct, _____?

9 There wasn't a lot of traffic, _____?

10 I'm right, _____?

11 You wouldn't like to go to a movie, _____?

12 She's not angry, _____?

Unit 7 ▶ phrasal verbs

7.1 ▶ phrasal verbs

DISCOVER

    a   John **took** the bus.

1   What is the verb in *a*?

    b   John **took off** his hat.

2   What is the verb in *b*?

    c   John **put** it **on**.

3   What is the verb in *c*?

    d   John **came up with** a good idea.

4   What is the verb in *d*?

LEARN

▶ Each of the examples above contains <u>one</u> verb. *B, c* and *d* are examples of *phrasal verbs*. Phrasal verbs are made from ordinary one-word verbs <u>plus</u> one and sometimes two other words called *particles*. You probably know many phrasal verbs already: *turn on, wake up, sit down* and *get up*, for example. For students, it is learning the <u>meanings</u> of new phrasal verbs that is most important. However, there are some things about the grammar of phrasal verbs that are important to understand too.

REMEMBER

▶ Phrasal verbs are a very common and a very important part of the English language. Students need to learn new verbs, so that means that they need to learn new phrasal verbs.

▶ Phrasal verbs are verbs. They are not *idioms*. (But they are *idiomatic*.) They are <u>not</u> always informal. In fact, they are usually <u>not informal</u>.

7.2 ▶ separable and inseparable phrasal verbs

DISCOVER

    a   Mary **put on** her hat.

    b   Mary **put** her hat **on**.

    c   Mary **put** it **on**.

1   Is it possible to separate the phrasal verb *put on*?

    d   Alex **fell off** his bicycle.

    e   Alex **fell off** it.

2   Is it possible to separate the phrasal verb *fall off*?

LEARN

▶ Some phrasal verbs are *separable*. This means that they can be separated by an object.
    *Mary **cleaned** her room **up**.*
    *= Mary **cleaned up** her room.*

▶ We know that pronouns can replace nouns. In this sentence, *it* can replace *her room*. However, there is a rule you must remember with separable phrasal verbs. Pronouns can <u>only</u> be placed <u>between</u> the verb and the particle.
    wrong → *Mary **cleaned up** it.*
    right →   *Mary **cleaned** it **up**.*

▶ Some phrasal verbs are *inseparable*. This means that they <u>cannot be separated</u> by a noun or an object pronoun.
    wrong → *The teacher **called** him **on**.*
    right →   *The teacher **called on** him.*

REMEMBER

▶ Many phrasal verbs are separable, and many are inseparable. There is no rule that students can learn so that they will always know. It is something that they have to pay attention to when they learn the meanings of new phrasal verbs.

Practice 1 All of the phrasal verbs in this exercise are separable. Use the objects in parentheses to write each sentence three ways.

    Example: Sam cut up. (the meat, it)   a Sam cut up the meat.

                                                                          b Sam cut the meat up.

                            c *Sam cut it up.*

1   I made up. (a story, it)   a

                            b

                            c

2   Carlos put away. (his shoes, them)   a

                            b

                            c

3   The teacher will call off. (the test, it)   a

                            b

                            c

4   The bank turned down. (Sarah, her)   a

                            b

                            c

5   He called back. (his friend, him)   a

                            b

                            c

6   Please clean up. (this mess, it)   a

                            b

                            c

7   They're tearing down. (the building, it)   a

                            b

                            c

8   Paul let down. (his father, him)   a

                            b

                            c

Practice 2 All of the phrasal verbs in this exercise are inseparable. Use the objects in parentheses to write each sentence two ways.

Example: Mark ran into. (a tree, it)   a *Mark ran into a tree.*

                                      b *Mark ran into it.*

1   Jack cheats on. (the tests, them)   a

                            b

2   She looked for. (her son, him)   a

                            b

3   The nurse is caring for. (Lucy, her)   a

                            b

4   I'll get on. (the horse, it)   a

                            b

▶ **phrasal verbs**

5   I'm counting on. (John, him)   a

                                            b

6   Don't fall for. (his lie, it)   a

                                            b

7   I dealt with. (the problem, it)   a

                                            b

8   Alex stepped on. (a banana, it)   a

                                            b

7.3 ▶ phrasal verbs used as nouns

DISCOVER

  a   The teacher will **hand out** the papers.
  b   The teacher will give **handouts** to the students.
1   Look at *a*. Is *hand out* a verb or a noun?
2   Look at *b*. Is *handout* a verb or a noun?

  c   The company is going to **lay** 100 employees **off**.
  d   The company announced 100 **layoffs**.
3   Look at *c*. Is *lay off* a verb or a noun?
4   Look at *d*. Is *layoffs* a verb or a noun?

LEARN

▶ Some phrasal verbs can be used as nouns. Sometimes the noun is written as one word. Sometimes the noun is written with a hyphen. There is no rule about this, and not everyone agrees about which way is correct.

  I **screwed up** the project.
  → This a big **screwup**.

  Michael likes to **show off**.
  → Michael is a **show-off**.

Practice 3 Decide which word is correct—the phrasal verb or the noun—and underline it.

  Examples: I'm going to (<u>stop over</u>/stopover) in Frankfort.

              I have a (stop over/<u>stopover</u>) in Frankfort.

1   There was a big (shake up/shakeup) at the office.

2   Sarah wants to (break up/breakup) with her boyfriend.

3   The salesperson made a (follow up/follow-up) call.

4   You should (back up/backup) your important computer files.

5   I was late for work because of a (break down/breakdown) on the highway.

6   The company is going to (lay off/layoff) 5,000 workers.

7   Please (hand out/handout) these tests to the students.

8   I had a (get together/get-together) at my house.

7.4 ▶ phrasal verbs used as adjectives

DISCOVER

  a   I **turned off** my computer.
  b   My computer is **turned off**.
1   Look at *a*. Is *turned off* a verb or an adjective?
2   Look at *b*. Is *turned off* a verb or an adjective?

  c   The student **spaced out** when the teacher asked her a question.
  d   The **spaced-out** student didn't know the answer to the teacher's question.

3   Look at *c*. Is *spaced out* a verb or an adjective?

4   Look at *d*. Is *spaced-out* a verb or an adjective?

LEARN

▶ The past participle of some phrasal verbs can be used as adjectives. Sometimes the adjective is written as two words. Sometimes the adjective is written with a hyphen. There is no rule about this, and not everyone agrees about which way is correct. (See Section 10.6 for more about past participles of verbs used as adjectives.)

*Larry **put** his toys **away**.*

→ *The toys are **put away**.*

*The job interview **stressed** me **out**.*

→ *I was very **stressed-out** after the job interview.*

Practice 4 Write *adj* in the blank if the words in *italics* are an adjective. Write *v* in the blank if the words in italics are a phrasal verb.

Examples: The application isn't *filled out*. ___*adj*___

  I *used up* all the printer paper. ___*v*___

1   Why is Francesca all *dressed up*? Is she going to a party? _____

2   We *fixed up* our old house before we sold it. _____

3   I was *locked out*. I had to break a window to get into my house. _____

4   Sarah *paid for* her sister's medical bills. _____

5   I am *mixed up*. I don't know what to do. _____

6   Alex bought a new monitor, but it isn't *hooked up* yet. _____

7   I was really *worn out* after the game. _____

8   Michael was sick, and he missed two weeks of school. He worked really hard to do all the work he missed, and now he is *caught up*. _____

(To learn more about phrasal verbs, see *The Ultimate Phrasal Verb Book* by Carl W. Hart.)

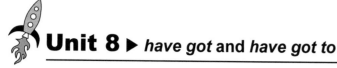# Unit 8 ▶ *have got* and *have got to*

8.1 ▶ *have = have got*

DISCOVER

    a   I **have** a car.

    b   I **have got** a car.

1 Do *a* and *b* have the same meaning?

LEARN

▶ The answer is that *a* and *b* have <u>exactly</u> the same meaning. How is this possible? *Have got* is an *idiom*. It does not follow any rules of grammar—it is something that students need to memorize. So, if *have got* means the same as *have*, what does *got* mean? The answer is that *got* means nothing. Nothing? Yes, that sounds crazy, but it is true. *Have got* is used by all native English speakers. Because it is <u>very common</u>, it is <u>very important</u> for students of English.

    They **have** a dog.

    = They **have got** a dog.

    = They**'ve got** a dog.

    She **has** three children.

    = She **has got** three children.

    = She**'s got** three children.

▶ *Have got* is <u>not</u> present perfect. It is used for the <u>present only</u>. Native speakers almost always use contractions of *have got* when they are speaking and usually when they are writing too. In informal pronunciation, native speakers often say *I got* instead of *I've got*. This is not correct grammar, but because it is very common, students must understand it when they hear it.

    I **have got** a cat.

    = I**'ve got** a cat.

    = I **got** a cat.

REMEMBER

▶ *Have got* is <u>not</u> informal English, it is <u>not</u> slang, and it is <u>not</u> "American" English. It is standard, correct English used by native speakers of English around the world. It is never necessary to use *have got*, but <u>it is necessary to understand it</u>.

Practice 1 Change the sentences so that they use *have got*. Use contractions.

Examples: We have a lot of work.

         We've got a lot of work.

         Larry has a good job.

         Larry's got a good job.

1 I have brown hair.

2 He has brown hair too.

3 We have a small house.

4 Paul has a broken arm.

5 Michael has three dogs.

6 Elephants have big ears.

7 Mark has an old book.

8 My car has a flat tire.

9 The boys have a new soccer ball.

10 I have a headache.

11 You have a big mouth.

8.2 ▶ *have got* in negative sentences

DISCOVER

    a   *I **do not have** a car.*

    b   *I **have not got** a car.*

1   How do we make negative sentences with *have got*? The same as with *have*? Differently?

LEARN

▶ Sentences with *have* and with *have got* are changed to negative in different ways.

    *They **do not have** a dog.*

    = *They **have not got** a dog.*

    = *They **haven't got** a dog.*

    *She **doesn't have** any children.*

    = *She **has not got** any children.*

    = *She **hasn't got** any children.*

REMEMBER

▶ In negative sentences with *have got*, native English speakers almost always use contractions. For that reason, you must understand them. Sometimes two contractions are possible.

    not common → *I**'ve not got** a book.*   **not common** → *She**'s not got** any money.*

    common →   *I **haven't got** a book.*   **common** →   *She **hasn't got** any money.*

Both contractions are possible, but in both examples, the second contraction is much more common.

Practice 2 Change the sentences so that they use *have got*. Use contractions.

Example: My sister doesn't have a cat.

        My sister hasn't got a cat.

1   Our house doesn't have a garage.

2   We don't have enough time.

3   Tom and Linda don't have any children.

4   Jack doesn't have a job.

5   My mother and father don't have a TV.

6   I don't have your dictionary.

7   The children don't have their homework.

8   Carlos doesn't have a calculator.

9   Snakes don't have legs.

10   Noura doesn't have a car.

8.3 ▶ *have got* in questions

DISCOVER

    a   ***Do** you **have** a car?*

    b   ***Have** you **got** a car?*

1   How do we make questions with *have got*? The same as with *have*? Differently?

LEARN

▶ Sentences with *have* and with *have got* are changed to questions in different ways.

    ***Do** they **have** a dog?*

    = ***Have** they **got** a dog?*

    ***Does** she **have** any children?*

    = ***Has** she **got** any children?*

Practice 3 Change the questions so that they use *have got*.

Example: Do you have a computer?

        Have you got a computer?

▶ *have got* **and** *have got to*

1   Does Francesca have a box of rocks?

2   Do you have enough money?

3   Does Lucy have a problem?

4   Does the hotel room have a balcony?

5   Do your sisters have tickets?

6   Does her house have a basement?

7   Do I have food in my teeth?

8   Does Mark have brown hair?

9   Do you have time to help me with my math homework?

8.4 ▶ *have to = have got to*

DISCOVER

     a   *Jim can't go to the beach tomorrow because he **has to** work.*

     b   *Jim can't go to the beach tomorrow because he **has got to** work.*

1   Do *a* and *b* have the same meaning? Think hard. Think very hard.

LEARN

▶ *Have to* and *have got to* have the same meaning. (See Section 11.6 for more about *have to* and *have got to*.)

   *I **have to** finish my work.*

   *= I **have got to** finish my work.*

   *= I**'ve got** to finish my work.*

   *Mary **has to** go to the doctor.*

   *= Mary **has got to** go to the doctor.*

   *= Mary**'s got to** go to the doctor.*

REMEMBER

▶ In informal pronunciation, native speakers often say *gotta* instead of *have got to*.

   *I **have got to** go.*

   *= I**'ve got to** go.*

   *= I **got to** go.*

   *= I **gotta** go.*

▶ Sometimes people use *gotta* in informal writing, but remember that *gotta* is never correct in serious, formal writing.

Practice 4 Change the sentences so that they use *have got to*. Use contractions.

Example: I have to work tomorrow.

          I've got to work tomorrow.

1   I have to take my son to soccer practice.

2   We have to take our cat to the vet.

3   Rosa has to do her homework.

4   The pilot has to fly to Norway.

5   The students have to take a test.

6   Michael has to clean his house.

7   I have to get to work early tomorrow.

8   You have to be quiet.

9   My father has to work on Sunday.

10   We have to wake up at 6:15.

11   Linda has to have an operation.

Practice 5 Change the sentences so that they use *have got to*. Use contractions.

Example: I don't have to help my father.

I haven't got to help my father.

1   She doesn't have to wake up early on Saturday.

2   I don't have to go to the meeting.

3   Carlos doesn't have to go to school on Thursday.

4   You don't have to do it.

5   The store doesn't have to return your money.

6   Susan and Noura don't have to go to the doctor.

7   Rosa doesn't have to work on July 4th.

8   They don't have to get there until 11:00.

9   John doesn't have to go shopping with his mother.

10   You don't have to be here until 10:00.

Practice 6 Change the questions so that they use *have got to*.

Example: Do you have to leave now?

Have you got to leave now?

1   Does he have to pay his tuition?

2   Do they have to fly to Moscow?

3   Does she have to be here early tomorrow?

4   Do the children have to brush their teeth?

5   Does the car have to be in the garage?

6   Do I have to wear a suit?

7   Does Mary have to pick up her friend at the airport?

8   Does Alex have to wash the car?

9   Do Francesca and Sofia have to go to school?

10   Does the milk have to be in the refrigerator?

11   Does she have to make a reservation?

Continue to Unit 8/advanced ↓ or go to Unit 9 →

8.5/a ▶ ellipsis examples and practice (See Section 1.9/a for more about ellipsis.)

DISCOVER

    a   Rosa: ***Have* you *got* a *DVD player*?**

            Ali: *No, I **don't**.*

                      *= No, I **[haven't got a DVD player]**.*

                      *No, I **haven't**.*

                      *= No, I **haven't** [got a DVD player].*

    b   Maria: ***Have* your children *got computers*?**

          Sofia: *Our son **does**, but our daughter **doesn't**.*

                      *= Our son **[has got a computer]**, but our daughter **[hasn't got a computer]**.*

                      *Our son **has**, but our daughter **hasn't**.*

                      *= Our son **has** [got a computer], but our daughter **hasn't** [got a computer].*

▶ *have got* and *have got to*

Practice 7/a Rewrite the B sentences with ellipsis. Write all possible answers.

Example: A: Have Sam and Lucy got a dog?

           B: No, they haven't got a dog.

                No, they don't.

                No, they haven't.

1   A: Has Linda got a pen?

     B: No, she hasn't got a pen.

2   A: Has your house got a basement?

     B: Yes, it's got a basement.

3   A: Have you and your wife got passports?

     B: I haven't got a passport, but my wife's got a passport.

4   A: Have you got jobs?

     B: I've got a job, but he hasn't got a job.

DISCOVER

  a   John: **Have you got to go to the meeting?**

        Sam: *Yes, I **do**.*

              = Yes, I['ve got to go to the meeting].

              Yes, I've got to.

              = Yes, I've got to [go to the meeting].

  b   Tom: **Have you and Mary got to work tomorrow?**

        Bill: *I **do**, but Mary **doesn't**.*

              = I['ve got to work tomorrow], but Mary [hasn't got to work tomorrow].

              *I've got to, but Mary **hasn't got to**.*

              *= I've got to [work tomorrow], but Mary **hasn't got to** [work tomorrow].*

Practice 8/a Rewrite the B sentences with ellipsis. Write all possible answers.

Example: A: Have you got to pick up Tom at the airport?

           B: Yes, I've got to pick up Tom at the airport.

                Yes, I do.

                Yes, I've got to.

1   A: Have you got to pay the bill?

     B: Yes, I've got to pay the bill.

2   A: Has your brother got to wear a tie at his new job?

     B: No, he hasn't got to wear a tie at his new job.

3   A: Have Carlos, Alex and John got to be here early tomorrow?

     B: Carlos and Alex have got to be here early tomorrow, but John hasn't got to be here early tomorrow.

4   A: Has Michael got to do it today?

     B: Yes, he's got to do it today.

# Unit 9 ▶ perfect tenses

9.1 ▶ present perfect

DISCOVER

a   I **ate** lunch.

b   I **have eaten** lunch.

1   Look at a and b. Are both of these sentences about the past?

c   Michael **saw** that movie five years ago.

d   Michael **has seen** that movie three times in the last five years.

2   Look at c and d. Are both of these sentences about the past?

LEARN

▶ A and c are about the past, but b and d are different. B and d are about the past <u>and the present</u>. How is this possible? B tells you information about the past. It tells you that I ate lunch. But it also tells you information about <u>the present</u>. It tells you that I am not hungry now. D tells you information about the past. It tells you that Michael saw that movie five years ago. But it also tells you information about <u>all the time since then</u>—<u>from five years ago until now</u>. It tells you that in these five years Michael saw the movie two more times.

▶ The present perfect is formed with have + the past participle (the third form) of the verb.

I'm not hungry now because I **have eaten**.
have + past participle

Maria is not here. She **has gone** to work.
have + past participle

▶ The best way to understand the present perfect is to think about it in two ways.

1   The present perfect is used to talk about the past when there is a <u>connection to the present</u>.

The plane **has arrived**. (It arrived in the past, and it is here now.)

We **have bought** a new car. (We bought a new car in the past, and we have a new car now.)

2   The present perfect is used to talk about the time <u>between a starting point in the past and the present</u>. Sometimes we use the present perfect to talk about how much time has passed <u>since the beginning of that time</u>.

Linda **has been working** on this project **since February**.

My sister **has been** married **for 24 years**.

Sometimes we use the present perfect to talk about something that has happened <u>during that time</u>.

Alex **has taken** his car to the mechanic **three times** since he bought it last year.

Sometimes we say when that time began.

I **have eaten** in that restaurant many times **since I moved to this city**.

Sometimes we do not say when that time began.

I **have eaten** in that restaurant many times.

REMEMBER

▶ The past form and past participle of regular verbs are the same. Both use -ed. (See the Appendix for past participles of irregular verbs.)

▶ In negative present perfect sentences, native English speakers almost always use contractions. For this reason, you must understand them. Sometimes two contractions are possible.

I**'ve not** eaten breakfast.   She**'s not** done her work.

= I **haven't** eaten breakfast.   = She **hasn't** done her work.

Both contractions are possible, but in both examples, the second contraction is much more common.

not common → They**'ve not** left.   **not common** → He**'s not** seen that movie.

common →   They **haven't** left.   **common** →   He **hasn't** seen that movie.

Be careful not to confuse contractions of has with contractions of is.

he <u>has</u>, she <u>has</u>, it <u>has</u>   = **he's, she's, it's**

he <u>is</u>, she <u>is</u>, it <u>is</u>   = **he's, she's, it's**

▶ In present perfect sentences, we do not talk about an exact time in the past. When we talk about an exact time in the past, we use the past simple.

present perfect → I **have eaten** lunch.   **present perfect** → Sarah **has gone** to Canada.

past simple →   I **ate** lunch at 12:30.   **past simple** →   Sarah **went** to Canada last year.

Practice 1 Change the sentences from past simple to present perfect. Use contractions.

Examples: Mark drove to New York.

Mark's driven to New York.

They had a party.

They've had a party.

1   She threw the ball.

2   Sofia wrote a letter.

3   We did our work.

4   Mary read the book.

5   The plant died.

6   Michael left.

7   Larry saw the movie.

8   The show began.

9   John took a taxi.

10   I cut my finger.

Practice 2 Change the sentences to questions.

Example: You've finished.

Have you finished?

1   You've ridden a camel.

2   They have gone home.

3   She's fallen asleep.

4   Sarah and her sister have seen that movie.

5   Francesca has painted her room pink.

6   We've been here before.

7   She's put her coat in the closet.

8   John's gotten a new dog.

9   Mary has done her work.

10   You've read this book.

Practice 3 Change the sentences to negative. Use contractions.

Example: The children have cleaned their room.

The children haven't cleaned their room.

1   They've been there before.

2   She's met him.

3   Jim's worn his new shoes.

4   We've had dinner.

5   I've taught this class.

6   Michael's done his work.

7   The store has closed.

8 I've talked to her.

9 She's flown to France.

10 They have lost their dog.

Practice 4 Complete the sentences with *have* or *has* and the correct form of the verbs. Some must be negative.

be   do   do   eat   fall   ~~give~~   ride   see   see   take   tell

Example: I don't know what my grade is. The teacher _____ hasn't _____ given _____ it to me.

1 I lost my keys. _____ you _____ them?

2 Look! A tree _____ _____ on that house.

3 I _____ _____ a camel only one time in my life.

4 Someone _____ _____ my pen. Was it you?

5 My wife doesn't know that I lost my job. I _____ _____ her yet.

6 You are so lazy! You _____ _____ anything all day!

7 Mary doesn't know where John is. She _____ _____ him.

8 I'm hungry. I _____ _____ all day.

9 How long _____ your sister _____ married?

10 What _____ she _____ with her hair? It looks awful.

9.2 ▶ *for* and *since*

DISCOVER
> a *I came here at 9:00. It is 11:00 now. I have been here **for two hours**.*
> b *I came here at 9:00. It is 11:00 now. I have been here **since 9:00**.*

1 Look at *a* and *b*. Which tells you about how much time has passed from a starting time until now? Which tells you about when the time began?

LEARN
▶ It is common to use *for* and *since* with the present perfect. *For* is used to talk about how much time has passed <u>since a starting time until now</u>. *Since* is used to say <u>when that time began</u>. For example, imagine that I got sick on Monday, and today is Wednesday. I can say this in two ways.
> *I have been sick **for three days**.*
> *I have been sick since **Monday**.*

REMEMBER
▶ Do not use *since* with other tenses.
> **wrong** → *I **am** sick since Monday.*
> **wrong** → *I **am being** sick since Monday.*
> **right** → *I **have been** sick since Monday.*

▶ *Since* is used to talk about the start of a time in the past only. <u>Do not</u> use *since* to talk about how much time has passed since the starting time. Use *for* to talk about how much time has passed since the starting time.
> **wrong** → *My grandfather has been dead **since** seven years.*
> **right** → *My grandfather has been dead **for** seven years.*

Practice 5 Choose *for* or *since*.

Examples: The baby has been asleep _____ since _____ 3:00.

The baby has been asleep _____ for _____ two hours.

1 I've lived here _____ a year.

2 She has worked there _____ February.

3 The children haven't eaten _____ breakfast.

4 I haven't changed my car's oil _____ six months.

5   Noura hasn't called me _____ last week.

6   I haven't seen her _____ a long time.

7   We've been married _____ 25 years.

8   They have been in the waiting room _____ only a few minutes.

Practice 6 Choose past simple or present perfect. Underline the correct answer.

Examples: Alex (<u>saw</u>/has seen) that movie last week.

Alex (saw/<u>has seen</u>) that movie many times.

1   I (ate/have eaten) in that restaurant twice since I moved to this city.

2   I (ate/have eaten) in that restaurant twice last week.

3   I (am/have been) here since 1:30.

4   Tom is married now. He (was/has been) married for 17 years.

5   Mary is single now. She (was/has been) married for 12 years.

6   Carlos (knew/has known) Larry since they were in high school together.

7   They (are/have been) sick for a long time.

8   He (left/has left) 10 minutes ago.

9.3 ▶ present perfect continuous

DISCOVER

> a   Michael *is studying*.
> b   Larry *has been studying* for three hours.

1   Which sentence tells you about something that is happening now?

2   Which sentence tells you about something that started in the past and is still happening now?

LEARN

▶ Verbs that are often continuous in the present simple and past simple are also often continuous in the present perfect.

▶ Present perfect continuous is formed with *have + been + -ing* form of the verb.

> Larry *has been working* for two hours.
> have + been + -ing form of the verb

Practice 7 Complete the sentences with present continuous or present perfect continuous. Use contractions.

Example: I (paint) _____'m painting_____ my house now. I ___'ve been painting___ it for two hours.

1   My mother (sleep) _____ now. She _____ since 11.00.

2   The girls (study) _____ in the library now. They _____ for two hours.

3   I (drive) _____ now. I _____ for five hours, and I'm really tired.

4   Paul (watch) _____ TV at the moment. He _____ TV all day.

5   We (look) _____ for John's house. We _____ for it for 20 minutes.

6   I (read) _____ a book about Russia at the moment. I started it two weeks ago, and

I _____ it since then.

7   We (work) _____ on our project now. We _____ on it since last week.

8   Sofia (ride) _____ her bicycle now. She _____ it all afternoon.

9.4 ▶ *just, yet* and *already*

DISCOVER

> a   Michael arrived at 11:30. It is 11:35 now. Michael has *just* arrived.

1   When did Michael arrive? A long time ago or a short time ago? What do you think *just* means?

> b   Mary has not called me *yet*.

2   Has Mary called? Does the speaker think that Mary will call later?

    c   *Mother: Go to your room and do your homework.*
        *John: I've **already** done my homework.*
        Mother: OK, I didn't know.

3   Did John's mother know that he did his homework before? Was this information a surprise to her?

LEARN

▶ It is common to use *just, already* and *yet* with the present perfect.

    Just is used to say that something happened <u>only a short time ago</u>.
      Larry: Are you lost?
      *Mary: Yes, I've **just** moved to this city, and I don't know where anything is.*

    Yet is used in questions to say that we <u>expect something to happen</u>. It hasn't happened, but <u>we think it will happen later</u>. *Yet* is also used in negative sentences for the same reason—to say that we expect something to happen.
      *Sofia: Have the children gone to bed **yet**?*
      *Lucy: No, they haven't gone to bed **yet**.*
      Sofia: It's late. Tell them to go to bed.
      *Lucy: I've **already** told them to go to bed three times, but they're still up.*

    Already is used to say that <u>something happened before that someone did not know about</u>. It is a surprise.
      Father: Mary, it's almost time for bed, and you haven't taken a bath yet.
      *Mary: I've **already** taken a bath.*
      Father: OK, I didn't know that.

REMEMBER

▶ *Already* and *just* are placed between *have* and the verb.
    *Sarah has **just** left.*
    *They have **already** finished.*

▶ *Yet* is usually placed at the end of the statements and questions.
    *Lucy: Have you seen this movie **yet**?*
    *John: No, I haven't seen it **yet**.*

▶ *Not yet* is a common answer to present perfect question with *yet*.
    *Larry: Have you washed the car **yet**?*
    *Noura: **Not yet.** I'll wash it later.*

Practice 8 Complete the conversations with *just, already* or *yet*. There may be more than one good answer.

1   A: When are you going to do your homework?

    B: I've _____ done it. I did it three hours ago.

2   A: Have you begun working on your project _____?

    B: Yes, I have. I started it last night.

3   A: Hello, may I speak with Maria please?

    B: Sorry, she was here five minutes ago, but she's _____ left.

4   A: Have you paid the gas bill _____?

    B: No, I haven't _____, but I will soon.

    A: Well, it's too late. The gas company has _____ turned off our gas.

5   A: Whoa! I almost broke my neck!

    B: Sorry, I didn't tell you. The floor is wet because I've _____ washed it. Be careful.

6   A: Hi, Mark. Have you eaten dinner _____?

    B: Not _____. I've _____ gotten home, and I haven't eaten dinner _____.

    A: Good. Let's go to that new restaurant on Main Street. Have you been there _____?

    B: Yes, I have. I've _____ eaten there, and it isn't very good.

9.5 ▶ *ever* and *been to*

DISCOVER

    *a   Have you **talked** to Carlos?*

1   Is it clear if the speaker is asking me about today, about a short time ago or about any time in my life?

    *b   Have you **ever talked** to Carlos?*

2   Is it clear if the speaker is asking me about today, about a short time ago or about any time in my life? How is *b* different from *a*?

    *c   Has Francesca **gone to** Mexico?*

    *d   Has Francesca **been to** Mexico?*

3   In one sentence, we know that Francesca is in Mexico now. Do you know which sentence? In the other sentence, we know she has returned from her trip to Mexico. Do you know which sentence?

LEARN

▶ It is very common to use *ever* in present perfect questions. We use it to be clear that a question is about <u>all time and not just recent time</u>. For example, if you ask me, *Have you talked to Tom?* I might think that you were asking about today. If you ask me, *Have you ever talked to Tom?* I would understand that you were asking about <u>any time</u> in my life.

    Sam: *Have you **ever** flown in a helicopter?*

    Linda: *Yes, I have. I've flown in a helicopter many times.*

▶ It is common to use *never* in negative answers to present perfect questions with *ever*.

    Alex: *Have you **ever** read this book?*

    Bill: *No, I have **never** read this book.*

▶ When we ask questions about people going to a place, and we think they are <u>still there</u>, we use *gone*. When we ask questions about people going to a place, and we think they are <u>not there now</u>, we use *been*.

    *Mary has **gone to** Poland. (She is still in Poland.)*

    *Alex has **been to** Turkey. (He went to Turkey, but he is not there now.)*

It is very common to use *been to* to talk about where people have traveled.

    Maria: *Have you ever **been to** Spain?*

    Alex: *No, I have never **been to** Spain. I've **been to** Europe many times, but I haven't **been to** Spain yet. What about you?*

    Maria: *I've **been to** Spain many times.*

Practice 9 Use *ever* and the words in parentheses to make present perfect questions.

    Example: (you, see, that movie)

               Have you ever seen that movie?

1   (John, write, a book)

2   (your father, drive, a truck)

3   (you, be to, Australia)

4   (you, eat, sushi)

5   (Carlos, read, this book)

6   (Mark, speak to, you)

7   (you, have, a broken heart)

8   (she, be, in the hospital)

9   (Larry, ride, a motorcycle)

10 (she, fly, a hot air balloon)

Practice 10 Complete the sentences with words from this list.

    am ~~are~~ been been been did ~~doing~~ go have have have have reading went

    Jim: Hi Bob. What _____*are*_____(1) you _____*doing*_____(2)?

    Bob: Hi Jim. I _____(3) _____(4) a book about India. _____(5) you ever

_____(6) to India?

Jim: Yes, I _____(7). India is a very interesting country.

Bob: When _____(8) you _____(9) there?

Jim: I _____(10) to India three years ago.

Bob: What about Nepal? _____(11) you ever _____(12) there?

Jim: No, I _____(13) never _____(14) to Nepal.

Practice 11 Mixed tense review. Complete the sentences in Lorena's email with the verbs in parentheses.

Hi,

My name is Lorena. I (live) _____*am living*_____(1) in Toronto. I (study) _____(2) English in high school now, so I need to practice. Right now, I (do) _____(3) my homework. Our teacher (tell) _____(4) us to write an email. That is why I (write) _____(5) to you now. _____(6) you ever (be) _____(7) to Toronto? My family (move) _____(8) to Toronto when I (be) _____(9) 13 years old. I (be) _____(10) 16 now, so that means we (live) _____(11) here for three years.

We (be) _____(12) to many places in Canada. Last year, we (go) _____(13) to the Rocky Mountains. It (be) _____(14) very beautiful. We (see) _____(15) lots of bears there. _____(16) you ever (see) _____(17) a bear?

I have to go. My brother (wait) _____(18) to use the computer. I (use) _____(19) it for two hours, and he (be) _____(20) angry with me.

Sincerely,

Lorena

9.6 ▶ past perfect

DISCOVER

a   **a few minutes ago**
    Mary: *Do you want to eat lunch?*
    Bill: *No, thank you. I **have eaten** lunch.*

b   **now**
    Sarah: *What did Bill say?*
    Mary: *He said that he **had eaten** lunch.*

1   Look at conversations a and b. Which one is about the present? Which one is about the past? How do you know? Why did *have eaten* change to *had eaten*?

c   **yesterday**
    Larry: *Have you seen this movie, Sam?*
    Sam: *Yes, I **have seen** it.*

d   **now**
    Tom: *Did Sam go to the movie with you yesterday?*
    Larry: *No, he didn't go with us because he **had** already **seen** it.*

2   Look at conversations c and d. Which one is about the present? Which one is about the past? How do you know? Why did *have seen* change to *had seen*?

LEARN

▶ The *past perfect* is similar to the present perfect with one important difference. The present perfect shows a connection between the past and the present. The past perfect shows a connection <u>between two times in the past</u>, and it shows you that <u>one happened before the other</u>.

▶ The past perfect is formed with *had* + the past participle of the verb.

*I **had seen** the movie already.*
   had + past participle

REMEMBER

▶ Everything you learned about *for, since, just, already* and *yet* and the present perfect is the same with the past perfect.

▶ In negative sentences with the present perfect, native English speakers almost always use contractions. For this reason, you must understand contractions. Sometimes two contractions are possible.

*He**'d not heard** that song.*

*= He **hadn't heard** that song.*

Both contractions are possible, but the second contraction is much more common.

not common → *She**'d not** eaten dinner.*

common →   *She **hadn't** eaten dinner.*

Practice 12 **Change the sentences from present perfect to past perfect. Use contractions.**

Example: I've been to France.

I'd been to France.

1   They've done their work.

2   She hasn't left yet.

3   We've been working for three hours.

4   He's lived in Chicago since 1985.

5   They've already had dinner.

6   I've never been to Timbuktu before.

7   We've never driven on that road.

8   Noura and Alex have just eaten.

9   I've never gone skiing before.

10   We've never watched that channel before.

Practice 13 **Change the sentences to questions.**

Example: She'd just left.

Had she just left?

1   Michael had finished.

2   Carlos had taken a shower.

3   They'd had breakfast.

4   She'd been there all day.

5   He'd given her some money.

6   You'd been reading.

7   Tom had already arrived.

8   Sofia had just gone to bed.

9   They'd already done it.

10   She'd been waiting a long time.

Practice 14 **Change the sentences to negative. Use contractions.**

Example: Mike had done it before.

Mike hadn't done it before.

1   She'd flown to Tibet.

2   The movie had begun.

3   Maria had spoken with her sister.

4   Carlos had been to Oman.

5   I'd told her the answer.

6   They'd been watching TV.

7   We'd taken the bus.

8   She had thought of the answer.

9   They'd already done it.

10   The train had left the station.

Practice 15 Write past perfect sentences as in the example. Be careful to put nouns and pronouns in the correct positions.

Example: Mary forgot to bring cash. Because of this, she couldn't pay for her lunch.

Mary couldn't pay for her lunch because she had forgotten to bring cash.

1   Larry's car broke down. Because of this, he was late for work.

2   Sofia went to bed. Because of this, I didn't talk to her when I called.

3   Bill didn't study for the test. Because of this, he failed it.

4   I forgot to bring my lunch to work. Because of this, I was hungry all day.

5   I didn't pay attention to the teacher. Because of this, I didn't know what to do.

6   I forgot Sarah's telephone number. Because of this, I couldn't call her.

7   Sam lost his keys. Because of this, he was locked out of his house.

8   Tom didn't listen to me. Because of this, he did it all wrong.

9   I didn't bring a map. Because of this, I didn't know where to go.

Practice 16 Complete the sentences as in the example. Use contractions.

Example: Last week Michael said, "I have already seen that movie."
            What did he say?

He said that he'd already seen that movie.

1   A few days ago Francesca said, "I've gotten married."
    What did she say?

2   Bill said, "I've never read that book."
    What did he say?

3   Yesterday Mark told his mother, "I have lost my watch."
    What did he tell his mother?

4   John said, "My sister's moved to Canada."
    What did he say?

5   Dr. Smith told Alex, "I have looked at your X-ray."
    What did she tell Alex?

6   Last night Sam's wife told him, "I've already washed the dishes."
    What did she tell Sam?

7   Lucy said, "Maria hasn't been to Africa."
    What did she say?

▶ **perfect tenses**

Practice 17 Complete the sentences with the past perfect or present perfect. Use the words in parentheses.

1 Sam: Why are you angry?

Father: I told you to clean your room, and your room is still a mess. Why (not, clean, yet) ___*haven't*___ (a)

you ___*cleaned*___ (b) it ___*yet*___ (c)?

2 Lucy: Yesterday I was shopping at the mall, and I ran into Mary. It was wonderful to see her. I (not, see)

_____(a) _____(b) her in many years.

Susan: Has she changed?

Lucy: A little. She (lose) _____(c) _____(d) some weight.

3 Maria: Why were you late to class?

Tom: I was almost at school, but then I had to go back to my house because I realized that I (forget)

_____(a) _____(b) my homework.

4 Alex: I noticed that Maria was crying this morning.

Mark: That's because she (just, have) _____(a) _____(b) _____(c) a fight

with her mother.

5 John: My boss was angry with me today.

Mary: Why?

John: Because she told me to finish my work before she returned from lunch, and when she returned, I still

(not, finish) _____(a) _____(b) it.

6 Ali: Hello, Noura? It's 5:00. You said you would be here at 4:00. Why (not, get, yet) _____(a)

you _____(b) here _____(c)?

Noura: I'm sorry. I (plan) _____(d) _____(e) to call you, but I couldn't find my cell phone.

I (look) _____(f) _____(g) everywhere, but I can't find it.

Ali: Really? If you (not, find) _____(h) _____(i) it, how are you talking to me now?

Continue to Unit 9/advanced ↓ or go to Unit 10 →

9.7/a ▶ future perfect

DISCOVER

    a *John:* *How long have you worked at this company?*

        Gary: *I started here in September of last year, and it's August now. That means I have worked here for 11*
*months and that next month I **will have** worked here for one year.*

1 Look at the conversation above. Has Gary worked at his company for one year? How long has he worked there?
When will it be one year? What is connected—two times in the past?, the past and present? the past and the future?

LEARN

▶ Remember that the present perfect connects the past and the present. The *future perfect* connects <u>the past and</u>
<u>the future</u>. It says how long a time which started in the past will be at a time in the future.

▶ The future perfect is formed with *will have* + the past participle of the verb.

    *Mary moved to Singapore nine years ago. Next year, she **will have lived** in Singapore for ten years.*
                                    will have + past participle

    *We began studying at 8:00, and it is 10:30 now. At 11:00 we **will have been studying** for three hours.*
                                      will have + past participle

    I want to go on vacation with my brother and sister in May, but I have to stay here at the university until I gradu-
*ate in June. In May I **will not have graduated** yet.*
                   will (not) have + past participle

REMEMBER

▶ The future perfect is not as common among native speakers as the present perfect and past perfect. Many native speakers never use it. It is not common to use contractions with the future perfect.

Practice 18/a Complete the sentences with the future perfect. Some are negative.

Example: We've lived in this city for 14 years, so next year we _____ will have lived _____ here for 15 years.

1 I'm sick. I got sick six days ago, so tomorrow I _____ sick for one week.

2 My parents were married 39 years ago, so next year they _____ married for 40 years.

3 It's 2:00. I want to go home at 4:00, but it will take me three hours to finish my work. I can't leave at 4:00 because

   I _____ my work yet.

4 Mary has been driving for six hours. In one hour she _____ for seven hours.

5 John's saving money to buy a new car. He wants to buy a new car next month, but he has to wait because by

   next month he _____ enough money.

6 Larry said he would come to my house at 6:00. It's 6:00 now, and he hasn't arrived yet, but he left at 5:00, and

   he lives very close, so I'm sure he _____ by 6:30.

7 I've been waiting for 55 minutes. In five minutes, I _____ for one hour.

8 I always get to my office at 8:15, so you can call me at my office at 8:30. I _____
   there yet.

9 I've been working on this book for a long time. In August, I _____ on it for three years.

9.8/a ▶ ellipsis examples and practice (See Section 1.9/a for an explanation of ellipsis.)

DISCOVER

a *We've been to Tibet. **Have you**?*
   = *We've been to Tibet. **Have you** [been to Tibet]?*

b *We've been to Tibet. **Have you been**?*
   = *We've been to Tibet. **Have you been** [to Tibet]?*

c *Sofia's eaten pineapple pizza, but **we haven't**.*
   = *Sofia's eaten pineapple pizza, but **we haven't** [eaten pineapple pizza].*

d *I'd heard that joke before, and Mary **had** too.*
   = *I'd heard that joke before, and Mary **had** [heard that joke before] too.*

Practice 19/a Write the ellipted words.

Example: The boys have cleaned their room, but the girls haven't _cleaned their rooms_ .

1 I haven't been there. Have you been _____?

2 I haven't been there. Have you _____?

3 John's finished dinner, but Mary hasn't _____.

4 He'd already left, but had she _____ too?

5 Alex had gotten there on time, but I hadn't _____.

6 He's lived in this town all his life. Have you _____?

7 Linda's been studying all day, but Sofia hasn't been _____.

8 Linda's been studying all day, but Sofia hasn't _____.

9 The children have had dinner, but we haven't _____.

10 I'd heard about the change, but I didn't know if he had _____.

Practice 20/a Combine the sentences as in the example. Use ellipsis. Write two answers for 2, 4 and 6.

Examples: Mary's left. Larry's left too.

Mary's left, and Larry has too.

My brother's been to Colombia. My sister hasn't been there.

My brother's been to Colombia, but my sister hasn't been.

My brother's been to Colombia, but my sister hasn't.

Sarah's mother has left. Mary's mother hasn't left.

Sarah's mother has left, but Mary's mother hasn't.

Sarah's mother has left, but Mary's hasn't.

1 Francesca has gone to school. Sofia has gone to school too.

2 Tom had been sleeping. Jerry hadn't been sleeping.

3 Paul's flown to Paris. Sam has flown to Paris too.

4 Sam's flight has arrived. Tom's flight hasn't arrived.

5 We'd finished. He had finished too.

6 You've been to Italy. I haven't been to Italy.

7 Tom had done his work. I had done my work too.

8 Maria and Sofia have flown in a hot air balloon. Larry has flown in a hot air balloon too.

🚀 Unit 10 ▶ adjectives

10.1 ▶ two ways to use adjectives

DISCOVER

    a   *I have a **red** car.*

    b   *The **tall** man is my brother.*

    c   *The hotel was **expensive**.*

    d   *The flowers smell **good**.*

    e   *Sarah looks **angry**.*

1   Look at *a* and *b*. Which words give information about the nouns *car* and *man*?

2   Look at *c*, *d* and *e*. Which words give information about the nouns *hotel*, *flowers* and *Sarah*?

3   Look at *a*, *b*, *c*, *d* and *e*. How is the grammar in *a* and *b* different from the grammar in *c*, *d* and *e*? What are the two ways that adjectives can be used in a sentence to give information about nouns?

LEARN (See Table 10a.)

▶ *Adjectives* give information about nouns—they describe and identify nouns. There are two basic ways that adjectives can be used in a sentence: before a noun or after words (sometimes called *linking verbs*) such as *be, smell, feel, taste, sound, seem, look, become* and *get*. (For more about this use of *get*, see Section 10.8.)

10a

two ways to use adjectives					
before a noun			**after a linking verb**		
	adjective	noun		linking verb	adjective
This is	*hot*	*coffee.*	*The water*	*is*	*cold.*
My son's got a	*new*	*job.*	*The flowers*	*smell*	*good.*
He is a	*good*	*dancer.*	*I*	*feel*	*hot.*
They have a	*big*	*house.*	*The cake*	*tastes*	*delicious.*
I saw a	*pink*	*elephant.*	*The music*	*sounds*	*wonderful.*
			Mary	*seems*	*angry.*
			Your hair	*looks*	*beautiful.*
			She	*became*	*sick.*
			Larry	*got*	*ready.*

REMEMBER

▶ There are no plural adjectives in English.

    wrong → *I have two **olds** cars.*   **wrong** → *The cookies are **goods**.*

    right →   *I have two **old** cars.*   **right** →   *The cookies are **good**.*

Practice 1 Complete the sentences.

   Example: Jim's shirt is orange.

              He has an _____*orange shirt*_____.

1   The perfume smells nice.

    It's _____.

2   The student got sick yesterday.

    She's a _____.

3   These shoes aren't comfortable.

    They're not _____.

4   Your idea sounds good.

    I think it's a _____.

5   This answer seems wrong.

   I think this a _____.

6   Your house looks fantastic.

   You have a _____.

7   The soup tastes salty.

   It's _____.

8   The man became very angry.

   He was a very _____.

Practice 2 Answer the questions.

Example: That's terrible music. How does the music sound?

        It sounds terrible.

1   I think Alex might be upset. How does Alex seem?

2   The baby has soft skin. How does the baby's skin feel?

3   Mary has beautiful hair. How does her hair look?

4   Carlos has stinky feet. How do his feet smell?

5   That restaurant has terrible food. How does their food taste?

6   I think Francesca has an interesting idea. How does her idea sound?

7   Michael is a sick man. How is Michael?

8   Larry was thin before, but now he is fat. How did Larry get?

10.2 ▶ comparative forms of adjectives

DISCOVER

   a   China is **bigger** than India.

1   How many countries are we talking about? Are we saying that they are the same or that they are different?

2   When we compare with a one-syllable adjective, how do we change the adjective?

   b   My sister is **more careful** than my brother.

3   When we compare with a two-syllable adjective, how do we change the adjective?

   c   Alex is **lazier** than Carlos.

4   When we compare with a two-syllable adjective which ends with -*y*, how do we change the adjective?

   d   John is **more polite** than Mark.

   e   John is **politer** than Mark.

5   When we compare with some two-syllable adjectives, what are two ways we change the adjectives?

   f   This book is **more difficult** than that book.

6   When we compare with a three- or more syllable adjective, how do we change the adjective?

LEARN (See Table 10b.)

▶ When we use adjectives to compare things or people, we change the spelling of the adjectives, or we use *more*. This form of the adjective is called the *comparative form*.

REMEMBER

▶ A small group of important adjectives are irregular in the comparative form. See Table 10b.

▶ Some two-syllable words have two comparative forms. In Table 10b, the examples in **bold** are less common.

Practice 3 Complete the sentences with the correct comparative form of the adjective in parentheses. When two forms are possible, use the more common form.

Example: (bad) My grade was _____*worse*_____ than yours.

1   (tall) I am _____ than my brother.

	adjective	comparative form		superlative form	
comparative and superlative forms of adjectives (examples) (When two forms of an adjective are shown, the form in **bold** is possible but is not common.)					
one-syllable adjectives	cold nice big small tall	colder nicer bigger smaller taller		coldest nicest biggest smallest tallest	
two-syllable adjectives	modern careful famous boring upset	more/less modern more/less careful more/less famous more/less boring more/less upset		most/least modern most/least careful most/least famous most/least boring most/least upset	
two-syllable adjectives ending with -y	happy easy crazy lazy lovely lonely	happier easier crazier lazier lovelier lonelier		happiest easiest craziest laziest loveliest loneliest	
two-syllable adjectives with two possible forms	angry common polite friendly quiet simple	angrier **commoner** **politer** friendlier quieter simpler	**more/less angry** more/less common more/less polite **more/less friendly** **more/less quiet** **more/less simple**	angriest **commonest** **politest** friendliest quietest simplest	**most/least angry** most/least common most/least polite **most/least friendly** **most/least quiet** **most/least simple**
two- or more syllable adjectives	difficult expensive dangerous interesting beautiful	more/less difficult more/less expensive more/less dangerous more/less interesting more/less beautiful		most/least difficult most/least expensive most/least dangerous most/least interesting most/least beautiful	
irregular adjectives	good well (healthy) bad far	better better worse farther/further		best best worst farthest/furthest	

2 (dangerous) Motorcycles are _____ than cars.

3 (easy) My math class is _____ than my English class.

4 (angry) She was really angry yesterday, and today she's even _____ than yesterday.

5 (well) I didn't feel well yesterday, but I feel _____ today.

6 (far) My house is close to the lake. Mark's house is much _____.

7 (quiet) My house is noisy. I'm going to the library to study because it's _____ than my house.

8 (nice) The hotel we stayed in last night was awful. I thought it was going to be _____.

Practice 4 Correct the mistakes in the sentences.

1 Your house is small. My house bigger.

2 Is Beijing more small than Shanghai?

▶ adjectives

3 BMWs are more expensives than Toyotas.

4 The book was gooder than the movie.

5 Spanish is more easier to learn than Portuguese.

6 I got a bad grade on the English test, but Mary's grade was worser.

7 Mark is lazy, but Larry is the lazier.

8 I play tennis better to Michael.

10.3 ▶ superlative forms of adjectives

DISCOVER

*a   Russia is the **biggest** country in the world.*

1 How many countries are we talking about? Are we comparing two countries, or are we comparing one country to all other countries? Are we saying that Russia is *bigger* than *all* other countries—that it is the maximum?

2 When we talk about the maximum with a one-syllable adjective, how do we change the adjective?

*b   All my classes are boring, but my accounting class is the **most boring**.*

3 When we talk about the maximum with a two-syllable adjective, how do we change the adjective?

*c   That was the **craziest** idea I've ever heard.*

4 When we talk about the maximum with a two-syllable adjective which ends with *-y*, how do we change the adjective?

*d   Mary is the **friendliest** person I know.*
*e   Mary is the **most friendly** person I know.*

5 When we talk about the maximum with some two-syllable adjectives, what are two ways we change the adjectives?

*f   Francesca is the **most intelligent** girl in her class.*

6 When we talk about the maximum with a three- or more syllable adjective, how do we change the adjective?

LEARN (See Table 10b.)

▶ When we use adjectives to talk about the maximum (or minimum), we change the spelling of the adjectives, or we use *most*. This form of the adjective is called the *superlative form*.

REMEMBER

▶ A small group of important adjectives are irregular in the superlative form. See Table 10b.

▶ Some two-syllable words have two superlative forms. In Table 10b, the examples in **bold** are less common.

Practice 5 Complete the sentences with the correct superlative form of the adjective in parentheses. When two forms are possible, use the more common form.

Example: (tall) Gary is the _____ *tallest* _____ player on the basketball team.

1 (small) Rhode Island is the _____ state in the USA.

2 (modern) We use only the _____ technology in our company.

3 (lovely) Noura has the _____ house in our neighborhood.

4 (simple) That was the _____ quiz that I ever took.

5 (expensive) What is the _____ car in the world?

6 (far) The _____ that I ever drove in one day was 700 miles.

7 (bad) This student's essay is the _____ that I have ever read.

8 (common) Do you know what the _____ disease in the world is?

9 (good) Which student had the _____ score?

Practice 6 Correct the mistakes in the sentences.

1 Is the Amazon River longest river in the world?

2 Sam is the most crazy guy I know.

3 I got a 99 on my quiz. That was the goodest grade in my class.

4　Mount Everest is highest mountain in the world.

5　Michael has messiest desk in our office.

6　My most young child is eight years old.

7　Yesterday was the worse day of my life.

8　Alex is more taller than Carlos.

10.4 ▶ modifying comparative forms of adjectives

DISCOVER

    a　Michael is **much taller than** John.
    b　Michael is **somewhat taller than** Mark.
    c　Michael is **as tall as** Larry.
    d　Michael is **almost as tall as** Carlos.
    e　Michael is **nowhere near as tall as** Alex.

1　We already saw that we use *-er* or *more* or *less* when we use adjectives to make comparisons, but what are some ways that we can add more information? For example, instead of saying only that something is *cheaper* or *more expensive* or *less expensive*, what are some ways we can say <u>how much</u> *cheaper* or <u>how much</u> *more expensive* or <u>how much</u> *less expensive*?

LEARN (See Table 10c.)

▶ The words shown in Table 10c are used to modify adjectives when they are used to make comparisons.

REMEMBER

▶ *Less* is not used with one-syllable adjectives. Use the opposite adjective instead.
    wrong → India is **less big** than China.
    right →　India is **smaller** than China.

Practice 7 Circle the letter of the best answer.

1　Sarah is 43 years old, and Mary is 11 years old. Sarah is _____ Mary.
    a　not nearly as old as
    b　a lot older than
    c　as old as
    d　slightly older than

2　Larry is a police officer. John is a teacher. John's job is _____ Larry's.
    a　far less dangerous than
    b　slightly less dangerous than
    c　far more dangerous than
    d　just as dangerous as

3　Linda is 1.7 meters tall, and her brother is 1.7 meters tall. Linda is _____ her brother.
    a　nearly as tall as
    b　just as tall as
    c　a bit taller than
    d　not as tall as

4　Michael's watch cost $150. My watch cost $145. My watch was _____ Michael's.
    a　not quite as cheap as
    b　just as cheap as
    c　a great deal cheaper than
    d　a bit cheaper than

5　My business made $500,000 last year, and yours made $10,000 last year. Mine is _____ yours.
    a　nowhere near as successful as
    b　a good deal more successful than
    c　a little bit more successful than
    d　considerably less successful than

modifying comparative adjectives					
one-syllable adjectives			**two- or more syllable adjectives**		
++	*much* *far* *a great deal* *a good deal* *considerably* *a lot* *lots* *way* (informal)	*bigger than*	**++**	*much more* *far more* *a great deal more* *a good deal more* *considerably more* *a lot more* *lots more* *way more* (informal)	*important than*
+	*slightly* *somewhat* *a bit* *a little* *a little bit*	*bigger than*	**+**	*slightly more* *somewhat more* *a bit more* *a little more* *a little bit more*	*important than*
=	*as* *just as*	*big as*	**=**	*as* *just as*	*important as*
–	(use opposite adjective)		**–**	*slightly less* *somewhat less* *a bit less* *a little less* *a little bit less*	*important than*
	not as *not quite as* *almost as* *nearly as*	*big as*		*not as* *not quite as* *almost as* *nearly as*	*important as*
– –	(use opposite adjective)		**– –**	*much less* *far less* *a great deal less* *a good deal less* *considerably less* *a lot less* *lots less* *way less* (informal)	*important than*
	not nearly as *nowhere near as*	*big as*		*not nearly as* *nowhere near as*	*important as*

6   There are only 2,000 people in my hometown. It's _____ than Los Angeles.
   a   way smaller
   b   slightly smaller
   c   almost as small as
   d   not quite as small as

7   Mark got a 97 on the test, and I got only a 62. My score was _____ Mark's score.
   a   somewhat worse than
   b   considerably worse than
   c   not quite as bad as
   d   not nearly as bad as

8   A mouse is _____ an elephant.
    a   much bigger than
    b   as big as
    c   almost as big as
    d   nowhere near as big as

10.5 ▶ using superlatives

DISCOVER

a   *Sofia:*   *Is Canada **the biggest** country **in the world**?*
    Mary: *No, Canada isn't **the biggest** country **in the world**, but it's **one of the biggest** countries **in the world**.*
    Sofia: *What is **the biggest** country **in the world**?*
    Mary: ***The biggest** country **of all** is Russia.*

1   How many countries are Sofia and Mary talking about? Are they comparing only two countries to each other, or are they comparing two countries to other countries in a group of all the other countries in the world?

2   What are two ways that we can say that one member of the group is number one—the maximum?

b   *Alex:*   ***I have seen** many movies.*
    Bill: *Have you seen Pale Rider?*
    Alex: *Yes, I have.*
    Bill: *Is it a good movie?*
    Alex: *Yes, Pale Rider is **one of the best** movies **that I have seen**.*

3   Alex is saying that *Pale Rider* is the best movie in a group of movies. What is the group of movies?

c   *Maria:*   *Oxford is **one of the oldest** universities **in the world**.*
    Mark: *Yes, **one of the oldest** universities **in the world** is Oxford.*

4   How are these sentences different? Do they have the same meaning?

d   *John:*   *Is North Dakota an expensive place to live?*
    Tom: *No, North Dakota is **one of the least expensive** places to live.*
    John: *Do you mean it's cheap?*
    Tom: *Yes, it's **one of the cheapest** places to live.*

5   What is the opposite of *most* in superlatives?

LEARN

▶ Superlatives are often used to say that something or someone is a member of a group that is <u>near the maximum</u> of the meaning of the adjective: *one of the longest, one of the worst, one of the most interesting,* etc.

▶ With adjectives with two or more syllables, we sometimes use *least* to say that one member of a group is <u>at the minimum</u> of the meaning of the adjective.
    *The **least busy** day at our restaurant is Monday.*

▶ It is common to say where this group exists: *in the world, in Europe, in this city, in my school,* etc.

▶ Sometimes, when we want to say very clearly that one member of a group is at the maximum or minimum of the meaning of the adjective, we say *of all*.
    *Jupiter is the biggest planet **of all**.*

▶ Sometimes we need to use a verb to describe the group. (These are a form of noun clause. See Unit 14 for more about noun clauses.)
    *The Pillars of the Earth is one of the best books **(that) I've read**.*

▶ It is possible to reverse the sentences.
    The Pillars of the Earth *is **one of the best books (that) I've read***.
    = ***One of the best books (that) I've read** is* **The Pillars of the Earth**.

Practice 8 **Use the correct maximum superlative form of the adjective in parentheses to complete the sentence.**

Example: (boring) This is one of the _____*most boring*_____ books I have ever read.

1   (hard) One of the _____ classes I ever took was economics.

2   (pretty) Francesca is one of the _____ girls in her school.

3   (hard) Diamonds are the _____ substance of all.

4   (stupid) That was one of the _____ things that I have ever done.

5   (beautiful) One of the _____ cities in the world is Venice.

6   (expensive) Moscow is one of the _____ cities in the world.

7   (large) The _____ ocean of all is the Pacific Ocean.

8   (interesting) I fell asleep during my geometry class. It was one of the _____ classes I have ever been in.

10.6 ▶ participle adjectives

DISCOVER

    a   John: *Have you **finished** your work?*

1   Is *finished* a verb or an adjective?

    b   Gary: *Yes, I am **finished**.*

2   Is *finished* a verb or an adjective?

LEARN

▶ The past participle (third form) of many verbs is also used as an adjective. Many common participle adjectives are given in the list below.

bored	*broken*	*burned*	*closed*	*confused*	*crowded*
divorced	*done*	*dressed*	*drunk*	*engaged*	*finished*
forbidden	*frightened*	*gone*	*hidden*	*hurt*	*interested*
invited	*involved*	*lost*	*married*	*mistaken*	*scared*
tired	*worried*	*written*			

Practice 9 Use the past participle of the verb in parentheses to complete the question, and then write *v* if the past participle is being used as a verb or *adj* if the past participle is being used as an adjective.

Examples: (break) I have to wear my old glasses today. I have _____*broken*_____ my new glasses. ____*v*____

             (break) I have to wear my old glasses today. My new glasses are _____*broken*_____. ___*adj*___

1   (worry) Where have you been? We've been very _____ about you. _____

2   (invite) How many people have you _____ to your wedding? _____

3   (marry) I'm _____, and I have three children. _____

4   (hide) I have _____ a key outside of my house. _____

5   (do) I can't go home yet. I'm not _____ with my work. _____

6   (lose) I've _____ my pen. Have you seen it? _____

7   (forbid) Some people say that _____ fruit is always sweeter. _____

8   (mistake) You are _____. My name isn't Tom. It's Tim. _____

9   (confuse) Can you help me? I'm _____. _____

10.7 ▶ adjective + preposition combinations

DISCOVER

    a   Mary: *Are you **bored**?*

    b   John: *Yes, I'm **bored with** my job.*

1   Look at the adjective *bored*. When there is an object (*my job*), is it necessary to use another word after the adjective?

    c   Sofia: *Is Sarah **married**?*

    d   Alex: *Yes, she's **married to** Mark.*

2   Look at the adjective *married*. When there is an object (*Mark*), is it necessary to use another word after the adjective?

LEARN

▶ Many adjectives must be used with a certain preposition when they are followed by an object. Sometimes changing the preposition changes the meaning of the adjective. Many common adjectives + preposition combinations are given in the list below.

    *Francesca isn't **ready**.*

    → *Francesca isn't **ready for** school.*

*Lucy is **worried**.*

→ *Lucy is **worried about** her sick father.*

absent from	angry about/with	bad for/at	bored with	confused about
curious about	different from	engaged to	finished with	frightened of
good for/at	happy about	hidden from	interested in	involved in
mad about/at	made of	married to	mistaken about	nervous about
ready for/to	responsible for	right about	scared of	sure about
tired of	used to	worried about	wrong about	

REMEMBER

▶ There is no rule that you can learn so that you will always know which preposition to use after an adjective.

▶ *Good for* and *bad for* mean something is good for your health or bad for your health.

Vegetables **are good for you**. = Vegetables **are good for your health**.

Smoking **is bad for you**. = Smoking **is bad for your health**.

▶ *Good at* and *bad at* mean that somebody does something well or does something badly.

Alex **is good at soccer**. = Alex **plays soccer well**.

Carlos **is bad at tennis**. = Carlos **plays tennis badly**.

▶ *Ready for* is for nouns. *Ready to* is for verbs.

He's **ready for** the test.

He's **ready to** take the test.

▶ *Mad at* and *angry with* are for people. *Mad about* and *angry about* are for things (especially situations).

I'm **mad at** my sister. = I'm **angry with** my sister.

I'm **mad about** what she said. = I'm **angry about** what she said.

I'm **mad at** my sister **about** what she said. = I'm **angry with** my sister **about** what she said.

Practice 10 Complete the sentences with the correct adjective + preposition combination from the list above. There may be more than one good adjective + preposition combination for some.

Example: I am very _____*confused about*_____ my homework. I don't understand it at all.

1 I was _____ class yesterday because I had to go to the doctor.

2 I'm sorry. What I told you yesterday was not correct. I was _____ it.

3 Are you _____ go yet? We need to leave now, or we will be late.

4 Carlos loves to read history books. He's very _____ history.

5 What Mary said to me yesterday was terrible. I am very _____ her.

6 This table looks like wood, but it isn't wood. It's _____ plastic.

7 I'm not _____ this, so you should check to make sure that I'm right.

8 My new shoes are hurting my feet. I'm not _____ them.

9 He said I was stupid, and I am very _____ him _____ it.

10 I packed my suitcases yesterday. I'm _____ my vacation.

10.8 ▶ *get* used with adjectives

DISCOVER

a *I was very thin when I was young, but I **got fat** after I turned 40.*

1 Is this sentence about being *thin*, about being *fat* or the <u>change from</u> being *thin* to being *fat*?

b *Is dinner almost ready? I'm **getting hungry**.*

2 Is this sentence about being *not hungry*, being *hungry* or the <u>change from</u> being *not hungry* to being *hungry*?

c *You're not ready yet? It's almost time to go, so **get ready**!*

3 Is this sentence about being *not ready*, being *ready* or the <u>change from</u> being *not ready* to being *ready*?

LEARN

▶ *Get* is used with adjectives to talk about the <u>change</u> from one condition to another condition. *Become* has the same meaning, but *get* is much more common.

*I haven't eaten anything today. I am **getting hungry**.*

▶ **adjectives**

*My father will **get angry** if I do not get an A on the test.*

*It **got** really **cold** last night, but now it's **getting warmer**.*

REMEMBER

▶ In American English, the past participle of *get* is *gotten*. In British English, it is *got*.

American English → *Put on a coat before you go outside. It has **gotten** cold.*

British English → *Put on a coat before you go outside. It has **got** cold.*

Practice 11 Complete the sentences with the correct form of *get*.

Example: Mary and Larry _____*got*_____ married last week. Now they're on their honeymoon.

1 I've been working all day. I'm _____ tired. I need to take a break.

2 Alex has food poisoning. He ate some bad food, and he _____ very sick yesterday.

3 Alex is still sick today, but he is _____ better now.

4 My father was driving in Boston, and he _____ totally lost.

5 Don't do that again! If you keep doing that, I'm going to _____ angry.

6 Don't wear your nice pants while you're working in the garden. They'll _____ dirty.

7 When I moved to Jeddah, it was difficult to _____ used to the hot weather.

8 It's 2:30 in the morning, and my daughter still hasn't come home. I'm _____ worried.

LEARN

▶ The adjective *used to* is very important, but is often a problem for students because they confuse it with a different meaning of *used to* (discussed in Section 11.11). When we say that we are *used to* something, we mean that it is normal, routine, not a problem. It <u>does not</u> mean that we like it; it means only that it is a routine, normal, regular part of our life. (See Section 18.11 for more about *get used to*.)

I'm not used to my new car. Everything is in a different place.

*When you get new glasses, it takes time to **get used to** them.*

*I've lived in Canada for three years, but I still **haven't gotten used to** the cold weather.*

REMEMBER

▶ *Used to* has the same meaning as *accustomed to*, but *used to* is much more common.

Practice 12 Complete the sentences with *used to*. Some are negative. Some also need *get*.

Examples: After we moved to this town, I didn't like it, but now I am _____*used to*_____ it.

I keep pushing the wrong buttons on my new remote control. I still haven't ____*gotten used to*____ it.

1 I've lived in Mexico for many years, so I am _____ spicy food now.

2 It's been hard to _____ the new system, but little by little, I am _____ it.

3 When I moved to England, it was a difficult to drive on the left. It took me a long time to _____ it.

4 The last time I saw your son, he was 12 years old. Now he's 23, and he is taller than I am! I can't

_____ how tall he is.

5 Everyone at my school is confused about the new schedule. We're not _____ it.

6 It takes a long time to _____ the time change when you fly from the USA to China.

10.9 ▶ *-ing/-ed* participle adjectives

DISCOVER

    a   *I was **bored** because the movie was **boring**.*

1 There are two adjectives in *a*—*bored* and *boring*. Which one is about the *cause* (= *reason*) for something? Which one is about the *effect* (= *result*) of that cause?

    b   *Alex is very **interested** in computers. He thinks computers are **interesting**.*

2 There are two adjectives in *b*—*interested* and *interesting*. Which one is about the cause/reason for something? Which one is about the effect/result of that cause?

3   Look at *a* and *b*. How do some adjectives change their spelling to show the difference between cause/reason and effect/result?

LEARN (See Table 10d.)

▶ Many adjectives have two forms: an *-ing* form to show the *cause* or *reason* for something and an *-ed* form to show the *effect* or *result* of something.

   *I am very **confused** because these instructions are **confusing**.*
   *Algebra is **boring**. I get **bored** in my algebra class.*

REMEMBER

▶ All *-ing/-ed* adjectives are made from verbs. The *-ing* form is the same as the continuous form (sometimes called the present participle) and the *-ed* form is the same as the past participle.

10d

-ing/-ed adjectives (examples)	
cause/reason form (present participle)	**effect/result form (past participle)**
amazing	amazed
amusing	amused
annoying	annoyed
boring	bored
challenging	challenged
confusing	confused
depressing	depressed
disappointing	disappointed
disgusting	disgusted
embarrassing	embarrassed
exciting	excited
exhausting	exhausted
fascinating	fascinated
frightening	frightened
insulting	insulted
interesting	interested
irritating	irritated
relaxing	relaxed
shocking	shocked
surprising	surprised
threatening	threatened

Practice 13 Complete the sentences with the correct form of the adjective.

Example: (surprise) Alex is an excellent student, so I was very ____*surprised*____ that he failed the exam.

1   (confuse) I don't understand my homework at all. It's very _____.

2   (annoy) I'm trying to study, and you keep talking. You are very _____.

3   (challenge) Calculus 404 is not an easy class. It will be very _____ for you.

4   (relax) After my holiday in Puerto Rico, I felt very _____.

5   (embarrass) Everybody laughed when I made the mistake. I was very _____.

6   (embarrass) Everybody laughed when I made the mistake. It was very _____.

7   (excite) I think traveling is very _____, and I'm _____ about my trip to Chile next week.

8   (frighten) That was a very _____ ghost story. I was very _____ when I heard it.

9   (irritate) Sarah did not think my joke about her big nose was funny. She was very _____.

10   (fascinate) This book is _____. I can't stop reading it.

▶ **adjectives**

10.10 ▶ nouns used as adjectives

DISCOVER

    a   *I have a **big** garden.*

1   *Big* gives you information about *garden*, right? Is *big* an adjective?

    b   *I have a **vegetable** garden.*

2   *Vegetable* gives you information about *garden*, right? Is *vegetable* an adjective?

3   Look at *a* and *b*. We know that *big* is an adjective because it gives us information about the noun *garden*. *Vegetable* is not an adjective—it is a noun—but it also gives us information about *garden*. Is it possible to use nouns as adjectives?

LEARN

▶ Sometimes nouns are used as adjectives.

    *We need to buy more **cat** food.*

    *Do you know where my **coffee** cup is?*

REMEMBER

▶ When nouns are used as adjectives, they are <u>always</u> singular.

    wrong → *I work in a **books** store.*

    right →   *I work in a **book** store.*

Practice 14 Complete the sentences.

    Example: I need a bowl for my soup. I need a _____ soup bowl _____.

1   They play baseball in that stadium. It's a _____.

2   I need a lighter for my cigarette. I need a _____.

3   Carlos likes juice from apples. He likes _____.

4   I watched a good show on TV yesterday. I watched a good _____ yesterday.

5   John wrote an article for a magazine. He wrote a _____.

6   I need an opener for this can. Do you know where the _____ is?

7   My father built a house in a tree. He built a _____.

8   Lucy teaches at a school. She is a _____.

9   Mark bought a cage for his bird. He bought a _____.

10   The school bought a bus. They bought a _____.

11   Sam is the driver of the school bus. He's the _____.

10.11 ▶ compound adjectives

DISCOVER

    a   *Larry stayed in an **expensive** hotel room.*

1   *Expensive* gives you information about *hotel room*, right? Is *expensive* an adjective?

    b   *Larry stayed in a **$500-a-night** hotel room.*

2   *$500-a-night* gives you information about the *hotel room*, right? Is *$500-a-night* an adjective?

3   Look at *a* and *b*. We know that *expensive* is an adjective because it gives us information about the noun *hotel room*. *$500-a-night* is not an adjective—it is a group of words which are connected by hyphens—but it also gives us information about the noun *hotel room*. Is it possible to use groups of words connected by hyphens as adjectives?

LEARN

▶ Sometimes a group of words can be connected by hyphens and used as adjectives. These are called *compound adjectives*.

    *I have a **nine-year-old** daughter.*

    *I read an **800-page** book.*

REMEMBER

▶ When nouns are used as adjectives, they are <u>always</u> singular.

    wrong → *Being a mother is a 24-**hours**-a-day job.*

    right →   *Being a mother is a 24-**hour**-a-day job.*

▶ In compound adjectives, dollar amounts are also singular.

    wrong → I have a **ten dollars**-an-hour job.

    right →   I have a **ten dollar**-an-hour job.

▶ Hyphens are used to create compound adjectives only when they come before the verb.

    It's a **six-hour** flight to Toronto.

    → The flight to Toronto is **six hours**.

    Sarah has a **20-year-old** cat.

    → Sarah's cat is **20 years old**.

Practice 15 Rewrite the sentences so that they use compound adjectives.

    Example: It takes 12 hours to fly to Thailand.

           It's a _____*12-hour*_____ flight to Thailand.

1   His salary is $50,000 a year.

    He has a _____ job.

2   The class lasted for two hours.

    It was a _____ class.

3   Mary lives in a house with four bedrooms.

    Mary lives in a _____ house.

4   The movie was in black and white.

    It was a _____ movie.

5   The race was 100 meters.

    It was a _____ race.

6   John gave a presentation that lasted 20 minutes.

    John gave a _____ presentation.

7   Rosa works four days a week.

    Rosa has a _____ job.

8   This story is well known.

    It's a _____ story.

9   The tour will last for three hours.

    It will be a _____ tour.

10.12 ▶ making comparisons with *same, similar, different, like* and *alike*

DISCOVER

    a   John and Mary have **the same** car. John's car is **the same as** Mary's. They are **the same**.

    b   Susan and Bob have **similar** cars. Susan's car is **similar to** Bob's. They are **similar**.

    c   Tom and Mark have **different** cars. Tom's car is **different from** Mark's. They are **different**.

    d   John's car is **like** Mary's. They are **alike**.

1   How are *same, similar, different, like* and *alike* used in sentences?

2   Which words sometimes come after *same, similar* and *different*?

LEARN

▶ *Same, similar, different, like* and *alike* are used to make comparisons.

▶ Notice how *same, similar, different, like* and *alike* are used in sentences.

    same

        My car and your car **are the same**.

        My car **is the same as** your car.

similar

> Larry's house and my house **are similar**.
> Larry's house **is similar to** my house.

different

> This pen and that pen **are different**.
> This pen **is different from** that pen. (Some people say *different than* and *different to* instead of *different from*.)

like/alike

> My dog **is like** your dog.
> My dog and your dog **are alike**.

▶ *Same, similar, different, alike* and *like* are always singular.

wrong → *Mary and Sarah like the **sames** music.*
right →   *Mary and Sarah like the **same** music.*

wrong → *My house and your house are **similars**.*
right →   *My house and your house are **similar**.*

wrong → *Tom and I live in **differents** cities.*
right →   *Tom and I live in **different** cities.*

Practice 16 Correct the mistakes in the sentences.

1   My house same as my sister's house.

2   Is this watch similars to your watch?

3   Carlos and Alex different from each other.

4   Austria and Australia are differents countries.

5   Spain and Mexico have same language.

6   North Korea and South Korea are very difference.

7   This book is different of that book.

8   My house and your house are not same.

9   Paul's bicycle is similar my bicycle.

10   These shoes are alike those shoes.

Practice 17 Use *be* and the words in parentheses to write two present tense sentences as in the example.

Example: (my coat, your coat, similar)

> My coat and your coat are similar.
> My coat is similar to your coat.

1   (New York City, Los Angeles, different)

2   (my tie, your tie, alike, like)

3   (Larry, his twin brother, same)

4   (my car, your car, similar)

5   (Spanish, Italian, similar)

6   (these shoes, those shoes, same)

7   (Canada, the USA, different)

8   (your idea, his idea, like, alike)

Continue to Unit 10/advanced ↓ or go to Unit 11 →

10.13/a ▶ adjectives modified by adverbs

DISCOVER

   a Tom: *Are you tired?*
   b Jerry: *Yes, I'm **a bit tired**, but I'm going to keep working.*

1   What does *a bit* tell you about how tired Jerry is?

   c Mary: *Are you sure?*
   d Larry: *Yes, I'm **fairly sure**, but I could be wrong.*

2   What does *fairly* tell you about how *sure* Larry is?

   e Sam: *Are you hungry?*
   f Tom: *Yes, I'm **pretty hungry**. Let's eat soon.*

3   What does *pretty* tell you about how *hungry* Tom is?

   g Ali: *Are you finished?*
   h Sofia: *Yes, I'm **totally finished**.*

4   If Sofia did not say *totally*, would the sentence have the same meaning? Why do you think she says *totally*?

LEARN (See Table 10e.)

▶ Some adverbs can be used to modify the meaning of adjectives. They can make the adjective weaker or stronger. With some adjectives, it is possible to be *a little, sort of* or *very*, etc., but with other adjectives it is not. For example, it is possible to be *a little hungry*, but it is not possible to be *a little dead*—people are either dead or they are not dead. However, for adjectives like *dead, unique, perfect, finished, impossible, pregnant, free*, etc., it is common to use adverbs which are listed under 100% in Table 10e to show how the speaker feels—to make the sentence stronger.

REMEMBER

▶ The adverb goes before the adjective.

   wrong → *He is **angry extremely**.*
   right → *He is **extremely angry**.*

10e

adjectives modified by adverbs			
weak	**moderate**	**strong**	**100%**
a bit *a little* *slightly*	*fairly* *kind of* *moderately* *rather* *reasonably* *somewhat* *sort of*	*awfully* *extremely* *highly* *pretty* *quite* *really* *terribly* *very*	*100%* *absolutely* *completely* *entirely* *totally*

Practice 18/a Underline the best adverb to finish the sentences. There may be more than one good answer. Be ready to explain your answer.

Example: My sister will not speak to me. She's (a bit / moderately / <u>pretty</u>) angry with me.

1   I'm (terribly / kind of / 100%) confused by my homework, but I think if I review Chapter 7 again, I will understand it.

2   I want to buy a new house, and today I looked at a house on Maple Street that is (kind of / very / absolutely) perfect.

3   It's not a good idea to let children play with guns. They are (fairly / very / totally) dangerous.

▶ **adjectives**

4   Francesca got a 98 on her test. That was a (slightly / somewhat / pretty) good score.

5   I was (a bit / terribly / completely) late to work—only five minutes.

6   John's mother died yesterday. He is (a bit / sort of / terribly) upset.

7   I want to buy my wife a big diamond ring, but they're (a little / kind of / extremely) expensive.

8   Sam had to go to the hospital yesterday. He was (a bit / sort of / very) sick.

9   My essay is (a little / rather / quite) short. The teacher said it should be 20 pages long, and mine is 19 pages long.

10 This is a disaster! You did everything wrong! Now I'll have to spend hours fixing this mess! It's (slightly / moderately / totally) screwed up!

Unit 11 ▶ modals and phrasal modals, part 1

INTRODUCTION

▶ We use *modal verbs* and *phrasal modal verbs*, which are similar to modal verbs, to say <u>how we understand</u> a situation. Sometimes one modal or phrasal modal can have many different meanings. Sometimes different modals or phrasal modals can have the same meaning. The best way for you to learn how to use modals is to <u>focus on situations</u> instead of individual modals or phrasal modals. For example, instead of focusing on the meanings of *would*, you should focus on learning the different ways *would* and other modals and phrasal modals are used in situations such as asking for permission, making requests or talking about how certain you are about something.

▶ Many contractions of modals and phrasal modals are possible, but some of them are not common.

11a

	contractions of modals and phrasal modals (The contractions in **bold** are possible but are not common.)	
	contractions with subject pronouns	**contractions with *not***
be able to be going to be supposed to can could had better have got to have to may might must ought to shall should used to will would	*I'm/you're/he's/she's/we're/they're able to* *I'm/you're/he's/she's/we're/they're going to* *I'm/you're/he's/she's/we're/they're supposed to* *I'd/you'd/he'd/she'd/we'd/they'd better* *I've/you've/he's/she's/we've/they've got to* *I'll/you'll/he'll/she'll/we'll/they'll* *I'd/you'd/he'd/she'd/we'd/they'd*	*isn't/aren't/wasn't/weren't able to* *isn't/aren't/wasn't/weren't going to* *isn't/aren't/wasn't/weren't supposed to* *can't* *couldn't* ***hadn't better*** *haven't got to* *don't have to* ***mayn't*** ***mightn't*** ***mustn't*** ***oughtn't to*** ***shan't*** *shouldn't* *didn't use to* *won't* *wouldn't*

11.1 ▶ asking for permission with *may*, *could* and *can*

DISCOVER

a ***May*** *I* ***use*** *your pencil?*

b ***Could*** *I* ***use*** *your pencil?*

c ***Can*** *I* ***use*** *your pencil?*

1 Do *a*, *b* and *c* have the same meaning or different meanings?

LEARN

▶ *A*, *b* and *c* have the same meaning. They are all asking for permission. In this situation (but not always!), *may*, *could* and *can* have the same meaning.

REMEMBER

▶ Common ways to answer requests for permission.

Yes, you may./No, you may not. (more formal and less common)

Yes, you can./No, you can't. (less formal and more common)

Sure.

OK.

Of course.

No problem.

▶ It is not possible to answer with *Yes, you could* or *No, you couldn't*.

Practice 1 What would you say in these situations? Write answers with *may*, *could* or *can*. Do not use the same modal for each answer. Practice using all of them.

Example: You are at my house, and you want to use my telephone. What do you say to me?

   May I use your telephone?

   Could I use your telephone?

   Can I use your telephone?

1   You want to open the window in my house. What do you say to me?

2   Your sister wants to use my car. What do you say to me?

3   You and your friend are at work, and you both want to go home early. What do you say to your boss?

4   We are at the zoo, and you want to use my camera. What do you say to me?

5   You are eating dinner at a friend's house, and you want another piece of cake. What do you say to your friend?

6   You want to use your friend's dictionary. What do you say to your friend?

7   You are at a friend's house, and you want a glass of water. What do you say to your friend?

8   You are talking to your teacher, and you want more time to finish your project. What do you say to your teacher?

9   You and I are at our friend's house, and we want to smoke. What do we say to our friend?

10   You want to ask me a personal question. What do you say to me?

11.2 ▶ asking for permission with *would you mind*

DISCOVER

   a   ***May I smoke** in your house?*
   b   ***Could I smoke** in your house?*
   c   ***Can I smoke** in your house?*
   d   ***Would you mind if I smoked** in your house?*
1   Does *d* have the same meaning as *a*, *b* and *c*?
2   How is the verb *smoke* different in *d* than it is in *a*, *b* and *c*?

LEARN

▶ *D* has the same meaning as *a*, *b* and *c*. It uses the verb *mind*. The meaning of *mind* is similar to *bother*, so another way to say *d* is *Would it bother you if I smoked in your house?* Notice that when *mind* is used, the grammar is a little different. It is necessary to use the past form of the verb. (This is a kind of conditional sentence. See Unit 20 for more about conditional sentences.)

REMEMBER

▶ The correct way to give a positive answer to a request with *mind* is with a negative sentence.
   Susan: *Would you mind if I smoked?*
   Mary: *No, I **wouldn't mind**.* (= Yes, you may.)

▶ It is also common to use *do* instead of *would* with the present form of the verb.
   Susan: *Do you mind if I smoke?*
   Mary: *No, I **don't mind**.* (= Yes, you may.)

Practice 2 Change these requests so that they use *would you mind*.

Example: May I sit down?

   Would you mind if I sat down?

1   Can I use your calculator?

2   May I close the door?

3   Can my son swim in your pool?

4   Can I be late for class tomorrow?

5   Could we watch the game at your house?

6   May I turn up the heat?

7   Could I use your phone?

8   Can I speak with your manager?

9   Can I not go shopping with you tonight?

10   Can I not be the best man at your wedding?

11.3 ▶ asking people to do something with *would*, *could*, *will* and *can*

DISCOVER
    a   **Would** you **help** me?
    b   **Could** you **help** me?
    c   **Will** you **help** me?
    d   **Can** you **help** me?

1   Do these questions have the same meaning or different meanings?

LEARN
▶ *A, b, c* and *d* have the same meaning. They are all ways to ask people to do something. In this situation (but not always!), *would, could, will* and *can* have the same meaning.

REMEMBER
▶ Common ways to answer requests from other people to do something.
  Yes, I will. / No, I won't.
  I'd be happy to.
  Sure.
  OK.
  Of course.
  No problem.

Practice 3 **What would you say in these situations? Write answers with *would, could, will* or *can*. Do not use the same modal for each answer. Practice using all of them.**

Example: You want your friend to give you a ride. What do you say to her?

    Would you give me a ride?
    Could you give me a ride?
    Will you give me a ride?
    Can you give me a ride?

1   You want me to fix your bicycle. What do you say to me?

2   You want your friend to help you with your homework. What do you say to him?

3   You want your son's teacher to talk to your son after class. What do you say to her?

4   You want me to close the window. What do you say to me?

5   You want me to get you a cup of coffee. What do you say to me?

6   You want your sister to turn off the TV. What do you say to her?

7   You want your son to be quiet. What do you say to him?

8   You want me to pick you up at the train station. What do you say to me?

9   You want me to feed the dog. What do you say to me?

10   You want a clerk in a store to help you. What do you say to him?

11.4 ▶ asking people to do something with *would you mind*

DISCOVER
    a   **Would** you **help** me?
    b   **Could** you **help** me?
    c   **Will** you **help** me?

▶ **modals and phrasal modals, part 1**

    d   **Can** you **help** me?

    e   **Would** you **mind helping** me?

1   Does *e* have the same meaning as *a, b, c* and *d*?

2   How is the verb *help* different in *e* than it is in *a, b, c* and *d*?

LEARN

▶ *E* has the same meaning as *a, b, c* and *d*. It uses the verb *mind*. The meaning of *mind* is similar to *bother*, so another way to say *e* would be *Would it bother you to help me?* Notice that when *mind* is used, the grammar is a little different. It is necessary to use the *-ing* form of the verb.

REMEMBER

▶ The correct way to give a positive answer to a request with *mind* is with a negative sentence.

   Susan: *Would you mind washing the dishes?*

   Mary: *No, I* **wouldn't mind**. (= Yes, I will.)

Practice 4 Change these requests so that they use *would you mind.*

   Example: Could you get me a sandwich?

                Would you mind getting me a sandwich?

1   Can you move this sofa for me?

2   Will you take us to the library?

3   Would you go shopping with me tomorrow?

4   Can you be here at 7:00?

5   Will you give me a ride to work?

6   Will you say that again?

7   Can you call me back?

8   Would you be quiet?

9   Can you not walk so fast?

11.5 ▶ using *borrow* and *lend*

DISCOVER

    a   I forgot my calculator. **May** I **take** yours?

    b   I forgot my calculator. **May** I **borrow** yours?

1   Do *a* and *b* have a similar meaning?

    c   I forgot my calculator. **Would you mind** if I **took** yours?

    d   I forgot my calculator. **Would you mind** if I **borrowed** yours?

2   Do *c* and *d* have a similar meaning?

    e   I forgot my calculator. **Can** you **give** me yours?

    f   I forgot my calculator. **Can** you **lend** me yours?

3   Do *e* and *f* have a similar meaning?

    g   I forgot my calculator. **Would you mind giving** me yours?

    h   I forgot my calculator. **Would you mind lending** me yours?

4   Do *g* and *h* have a similar meaning?

LEARN

▶ It is very common to use *borrow* and *lend* when making requests, but many students have difficulty using *borrow* and *lend* correctly. *Borrow* is similar to *take*. *Lend* is similar to *give*. The meanings of *borrow* and *lend* are opposite, but they can be used to say the same thing.

   Can **I borrow** $10?   Would **you mind if I borrow** $10?

   = Can **you lend me** $10?   = Would **you mind lending me** $10?

REMEMBER

   wrong → Can **you borrow me** your calculator?

   right →   Can **I borrow** your calculator?

   right →   Can **you lend me** your calculator?

Practice 5 Circle the letter of the best answer.

1   I don't have any money. _____ $20?
    a   Could you lend
    b   Could I lend me
    c   Could I borrow
    d   Could you borrow me

2   I forgot my pen. _____ your pen?
    a   Would you mind lending me
    b   Could you mind lending
    c   Would you borrow me
    d   Would you mind me borrowing

3   My father's car is at the mechanic. _____ your car?
    a   Can you lend
    b   Can you lend him
    c   Can he lend you
    d   Can you borrow him

4   I forgot my umbrella. _____ your umbrella?
    a   Would I mind if you borrowed
    b   Would you mind if lent
    c   Would you mind borrowing me
    d   Would you mind if I borrowed

5   Mary forgot her tennis racket. _____ yours?
    a   Would you borrow her
    b   Would she borrow you
    c   Would you lend her
    d   Would she lend you

Practice 6 What would you say in these situations? Write one answer with *borrow* <u>and</u> one answer with *lend*.

Example: You want your friend to give you some money.

      (may) *May I borrow some money?*

      (would, mind) *Would you mind lending me some money?*

1   You want to use your friend's bicycle.

    (can, borrow)

    (would, mind, lend)

2   You want to use your sister's football.

    (would, lend)

    (may, borrow)

3   You want your friend to give you her dictionary.

    (would, mind, borrow)

    (will, lend)

4   You want your friend to give you his snow shovel.

    (could, borrow)

    (will, lend)

5   You want to use your neighbor's grill.

    (would, mind, borrow)

    (would, mind, lend)

▶ **modals and phrasal modals, part 1**

11.6 ▶ saying something was necessary in the past with *had to*

DISCOVER

  a   I **had to work** yesterday, and I **must work** today.
  b   We **had to take** a test last week, and we **have to take** another test next week.
  c   Mary **had to go** to a meeting last month, and she **has got to go** to a meeting tomorrow.

1   How many ways do you see to say something is necessary in the present and future?
2   How many ways do you see to say something was necessary in the past?

LEARN (See Table 11b.)

▶ *Must, have to* and *have got to* are used to talk about *necessity*—something that is *required*, something that some-body *must* do. *Have to* and *have got to* are much more common than *must*. Because *have got* and *have got to* are very important, they have already been discussed in Unit 8. (Another very important and much more common way to use *must* is discussed in Section 12.1 and in Section 12.2.) *Must* and *have got to* are <u>not</u> used to talk about the past. Only *had to* is used for the past.

11b

necessity in the past, present or future	
past	**present or future**
had to	*have to* *have got to* *must*

Practice 7 Change the sentences to past simple.

  Examples: Sarah has to go to the library.

  Sarah had to go to the library.

  I must pay my telephone bill.

  I had to pay my telephone bill.

  My father's got to go to the dentist.

  My father had to go to the dentist.

1   Mark must do his homework.

2   I've got to go to the airport.

3   He's got to help his father.

4   Do you have to wake up early?

5   Have you got to make dinner?

6   Does she have to go shopping?

7   I don't have to practice the piano.

8   We don't have to turn in our homework.

9   Does it have to be typed?

11.7 ▶ saying something is not necessary with *have to* or is not allowed with *must*

DISCOVER

  a   You **must not talk** to John.
  b   You **don't have to talk** to John.

1   Do these sentences have the same meaning?

LEARN

▶ *A* and *b* do not have the same meaning. When *must* and *have to* are used in negative present simple sentences, their meaning is not the same (*have got* is not common for this meaning). *You must not talk to John* means that it is not allowed, it is *prohibited*. *You don't have to talk to John* has a different meaning. It means that you may talk to him if you want to, but you are not required to—it is *optional*—you have a choice.

Practice 8 Write *NN* after the sentence if it means that something is not necessary. Write *NA* in the blank if it means that something is not allowed.

Examples: You don't have to go to the meeting. __NN__

You must not talk to anyone during the exam. __NA__

1   Sarah doesn't have to take her brother to work. _____

2   You must not smoke in a supermarket. _____

3   I don't have to go with my brother. _____

4   You must not drink and drive. _____

5   You must not let your cat jump on the dinner table. _____

6   You don't have to go to church with your mother. _____

7   You must not tell anyone. _____

8   Larry doesn't have to help his sister. _____

11.8 ▶ saying something is a good idea or a bad idea in the present or future with *should, ought to* and *had better*

DISCOVER
a   You **should eat** less salt.
b   You **ought to eat** less salt.
c   You **had better eat** less salt.

1   Do *a, b* and *c* have the same meaning?

LEARN
▶ *A, b* and *c* have the same basic meaning. *Should, ought to* and *had better* are all used to give advice, to say that something is a good idea. The only difference is that *had better* is stronger than *should* and *ought to*. With *had better*, there is usually an idea that something bad will happen if the advice is not taken.

REMEMBER
▶ *Ought* is <u>not</u> the same as *should*. *Ought <u>to</u>* is the same as *should*.

▶ It is not common to use *ought to* in negative sentences.

▶ *Ought to* is usually pronounced as *otta* in informal English.

▶ Only *should* is used in questions.

▶ The contraction of *had* is *'d*, but in spoken English, the *'d* is often completely silent. In informal speech, it is very common to hear, for example, *You better* or *I better* instead of *You'd better* or *I'd better*.
   *The boss is coming! We **better get** to work!*

▶ *Had better* is an idiom. Do not try to understand the grammar. Although *had* is the past form of *have*, *had better* is <u>not</u> about the past.

▶ *Had better* is stronger than *should* and *ought to*. It is used only when there is a reason to be extra strong—when we want to say that if something does not happen, there will be a negative consequence (a bad result).
   *You'd **better slow** down. If you don't, **you'll have an accident**.*

Practice 9 What would you say in these situations? Use *should, ought to* or *had better* to complete the sentences. There may be more than one good answer for some. Be ready to explain your answer.

1   Fire! You _____ call the fire department right now!

2   Your hands are dirty. You _____ wash them before you make dinner.

3   You're sick. You _____ wash your hands before you make dinner.

4   Michael, you _____ not eat with your mouth open.

5   I'm getting angry. You _____ not say that again!

6   We still have a quarter tank of gas, but we _____ get gas soon.

7   We're almost out of gas! We _____ get gas right now.

8   It's 8:50? Oh no! I didn't know it was so late. I have to be at work at 9:00. I _____ go.

9   Your left rear tire is a little low. You _____ put air in it.

10 Your left rear tire is almost flat. You _____ put air in it.

11.9 ▶ saying something was a good idea or a bad idea in the past with *should*

DISCOVER

    a   *I got a bad grade on the test. I didn't study for the test. That was a mistake. I **should have studied**.*

    b   *Mary was late for work. She **should've left** earlier.*

    c   *I feel sick. Maybe I **shouldn't have eaten** two hot dogs, three cheeseburgers and four slices of pizza.*

1   How do we say that doing something was a good idea in the past, but that somebody did not do it (or the opposite—that something was not a good idea but somebody did do it)?

2   Which word always follows *should*? Which form of the main verb follows *have*?

LEARN

▶ When we want to say that something was a good idea in the past, but it did not happen or somebody did not do it, we use *should* + *have* + past participle.

    *This traffic is terrible! We **should have taken** the train.*

          should + *have* + past participle

REMEMBER

▶ *Had better* is not used to talk about the past. It is possible to use *ought to have* to talk about the past, but it is not common. *Should have* is much more common.

▶ In speech, *should have* (*should've*) is often pronounced as *shoulda*.

Practice 10 What would you say about the people in these situations? Use *should have* to say what they should have done or *should not have* to say what they should not have done. You are giving advice, so there may be more than one possible answer for some. Be ready to explain your answer.

Examples: I didn't go to the party, and now my friends are telling me that it was a great party.

    You should have gone to the party.

    Maria locked her keys inside her house, and she had to break a window to get in.

    She shouldn't have locked her keys inside her house.

1   I didn't eat breakfast. Now I'm hungry.

2   I exercised for two hours yesterday. Now my muscles hurt.

3   Noura didn't keep her big mouth shut. Now her sister is very angry with her.

4   Alex didn't call his father. Now his father is upset.

5   I ate six pieces of chocolate cake. Now I feel sick.

6   Carlos forgot to bring his glasses to the movie theater. Now he can't see the movie.

7   I didn't buy coffee yesterday. Now we don't have any.

8   I tried to start a fire with gasoline. Now I'm in the hospital.

9   Larry jumped off the roof, and he broke his arm.

10 My wife asked, "Am I fat?" and I said, "yes." Now she won't talk to me.

11.10 ▶ talking about ability in the past, present and future with *can, could* and *be able to*

DISCOVER

    a   *I **can speak** English now. I learned when I was in high school.*

    b   *I **am able to speak** English now. I learned when I was in high school.*

1   Look at *a* and *b*. How do we talk about ability in the present?

    c   *I **could not speak** English before I learned it in high school.*

    d   *I **was not able to speak** English before I learned it in high school.*

2   How do we talk about ability in the past?

    e   *I'm busy now, but I **can help** you move your sofa later.*

    f   *I'm busy now, but I **will be able to help** you move your sofa later.*

3   How do we talk about ability in the future?

LEARN

▶ *Can* and *be able to* have the same meaning when we are talking about ability (but not always!). *Could* and the past forms of *be able to* are used to talk about ability in the past.

Practice 11 Complete the sentences with *can* or *could*.

1   I'm really tired. I (not, sleep) _____ last night.

2   Sarah (walk) _____ when she was only six months old.

3   (understand) _____ you _____ what the teacher was talking about?

4   (tell) _____ you _____ me what this says? I forgot my glasses, and

    now I (not, read) _____ it.

5   (reach) _____ you _____ that book on the top shelf?

6   I (not, open) _____ this jar. (do) _____ you _____ it?

7   Mary has to work Friday night. She (not, come) _____ to the party.

8   (figure out) _____ you _____ what's wrong with my car?

9   Ali (do) _____ it now, but he (not, do) _____ it when he was younger.

10   I forgot my cell phone, so I (not, call) _____ you last night.

Practice 12 Rewrite the sentences using the correct form and tense of *be able to*.

Examples: I can't do it.

    I'm not able to do it.

    Could you hear what he said?

    Were you able to hear what he said?

1   Can you walk with that broken leg?

2   I can't sleep on airplanes.

3   Gary couldn't see the play from the back row of the theater.

4   Could the tech guy figure out what was wrong with your computer?

5   Linda can speak several languages.

6   I can see a lot better with my new glasses.

7   We couldn't make any sense out of the instructions.

8   The doctors couldn't save him.

9   I couldn't get my car started.

10   Can you walk and chew gum at the same time?

11.11 ▶ talking about repeated past actions and past situations with *used to* and *would*

DISCOVER

    a   *When I was young, I **would/used to go** swimming every Saturday.*

1   Is this sentence about something I <u>did</u> in the past, or is it about <u>a situation</u> in the past?

    b   *I **used to live** in the Middle East, but now I live in Indiana.*

2   Is this sentence about something I <u>did</u> in the past, or is it about <u>a situation</u> in the past?

LEARN

▶ *Would* and *used to* are both used to talk about repeated past actions.

*We **used to go** camping in Wisconsin every summer when we lived in Chicago.*

*When my wife was a college student, she **would study** all night long.*

▶ *Used to* is also used to talk about a situation that existed in the past but does not exist today.

*Mary **used to work** at a bank, but now she works at a hospital.*

*I **used to be** thin, but now I'm fat.*

REMEMBER

▶ *Used to* is different from *be used to* discussed in Section 10.8.

▶ We use *would* and *used to* only when we do not say the time of the past actions or the past situation. When we do say the time of the past action or the past situation, we use the past simple.

wrong → *I **used to be** a truck driver **from 1999 to 2005**.*

right → *I **was** a truck driver **from 1999 to 2005**.*

Practice 13 Underline *would* or *used to*. If both are correct, underline both.

Example: I (would / <u>used to</u>) love basketball when I was young. I (<u>would</u> / <u>used to</u>) play whenever I had a chance.

1 Sarah (would / used to) be married to a guy named Bill.

2 My sister (would / used to) have five dogs. They (would / used to) bark all night and wake up the neighbors.

3 I (would / used to) to work at the First National Bank on Main Street. When I worked there, I (would / used to) eat lunch at Sam's restaurant across the street almost every day.

4 When my grandfather was young, he (would / used to) travel around the country looking for work.

5 Michael (would / used to) be thin, but he's gained a lot of weight in the last few years.

6 When I shared an apartment with my brother, he (would never / never used to) help me clean.

7 My uncle (would / used to) tell the same jokes again and again.

8 When I was young, my parents (wouldn't / didn't use to) let me go out on school nights.

11.12 ▶ using modals with phrasal modals

DISCOVER

    a *I failed my math exam, and now I'm not sure that I **will be able to graduate** in June.*

    b *I think there's something wrong with my car. I **might have to take** it to a mechanic soon.*

1 What are the modals? What are the phrasal modals?

LEARN

▶ It is never correct to use two modals together, but it is very common to use the modals *will, would, might, may* and *should* with the phrasal modals *be able to* and *have to*.

*If you were taller, you **would be able to reach** the top shelf.*

*I want customers in my restaurant to get good service. They **shouldn't have to wait** a long time for their food.*

REMEMBER

▶ It is not common to use phrasal modals with *ought to*.

▶ It is not possible to use modals with *have got to*.

Practice 14 Complete the sentences with the words in parentheses.

Example: Tom is going to try to fix my TV, so I (not, have to, buy, may) ___*may not have to buy*___ a new one.

1 Carlos told me that he (come, be able to, not, will) _____ to my wedding.

2 If you're over 65, you (not, have to, might, pay) _____ full price. You (get, might, be able to) _____ a discount.

3 I'm sorry, but your essay wasn't very good. You (have to, will, rewrite) _____ it.

4 After you finish your driver's education course, you (pass, be able to, should) _____ the driver's license exam.

5   When you're in Norway, you (be able to, might, see) _____ the Northern Lights.

6   Our flight is at 3:00 in the morning, so we (leave, have to, will) _____ for the airport around 1:00.

7   Alex is very smart. You (have to, not, should, explain) _____ the plan to him more than once. He'll understand.

8   July and August are the busy season, so we (be able to, not, fly, might) _____ to France when we want to.

9   John lived in Greece for 20 years, so he (speak, should, be able to) _____ Greek.

10 If you plan to graduate from college in only three years, you (take, have to, will) _____ classes in the summer.

11 If you arrive at the opera after 7:30, you (enter, be able to, not, may) _____. You may have to wait until the intermission.

12 I'd like to give you a ride to work tomorrow, but I (not, would, be able to) _____ until 8:00.

> ## Continue to Unit 11/advanced ↓ or go to Unit 12 →

11.13/a ▶ talking about preferences with *would rather*

DISCOVER

    a   Mary: *Where **would** you **rather go**—to the beach or to the park?*
          Tom: *I **would rather go** to the beach than the park.*

1   Are the speakers talking about preferences—which choice Tom prefers?

2   Is it necessary to repeat *to* (or *go to*) in the answer?

    b   Alex: ***Would** you **rather eat** Chinese food or Mexican?*
          Sam: *I'**d rather eat** Mexican food than Chinese.*

3   Would it be possible to repeat *eat* and *food* in the answer?

    c   Sofia: *What do you want to do—play basketball or watch TV?*
          Ali: *I'**d rather play** basketball.*

4   Would it be possible to add *than watch TV* to the answer?

    d   Carlos: *Do you want to go shopping with me?*
          Rosa: *I'**d rather not**.*

5   Is there anything that could be repeated in Rosa's answer?

LEARN

▶ *Would rather* is used with the present simple to talk about preferences. *Would* is often contracted to *'d* (*I'd, He'd*, etc.).

▶ Ellipsis is often used with *would rather*, so it is important to understand the many ellipsis possibilities. When one verb is used with two or more objects, often the objects are repeated but not the verb.

    *I'd rather play tennis than **[play]** soccer.*
    *He'd rather be studying medicine than **[be studying]** law.*

In conversation, often everything after the first object is not repeated.

    A: *What would you rather do—play tennis or play soccer?*
    B: *I'd rather play tennis.*
         *= I'd rather play tennis **[than play soccer]**.*

    A: *Would Mark rather be studying medicine or studying law?*
    B: *He'd rather be studying medicine.*
         *= He'd rather be studying medicine **[than be studying law]**.*

Sometimes the choice is between <u>something</u> and <u>nothing</u>.

    A: *Would you like to help me give my cat a bath?*
    B: *I'd rather not.*
         *= I'd rather not **[help you give your cat a bath]**.*

Without ellipsis, conversations *b*, *c* and *d* in Discover would be

    b   Alex: *Would you rather eat Chinese food or Mexican?*

▶ modals and phrasal modals, part 1   115

= *Would you rather eat Chinese food or [eat] Mexican [food]?*

Sam: *I'd rather eat Mexican food than Chinese.*

= *I'd rather eat Mexican food than [eat] Chinese [food].*

c Sofia: *What do you want to do—play basketball or watch TV?*

   Ali: *I'd rather play basketball.*

        = *I'd rather play basketball [than watch TV].*

d Carlos: *Do want to go shopping with me?*

   Rosa: *I'd rather not.*

         = *I'd rather not [go shopping with you].*

▶ Four patterns are common when *would rather* is used in questions. (See Section 6.9/a for more about negative questions.)

*What **would** you **rather** have—chocolate ice cream or vanilla ice cream?*

***Would** you **rather** have chocolate ice cream **or** [have] vanilla ice cream?*

***Would** you **rather** have chocolate ice cream **than** [have] vanilla ice cream?*

***Wouldn't** you **rather** have chocolate ice cream **than** [have] vanilla ice cream?*

Practice 15/a Ask questions with *would rather*.

Examples: A: What _____ *would you rather have—apple juice or orange juice* _____ ?

           B: I'd rather have apple juice [than have orange juice].

           A: What _____ *would you rather do—walk to the store or drive there* _____ ?

           B: I'd rather walk to the store [than drive there].

           A: Would _____ *you rather go to a movie than visit my mother* _____ ?

           B: I'd rather go to a movie [than visit your mother].

           A: Wouldn't _____ *you rather watch TV than clean the garage* _____ ?

           B: Yes, I'd rather watch TV [than clean the garage].

1 A: What _____ ?

   B: I'd rather stay home [than go to the library].

2 A: Wouldn't _____ ?

   B: Yes, I'd rather go to the beach [than go shopping].

3 A: When _____ ?

   B: I'd rather leave tomorrow [than leave today].

4 A: Would _____ ?

   B: He'd rather drive all night [than stop at a hotel].

5 A: Where _____ ?

   B: He'd rather go to Munich [than go to Berlin].

6 A: Wouldn't _____ ?

   B: No, she wouldn't rather be married [than be single].

7 A: What _____ ?

   B: She'd rather have onion rings [than potato chips].

8 A: Would _____ ?

   B: They'd rather live in a small town [than live in a big city].

Practice 16/a Write two answers to the questions. In the first answer, do not use ellipsis. In the second answer, use ellipsis as much as possible. Often there is ellipsis in the question. Try to replace the ellipted words in the B1 answer as in the example.

Example: A: Would you rather have coffee or tea?

          (You prefer tea.)

          B1: I'd _____ *rather have tea than have coffee* _____ .

          B2: I'd _____ *rather have tea* _____ .

1 A: Would he rather go to London or Paris?
(He prefers London.)

B1: He'd _____.

B2: He'd _____.

2 A: What would you rather do—play tennis or go swimming?
(You prefer to play tennis.)

B1: I'd _____.

B2: I'd _____.

3 A: Wouldn't you rather drive to the beach than walk to the beach?
(You prefer to walk to the beach.)

B1: Yes, I would _____.

B2: Yes, I would _____.

4 A: Would you rather buy a new TV or get this one fixed?
(You prefer to buy a new TV.)

B1: I'd _____.

B2: I'd _____.

5 A: What would she rather do—take a taxi or go in my car?
(She prefers to take a taxi.)

B1: She'd _____.

B2: She'd _____.

6 A: Do you want to go out for dinner?
(You don't want to go out for dinner.)

B1: I'd _____.

B2: I'd _____.

7 A: Wouldn't you rather eat at 6:00 than wait until 7:00?
(You prefer to wait until 7:00.)

B1: No, I'd _____.

B2: No, I'd _____.

8 A: Would Alex rather live in Chicago or New York?
(He prefers Chicago.)

B1: He'd _____.

B2: He'd _____.

9 A: Would Carlos like to go shopping with his mother?
(He doesn't want to.)

B1: He'd _____.

B2: He'd _____.

10 A: What would you rather have for dinner—beef or chicken?
(You prefer chicken.)

B1: I'd _____.

B2: I'd _____.

▶ **modals and phrasal modals, part 1**

11 A: Would you rather be doing your homework or watching TV?
    (You prefer watching TV.)

    B1: I'd _____.

    B2: I'd _____.

12 A: Would you rather be eaten by a tiger or a shark?
    (You prefer to be eaten by a shark.)

    B1: I'd _____.

    B2: I'd _____.

11.14/a ▶ ellipsis examples and practice (See Section 1.9/a for more about ellipsis.)

DISCOVER

a   Linda: *May/can/could we leave the class early?*
    Lucy: *Yes, you may/can.*
            = Yes, you may/can [leave the class early].

b   Mary: *Can you speak Russian?*
    Larry: *I can't, but my sister can.*
            = I can't [speak Russian], but my sister can [speak Russian].

c   Tom: *Did you have to help clean the garage?*
    Sam: *No, I didn't have to, but my brother had to.*
            = No, I didn't have to [help clean the garage], but my brother had to [help clean the garage].
            No, I didn't, but my brother did.
            = No, I didn't [have to help clean the garage], but my brother [had to help clean the garage].

d   Alex: *Should I study Chapter 12 for the test?*
    Sofia: *Yes, you should/ought to.*
            = Yes, you should/ought to [study Chapter 12 for the test].

e   Bill: *Do you want to stop for breakfast on the way to work?*
    Sarah: *We'd better not. We might be late for work again.*
            = We'd better not [stop for breakfast on the way to work]. We might be late for work again.

f   Sam: *Yesterday was the first of the month. Did you pay the rent?*
    Noura: *I forgot. I should have, but I didn't.*
            = I forgot [to pay the rent]. I should have [paid the rent], but I didn't [pay the rent].

g   Ali: *Were you able to get your work done today?*
    Rosa: *No, I wasn't able to, but I will tomorrow.*
            = No, I wasn't able to [get my work done today], but I will [be able to get my work done] tomorrow.

Practice 17/a Rewrite the B sentences with ellipsis. There is more than one good answer for some.

    Example: A: Did you call your mother? Yesterday was her birthday.

                 B: I should have called my mother, but I didn't call my mother.

                      I should have, but I didn't.

1   A: Did John and Carlos have to go to school yesterday?

    B: John had to go to school yesterday, but Carlos didn't have to go to school yesterday.

2   A: Will you be able to help me tomorrow?

    B: No, I won't be able to help you tomorrow.

3   A: You should quit smoking.

    B: I know I should quit smoking. I want to quit smoking, but I can't quit smoking.

4   A: Look at those dark clouds. I think it might rain soon. You'd better take an umbrella with you when you go out.

    B: You're right. I'd better take an umbrella with me when I go out.

5   A: Can I use your car tomorrow?

    B: No, you can't use my car tomorrow. I'm going to be using it.

6 A: Did you really tell your boss that he's stupid?
   B: Yes, I shouldn't have told my boss that he's stupid, but I told my boss that he's stupid.

7 A: Can you understand Paul?
   B: No, I can't understand him. Nobody can understand him.

8 A: Are you going to clean your house today? It's very dirty.
   B: I'd better clean my house today. My mother is coming to visit tonight.

9 A: Should you have bought that car?
   B: No, I shouldn't have bought this car. It was a big mistake.

10 A: Is it a good idea to go to that neighborhood so late at night? It's dangerous.
   B: No, I'd better not go to that neighborhood so late at night. If I do go to that neighborhood so late at night, I might get robbed. (If you are confused by *If I do go*, see Section 3.8/a.)

▶ **modals and phrasal modals, part 1**

Unit 12 ▶ modals and phrasal modals, part 2

12.1 ▶ certainty: saying that you are sure about something in the present with *must, have to, have got to, may, might* and *could*

DISCOVER

    *a   The teacher is wearing a wedding ring. He has never told me that he is married, but if he's wearing a wedding ring, he **must/has to/has got to be** married.*

1   How sure am I that the teacher is married?

    *b   Michael **might/may/could speak** French. He's from Canada, and many Canadians speak French.*

    *c   Michael **might not/may not speak** French. He's from Canada, but not everyone in Canada speaks French.*

2   How sure am I that Michael speaks French?

    *d   Alex isn't answering the telephone. He **must not be** home.*

3   How sure am I that Alex is not home?

    *e   That man across the street looks like John, but it **couldn't/can't be** John. John is in prison now.*

4   How sure am I that the man across the street is not John?

LEARN (See Table 12a.)

▶ *Must, have to, have got to, might, may* and *could* are used to talk about how certain (sure) we are about something in the present.

12a

degrees of certainty about the present

+ **100% SURE:** When we are 100% certain, we do not use modals or phrasal modals.
    *Mary **is** sick.*
    *Carlos **speaks** Spanish.*
 	
    VERY CERTAIN: When we are very certain, we use *must, have to* or *have got to*. The meanings you see here are different from the meanings discussed in Section 11.6. They are <u>not</u> about obligation (*I have to work tomorrow*). They are about how certain we are about something. *Must* is the most common. *Have to* and *have got to* are used only when we want extra emphasis to make what we say stronger.
    *Maria's from Italy. I've never heard her speak Italian, but if she's from Italy, she **must speak** Italian.*
    *It takes an hour to drive to the mall, and they left three hours ago, so they **have to be** there now.*
    *That's the craziest thing I have ever heard! You**'ve got to be** joking.*
 	
    MAYBE: When we are not certain, we use *might, may* or *could*. There is no difference in meaning.
    *Larry is often absent from class, and he's absent today. He **might be** sick, but I'm not sure.*
    *John knows a little about French history, so he **may know** the answer to your question.*
?   *Where are my keys? They **could be** under the sofa, or they **could be** in my coat pocket.*

? **MAYBE:** When we are not certain, we use *might not* and *may not* (but not *could not*) in negative sentences. The contractions *mightn't* and *mayn't* are possible, but they are not common.
    *The mechanic told me that my car would be ready around 2:00, and it's 1:50 now, so it **might not be** ready yet.*
    *I asked that man for directions to the bank, but he just smiled and kept walking. I think he **may not speak** English.*
 	
    VERY CERTAIN: When we are very certain, we use *must not*. Notice that *have to* and *have got to* are not used in negative sentences. The contraction *mustn't* is possible, but it is not common.
    *John isn't eating any of the food on his plate. He **must not be** hungry.*
 	
    ALMOST 100% SURE: When we are almost 100% sure, we use *cannot* or *could not*. Notice how the meaning of **could** is different in negative sentences than it is in affirmative sentences.
    *Your husband wants to quit his job at the bank and become a circus clown? You **can't be** serious.*
    *Somebody told you that he invented a car that runs on sea water? That **couldn't be** true. I think you made a mistake.*
 	
    100% SURE: When we are 100% certain, we do not use modals or phrasal modals.
    *Sofia **is not** here.*
—   *John **doesn't live** in California.*

REMEMBER

▶ *May be* is not the same as *maybe*, but they have a similar meaning.

    Maybe Sarah **is** sick.   **Maybe** I **will go** the library tomorrow.

    = Sarah **may be** sick.   = I **may go** to the library tomorrow.

Practice 1 What would you say in these situations? Study Table 12a to better understand when each modal is used. Then underline the words that you think are the best in each situation.

1   Noura sometimes goes to the gym in the evening. It's 7:30 p.m. now, so she (might be / is) there now.

2   I forgot my dictionary, and I need one for the English test. Francesca sometimes has a dictionary, so I'll ask her. She (may have / has got to have) one.

3   I'm trying to contact an old friend named Bob Jones. There's a man named Bob Jones in the telephone book. He (is / could be) the guy I'm looking for, but that's a very common name, so I can't be sure.

4   Michael always smells like cigarettes. He (must smoke / may smoke) a lot.

5   That movie was fabulous! I loved it! It (might be / has to be) the best movie in the universe!

6   Alex never goes in the deep end of the swimming pool. He (doesn't know / must not know) how to swim.

7   It's 9:00 p.m. I just called my sister, but there was no answer. She (may be / must be) sleeping.

8   It's 2:00 a.m. I just called my sister, but there was no answer. She (may be / must be) sleeping.

9   I can't remember his name. It (might be / must be) Tim or Tom.

10   Carl ate everything on his plate except the mushrooms. He (may not like / must not like) mushrooms.

11   Your 18-year-old daughter is going to marry an 83-year-old man? You (can't be / aren't) serious! You (have got to be / could be) joking!

12   Look at that man over there. He's buying 10 big bags of dog food. He (might have / must have) a lot of dogs.

12.2 ▶ certainty: saying that you are sure about something in the past with *must, have to, have got to, may, might, can* and *could*

DISCOVER

    a   *The stove's been on all night! My son was cooking last night. He **must have forgotten** to turn the stove off.*

1   How sure am I that my son forgot to turn off the stove?

    b   *I don't know where Larry is. He **might have / may have / could have gone** to the beach, but I'm not sure.*

2   How sure am I that Larry went to the beach?

    c   *The police aren't sure what caused the accident, but they think the driver **might not have / may not have seen** the red light.*

3   How sure are the police that the driver did not see the red light?

    d   *Mary failed the final exam. She **must not have studied**.*

4   How sure am I that Mary did not study?

    e   *Yesterday my English teacher told me, "You **cannot have / could not have written** this essay yourself. It's too good. You must have copied it from the internet."*

5   How sure is my English teacher that I did not write my essay?

LEARN (See Table 12b.)

▶ *Must have, might have, may have, could have* and *cannot have* are used to talk about how certain (sure) we are about something in the past.

Practice 2 What would you say in these situations? Study Table 12b to better understand when each modal is used. Then underline the words that you think are the best in each situation.

1   Jim's not in his office. It's 1:00 p.m. He (must have gone / may have gone) home.

2   Jim's not in his office. It's 6:00 p.m. He (must have gone / may have gone) home.

3   It takes three hours to fly to Paris from here, and Sarah left five hours ago. She (must have arrived / might have arrived) in Paris.

degrees of certainty about the past

+ **100% SURE:** When we are 100% certain, we do not use modals or phrasal modals.

*Carlos **has eaten** dinner.*

*Mark **was** here yesterday.*

*My brother **went** to the library.*

VERY CERTAIN: When we are very certain, we use *must have*. The meaning of *must* you see here is different from the meaning discussed in Section 11.6. It is <u>not</u> about obligation. It is about how certain we are about something. *Have to have* and *have got to have* are possible, but they are not common.

*Sarah isn't answering her telephone. She **must have gone** to bed.*

MAYBE: When we are not certain, we use *might have, may have* or *could have*. There is no difference in meaning.

*John didn't come to work today. I think he **might have gone** to the baseball game.*

*I hurt my finger badly today. I'm going to go the hospital because I think I **may have broken** it.*

? *Somebody called but didn't leave a message. It **could have been** my son calling to wish me happy birthday.*

? **MAYBE:** When we are not certain, we use *might not have* and *may not have* (but not *could not have*) in negative sentences. The contractions *mightn't have* and *mayn't have* are possible, but they are not common.

*I left a message for Mary to call me tonight, but she hasn't called me yet. I think she **might not have gotten** the message.*

*Our teacher told all of us to come to the library today, but Carlos isn't here. He **may not have been listening** when the teacher told us to come here.*

VERY CERTAIN: When we are very certain, we use *must not have*. Notice that *have to* and *have got to* are not used in negative sentences. The contraction *mustn't have* is possible, but it is not common.

*Ali got a bad grade on his English test. He **must not have studied**.*

ALMOST 100% SURE: When we are almost 100% sure, we use *cannot have* or *could not have*. Notice how the meaning of *could have* is different in negative sentences than it is in affirmative sentences.

*Your teacher told you that the sun rises in the west? You **cannot have heard** her correctly.*

*Carlos says that he read a 500-page book last night, but he **couldn't have read** such a long book in one night.*

100% SURE: When we are 100% certain, we do not use modals or phrasal modals.

*John **hasn't been** here all day.*

*Michael and Sarah **weren't** at the party.*

– *They **didn't go** to the park.*

---

4   It takes three hours to fly to Paris from here, and Alex left three hours ago. He (must have arrived / might have arrived) in Paris.

5   It takes three hours to fly to Paris from here, and Michael left two hours ago. He (cannot have arrived / might not have arrived) in Paris.

6   I left a message for Jim about my party. I was sure he would come, but he didn't. He (may not have gotten / did not get) my message.

7   I wonder if Bill has finished that project yet. It was a very small project, and he started working on it almost three months ago. He (must have finished / finished) it a long time ago.

8   *Zombies Ate My Brain* is my favorite movie! I (must have seen / could have seen) it 25 times.

9   I know John has a meeting at 2:00, and it's 1:50 now. I just saw him walking toward the meeting room, so he (must have been / could have been) going to the meeting.

10   I don't know if Sam was invited to the meeting at 2:00, but I just saw him walking toward the meeting room, so he (must have been / might have been) going to the meeting too.

11   You did it wrong. That's not what I told you to do. You (must not have been / might not have been) listening to me.

12   I saw Linda across the street. I waved to her, but she didn't wave back. She (didn't see / may not have seen) me.

13   Maria didn't answer her phone. She (didn't hear / might not have heard) it ringing.

14   I crashed my car today. I (didn't see / must not have seen) the red light.

12.3 ▶ certainty: saying that you are sure about something in the future with *will, be going to, might, may* and *could*

DISCOVER

     a   Alex **will/is going to go** to Sarah's party. He told me.

1   How sure am I that Alex will go to Sarah's party?

     b   Carlos **might/may/could go** to Sarah's party. He said he wasn't sure.

     c   Carlos **might not/may not go** to Sarah's party. He said he wasn't sure.

2   How sure am I that Carlos will go to Sarah's party?

     d   Francesca **will not/is not going to go** to Sarah's party. She told me.

3   How sure am I that Francesca will not go to Sarah's party?

LEARN (See Table 12c.)

▶ *Will, be going to, might, may* and *could* are used to talk about how certain (sure) we are about something in the future.

REMEMBER

▶ *Will, be going to* and other ways to talk about the future are discussed in Unit 4.

▶ It is common to use *probably* with *will* and *be going to*. The meaning of *probably* is *more than maybe but not for sure*.

    + 100%   Alex **will/is going to go** to Sarah's party.

       90%   Larry **will probably/is probably going to go** to Sarah's party.

       50%   Carlos **might/may/could go** to Sarah's party.

       50%   Carlos **might not/may not go** to Sarah's party.

       90%   Sofia **probably will not/probably is not going to go** to Sarah's party.

    − 100%   Francesca **will not/is not going to go** to Sarah's party.

12c	
degrees of certainty about the future	

+	**100% SURE:** When we are 100% certain, we use *will* and *be going to*. Maria **will make** an apple pie. They**'re going to win** the game. **MAYBE:** When we are not very certain, we use *might, may* or *could*. There is no difference in meaning. I think it **might rain** soon. The meeting tomorrow **may be** canceled. **?** My grandfather is very sick. He **could die** at any moment.
?	**MAYBE:** When we are not very certain, we use *might not* and *may not* (but not *could not*) in negative sentences. The contractions *mightn't* and *mayn't* are possible, but they are not common. Larry **might not like** this shirt that I got him for his birthday. Are you sure you want to go to a Japanese restaurant? You **may not like** the food. **100% SURE:** When we are 100% certain, we use *will not* and *be not going to*. The store **won't be** open when we get there. **−** My speech **isn't going to last** longer than 30 minutes.

Practice 3 What would you say in these situations? Study Table 12c to better understand when each modal is used. Then use *will, be going to, might, may* or *could* to complete the sentences. Use *not* and *probably* when you think they are necessary. Remember that modals are used to say how we understand a situation, so it is possible for different people to understand the same situation in different ways. For this reason, there may be more than one good answer for some. Be ready to explain your answer.

1   Francesca _____ help me. She promised, and she never breaks a promise.

2   Today is Sunday, and sometimes stores are closed on Sunday, so if we go shopping, some of the stores

     _____ be closed.

3   I'm feeling a little sick. I _____ go to work tomorrow.

4   I'm feeling very sick. I _____ go to work tomorrow.

5   Gary wants to go to the gym tonight, but he's very busy, so he _____ go.

6   My doctor's appointment is at 9:00, and the meeting starts at 10:00, so I _____ be late for the meeting.

7   My doctor's appointment is at 9:00, and the meeting starts at 3:00, so I _____ be late for the meeting.

8   Look at all this traffic! We _____ get to the movie before it starts.

9   Michael's car won't start, so he _____ take a taxi to work.

10 I _____ go with you and your friends to the restaurant tomorrow. I don't like Korean food.

11 Maria spilled coffee on her white blouse. She _____ be able to get the stain out.

12 Oh no! I wanted to make tacos, but I've got only five tortillas. That _____ be enough.

13 An elephant stepped on my foot yesterday. I _____ play basketball with you tomorrow.

12.4 ▶ predictions: talking about expectations based on previous knowledge or experience with *should* and *ought to*

DISCOVER

a   *I'm getting worried about my wife. It's 6:00, and she always comes home from work at 4:00. She **should have/ought to have come** home two hours ago. Where is she?*

1   What was the speaker's expectation? Did it happen?

b   *Larry had a test yesterday. I haven't talked to him, so I don't know how the test went, but he's a really good student, so the test **should have/ought to have been** easy for him.*

2   What is the speaker's expectation? Did it happen?

c   *John flew to Los Angeles this morning. He left four hours ago, and it usually takes two hours, so he **should have/ought to have arrived** by now.*

3   What is the speaker's expectation? Did it happen?

d   *Lucy, this was a small project. You took two weeks to finish it. It **shouldn't have taken** you more than one week.*

4   What was the speaker's expectation? Did it happen?

e   *Sarah asked John to give her a ride to the bank. He was going to go to the library anyway, and the library is next to the bank, so that **shouldn't have been** a problem for John.*

5   What is the speaker's expectation? Did it happen?

f   *Francesca's father told her to finish her homework before dinner. She had just a little homework, so she **shouldn't have needed** more than 15 minutes to finish it.*

6   What is the speaker's expectation? Did it happen?

g   *He told me he planned to come to this party, so where is he? He **should/ought to be** here now, but he isn't.*

7   What is the speaker's expectation? Has it happened?

h   *I don't know the answer to your question, but Maria knows a lot about that subject. Let's ask her. She **should/ought to know**.*

8   What is the speaker's expectation? Will it happen?

i   *Can you believe it? The USA is playing Brazil in the World Cup final, and the USA is ahead 6 to 0. This **shouldn't be** happening!*

9   What is the speaker's expectation? Is it happening?

j   *I don't want to see Linda at the gym. She always goes there in the morning. It's 3:00 in the afternoon now, so if I go to the gym now, she **shouldn't be** there.*

10 What is the speaker's expectation? Will it happen?

k   *Follow these directions to get to the clinic: First, drive three miles north on Main Street. Then turn left on Oak Street and go about one mile. You **should/ought to see** the clinic on the right.*

11 What is the speaker's expectation? Will it happen?

l   *I'm going to travel to Dubai soon. Dubai's really hot in the summer, but I'm going there in the winter. It **shouldn't be** very hot then.*

12 What is the speaker's expectation? Will it happen?

LEARN (See Table 12d.)

▶ Sometimes we use *should* and *ought to* to make predictions about people or situations which we <u>already know about and understand</u>. We want to say we are certain about something because we <u>already</u> have experience with or knowledge of these people or situations.

▶ How did you answer the questions *Did it happen, Will it happen,* etc.? Some of your answers should have been *No* and some of your answers should have been *I don't know*. This is because *should* and *ought to* are used in two ways: when we <u>do not know</u> if what we predicted really happened

  It usually takes ten minutes to drive to the bank, and John left an hour ago, so he ***should/ought to be*** *there now.*

and when what we predicted <u>did not</u> happen.

  I'm worried. My sister calls me every morning, and it's 2:00 p.m. now. She ***should have/ought to have called*** *me.*

The questions that you answered with *I don't know* were *unconfirmed* expectations—the speaker does not know if what he or she or someone else expected really happened. The questions that you answered with *No* were *unfulfilled* expectations—what the speaker expected did not happen.

12d

	predictions based on previous knowledge or experience		
	past	**present**	**future**
+	*should have* *ought to have*	*should* *ought to*	*should* *ought to*
−	*should not have*	*should not*	*should not*

REMEMBER

▶ In Section 4.1 we learned that *will* and *be going to* are used to make predictions. How are *should* and *ought to* different? They are similar, but with *should* and *ought to*, we are making it clear that we have some <u>knowledge or experience</u> to support our prediction. I can predict that *The sun is going to blow up tomorrow* or *You will win the lottery*, but these predictions are not based on any knowledge or experience, so it would <u>not</u> make sense to use *should* or *ought to* in these predictions.

▶ *Ought* is <u>not</u> the same as *should*. *Ought <u>to</u>* is the same as *should*.

▶ It is not common to use *ought to* in negative sentences.

Practice 4 What would you say in these situations? Use *should, should have* or *ought to* and the correct form of the verb in parentheses to complete the sentences. Write all possibilities. Some are negative. Remember that it is not common to use *not* with *ought to*.

1 The train is supposed to come at 7:14, and it's already 7:24. The train (come) _____ soon.

2 It's really easy to do this. It (take) _____ you more than a few minutes last night, so what was the problem?

3 Francesca and her husband went to Joe's Diner. That isn't a very expensive restaurant, so dinner for two people

  (cost) _____ more than $40.

4 It's really easy to do this. It (take) _____ you more than a few minutes tonight, but call me if you have a problem.

5 I'm flying to Argentina tomorrow. I'm going to leave at 7:30. An hour is usually enough time to drive to the airport.

  It (take) _____ longer than that.

6 The mail is delivered every morning at 10:00, and it's 11:30 already. It (come) _____ by now.

7 It's usually very cold here in February, but it's quite warm today. It (be) _____ colder now.

8 Look! The light is on in our neighbors' house. They're on vacation now. The light (be) _____ on now.

9 Let's visit Larry and Mary. They usually eat dinner at 6:00, and it's 8:00 now, so they (be) _____ finished with dinner by now.

▶ modals and phrasal modals, part 2

10 Using this program isn't difficult. You (have) _____ any problem when you try it.

11 I drove downtown on Sunday at 5:00 in the morning, and there was a lot of traffic. I was surprised. There (be) _____ so much traffic on a Sunday morning.

12 Alex is going to spend six months traveling around Europe. That (be) _____ a lot of fun.

13 My wife loves to make Italian food, so she (love) _____ this pasta maker I am buying for her.

12.5 ▶ plans: talking about past plans with *be going to*

DISCOVER

    a   *I **was going to make** a chocolate cake last night, but I didn't.*

1   What was the plan? Did it happen?

    b   *You **were going to be** here at 8:00, but you came at 9:00. Why were you late?*

2   What was the plan? Did it happen?

    c   *Look! Larry got a tattoo! He said he **wasn't going to get** a tattoo, but he did.*

3   What was the plan? Did it happen?

    d   *Sarah **wasn't going to be** at the meeting, but she was.*

4   What was the plan? Did it happen?

    e   *Sam:*   *Were your friends going to eat at that new French restaurant last night?*
    f   *Dave:*   *Yes, they **were going to eat** there, but I don't know if they did.*

5   What was the plan? Did it happen?

    g   *I need to know what happened at the conference yesterday. Mary **was going to be** there. I'm going to call her to see what happened.*

6   What was the plan? Did it happen?

    h   *Gary, why are you smoking? You told me you **weren't going to smoke** anymore, remember?*

7   What was the plan? Did it happen?

    i   *Francesca **was going to go** shopping today, but she changed her mind and stayed home.*

8   What was the plan? Did it happen?

    j   *Tom:*   *Is Noura here?*
    k   *Jerry:*   *Noura **was going to be** here, but she isn't.*

9   What was the plan? Did it happen?

    l   *John wanted to make an appointment to see his doctor today, but he couldn't. The doctor **was going to be** in surgery at the hospital.*

10   What was the plan? Did it happen?

    m   *Don't call Carlos. He's not home. He **was going to go** to the museum today.*

11   What was the plan? Did it happen?

    n   *Sam:*   *Is your sister at work now?*
    o   *Alex:*   *She **wasn't going to go** to work today, but I just called her, and she isn't home, so maybe she did go.*

12   What was the plan? Did it happen?

LEARN

▶ In Section 4.1, we learned that *be going to* is used to talk about future plans. If we plan something and then what we plan happens, we use the past simple to talk about it.

    Sunday: *I'm going to call my mother tomorrow.*
    Tuesday: *I called my mother yesterday.*

But what if we want to talk about a plan that <u>did not</u> happen? What if we <u>do not know</u> if it happened? Then we use the past forms of *be going to*—*was going to* and *were going to*.

▶ How did you answer the questions *Did it happen?* Some of your answers should have been *No* and some of your answers should have been *I don't know*. The questions that you answered with *No* were unfulfilled plans—the plan did not happen.

    *I **was going to wash** my car yesterday, but I didn't.*

The questions that you answered with *I don't know* were unconfirmed plans—the speaker does not know if what he or she or someone else planned really happened.

    *My brother **was going to ask** his girlfriend to marry him. I hope she said yes.*

Sometimes an expectation is unfulfilled because the possibility to fulfill it is <u>in the future</u>—we are talking about a plan that was made in the past to do something that has not happened yet. It is still in the future.

*They said they **were going to deliver** my new sofa tomorrow.*

REMEMBER

▸ *Plan to, be planning to* and *intend to* have a similar meaning.

  I **was going to wash** my car yesterday, but I didn't.

  = I **planned to wash** my car yesterday, but I didn't.

  = I **was planning to wash** my car yesterday, but I didn't.

  = I **intended to wash** my car yesterday, but I didn't.

▸ Sometimes *would* is used in a way that is similar to *was going to* and *were going to*. (See Section 14.7).

Practice 5 Complete the sentences with *be going to*. **Some are negative.**

Example: A: I'm surprised to see you here, Carlos. You _____<u>weren't going to</u>_____ come, but here you are.

  B: You're right. I _____<u>was going to</u>_____ stay home tonight, but I changed my mind.

1 A: Did Mark and Sarah go to Thailand last year?

  B: They _____ go, but they didn't.

2 A: Why are you here at work? You _____ take today off, right?

  B: No, I _____ take today off. Sam _____ take today off.

3 A: You lost your job? When _____ you _____ tell me?

  B: Yes, I lost my job. I _____ tell you tomorrow.

4 A: Alex! What a surprise to see you here at the beach. You _____ stay home.

  B: Yeah, I _____, but I didn't.

5 A: My parents visited me last night, so I had to cancel all my plans.

  B: What _____ you _____ do?

  A: I _____ have dinner with Lucy, and then we _____ go dancing.

12.6 ▸ talking about expectations with *be supposed to*

DISCOVER

  a *Sarah **was supposed to meet** me for lunch yesterday, but she didn't come. She told me later that she forgot.*

  b *Michael's plane **is supposed to arrive** at 12:20. I hope it's not late.*

  c *You **are supposed to wash** this sweater in cold water.*

  d *My son **is supposed to take out** the garbage every day.*

1 Which sentence is about something somebody with power or authority has told somebody to do and expects somebody to do because he or she is the boss?

2 Which sentence is about what somebody expected to happen in the past because it was a plan or something on a schedule, but it did not happen?

3 Which sentence is about what somebody expects to happen because it is the correct way to do it?

4 Which sentence is about what somebody expects to happen in the future because it is a plan or something on a schedule?

LEARN

▸ *Be supposed to* is used to talk about what we expect because it is a rule or a law.

  *You**'re supposed to stop** when the light is red.*

  *You**'re not supposed to smoke** in a movie theater.*

▸ *Be supposed to* is used to talk about what we expect because it is the correct way to do something.

  *You**'re supposed to take** this medicine twice a day.*

  *Parents **are supposed to teach** their children about right and wrong.*

▸ *Be supposed to* is used to talk about what we expect because it is a plan or a schedule.

  *The meeting tomorrow **is supposed to start** at 10:00.*

  *I'm waiting for Maria. She**'s supposed to meet** me here at 11:30, and then we're going to eat lunch.*

▸ **modals and phrasal modals, part 2**

▶ *Be supposed to* can also be used to talk about unfulfilled plans

   *The meeting yesterday **was supposed to start** at 10:00, but it started late.*

and unconfirmed plans.

   *John **was supposed to meet** Mary this morning at 8:00. I hope he remembered.*

▶ *Be supposed to* is used to talk about the past, present and future, but only the past simple and present simple form of *be* are used. (*My sister is supposed to call me tomorrow.*) It is never continuous.

REMEMBER

▶ Always *supposed*. Never *suppose*.

   wrong → *You're not **suppose** to go in that room.*

   right → *You're not **supposed** to go in that room.*

Practice 6 Correct the mistakes in the sentences.

1   I supposed to finish this work before I go home.

2   You're not suppose to talk in a library.

3   John will be supposed to give a presentation next week.

4   Are we supposed read Chapter 5 or Chapter 6 for our homework?

5   The show is supposing to start at 9:00.

6   I have to go home. I not supposed to stay out after midnight.

7   You supposed to take your hat off inside a building.

8   I don't understand. What I am supposed to do?

Practice 7 Complete the sentences with *be supposed to*. Some are negative.

Example: A: Why is Mark angry with you?

               B: Because I _____*was supposed to*_____ take him to the airport, and I forgot.

1   A: When does the meeting begin?

    B: It _____ begin at 11:00.

2   A: Did Mary meet you at the mall this morning?

    B: She _____, but she didn't.

3   A: How long should I cook this cake for?

    B: You _____ cook it for 45 minutes.

4   A: Is it OK to smoke here?

    B: No, you _____.

5   A: When _____ we _____ be at the party tonight?

    B: We _____ be there at 8:30.

6   A: _____ you _____ do that?

    B: No, I wasn't. Don't tell anybody, OK?

7   A: When _____ I _____ be home tonight?

    B: I already told you. You _____ be home at midnight.

8   A: Is it OK to put metal in a microwave oven?

    B: No, you _____. It's dangerous.

9   A: Why isn't Linda here?

    B: I don't know. She _____ be here 15 minutes ago.

12.7/a ▶ talking about expectations with *be to*

DISCOVER

    a   The President **is to speak** to the nation at 8:00 Tuesday evening.

    b   This is secret. You **are not to tell** anyone. Do you understand?

    c   The meeting **was to have ended** at 4:00, but it didn't end until 5:30.

    d   You **were to finish** your homework assignment three days ago. Why haven't you finished yet?

1   Which sentence is about something that is expected because it is an order or a rule?

2   Which sentence is about something that is expected because it is an official plan or arrangement?

3   Which sentence is about something that was expected, but it did not happen?

4   Which sentence is about something that was expected, but we do not know if it happened?

LEARN

▶ The phrasal modal *be to* is very common in formal English, but it is very seldom studied by students.

▶ It is common to use *be to* in formal English to talk about what people expect to happen because it is an order or rule.

    Students **are to complete** the first part of the exam before 10:30 and the second part before 11:15.

    You **are not to open** this door when the red light is on. Do you understand?

    Major Payne **was to report** to General Mills at 0200.

▶ It is common to use *be to* in formal English to talk about what people expect to happen in the future because it is an official plan or arrangement.

    The president of the company **is to speak** to the conference at 9:00.

    The king and the prime minister **were to meet** yesterday in the royal palace.

▶ It is common to use the present perfect with *be to* in the past. There is no difference in meaning between the past simple and the present perfect.

    The king and the prime minister **were to meet** yesterday in the royal palace.

    = The king and the prime minister **were to have met** yesterday in the royal palace.

    He **was to be** in his lawyer's office at 1:00.

    = He **was to have been** in his lawyer's office at 1:00.

When we are talking about plans and arrangements in the past, and we know that what was planned or arranged really happened, we use the past simple.

    The king and the prime minister **met** yesterday in the royal palace.

    He **was** in his lawyer's office at 1:00.

Past forms of *be to* are usually used for unrealized expectations

    The president of the company **was to have spoken** to the conference at 9:00, however her speech was canceled.

and unconfirmed expectations.

    He **was to have been** in his lawyer's office at 1:00, but I don't know if he went.

Practice 8/a You *are to* use the correct form of *be to* to complete the sentences. Some are negative.

Examples: You _____*were to*_____ be at the meeting yesterday. Where were you?

           You _____*were to have*_____ been at the meeting yesterday. Where were you?

           You _____*are to*_____ be at the meeting tomorrow. Is that clear?

1   You _____ sit here, do your work and be quiet. Do you understand?

2   My teacher told us that we _____ read Chapter 3 tonight.

3   This information is secret. You _____ discuss it with anyone. Is that clear?

4   The flight from Madrid to Mexico City _____ arrived at 2:10, but it didn't. In 30 minutes an

    airline official _____ announce some important information about the missing plane.

5   Government officials _____ fly over the earthquake zone tomorrow and then meet with the
    president after that.

6   You _____ submitted your report by yesterday. Why didn't you?

7 The judge _____ announced her decision today, but she postponed it until tomorrow.

8 Several executives of our company are going to speak at the conference tomorrow. The advertising manager _____ speak about the new advertising campaign, and then David Bacherman, Ted Macdonald and Bill Kline _____ give a presentation about plans for the next year. Becky Shelton, the CEO of the company, _____ spoken at the conference as well, but she had to cancel.

12.8/a ▶ ellipsis examples and practice (See Section 1.9/a for more about ellipsis.)

DISCOVER

a Mary: *Is the supermarket **open now**?*
   John: *It **must be**. It's open 24 hours a day.*
          *= It **must be [open now]**. It's open 24 hours a day.*

b Tom: *Susan works at the same company as your brother. Do you think she **knows him**?*
   Ali: *She **must**. It's a very small company.*
         *= She **must [know him]**. It's a very small company.*

c Sam: *Misaki is from Japan. Does she **speak Japanese**?*
   Sofia: *She **must/has to/has got to**. How could she be from Japan and **not**?*
           *= She **must/has to/has got to [speak Japanese]**. How could she be from Japan and **not [speak Japanese]**?*

d Bill: *I called Carlos five times last week, but there was no answer. I wonder if he was **on vacation**.*
   Alex: *He **might/may/could have been**.*
          *= He **might have/may have/could have been [on vacation]**.*

e Gary: *Has Mary **gone to bed**?*
   Tom: *It's almost midnight. She **must have**.*
         *= It's almost midnight. She **must have [gone to bed]**.*

f Sarah: *Are you still going to **go to the doctor tomorrow**?*
   John: *I **might not/may not**. I'm feeling a lot better.*
          *= I **might not/may not [go to the doctor tomorrow]**. I'm feeling a lot better.*

g Linda: *Is Francesca **here**?*
   Rosa: *She **ought to be**, but she **isn't**.*
          *= She **ought to be [here]**, but she **isn't [here]**.*

h Mark: *Has Sarah **called you** yet? She said she would call at 4:30, and it's 5:00 now.*
   Noura: *She **should have** by now, but she **hasn't**.*
           *= She **should have [called me]** by now, but she **hasn't [called me]**.*

i John: *Did you **go shopping last night**?*
   Maria: *I **was going to**, but I **didn't**.*
           *= I **was going to [go shopping last night]**, but I **didn't [go shopping last night]**.*

j Lucy: *Did you **return the library book yesterday**?*
   Joe: *I was **supposed to**, but I **didn't**.*
         *= I was **supposed to [return the library book yesterday]**, but I **didn't [return the library book yesterday]**.*

k Ali: *The members of the committee **were to have met yesterday**. Is that correct?*
   Sam: *Yes, that is correct. They **were to have**, but I don't know if they **did**.*
         *= They **were to have [met yesterday]**, but I don't know if they **[met yesterday]**.*

Practice 9/a Rewrite the B sentences with ellipsis.

Example: A: Can I park here?

          B: No, you're not supposed to park here.

              No, you're not supposed to.

1 A: Larry left for Medford two hours ago. I wonder if he has arrived.
   B: Medford is only 15 kilometers from here. He must have arrived by now.

2 A: Look! Is that Michael's car?
   B: It's got to be Michael's car. It looks exactly like his car.

3   A: Have Lucy and Sam moved? I haven't seen them for a long time.

      B: I don't know. They might have moved.

4   A: Are Rosa and Sofia in the classroom?

      B: They ought to be in the classroom, but they're not in the classroom.

5   A: Has Larry left yet?

      B: It's after 5:00, so he should have left by now, but I don't know if he has left yet.

6   A: Your father asked you to cut the grass today. Did you?

      B: I wanted to cut the grass today, I was going to cut the grass today, and I should have cut the grass today, but I didn't cut the grass today.

7   A: Did you take your kids to the movie last night?

      B: I was going to take my kids to the movie last night, but I was busy, so I didn't take my kids to the movie last night.

8   A: Did you pay the rent yesterday?

      B: I was supposed to pay the rent yesterday, but I didn't pay the rent yesterday.

9   A: Wasn't the sales manager to have completed her monthly sales report by the end of the month?

      B: Yes, she was to have completed her monthly sales report by the end of the month, but she didn't complete her monthly sales report by the end of the month.

10   A: Do you think Mary's home now?

      B: She should be home now. She never goes anywhere in the evening.

11   A: Is Larry going to go to France next summer?

      B: He may go to France next summer. He's not sure.

12   A: Did the judges announce their decision yesterday? That was the plan, wasn't it?

      B: Yes, the judges were to have announced their decision yesterday, but they postponed their decision.

13   A: Jack is a very bad student, and he got a 100 on the test. Do you think he cheated?

      B: He must have cheated.

▶ modals and phrasal modals, part 2

Unit 13 ▶ adjective clauses

INTRODUCTION

▶ *Adjective clauses* (also called *relative clauses*) are a way to connect sentences. An adjective clause is a group of words which do the same job that regular adjectives like *big*, *hot* or *expensive* do: They describe or identify nouns.

13.1 ▶ subject adjective clauses

DISCOVER

    a   I saw a man. **He was tall.**
    b   = I saw a man **who was tall**.
    c   = I saw a man **that was tall**.

1   Look at *b* and *c*. Which words give you information about *a man*?
2   How are *b* and *c* different?
3   The subject of the **bold** sentence in *a* is *he*. Do you see *he* in *b* and *c*?

    d   The computer doesn't work. **It is in the lab.**
    e   = The computer **which is in the lab** doesn't work.
    f   = The computer **that is in the lab** doesn't work.

4   Look at *e* and *f*. Which words tell you which computer the speaker is talking about?
5   How are *e* and *f* different?
6   The subject of the **bold** sentence in *a* is *it*. Do you see *it* in *e* and *f*?

LEARN

▶ If I say *The book is mine*, you might say *Which book?* To identify which book I am talking about, I can say *It is on the table.* I can say this with two sentences,

    The book is mine. **It is on the table.**

or I can cancel the subject of *It is on the table* (*It*) and say one sentence with a subject relative pronoun

    The book **<u>which</u> is on the table** is mine.

or I can say

    The book **<u>that</u> is on the table** is mine.

Because *it*, the <u>subject</u> of *It is on the table,* is canceled when *It is on the table* is changed to an adjective clause, this adjective clause is a *subject adjective clause*.

▶ The adjective clause always goes directly after the noun that it gives information about.

    wrong → The **computer** doesn't work **that is in the lab.**
    right →   The **computer that is in the lab** doesn't work.

▶ Use the subject relative pronouns *who* or *that* for people and *which* or *that* for things. *Who* is more common for people, and *that* is more common for things.

    wrong → I know a man **which** lived in Antarctica.   **wrong** → Where is the book **who** was on the table?
    right →   I know a man **who** lived in Antarctica.   **right** →   Where is the book **which** was on the table?
    right →   I know a man **that** lived in Antarctica.   **right** →   Where is the book **that** was on the table?

REMEMBER

▶ Remember to cancel the subject of sentences that are changed to subject adjective clauses.

    wrong → The people who **they** were hurt in the accident went to the hospital.
    right →   The people who were hurt in the accident went to the hospital.

Practice 1 Cross out the word in the second sentence that would be canceled in a subject adjective phrase.

Example: The student is absent today. ~~She~~ was sick yesterday.

1   A man is very lazy. He works in my office.

2   I bought a car. It cost $25,000.

3   The people make a lot of noise. They live next to me.

4   What did the man say? He called you.

5   I know a girl. She is from Russia.

6 Do you know the people? They live in that house.

7 The girl was crying. She fell out of a tree.

8 We ate dinner in the Italian restaurant. It is on Maple Street.

Practice 2 Write *who/that* or *which/that* in the blanks. Then put parentheses around the adjective clause.

Example: The student (____who/that____ was sick yesterday) is absent today.

1 Some people _____ live near me were hurt in an accident.

2 Ali read a book _____ was 450 pages long.

3 I heard a joke _____ was really funny.

4 The waiter _____ waited on us wasn't friendly.

5 John told us a crazy story _____ didn't make any sense at all.

6 Who is the woman _____ works in Office 307?

7 The people _____ were killed in the plane crash were from Texas.

8 Do you know the man _____ lives in the big house next to the library?

9 I attended a lecture by Richard Stone _____ was very interesting.

Practice 3 Combine the sentences using the second sentence as an adjective clause. Use only *who* or *that*.

Example: The boy broke his arm. He fell out of a tree house.

> *The boy who fell out of a tree house broke his arm.*

1 A woman speaks French. She lives in my building.

2 She told me a story. It was interesting.

3 My wife bought some shoes. They cost $50.

4 People should wear helmets. They ride motorcycles.

5 The man is a liar. He sold me his car.

6 A person is bilingual. He speaks two languages.

7 The people talked a lot. They sat behind us at the movie theater.

8 How many people speak Spanish? They live in Florida.

9 The teacher asked me a question. It was very difficult.

10 Did the searchers find the woman? She was lost in the forest.

13.2 ▶ object adjective clauses

DISCOVER

    *a She knows a man. **He speaks Swahili.***
    *b = She knows a man **who speaks Swahili.***

1 Look at *a* and *b*. Are the subject *he* in *a* and *who* in *b* in the same place?

    *c Mary talked about a man. **I don't like him.***
    *d = Mary talked about a man **who(m) I don't like**.*

2 Look at *c* and *d*. Are the object *him* in *c* and *who(m)* in *d* in the same place? Is something different?

    *e Larry has some pictures. **They are very beautiful.***
    *f = Larry has some pictures **which are very beautiful**.*

3 Look at *e* and *f*. Are the subject *they* in *e* and *which* in *f* in the same place?

    *g Rosa baked the cookies. **I ate them.***
    *h = Rosa baked the cookies **which I ate**.*

4 Look at *g* and *h*. Are the object *them* in *g* and *which* in *h* in the same place? Is something different?

LEARN

▶ In the adjective clauses we studied before, the relative pronoun was the subject of the adjective clause. For example, in *b* and *f, who* and *which* are replacing the subjects of the sentences. However, in *d* and *h, who(m)* and *which* are replacing the <u>objects</u> of the sentences.

▶ For people, it is possible to use three object relative pronouns: *who, whom* or *that.* It is also possible to use no pronoun at all. *Whom* is more formal, however few native speakers understand how to use *whom* correctly, so they usually use *who* or no pronoun at all.

    The people were interesting. **I met <u>them</u> at a party last night.**
    = *The people* **<u>whom</u> I met at the party last night** *were interesting.*
    = *The people* **<u>who</u> I met at the party last night** *were interesting.*
    = *The people* **<u>that</u> I met at the party last night** *were interesting.*
    = *The people* **I met at the party last night** *were interesting.*

▶ For things, it is possible to use two object relative pronouns: *which* or *that.* It is also possible to use no pronoun at all. It is more common to use *that* or no pronoun than it is to use *which.*

    The car cost a lot of money. **Mark bought <u>it</u> last week.**
    = *The car* **<u>which</u> Mark bought last week** *cost a lot of money.*
    = *The car* **<u>that</u> Mark bought last week** *cost a lot of money.*
    = *The car* **Mark bought last week** *cost a lot of money.*

REMEMBER

▶ The object relative clause always goes directly after the noun which it gives information about.

    wrong → *The* **homework** *was very difficult* **which I did last night.**
    right →   *The* **homework which I did last night** *was very difficult.*

Practice 4 Cross out the word in the second sentence that would be canceled in an object adjective phrase.

Example: The books are about Spain. I got ~~them~~ at the library.

1   The potato salad was delicious. We ate it at the picnic.

2   The man is not friendly. I live next to him.

3   A woman came to my office. I had never met her before.

4   What did the people say? You were talking to them.

5   I'm not used to the shoes. I bought them yesterday.

6   Have you seen the book? Your sister took it out of the library this morning.

7   A man is a retired professor of history. I know him.

8   The band was awful. We saw them last night.

9   Was the exhibit good? You saw it at the museum.

Practice 5 Write *who(m)/that* or *which/that* in the blanks. Then put parentheses around the adjective clause.

Example: The student (____who/that____ was sick yesterday) is absent today.

1   The tacos _____ we had last night weren't very good.

2   Did you see the dress _____ she wore to the party?

3   The flight attendant _____ I talked to was from Montreal.

4   The soup _____ he made was too salty.

5   The guy _____ I sat next to on the plane had bad breath.

6   Is that the girl _____ you told me about?

7   Where is the pen _____ I was using before?

8   Don't talk to people _____ you don't know.

9   The excuse _____ she gave to the police didn't make any sense.

Practice 6 Combine the sentences using the second sentence as an adjective clause. Give all possible answers.

Example: The girl was pretty. I saw her.

The girl whom I saw was pretty.

The girl who I saw was pretty.

The girl that I saw was pretty.

The girl I saw was pretty.

1 The mechanic said it would cost $1,000 to fix my car. I talked to him.

2 We don't understand the language. She speaks it.

3 Some people never take a bath. I know them.

4 The guy is interesting. I live next to him.

5 The man was very tall. I saw him.

6 The questions were difficult. Gary asked them.

7 The bread was delicious. My wife baked it.

8 Nobody believed me. I talked to them.

9 The book was very boring. I took it with me to read on the plane.

▶ adjective clauses

135

13.3 ▶ *whose* in subject adjective clauses

DISCOVER

    a   *I saw a girl. **Her** hair was blue.*

    b   *= I saw a girl **whose** hair was blue.*

    c   *The family stayed in a hotel. **Their** house burned down.*

    d   *= The family **whose** house burned down stayed in a hotel.*

1   Look at *b*. Which words give you information about the girl?

2   Look at *d*. Which words tell you which family I am talking about?

3   Look at *b* and *d*. What kind of pronouns do you think *whose* replaces?

LEARN

▶ Until now, we have seen how *who, which* and *that* can replace the subject pronouns *he, she, it* and *they*. Now we will see how *whose* can replace the possessive adjectives *his, her, its* and *their*.

    *The coach was very happy. **Her** team won the game.*

    *= The coach **whose** team won the game was very happy.*

REMEMBER

▶ Be careful with spelling. Many students confuse *whose* and *who's*. They sound the same, but they are not the same.

Practice 7 Combine the sentences. Use the second sentence as an adjective clause. Use only *whose*.

Examples: The woman called the police. Her son was lost.

                     The woman whose son was lost called the police.

1   I talked to a man. His wife is a heart surgeon.

2   Did the woman go to the doctor? Her arm was broken.

3   The airplane crashed. Its wing fell off.

4   I know a girl. Her father is a naval officer.

5   People can learn Italian easily. Their native language is Spanish.

6   The guy was taken to the hospital. His hair was on fire.

7   Where is the man? His wallet was stolen.

8   I sat next to a woman. Her daughter is a violinist.

9   The actor was working as a waiter. His show was canceled.

10   The woman was very upset. Her husband was hurt in the accident.

13.4 ▶ *where* and *when* used in adjective clauses

DISCOVER

    a   *The town is very small. **I live there.***

    b   *= The town **where** I live is very small.*

1   Which words in *b* give you information about the town?

2   Which word do we use for places?

    c   *The day was the best day of my life. **I met my wife then.***

    d   *= The day **when** I met my wife was the best day of my life.*

3   Which words in *d* give you information about *the best day*?

4   Which word do we use for time?

LEARN

▶ Sometimes we can use *where* to make an adjective clause about a place. Sometimes we can use *when* to make an adjective clause about a time.

    *The office is on the fifth floor. **I work there.***

    *= The office **where** I work is on the fifth floor.*

    *There is no day next week. **I can meet you for lunch then.***

    *= There is no day next week **when** I can meet you for lunch.*

Practice 8 Combine the sentences. Use the second sentence as an adjective clause. Use only *where* or *when*.

Examples: Saturday is the day. Many people do their shopping then.

Saturday is the day when many people do their shopping.

That is the building. I work there.

That is the building where I work.

1 January is the month. We always go to Florida then.

2 That's the park. We play soccer there sometimes.

3 I can't remember the place. I took this picture there.

4 Do you know a store? I can buy extra large shoes there.

5 I still remember the day. My son was born then.

6 Is there a day? I can meet with you then.

7 August 4th is the day. I will fly back to Chicago then.

8 Is this the place? The crime happened there.

9 Did he tell you? He went there.

10 The day was the worst day of my life. My parachute didn't open then.

Continue to Unit 13/advanced ↓ or go to Unit 14 →

13.5/a ▶ subject adjective clauses with *be* reduced to adjective phrases

DISCOVER

    a   Students **who are** taking the TOEFL test must register before Friday.

    b   = Students taking the TOEFL test must register before Friday.

1 How are *a* and *b* different?

    c   I live in a house **which is** made of stone.

    d   = I live in a house made of stone.

2 How are *c* and *d* different?

LEARN

▶ Adjective clauses can be *reduced* (changed so they are shorter) to adjective phrases. If there is a form of *be* in the adjective clause, the form of *be* and the subject relative pronoun can be canceled.

    *The girl **who is dancing** with my brother is Gary's sister.*

    = The girl ~~who is~~ dancing with my brother is Gary's sister.

    *Pizzas **which are not sold** before the restaurant closes are given to poor people.*

    = Pizzas ~~which are~~ not sold before the restaurant closes are given to poor people.

    *I am reading a book **which is about** Henry Morton Stanley.*

    = I am reading a book ~~which is~~ about Henry Morton Stanley.

Practice 9/a Draw lines through the words which can be canceled.

Example: The clothes ~~which are~~ in this box are too small for me.

1 The cat which is sleeping on the sofa is 14 years old.

2 The people who are coming to our dinner party are really boring.

3 A man who was riding a bicycle on the highway was run over by a bus.

4 Don't use the dishes which are on the top shelf.

5 The woman who was interviewed on TV was from England.

6 The guys who were not chosen for the show were disappointed.

7 Cars which are made in Germany are usually expensive.

▶ adjective clauses

8   I like the song which is on the radio now.

9   Many of the buildings which were destroyed in the earthquake were never rebuilt.

10   Applications which are not submitted before the deadline will not be accepted.

13.6/a ▶ subject adjective clauses with other verbs reduced to adjective phrases

DISCOVER

    *a   People **who live** in Alaska are used to cold weather.*

    *b   = People **living** in Alaska are used to cold weather.*

1   How are *a* and *b different?*

    *c   Students **who do not go** on the field trip must work on their projects in the library.*

    *d   = Students **not going** on the field trip must work on their projects in the library.*

2   How are *c* and *d different?*

LEARN

▶ If there is a main verb in the adjective clause, the main verb can be changed to the *-ing* form and the subject relative pronoun can be canceled.

    *The people **who work** in my office aren't friendly.*

    *= The people **working** in my office aren't friendly.*

    *Anyone **who disagrees** with me is wrong.*

    *= Anyone **disagreeing** with me is wrong.*

    *People **who don't have** tickets cannot get on the train.*

    *= People **not having** tickets cannot get on the train.*

Practice 10/a Change the adjective clauses to adjective phrases.

Example: Anyone who goes to that country must have a visa.

               Anyone going to that country must have a visa.

1   The family which lives next to us has a swimming pool.

2   Drivers who don't wear seat belts are risking their lives.

3   Anyone who does that is crazy.

4   Students who want to try out for the soccer team should talk to the coach.

5   I have a lot of friends who work in that factory.

6   Anyone who smokes in the theater will be kicked out.

7   Kids who go to that school have to wear uniforms.

8   Any student who doesn't turn in his or her project by Friday will get an F.

9   Anybody who doesn't have identification cannot enter the building.

10   There were so many kids who made noise outside that I couldn't sleep.

13.7/a ▶ punctuation of adjective clauses

DISCOVER

    *a   A woman **who lives in my building** speaks French.*

1   Do we know the woman's name? Is *who lives in my building* necessary to identify the girl, or is it just extra information?

    *b   Marie, **who lives in my building,** speaks French.*

2   Do we know Marie's name? Is *who lives in my building* necessary to identify Marie, or is it just extra information?

3   How are *a* and *b different?*

LEARN

▶ When the adjective clause is used <u>only</u> to give extra information, and is <u>not</u> used for identification, we put commas around the adjective clause. When commas are necessary, it is <u>not</u> possible to use *that* or to use no pronoun.

    A woman who works in my office is from Costa Rica.

    Cristina Ramos, who works in my office, is from Costa Rica.

REMEMBER

▶ When commas are necessary, you must use either *which, who, whom* or *where*.

wrong → *Cairo, **that** is the largest city in Africa, is in Egypt.*

right → *Cairo, **which** is the largest city in Africa, is in Egypt.*

wrong → *Thomas Edison, **that** was an American inventor, invented the light bulb.*

right → *Thomas Edison, **who** was an American inventor, invented the light bulb.*

wrong → *Phil Shepardson, **that** I work with, speaks Arabic.*

right → *Phil Shepardson, **whom** I work with, speaks Arabic.*

Practice 11/a Put commas around the adjective clauses that are only for extra information and not identification.

Examples: The man who called yesterday wants to talk to me about a job.

no change

Larry Smith who called yesterday wants to talk to me about a job.

Larry Smith, who called yesterday, wants to talk to me about a job.

1   The man who had escaped from prison was captured by the police.

2   Professor Grant who is my history teacher has written several books.

3   Elephants which are native to Africa and India are very intelligent.

4   My boss whom I met with yesterday told me that she is planning to retire next year.

5   Mary Johnson whose husband is the mayor of this city was my college roommate.

6   The boy who was bitten by a dog was crying.

7   My house which was built in 1685 is the oldest building in our town.

8   Coffee which originally came from the Middle East is now grown in many countries.

9   Abraham Lincoln who was born in 1809 was the 16th president of the United States.

10   The city where I live now is very boring.

11   Riverwoods where I grew up is a small town.

12   A man whom I used to work with called me last night.

13.8/a ▶ object adjective clauses with verb + preposition combinations

DISCOVER

a   *The woman is very nice. I **work <u>with</u>** her.*

b   = *The woman **who(m)** I **work <u>with</u>** is very nice.*

c   = *The woman **that** I **work <u>with</u>** is very nice.*

d   = *The woman I **work <u>with</u>** is very nice.*

e   = *The woman **<u>with</u> whom** I **work** is very nice.*

1   Look at a, b, c and d. Where is the preposition *with*?

2   Look at e. Where is the preposition *with*?

f   *I didn't like the movie. We **went <u>to</u>** it last night.*

g   = *I didn't like the movie **which** we **went <u>to</u>** last night.*

h   = *I didn't like the movie **that** we **went <u>to</u>** last night.*

i   = *I didn't like the movie we **went <u>to</u>** last night.*

j   = *I didn't like the movie **<u>to</u> which** we **went** last night.*

3   Look at f, g, h and i. Where is the preposition *to*?

4   Look at j. Where is the preposition *to*?

LEARN

▶ Many verbs must be used with a certain preposition when they are used with an object. When these verb + preposition combinations are used in adjective clauses, the preposition can be moved so that it is before the relative pronoun. When the preposition is moved, <u>only</u> *whom* or *which* is used. It is not correct to use *that, who* or nothing.

look <u>for</u> the car →   *The car **<u>for</u> which** I **looked** was red.*

listen <u>to</u> music →   *The music **<u>to</u> which** I **listened** was beautiful.*

▶ adjective clauses

*work **with** Phil Shepardson →*   *Phil Shepardson, **with whom** I **work**, speaks Arabic.*
*fly **over** the city →*   *The city **over** **which** we **flew** had been destroyed by a tornado.*
*live **next to** a man →*   *The man **next to** **whom** we **live** has a big dog.*

▶ Sometimes there is an object between the verb and the prepositional phrase.

***receive** a letter **from** the lawyer →*   *The lawyer **from** **whom** we **received** a letter has an office in New York.*
***make** a cake **for** the wedding →*   *The wedding **for** **which** my mother **made** a cake was canceled.*
***send** an email **to** Alex →*   *Alex, **to** **whom** I **sent** an email, is a college student.*
***write** your name **on** the paper →*   *Where is the paper **on** **which** you **wrote** your name?*
***fix** my car **with** my father →*   *My father, **with** **whom** I **fixed** my car, is a mechanic.*

REMEMBER

▶ It is never necessary to move prepositions in this way, but because it is common in formal writing and speaking, it is a good idea to understand it.

Practice 12/a Change the adjective clauses so that the preposition is before the relative pronoun. Use only which or whom.

Example: The house that I live in is very old.

     The house in which I live is very old.

     General Mills, whom Captain Cook served under, was killed during the war.

     General Mills, under whom Captain Cook served, was killed during the war.

1   The boy whom I sat behind in grammar school is a lawyer now.

2   Blue Lake, which we live near, flooded last summer.

3   I didn't get the job I applied for.

4   The woman I work with is from Lebanon.

5   The guy I voted for lost.

6   Peter Martin, whom I used to work with, speaks Chinese.

7   The subject she gave a presentation about was interesting.

8   The opera I slept during was by Wagner.

Practice 13/a Combine the sentences using the second sentence as an adjective clause with the preposition before the relative pronoun. Be careful about punctuation.

Example: The city was very small. I grew up in it.

     The city in which I grew up was very small.

1   I don't know the man. You were talking to him.

2   Main Street is a very busy street. I live on it.

3   The car is blue. The police are looking for it.

4   The student is from Germany. I sit in front of him.

5   The man is not here. I was talking about him.

6   John lives in Rome. I got a letter from him.

7   The boys live next to me. I was playing football with them.

8   I saw a movie with some friends. I work with them.

9   The woman plays loud music all night. We live under her.

10   Lucy will be 9 years old. We bought a birthday gift for her yesterday.

11   It is an amazing story. Many books have been written about it.

12   The people are idiots. I have to work with them on this project.

13.9/a ▶ *which* used to modify an entire sentence

DISCOVER

    a   *My pregnancy test was positive.* ***It was a big surprise.***

    b   *= My pregnancy test was positive,* ***which was a big surprise***.

    c   *Alex was admitted to Stanford University.* ***This made his parents very happy.***

    d   *= Alex was admitted to Stanford University,* ***which made his parents very happy***.

1   Look at *b* and *d*. Which part of the sentences gives information? Which part of the sentences tells you how somebody feels about the information?

LEARN

▶ Sometimes we say how we feel about some information by adding a comment after an entire sentence with *which*. The first clause must be an independent clause (a complete sentence), and the additional information is added after a comma. Only *which* is used—not *that*.

    He said yes. ***This surprised me.***

    = He said yes, ***which surprised me***.

    Linda and Sam got married. ***Linda's parents were not happy about this.***

    = Linda and Sam got married, ***which Linda's parents were not happy about***.

Practice 14/a Combine the sentences. Use the second sentence as an adjective clause. Be sure to cancel *this*.

Example: I forgot my wife's birthday. This made her angry.

          I forgot my wife's birthday, which made her angry.

1   A man helped me fix my bicycle. This was very nice of him.

2   Francesca got an A on her final exam. This didn't surprise me.

3   Sarah is very sick. This makes me worry.

4   Michael crashed his car. This didn't surprise me because he always drives too fast.

5   I forgot to bring my homework to class yesterday. This wasn't very smart and made my teacher angry.

6   The doctor said my friend doesn't have cancer anymore. This was great news.

7   It will cost $3,000 to fix my car. This is more than the car is worth.

8   Our team won a game. This was a miracle.

9   The men in our office make more than the women. This, if you ask me, is very unfair and illegal.

10   Last year we went to Venice. This, in my opinion, is the most beautiful city in the world.

Practice 15/a Combine the sentences. Use the second sentence as an adjective clause. Be sure to cancel *this*.

Example: A man told me that he was from Mars. I found this impossible to believe.

          A man told me that he is from Mars, which I found impossible to believe.

1   Our neighbors have a big dog. I don't like this at all.

2   My daughter dropped out of high school. I was, of course, very angry about this.

3   We spent last summer traveling in Italy. We really enjoyed this.

4   I wear the same socks every day for a week. My wife thinks this is disgusting.

5   My husband wants to buy a horse. I think this is a crazy idea.

6   The guy who works next to me never stops talking. I find this very annoying.

7   Ali spent three hours helping me with my homework. I really appreciated this.

8   My son got in trouble at school. I'm not happy about this.

9   Larry told his boss that her idea wasn't very good. I think this was a pretty dumb thing to do.

10   He believed me when no one else did. I will never forget this.

Unit 14 ▶ noun clauses

14.1 ▶ noun clauses beginning with a question word

DISCOVER

  a   Mary: Did you hear **the story**?

  b   Larry: Yes, I heard **the story**.

  c   Mary: Was **the story** interesting?

  d   Larry: Yes, **the story** was interesting.

1   Look *a, b, c* and *d*. Is *the story* a verb, an adjective, a noun or an adverb?

  e   Susan: **What did he say?** Did you hear **what he said**?

  f   Alex: Yes, I heard **what he said**.

  g   Susan: Was **what he said** interesting?

  h   Alex: Yes, **what he said** was interesting.

2   Look at *e*. Look at *What did he say?* In Unit 6 you learned that this is how to ask a question, but now look at *f, g* and *h*. Look at the **bold** words. Are they the same as in *What did he say?* Are they different? Why?

  i   Maria: Do you know where **did he go**?

  j   Sofia: Do you know where **he went**?

  k   Ali: **He went** to the supermarket.

3   Look at Maria and Sofia's questions (*i* and *j*). One of them is making a mistake in her grammar. Is it Maria or Sofia?

LEARN

▶ A *noun clause* is a group of words which contains a subject and a verb that does the job of a noun in a sentence. Noun clauses can be the subject or the object of a sentence the same way that a noun or a noun phrase can.

noun subject →	**Elephants** eat peanuts.
noun phrase subject →	**A diamond ring** costs a lot of money.
noun clause subject →	**What Sarah told me yesterday** was a big surprise.
noun object →	I like **chocolate**.
noun phrase object →	I drove **my sister's car**.
noun clause object →	I don't know **where Michael lives**.

▶ The easiest way to make a noun clause about an information question correctly is to ask yourself, *how could I answer the question?* The grammar you would use in the answer is the same grammar you should use in the noun clause.

  wrong noun clause grammar → I asked Mark when **does the movie begin**.

                     possible answer grammar → | The movie begins | at 8:00.

  = **right** noun clause grammar → I asked Mark when | the movie begins |.

  wrong noun clause grammar → Do you know where **is Joe**?

                     possible answer grammar → | Joe is | in the hospital.

  = **right** noun clause grammar → Do you know where | Joe is | ?

REMEMBER

  wrong → I asked Mary where **did she go**.   **wrong** → Do you know what time **is it**?

  right →   I asked Mary where **she went**.   **right** →   Do you know what time **it is**?

Practice 1 First look at the answer to the questions. Then circle the letter of the correct question.

  Example: A1: Do you know how many dogs does he have?

           (A2:) Do you know how many dogs he has?

            B: He has four dogs.

1   A1: Do you know where he lives?

    A2: Do you know where does he live?

    B: He lives in Los Angeles.

2   A1: Do you know when can she do it?

    A2: Do you know when she can do it?

    B: She can do it tomorrow.

3 A1: Is what the teacher said important?

   A2: Is what did the teacher say important?

   B: Yes, the teacher said there is an exam tomorrow.

4 A1: I don't know where is Carlos. Do you know?

   A2: I don't know where Carlos is. Do you know?

   B: I think Carlos is in the kitchen.

5 A1: Do you know when does the game start?

   A2: Do you know when the game starts?

   B: The game starts at 1:00.

6 A1: I don't know what Sofia should do to get better grades. Can you give me some advice?

   A2: I don't know what should Sofia do to get better grades. Can you give me some advice?

   B: Sofia should study more.

7 A1: Did Michael tell you where he will go?

   A2: Did Michael tell you where will he go?

   B: He said that he will go to Brazil.

8 A1: Do you know how much does it cost?

   A2: Do you know how much it costs?

   B: It costs $25.

Practice 2 First look at the answer to the questions. Then complete the noun clause in the question.

Example: A: Do you know where _____ she works _____?

           B: She works in a supermarket.

1 A: Can you tell me what time _____?

   B: It is 3:30.

2 A: Do you remember how many children _____?

   B: I think he has three children.

3 A: Did Larry tell you where _____?

   B: He told me that he's going to Hong Kong.

4 A: I didn't hear what _____. Did you?

   B: The teacher said to read pages 22 to 38 in our biology book.

5 A: Do you know when _____?

   B: The game starts at 1:00.

6 A: Do you know why _____?

   B: He was late because he had car problems.

7 A: I don't know where _____? Do you know?

   B: I think Noura lives in Abu Dhabi.

8 A: Did Sarah tell you why _____ on Sunday?

   B: She's got to work on Sunday because her company got a big order.

9 A: I can't remember what _____. Do you know?

   B: Sorry, I don't know what you're supposed to do.

▶ **noun clauses**   143

Practice 3 Change the questions to noun clauses. If you are not sure, remember to ask yourself, *How could I answer this question?* Because these are conversations, be sure to use the appropriate pronouns.

> *Example:* A: Why was John upset with you?
>
> B: I don't know _____ *why he was upset with me* _____.

1 A: What time is it?

   B: I don't know _____.

2 A: Where did Paul go?

   B: I'm not sure _____.

3 A: What is Sofia's telephone number?

   B: I have no idea _____. Look in the phone book.

4 A: When does the movie start?

   B: I can't remember _____.

5 A: When are we going to eat dinner?

   B: I don't know. Ask your mother _____.

6 A: Why was he angry?

   B: I don't know. _____ is a good question.

7 A: When did World War II begin?

   B: I can't remember. Ask your father _____. Maybe he knows.

8 A: Where has your brother gone?

   B: I'm not sure _____.

9 A: When does John's soccer game begin?

   B: He didn't tell me _____.

10 A: Sorry professor, what did you say?

   B: _____ was "we're going to have a quiz on Friday."

11 A: Who did Alex go to the library with?

   B: I don't know _____.

Practice 4 Some of the sentences contain mistakes. Find the incorrect sentences and correct them.

1 I asked Ali what does he want for dinner.

2 Do you know what is his name?

3 What the student wrote didn't make sense.

4 Ask Carlos how much money does he have.

5 I'm not sure when will Maria get here.

6 Do you know when she is going to come?

7 Please tell me how much money does he need.

8 I did not understand what was he talking about.

9 I'm not sure how long the movie is.

10 Do you know whose car is that?

14.2 ▶ noun clauses beginning with *if* or *whether (or not)*

DISCOVER

    a   Sam: ***When does** the train arrive?*

    b   Larry: *I don't know **when the train arrives**.*

    c   John: ***Does** the train arrive at 4:30?*

    d   Paul: *I don't know **if/whether the train arrives** at 4:30.*

1   Look at *a* and *c*. Which is an information question? Which is a *yes/no* question?

2   Look at *b* and *d*. How are the answers different?

LEARN

▶ In Section 14.1, the noun clauses all contained question words because they were based on information question. Now we will look at noun clauses which are based on *yes/no* questions. Noun clauses based on *yes/no* questions begin with *if* or *whether*.

    Maria: *Did Paul come to the party?*

    Sofia: *I don't know **if/whether** Paul came to the party.*

REMEMBER

▶ Sometimes *or not* is also used with noun clauses beginning with *if* or *whether*.

    *I don't know **whether or not** Paul came to the party.*

    *I don't know **if** Paul came to the party **or not**.*

    *I don't know **whether** Paul came to the party **or not**.*

  It is not correct to use *or not* with *if*.

    wrong → *I'm not sure **if or not** she is married.*

    right →   *I'm not sure **if** she is married **or not**.*

▶ When the noun clause is the subject of the sentence (and begins the sentence), only *whether* is possible.

    wrong → ***If** Sarah calls me is not something I care about.*

    right →   ***Whether** Sarah calls me is not something I care about.*

Practice 5 Change the question to a noun clause. If you are not sure, remember to ask yourself *How could I answer the question?* Practice using *if, whether* or *whether or not*.

Examples: A: Was Mary sick yesterday?

          B: I don't know _____*if/whether she was sick yesterday*_____.

          A: Is Jack telling the truth?

          B: _____*Whether or not he is telling the truth*_____ is something I can't be sure of.

1   A: Is she going to work tomorrow?

      B: I'm not sure _____.

2   A: Does Tom have a car?

      B: I don't know _____.

3   A: Does she believe you?

      B: No, but I don't care _____.

4   A: Does your ex-wife still think about you?

      B: Good question. I wonder _____.

5   A: Are cats smarter than dogs?

      B: I don't know. I will ask my cat _____.

6   A: Should you call her?

      B: _____ has been on my mind all day.

7   A: Has Francesca done her homework?

      B: I don't know _____.

8 A: Were Sam and Dave talking about you?

   B: I'd like to know _____.

9 A: Does the show start at 9:00?

   B: I have no idea _____.

10 A: Has Mary got a boyfriend?

   B: _____ is none of your business.

11 A: Is he the new teacher?

   B: I can't tell you _____.

12 A: Would Michael like to go to the beach with us?

   B: I'll ask him _____.

Practice 6 Some of the sentences contain mistakes. Find the incorrect sentences and correct them.

1 I want to know will he come to the party.

2 Can you tell me is Paul going to be here tomorrow?

3 Whether you come to the party or not doesn't matter to me.

4 I don't remember we are supposed to read this book or that book.

5 Does Michael speak French is not something I know.

6 I don't know if I will do it or not.

7 I wonder do they know the answer.

14.3 ▶ noun clauses with question words and infinitives

DISCOVER
   a *I don't know which book **I should read**.*
   b *I don't know which book **to read**.*
1 How are *a* and *b* different?
   c *Mary doesn't know where **she can buy** extra large baby shoes.*
   d *Mary doesn't know where **to buy** extra large baby shoes.*
2 How are *c* and *d* different?
   e *My mother isn't sure whether **she ought to say** yes or no.*
   f *My mother isn't sure whether **to say** yes or no.*
3 How are *e* and *f* different?

LEARN
   ▶ When noun clauses begin with question words which contain a subject and the modal verbs *can, could, ought to* or *should*, the subject and modal can be replaced with an infinitive (the base form of the verb).
   *Do you know where **I can buy** cat food? = Do you know where **to buy** cat food?*

Practice 7 Change the sentences so that they have the same meaning by using infinitives.

   Example: Please tell me what I should do.
              Please tell me what to do.

1 Mark told me what I should do.

2 Can you tell me where I can get my car fixed?

3 I've told you everything I know. I don't know what else I can say.

4 The recipe doesn't say how long I should cook it.

5 I've been thinking about what I should do about this problem for many days.

6 I told Carlos where he could cash a check.

Practice 8 Use your own words to complete the sentences with infinitives.

1   Everything in this restaurant looks so good. I don't know what _____.

2   Do you have any idea how _____ this problem?

3   I can't decide whether _____ a new car or _____ my old one.

4   Do you know how _____ to the mall from here?

5   Both of these books look very interesting. I don't know which one _____.

6   Tom told me I should come to the meeting early, but he didn't say how early _____.

14.4 ▶ object noun clauses beginning with *that*

DISCOVER
    a   ***Yesterday was my wife's birthday.***
    b   *I forgot **(that) yesterday was my wife's birthday**.*

1   Is *a* the object of the verb *b*?

    c   ***Carlos was born in Saudi Arabia.***
    d   *Nobody knows **(that) Carlos was born in Saudi Arabia**.*

2   Is *c* the object of the verb *d*?

    e   ***It's going to be cold tomorrow.***
    f   *The weatherman said **(that) it's going to be cold tomorrow**.*

3   Is *e* the object of the verb in *f*?
4   Look at *b*, *d* and *f*. Can an entire independent clause be the object of a sentence?

LEARN
▶ A noun clause that is an independent clause can be the object of another sentence. In other words, one sentence can be the object of another sentence. They often begin with *that*, but *that* is optional, and in informal speech many native speakers do not use *that*.
    *I told the doctor **I had a pain in my stomach**.*

Practice 9 Choose any sentence and use it as a noun clause to complete the sentences.
    ~~*Cats are smarter than dogs.*~~
    Ghosts are real.
    Amsterdam is a beautiful city.
    The USA will win the World Cup someday.
    I am smart.

1   Everybody knows (that) _____ *cats are smarter than dogs* _____.

2   I don't believe (that) _____.

3   Some people think (that) _____.

4   Do you agree (that) _____?

5   Most people don't think (that) _____.

14.5 ▶ subject noun clauses beginning with *that*

DISCOVER
    a   ***Mary failed the test.***
    b   ***That Mary failed the test** was a big surprise.*
    c   *It was a big surprise **(that) Mary failed the test**.*

1   Is *a* the subject of *b*?
2   Do *b* and *c* have the same meaning?

    d   ***Mary needs to study more.***
    e   ***That Mary needs to study more** is clear.*
    f   *It's clear **(that) Mary needs to study more**.*

3   Is *d* the subject of *e*?
4   Do *e* and *f* have the same meaning?
5   Look at *b* and *e*. Can an entire independent clause be the subject of a sentence?

▶ noun clauses

LEARN

▶ A noun clause that is an independent clause can be the subject of another sentence. In this case, *that* is necessary, not optional. It is much more common, however, to put the noun clause at the end of the sentence and to use *it* as the subject.

less common → ***That you need to study more*** *is clear.*

more common → ***It*** *is clear* ***(that) you need to study more***.

Practice 10 Choose any sentence and use it as a noun clause to complete the sentences.

~~*Dogs are not as smart as cats.*~~
There is life on other planets.
Smoking is bad for your health.
The Chicago Cubs will never win the World Series.
Professor Jones is a good teacher.
Americans eat only cheeseburgers.

1 That _____ dogs are not as smart as cats _____ is obvious.

It is obvious that _____ dogs are not as smart as cats _____.

2 That _____ is believed by everyone.

It's believed by everyone _____.

3 That _____ is a fact.

It is a fact that _____.

4 That _____ is well known.

It's well known _____.

5 That _____ is true.

It is true that _____.

6 That _____ is not true.

It's not true that _____.

14.6 ▶ noun clauses used in reported speech

DISCOVER

a **last week**

Tom: ***I want*** *to eat in the new Italian restaurant in the mall.*

John: *OK, let's go someday.*

today

John: *Last week Tom said* ***(that) he wanted*** *to eat in the new Italian restaurant in the mall.*

Harry: *I'd like to go there too.*

1 Why did the verb *want* change from present to past?

b **five minutes ago**

Sam: ***I work*** *in a museum.*

Lucy: *That's interesting.*

now

Ali: *What did Sam say? I didn't hear him.*

Lucy: *He said* ***(that) he works*** *in a museum.*

2 Why <u>didn't</u> the verb *work* change from present to past?

c **yesterday**

Noura: ***I live*** *in a 300-year-old house.*

Gary: *Really? That's very old.*

now

Gary: *Yesterday Noura told me* ***(that) she lives*** *in a 300-year-old house.*

Larry: *Wow, that's very old.*

3 Why <u>didn't</u> the verb *live* change from present to past?

LEARN (See Table 14a.)

▶ Noun clauses are used in *reported speech*. Reported speech is when we repeat what somebody said earlier. It is not a direct quotation. In a direct quotation, you are repeating <u>exactly</u> what the person said. In reported speech (also called *indirect speech*), we are changing the pronouns and <u>sometimes</u> the tense of the verb.

direct quotation →   *Michael said, **"I will help you."***

reported speech →   *Michael said **(that) he would help me.***

▶ Why do we change the tense of the verb only sometimes? When we talk in the present about something that was said in the past and is finished, we often change the tense of the verb to the past.

*I talked to John last week, and he said (that) he **would** help me.*

However, when we talk about something that was said in the <u>recent past</u> or about something that is <u>still true</u>, we often do not change to the past.

*I talked to Michael a few minutes ago, and he said (that) he **will** help me.*

*Yesterday my neighbor told me (that) she **works** in a bakery.*

Often either past or present is correct. It depends on the situation and the preference of the speaker.

14a

quoted and reported speech		
quoted speech	reported speech—past	reported speech—recent past / still true
*I **eat** fruit.*	*He said (that) **he ate** fruit.*	*He said (that) **he eats** fruit.*
*I **am eating** fruit.*	*He said (that) **he was eating** fruit.*	*He said (that) **he is eating** fruit.*
*I **ate** fruit.*	*He said (that) **he had eaten** fruit.*	*He said (that) **he ate** fruit.*
*I **have eaten** fruit.*	*He said (that) **he had eaten** fruit.*	*He said (that) **he has eaten** fruit.*
*I **had eaten** fruit.*	*He said (that) **he had eaten** fruit.*	*same*
*I **will eat** fruit.*	*He said (that) **he would eat** fruit.*	*He said (that) **he will eat** fruit.*
*I **am going to eat** fruit.*	*He said (that) **he was going to** eat fruit.*	*He said (that) **he is going to** eat fruit.*
*I **can eat** fruit.*	*He said (that) **he could eat** fruit.*	*He said **he can eat** fruit.*
*I **may eat** fruit.*	*He said (that) **he might eat** fruit.*	*same*
*I **might eat** fruit.*	*He said (that) **he might eat** fruit.*	*same*
*I **must eat** fruit.*	*He said (that) **he had to eat** fruit.*	*He said (that) **he has to eat** fruit.*
*I **have to eat** fruit.*	*He said (that) **he had to eat** fruit.*	*He said (that) **he has to eat** fruit.*
*I **should eat** fruit.*	*He said (that) **he should eat** fruit.*	*same*
*I **ought to eat** fruit.*	*He said (that) **he ought to eat** fruit.*	*same*

Practice 11 Complete the sentences with reported speech. If two answers are possible, use the one that you think is best. Be ready to explain your answer.

Example: Noura: I have to get a job.

           Last month Noura told me that _____ *she had to get a job* _____.

1   Paul: I will be the next head of the sales department.

    Yesterday Paul said that _____.

2   Linda: I have nine children.

    Linda told me that _____.

3   Carlos: I'm going to work harder in school.

    When I talked to Carlos last week, he promised me _____.

4   Alex: I've bought a new car.

    I just talked to Alex, and he said that _____.

5   Sofia: My father lost his wallet.

    Sofia told me that _____.

▶ noun clauses

6   Mary: I may call you tomorrow.

Mary told me that _____.

7   Tom: I have to read 100 pages tonight.

Did you hear that? Tom said _____.

8   Larry: My father will not let me use his car next weekend.

I talked to Larry yesterday, and he told me that _____.

9   Rosa: My grandfather called me this morning.

Rosa said _____.

10 Mark: I don't have time to help you.

Last night Mark said that _____.

14.7 ▶ plans: talking about past plans with noun clauses with *would*

DISCOVER

Monday

a   John: When are you going to wash your car?
b   Gary: I **will**/**am going to** wash my car on Wednesday.

Friday

c   John: Gary **was going to** wash his car on Wednesday, but he didn't.
d   Sofia: Did he say (that) he **would**/**was going to** wash his car on Wednesday?
e   John: Yes, he told me (that) he **would**/**was going to** wash his car on Wednesday.

1   Look at *d* and *e*. Is it possible to use *would* to talk about past plans in a noun clause?
2   Look at *c*. Is it possible to use *would* to talk about past plans in an independent clause?

LEARN

▶ We saw in Section 4.1 that both *will* and *be going to* are used to talk about future plans. We saw in Section 12.5 that the past form of *be going to* is used to talk about unrealized and unconfirmed past plans. But what about using *would* to talk about unrealized and unconfirmed past plans? *Would* can also be used to talk about past plans, but <u>only</u> when it is part of a noun clause.

*Michael **was going to** call me.*
→ *Michael said (that) he **would**/**was going to** call me.*

*I **was going to** help you.*
→ *I told you (that) I **would**/**was going to** help you.*

*You **were going to** do it, but you didn't.*
→ *I thought (that) you **would**/**were going to** do it, but you didn't.*

Practice 12 Complete the sentences with *would*. Be sure to change pronouns when it is necessary.

Example: Nick: I am going to support you.

Nick lied when he told me that _____ *he would support me* _____.

1   Rosa: Tom is going to cook dinner.

Rosa told me that _____.

2   Carlos: She'll arrive at 3:15.

I think Carlos said _____, but I'm not sure.

3   Alex: Larry is going to take out the garbage.

Alex said that _____.

4   Michael: I'll meet you at the library at 7:30.

I'm pretty sure that Michael said _____.

5 Lucy: I'm going to call you later.

Lucy told me that _____.

6 John: I'll do my homework after dinner.

John said that _____, but he didn't.

7 Sam: My sister was going to be there.

I just talked to Sam, and he said _____.

8 Bob: They'll be there at 9:00.

Bob told me that _____.

14.8 ▶ noun clauses with question words and *-ever*

DISCOVER

    a   *Bill:*   *You can do **whatever** you want.*
    b   *Sam:*   *What did you say?*
    c   *Bill:*   *I said that you can do **anything** you want.*

1   Do *whatever* and *anything* have the same meaning in this conversation?

    d   *Rosa:*   ***Whoever** believes that story is crazy.*
    e   *Alex:*   *What did you say?*
    f   *Rosa:*   *I said **anyone** who believes that story is crazy.*

2   Do *whoever* and *anyone* have the same meaning in this conversation?

LEARN

▶ Words like *whatever*, *whenever* and *however*, etc., can <u>sometimes</u> be used in the same way as *anything*, *any time* and *any way*, etc.

whoever	=	anyone (who / that) / anybody (who / that)
whomever	=	anyone (whom / that) / anybody (whom / that)
whatever	=	anything (which / that)
whichever	=	any [of a group] (which / that) / any one (which / that)
whenever	=	any time (when / that)
wherever	=	anyplace (where / that) / anywhere (where / that)
however	=	any way (which / that)

REMEMBER

▶ Do not confuse *any one* with *anyone* or *any way* with *anyway*.

Practice 13 Change the sentences as in the example.

Example: You can eat anything you want.

        You can eat whatever you want.

1   Any time you want to eat dinner is OK with me.

2   Bob tells the same joke to anyone he meets.

3   Anybody who comes to the party needs to bring something to eat or drink.

4   I hate this city, so anyplace I move to would be better than this place.

5   You can sit in any chair you like.

6   My daughter cannot do anything she wants. She's only 14.

7   These are all the same. You can use any one you want.

8   Any way you drive to Chicago, the traffic is going to be very slow.

9   Jack is a liar. You can be sure anything he says is not true.

10   Any way you want to do it is fine. Just get the job done.

 **Unit 15 ▶ the passive**

15.1 ▶ forms of the passive

DISCOVER

    *a   Sofia **rides** horses.*

1   What is the subject of the sentence? What is the object of the sentence?

2   Is *rides* in the present tense?

    *b   Horses **are ridden** by Sofia.*

3   What is the subject of the sentence? What is the object of the sentence?

4   How are *a* and *b* different?

LEARN (See Table 15a.)

▶ *A* is in the *active voice*. *B* is in the *passive voice*. The passive voice is formed by *be* + past participle. *Be* can be any tense and can be combined with modals and phrasal modals.

15a

basic patterns of the passive			
tense	subject	verb	object
simple present — active	Lucy	eats	pizza.
simple present — passive	Pizza	**is** eaten	by Lucy.
present continuous — active	Lucy	is eating	pizza.
present continuous — passive	Pizza	**is being** eaten	by Lucy.
present perfect — active	Lucy	has eaten	pizza.
present perfect — passive	Pizza	**has been** eaten	by Lucy.
simple past — active	Lucy	ate	pizza.
simple past — passive	Pizza	**was** eaten	by Lucy.
past continuous — active	Lucy	was eating	pizza.
past continuous — passive	Pizza	**was being** eaten	by Lucy.
past perfect — active	Lucy	had eaten	pizza.
past perfect — passive	Pizza	**had been** eaten	by Lucy.
future will — active	Lucy	will eat	pizza.
future will — passive	Pizza	**will be** eaten	by Lucy.
future be going to — active	Lucy	is going to eat	pizza.
future be going to — passive	Pizza	**is going to be** eaten	by Lucy.

REMEMBER

▶ It is easy to form the passive. Simply reverse the subject and object of the active sentence, then look at the tense of the verb in the active sentence and use that same tense with the correct form of *be* and the past participle of the verb in the active sentence.

Practice 1 Change these active sentences to passive by writing the correct form of *be*.

   Examples: A mouse ate the cheese.

             The cheese _____*was*_____ eaten by a mouse.

             She is using the dictionary.

             The dictionary _____*is being*_____ used by her.

1   Larry drives the truck every day.

      The truck _____ driven by Larry every day.

2 I didn't do the work.

The work _____ done by me.

3 They are taking the class now.

The class _____ taken by them now.

4 He will go over the test results on Friday.

The test results _____ gone over by him on Friday.

5 We have written the answers.

The answers _____ written by us.

6 Ms. Martin was teaching French.

French _____ taught by Ms. Martin.

7 He is going to fly the airplane.

The airplane _____ flown by him.

8 Sarah and he had finished dinner.

Dinner _____ finished by Sarah and him.

Practice 2 Change these active sentences to passive. Be sure to change pronouns when it is necessary.

Examples: He speaks Chinese.

Chinese is spoken by him.

Mary doesn't eat meat.

Meat isn't eaten by Mary.

1 I teach English.

2 The boss didn't approve my request.

3 Many people take the bus.

4 We don't drink milk.

5 Francesca reads many books.

6 Carlos draws pictures.

7 He doesn't use this computer.

8 Noura manages the store.

Practice 3 Change these active sentences to passive. Be sure to change pronouns when it is necessary.

Examples: Sofia is riding a horse.

A horse is being ridden by Sofia.

They aren't doing the work.

The work isn't being done by them.

1 John is hiding the money.

2 The children are putting away the toys.

3 I'm not doing it.

4 The coach is choosing players.

5 They're sending the letters.

6 She's not writing the report.

▶ **the passive**

7 Larry is doing nothing.

8 We aren't taking the train.

Practice 4 Change these active sentences to passive. Be sure to change pronouns when it is necessary.

Examples: Sam has paid the bill.

The bill has been paid by Sam.

She hasn't written the contract.

The contract hasn't been written by her.

1 The kids have eaten the cookies.

2 We have started a new company.

3 Michael hasn't read the letter.

4 Professor Flagg has helped us.

5 A dog has bitten me.

6 I haven't seen that movie.

7 We haven't cleaned our rooms.

8 She has broken the window.

Practice 5 Change these active sentences to passive. Be sure to change pronouns when it is necessary.

Examples: Lucy saw the accident.

The accident was seen by Lucy.

She didn't ride the red bicycle.

The red bicycle wasn't ridden by her.

1 Jack stole my car last week.

2 She didn't make the sandwiches.

3 The police caught a criminal.

4 I took Rosa to the hospital.

5 The pilot flew the airplane.

6 They didn't do it.

7 He didn't give the correct answer.

8 An octopus ate Henry.

Practice 6 Change these active sentences to passive. Be sure to change pronouns when it is necessary.

Examples: Larry was cooking the hamburgers.

The hamburgers were being cooked by Larry.

We weren't listening to the music.

The music wasn't being listened to by us.

1 Francesca was riding a bicycle.

2 He wasn't driving the car.

3 The people at the party were making a lot of noise.

4 The teacher wasn't grading the tests.

5 My father was fixing the broken window.

6 You were watching a movie.

7   Noura and I weren't doing the dishes.

8   The judges were choosing the winner.

Practice 7 Change these active sentences to passive. Be sure to change pronouns when it is necessary.

Examples: The students had already read the book.

The book had already been read by the students.

He hadn't called her.

She hadn't been called by him.

We had never seen it.

It had never been seen by us.

1   Everyone had already heard the news.

2   Linda hadn't set up a meeting.

3   I'd done the work.

4   They had never seen a zebra.

5   The company hadn't paid the workers.

6   John and I had never eaten Indian food.

7   Ali had already finished the exam.

8   We'd already ridden the motorcycle.

Practice 8 Change these active sentences to passive. Be sure to change pronouns when it is necessary.

Examples: Sarah will do all the work.

All the work will be done by Sarah.

They won't do it.

It won't be done by them.

1   The manager will explain the new plan at the meeting.

2   She won't cook dinner.

3   He'll change the light bulb.

4   John and he will give a speech.

5   I won't write the report.

6   He won't steal your money.

7   I'll speak to him later.

8   The doctor will see the patient at 11:00.

Practice 9 Change these active sentences to passive. Be sure to change pronouns when it is necessary.

Examples: Rosa is going to help me.

I'm going to be helped by Rosa.

They aren't going to do it.

It's not going to be done by them.

1   Paul is going to organize a conference.

2   The students aren't going to take a test today.

3   The news is going to surprise you.

4   I'm going to bring the hot dogs.

5   We're not going to pay for their wedding.

6   They're going to take the bus.

7   He was going to drive the car.

8   Carlos was going to fly the helicopter.

15.2 ▶ meanings of the passive

DISCOVER

    a   **Jack** stole my car.
    b   My car was stolen **by Jack**.

1   Look at *a*. Do I know the name of the person who stole my car?

2   Look at *b*. I know the name of the person who stole my car, so is there a good reason to say *by Jack*?

    c   **Somebody** stole my truck.
    d   My truck was stolen.

3   Look at *c*. Do I know the name of the person who stole my truck?

4   Look at *d*. I do not know the name of the person who stole my truck, so is there a good reason to say *by somebody*?

    e   **People** grow coffee in Brazil.
    f   Coffee is grown in Brazil.

5   Look at *e*. What information is more important—that <u>people</u> grow coffee in Brazil or that people grow coffee <u>in Brazil</u>?

6   Look at *f*. Because *people* is not important or obvious (of course people do it, not monkeys or robots), is there a good reason to say *by people*?

    g   **I** made a mistake.
    h   A mistake was made.

7   Look at *g*. Do you think that I enjoy telling people that I made a mistake? Do you? Does anyone?

8   Look at *h*. Does the passive let me say that somebody made a mistake without saying that I made it?

LEARN

▶ Why do people sometimes use the passive? It is common to use the passive when we think that who or what is <u>receiving</u> the action of the verb is more important than who or what is <u>doing</u> the action of the verb,
    The apple pie was made by my wife.

when we <u>do not know</u> who did something,
    The jewelry store was robbed yesterday. (By somebody, of course, but we don't know who it was.)

when it is <u>not important</u> or when it is <u>obvious</u>
    Japanese is spoken in Japan. (By Japanese people, of course.)

or when we <u>do not want to say</u> who did something.
    Mistakes were made. (By me, but I don't want anybody to know!)

Practice 10 Change these active sentences to passive. If you think there is a good reason for a *by*-phrase, include it in your answer. If you think there is not a good reason for a *by*-phrase, do not include it. Be ready to explain your answer.

Examples: Mary Smith wrote this book in 1993.

      This book was written by Mary Smith in 1993.

      Somebody built my house in 1898.

      My house was built in 1898.

1   People invented gunpowder in China.

2   Michael will cook dinner.

3   Teachers teach Spanish in my high school.

4   I broke the photocopier.

5   A man delivered a package this morning.

6   Somebody robbed the bank.

7   A man with red hair robbed the bank.

8   My grandfather paid for my education.

9   Somebody is going to open a new restaurant on Main Street.

10 Pirates buried the treasure.

15.3 ▶ passive modals (See Table 15b.)

DISCOVER

    a   *This bill **is paid** every month.*

    b   *This bill **must be paid** before the end of the month.*

1   Why does *is* in *a* change to *be* when it is after a modal in *b*?

    c   *The work **was done** yesterday.*

    d   *The work **should have been done** three days ago.*

2   Why does *was* in *c* change to *have been* in *d*?

LEARN (See Table 15b.)

▶ *A* and *c* do not contain modals. *B* and *d* contain modals. Present and future passives with modals follow the pattern: modal + *be* + past participle.

    Gary **should call** the customer.

    → The customer **should be called** by Gary.
            modal + *be* + past participle

Past passives with modals follow the pattern: modal + *have been* + past participle.

    Larry **must have** made a mistake.

    → A mistake **must have been made** by Larry.
            modal + *have been* + past participle

REMEMBER

▶ It is common to use *already* with past passive modals.

    *Your homework should **already** have been done.*

Practice 11 Change the active sentences to passive.

Example: The kids must have eaten the chocolate cake.

           The chocolate cake must have been eaten by the kids.

1   Mary might take a taxi.

2   The plumber was supposed to fix the hot water heater.

3   Paul may already have found a better job.

4   The pilot had better check the fuel level.

5   The manager should already have contacted you.

6   She must not have seen my note.

7   A doctor has got to look at your leg.

8   You should not have read her diary.

9   Anyone could have done this.

10 He will not have finished the project.

Practice 12 Mixed tense review. Complete the sentences with the words in parentheses.

Example: Who opened this letter? It (shouldn't, open) _____*shouldn't have been opened*_____ by anyone.

1   My stapler is not on my desk. It (must, borrow) _____ by one of my kids.

2   I think I (may, transfer) _____ by my company to Vancouver soon.

3   These boxes (be supposed to, put on) _____ the truck tomorrow.

4   You (might, bite) _____ by the snake you were holding yesterday.

5   My speech for the conference tomorrow (has got to, finish) _____ tonight.

the passive with modals and phrasal modals				
present / future	subject	modal or phrasal modal	verb	object
will active	Mary	will	finish	the project.
will passive	The work	will	**be** finished	by Mary.
can active	John	can	drive	the truck.
can passive	The truck	can	**be** driven	by John.
should active	He	should	clean	the room.
should passive	The room	should	**be** cleaned	by him.
ought to active	Ali	ought to	fix	these mistakes.
ought to passive	These mistakes	ought to	**be** fixed	by Ali.
may active	Mark	may	buy	a house.
may passive	A house	may	**be** bought	by Mark.
might active	Francesca	might	ride	an elephant.
might passive	An elephant	might	**be** ridden	by Francesca.
had better active	You	had better	write	this essay.
had better passive	This essay	had better	**be** written	by you.
have to active	Noura	has to	give	permission.
have to passive	Permission	has to	**be** given	by Noura.
have got to active	He	has got to	do	this work now.
have got to passive	This work	has got to	**be** done	by him now.
be supposed to active	Nobody	is supposed to	open	this door.
be supposed to passive	This door	is not supposed to	**be** opened	by the anybody.
be going to active	The company	is going to	build	a new factory.
be going to passive	A new factory	is going to	**be** built	by the company.
past	subject	modal	verb	object
should have active	Michael	should	have called	you.
should have passive	You	should	**have been** called	by Michael.
could have active	Nobody	could	have helped	them.
could have passive	They	could not	**have been** helped	by anyone.
would have active	He	would	never do	that.
would have passive	That	would never	**have been** done	by him.
must have active	The traffic	must	have delayed	her.
must have passive	She	must	**have been** delayed	by the traffic.
may have active	Mary	may	have seen	the movie.
may have passive	The movie	may	**have been** seen	by Mary.
might have active	The doctor	might	have made	a mistake.
might have passive	A mistake	might	**have been** made	by the doctor.

6   I'm really angry. This work (should, do) _____ a long time ago!

7   There's something wrong with this microwave. It (can't, use) _____ .

8   The teacher told us that the homework (had better, turn in) _____ on time.

9   I still haven't received my mother's package. I think it (may, send) _____ to the wrong address.

10   Don't forget about this bill. It (has got to, pay) _____ by the 21st.

11   A new school (be going to, build) _____ on Oak Street next year.

12   The tires on your car are very worn. They (have got to, replace) _____ soon.

13   A lot of people think that the company (might, sell) _____ in a few months.

14   Here is your medicine. It (ought to, take) _____ four times a day.

15   I ordered a book, but it (won't, deliver) _____ until next week.

15.4 ▶ passives with *get*

DISCOVER

    a   Jack **was arrested** by the police.

    b   Jack **got arrested** by the police.

1   Look at *a* and *b*. Do they have the same meaning?

LEARN

▶ *Get* is sometimes used with the passive instead of *be*. There is often little difference in meaning, but sometimes, when *get* is used, there is an idea that the person who is the subject of the sentence is somehow <u>responsible for</u> what happened.

▶ Sometimes, when the speaker wants to make this idea of responsibility clear, reflexive pronouns are used. For example, in the sentence *Jack got himself arrested by the police*, it is clear that it was Jack's fault—he did something to make this happen.

▶ This use of *get* is similar to the use of *get* discussed in Section 10.8. There we saw that *get* is often used with adjectives—sometimes adjectives formed from past participles. What makes this use of *get* different is that a *by*-phrase is possible (but not always necessary). For that reason, the past participles used in this way are verbs and not adjectives.

REMEMBER

▶ Remember that a *by*-phrase is often not necessary.

    Somebody robbed me yesterday.

    = I **got** robbed yesterday.

Practice 13 Change the active sentences to passive sentences with *get*. Use a *by*-phrase only if you think there is a good reason for it.

Example: A mosquito bit me.

    I got bitten by a mosquito.

1   Something hurt Michael in a rugby game.

2   My boss fired me.

3   The police said someone killed two guys last night.

4   A truck hit Paul.

5   I forgot to lock up my motorcycle, and somebody stole it.

6   Somebody hurt Mark in a fight.

7   Somebody shot me.

8   The police arrested him.

9   Somebody kicked him out of the party.

10   A monster ate Henry.

Unit 16 ▶ adverbs, adverb clauses, adverb phrases and more, part 1

16.1 ▶ adverbs and adverb clauses

DISCOVER

    *a   Sarah sings **beautifully**.*

    *b   Sarah sings **while she is in the shower**.*

1   Which word in *a* gives you information about the verb *sings*?

2   Which words in *b* give you information about the verb *sings*?

    *c   Carlos worked **hard**.*

    *d   Carlos worked **even though he was tired**.*

3   Which word in *c* gives you information about the verb *worked*?

4   Which words in *d* give you information about the verb *worked*?

LEARN

▶ In *a* and *c*, the words that give information about verbs (*beautifully* and *hard*) are *adverbs*. In *b* and *d*, the words that give information about verbs (*while she is in the shower* and *even though he was tired*) are *adverb clauses*. Adverb clauses are groups of words which contain a subject and a verb which together do the same job that adverbs do: They modify (give information about) verbs. Adverb clauses are connected to *independent clauses* by words (called *subordinating conjunctions*) such as *before, after, because, although, while* and *if*.

    After *I eat dinner,* *I'm going to watch TV.*
    subordinating   independent clause
    conjunction

             adverb clause
    (a kind of dependent clause)

Independent clauses <u>make sense alone</u>. If I say <u>only</u> *I'm going to watch TV*, that makes sense. But if I say <u>only</u> *After I eat dinner*, it <u>does not make sense</u>. This means that adverb clauses are *dependent clauses*—they do not make sense alone. They must be in a sentence with an independent clause to make sense.

▶ Dependent and independent clauses can be reversed. When the dependent clause is first, a comma comes after it.

    I went to the doctor **because I was sick**. = **Because I was sick,** *I went to the doctor.*
    independent clause   dependent clause   dependent clause   independent clause

REMEMBER

▶ Both independent and dependent clauses contain a <u>subject and a verb</u>.

    ***My husband made** dinner.* ***I watched** TV.*
    independent clause   independent clause

    ***My husband made** dinner <u>while **I watched** TV</u>.*
    independent clause   dependent clause

    <u>*While **I watched** TV*</u>, *my husband made dinner.*
    dependent clause   independent clause

Practice 1 Underline the adverb clauses and add commas where they are necessary.

Examples: <u>Before I go to bed</u>, I always take a shower.

             I failed the test <u>even though I studied a lot</u>.

1   Although I was very angry I didn't say anything.

2   You can go home when you are finished.

3   As soon as I saw the fire I called the fire department.

4   I've taught French since I graduated from college.

5   In case my ATM card doesn't work I always take cash when I travel.

6   I'm going to watch TV now that I've finished my homework.

7   Every time I think about what Sam said about me I get angry.

8   I took a shower before I jumped into the swimming pool.

9   Until you have completed the first level you can't go on to the second.

10   The next time we go to that restaurant we should try the sushi tacos.

16.2 ▶ adverb clauses about time

DISCOVER

a   ***After Michael finished dinner,*** *he watched TV.*

1   What is the adverb clause about? What information does it give you about the independent clause?

b   *John checks his email* ***as soon as he gets out of bed***.

2   What is the adverb clause about? What information does it give you about the independent clause?

LEARN

▶ Several subordinating conjunctions are about time. (See Section 4.4/a for more about future time clauses.)

after

After *Larry saw the accident, he called the police.*

The children should do their homework ***after*** *they finish dinner.*

as (= while)

As *Noura was sleeping, the burglar stole her jewelry.*

I thought about what you said to me last night ***as*** *I drove to work this morning.*

as long as

As long as *I live, I will never forget this day.*

You can stay here ***as long as*** *you want to.*

as soon as (= immediately after)

As soon as *the hiker saw the bear, he climbed a tree.*

I'll call you ***as soon as*** *I arrive in Milan.*

before

Before *I ate breakfast, I took a shower.*

Mary will finish her work ***before*** *she goes home.*

by the time (that) (= when)

By the time that *you graduate from college, you'll be 23 years old.*

I hope dinner is ready ***by the time*** *we get home.*

every time (that)

Every time that *I hear that song, I remember my high school years.*

My car is hard to start ***every time*** *it gets really cold outside.*

once (= when, after)

Once *you have completed Part A of your exam, begin Part B.*

You can watch TV ***once*** *you have finished your homework.*

since (= from the time)

Since *I moved to Indiana, I have been very bored.*

Alex has grown a lot ***since*** *you were here before.*

the first time (that) / the next time (that) / the last time (that), etc.

The first time that *I came to this city, I hated it.*

I'll call you ***the next time*** *I need some advice.*

until

Until *I have enough money to buy a house, I will have to rent an apartment.*

We'll play football ***until*** *it gets too dark to play.*

when (sometimes = while)

When *the TV show is over, I want you to go to bed.*

I'm very busy now. I'll do it ***when*** *I have time.*

I never talk on my mobile phone ***when*** *I am driving. (= I never talk on my mobile phone* ***while*** *I am driving.)*

whenever (= any time)

Whenever *I feel sad, I call my mother.*

I always visit my brother ***whenever*** *I am in New York City.*

while

While *you are washing your car, I'll work in the garden.*

The teacher watched the students ***while*** *they were taking the test.*

Practice 2 Only one of the subordinating conjunctions makes sense. Underline the correct subordinating conjunction.

Example: (<u>As soon as</u>/before) I saw the fire, I called the fire department.

1   (Until/While) you are working at your desk, you can listen to the radio.

2   He gets very sick (by the time/every time) he eats peanuts.

3   I got out of bed (while/as soon as) my alarm clock went off.

4   The meeting is going to be almost over (by the time/every time) we get there.

5   (Whenever/Once) you have gotten your bachelor's degree, you should think about getting a master's degree.

6   (As/The last time) I was sitting in class this morning, I thought about what to cook for the party.

7   Paul has been in the hospital (as long as/since) he fell off the roof of his house.

8   (As long as/Once) he lives, he won't forget the day he saw a ghost in the cemetery.

9   (After/Since) she finishes her work, she's going to go home.

10 (Before/Whenever) I am really hungry, I eat an entire large pizza.

11 In my country, you cannot drive (since/until) you are 16.

12 You'd better clean your room (before/when) you go out with your friends!

13 I'm going to make dinner (when/while) I get home.

14 (By the time/The last time) I ate at that restaurant, the food was terrible.

Practice 3 Use the sentences and the subordinating conjunction in parentheses to make sentences with adverb clauses. Write both possible sentence patterns. Be careful about punctuation, and be sure to change pronouns when it is necessary.

Example: The rice is ready. We can't eat dinner. (until)

　　　　Until the rice is ready, we can't eat dinner.
　　　　We can't eat dinner until the rice is ready.

1   Your mother is ready. We can go. (when)

2   She says that. It makes me angry. (every time)

3   You take the test. You should review. (before)

4   You live in my house. You will follow my rules. (as long as)

5   I got to work. I started to feel sick. (after)

6   You need my car. You can borrow it. (whenever)

7   Noura was finishing her homework. I went to the store. (while)

8   We bought this printer. We have been having problems with it. (since)

16.3 ▶ adverb clauses about reasons

DISCOVER

    a   *I went to the dentist **because I had a toothache**.*

1   What is the adverb clause about? What information does it give you about the independent clause?

    b   ***Since I didn't have any cash,** I used my credit card.*

2   What is the adverb clause about? What information does it give you about the independent clause?

LEARN

▶ Some subordinating conjunctions are about the cause, or reason, for something.

as (= ***because***)

    ***As** my car was out of gas, I had to walk to work.*

    *I took my umbrella with me this morning **as** I had heard that it might rain today.*

because

    ***Because** Mary was late for class, she didn't have enough time for the quiz.*

    *Larry didn't go to work **because** he was sick.*

now that (= ***because it is now true that***)

    ***Now that** you have finished your work, you can go home.*

    *I feel much better **now that** I have lost 10 kilograms.*

since (= ***because***)

    ***Since** you don't like my cooking, you can do all the cooking from now on!*

    *The teacher gave me a zero **since** I had cheated on the test.*

Practice 4 Use the sentences and the subordinating conjunction to make sentences with adverb clauses. Write both possible sentence patterns. Be careful about punctuation, and be sure to change pronouns when it is necessary.

Example: Michael forgot his key. He couldn't open the door. (since)

         Since Michael forgot his key, he couldn't open the door.

         Michael couldn't open the door since he forgot his key.

1   You are married. You had better get life insurance. (now that)

2   You asked me. I will tell you the truth. (since)

3   I wasn't careful. I cut my hand. (because)

4   It was raining. The picnic was canceled. (as)

5   You have failed the final exam. You cannot pass the class. (since)

6   The war has ended. It's now safe to travel in that country. (as)

7   The party is over. We have to clean up the house. (now that)

8   He is 21 years old. He can do whatever he wants. (as)

9   Carl is an English teacher. He doesn't make a lot of money. (because)

16.4 ▶ adverb clauses about opposites

DISCOVER

    a   **Even though I was hungry,** *I didn't eat anything.*

1   What is the adverb clause about? Does the speaker think that *was hungry* and *didn't eat* have a similar or an opposite meaning?

    b   *I will go shopping with you* **although I don't want to.**

2   What is the adverb clause about? Does the speaker think that *will go shopping* and *don't want to* have a similar or an opposite meaning?

LEARN

▶ When people do things that are what we expect them to do, we use *because*.

    Because *I was hungry,* **I ate** *lunch.*

But some subordinating conjunctions have an opposite meaning. *Even though, although* and *though* tell you that what was true (or is true or will be true) or what happened (or is happening or will happen) is the <u>opposite of what you expect</u>. *Even though, although* and *though* have the same meaning, but *even though* is the most common, and *though* is the least common.

    Even though *I was hungry, I* **didn't eat** *lunch.*

      = **Although** *I was hungry, I* **didn't eat** *lunch.*

      = **Though** *I was hungry, I* **didn't eat** *lunch.*

    although

      Although *I need a new car, I don't have enough money to buy one.*

      Mark gave me a ride to the airport **although** *he wanted to stay home and watch the game on TV.*

    even though

      Even though *I explained everything again and again, he still did it wrong.*

      Sarah told Michael that she believes him **even though** *she really thinks he is lying.*

    though

      Though *he studied very hard for the test, he failed.*

      I have to go now **though** *I really would like to stay longer.*

REMEMBER

▶ Be careful not to confuse *though* with *thought* (the past form of *think*).

▶ Usually a noun is used in the first clause and a pronoun in the second clause.

    Although **John** *was born in France,* **he** *can't speak French.*

    = **John** *can't speak French although* **he** *was born in France.*

Practice 5 Use the subordinating conjunction in parentheses to write sentences with adverb clauses. Write both possible sentence patterns. Be careful about punctuation.

Example: My wife is still angry with me. I apologized to her about 10 times. (even though)

    Even though I apologized to my wife about 10 times, she is still angry with me.

    My wife is still angry with me even though I apologized to her about 10 times.

1   We looked everywhere for our dog. We couldn't find her. (even though)

2   I had a map. I still got lost. (although)

3   I left for the airport three hours before my flight. I still missed my plane. (even though)

4   She makes a lot of money. She's always broke. (even though)

5   I hate basketball. I promised to go to a game with my husband. (although)

6   You have a headache. Do you still want to go to the movie? (even though)

7   He offered to pay me $75,000 for my car. I said no. (although)

8   The doctors did everything they could. She didn't get better. (though)

16.5 ▶ adverb clauses about condition

DISCOVER

>   a   ***If I eat a big lunch,*** *I fall asleep at my desk.*
>   b   *The coach will cancel the game* ***if it rains tomorrow****.*

1   Look at *a* and *b*. Which sentence is about something that always happens? Which sentence is about something that might happen only one time?

2   Look at *a*. What is the tense of the adverb clause? What is the tense of the independent clause?

3   Look at *b*. What is the tense of the adverb clause? What is the tense of the independent clause?

LEARN

▶ Some subordinating conjunctions have a *conditional* meaning. The word *condition* has many meanings in English. Here condition means something that must happen or must be true before something else can happen or can be true. In *a*, *eat a big lunch* must happen for *fall asleep at my desk* to happen. In *b*, *rain* must happen for *cancel the game* to happen. Notice that when the sentence is about something that <u>always</u> happens or is <u>alway</u> true, both clauses are in the <u>present tense</u>.

>   ***Unless*** *it rains, the children* ***play outside*** *after school.* (The speaker is talking about something that is always true.)

▶ Notice that when the sentence is about something that <u>might happen only one time</u>, the independent clause is in the <u>future tense</u>, but the adverb clause is in the <u>present tense</u>. (See Unit 20 for more about conditional sentences.)

>   ***Unless*** *it rains, the children* ***will play outside*** *after school.* (The speaker is talking about today only.)

>   ***even if***
>   ***Even if*** *you ask me a million times, the answer will still be no.*
>   *We're going to the beach tomorrow* ***even if*** *it's cold.*

>   ***if***
>   ***If*** *we win this game, we'll go to the semi-finals.*
>   *My mother worries* ***if*** *I am late.*

>   ***whether or not***
>   ***Whether or not*** *you come with me, I am going to the party.*
>   *The teacher is going to start the test at 10:00* ***whether or not*** *all the students are there.*

>   ***unless***
>   ***Unless*** *you apologize, I'm never going to speak to you again.*
>   *We eat dinner at 6:30* ***unless*** *our father comes home late.*

REMEMBER

▶ The conditional adverb clause should <u>not</u> be in the future tense.
>   **wrong** → *If you* ***will have*** *a problem, I will help you.*
>   **right** →   *If you* ***have*** *a problem, I will help you.*

Practice 6 Only one of the subordinating conjunctions makes sense. Underline the correct subordinating conjunction.

Example: (<u>If</u>/Unless) you are sick, you should go to the doctor.

1   You should take an umbrella (even if / in case) it rains.

2   (Unless / Whether or not) you pay the bill soon, your telephone will be disconnected.

3   (Unless / Whether or not) we win the game, we will still have fun playing.

4   (Whether or not / In case) there is a fire, call the fire department immediately.

5   I will lend you some money (if / unless) you don't have enough.

6   I'm going to finish this project (even if / in case) I have to stay up all night.

7   (Unless / In case) you forget your password, you should write it on a piece of paper.

8   I'll be there at 11:00 (unless / if) the traffic is really bad.

9   I'm going to tell my boss what I think (even if / in case) she fires me.

10 (Unless / If) my wife says I have to stay home, I'll go fishing with you on the weekend.

16.6 ▶ *well*

DISCOVER
> a   *They **are good** dancers. They **dance well**.*
> b   *Alex **is** a **good** soccer player. He **plays** soccer **well**.*

1   In each sentence, is *good* an adjective or an adverb? How do you know? Is *well* an adjective or an adverb? How do you know?

> c   *I don't feel **well**. Maybe I'm going to be sick tomorrow.*
> d   *I'm sorry that your sister was in the hospital. I hope she is **well** now.*

2   In each sentence, is *well* an adjective or an adverb? How do you know?

LEARN

▶ *Well* is an adjective <u>and</u> an adverb. The adjective *well* means *in good health*. The opposite is *bad* (not *badly*). Like other adjectives, the adjective *well* is used with *be, feel, look, seem,* etc. Like other adverbs, the adverb *well* gives information about verbs—how somebody or something <u>does</u> something. The opposite is *badly* (not *bad*). (See Unit 10 for more about adjectives.)

▶ It is common to use *not* + verb + *(very) well* instead of *badly*. The meaning is the same, but less strong, and for that reason, a little softer and more polite.

> *You speak Spanish **badly**.*
> = *You **don't** speak Spanish **well**.*
> *Your daughter sings **badly**.*
> = *Your daughter **doesn't** sing **very well**.*

Practice 7 Answer the questions. If the sentence is negative, write two possible answers.

Examples: Bob is a good football player. What can you say about him?

> He plays football well.

Sarah is a bad tennis player. What can you say about her?

> Sarah plays tennis badly.
> Sarah doesn't play tennis well.

1   Mary is a good driver. What can you say about her?

2   Carlos is a bad chess player. What can you say about him?

3   Tom and Jerry are good singers. What can you say about them?

4   Larry was a bad teacher. What can you say about him?

5   Some people think Sofia's a good dancer. What do they think about her?

6   We're bad writers. What can you say about us?

7 Jim was a good swimmer. What can you say about him?

8 Michael is a bad cook. What can you say about him?

16.7 ▶ *fast, hard* and *late*

DISCOVER

    *a I have a **fast** car. I drive **fast**.*

1 Is *fast* an adjective or an adverb? How do you know?

    *b Alex's homework is **hard**. Alex works **hard**.*

2 Is *hard* an adjective or an adverb? How do you know?

    *c I have a **late** class at the university. I get home **late** from my class.*

3 Is *late* an adjective or an adverb? How do you know?

LEARN

▶ *Fast, hard* and *late* are adjectives <u>and</u> adverbs. They have similar meanings whether they are adjectives or adverbs. In *b* and *c*, *lately* and *hardly* would <u>not</u> be correct. They have different meanings from *hard* and *late*. (See Section 16.8 for more about *lately* and *hardly*.)

    wrong → *Maria works **hardly**.*

    right → *Maria works **hard**.*

    wrong → *My son came home **lately** last night.*

    right → *My son came home **late** last night.*

Practice 8 Write *adj* after the sentence if the word in *italics* is an adjective. Write *adv* after the sentence if the word in italics is an adverb.

    Examples: I got to work *late* yesterday. ___*adv*___

                My boss is angry because I was *late* yesterday. ___*adj*___

1 If you work *fast*, you will make more mistakes. _____

2 That airplane is really *fast*. _____

3 I told my daughter not to come home *late* from the party. _____

4 My flight from Vienna was *late*. _____

5 This is *hard* work. _____

6 I'm tired because I stayed up *late* last night. _____

7 My idea sounds *hard*, but I think it will be easy. _____

8 I tried *hard* to finish my work today, but I couldn't. _____

9 I couldn't understand what Maria said because she always talks so *fast*. _____

16.8 ▶ *lately* and *hardly*

DISCOVER

    *a Sofia: Have you been to New York **lately**?*

    *b Mary: No, not **lately**.*

    *c John: Have you been to Boston **recently**?*

    *d Susan: No, not **recently**.*

1 Look at *b* and *d*. In these sentences, do *lately* and *recently* have the same meaning?

    e Tom: Did you understand what Larry said yesterday?

    *f Jerry: No, Larry's English is really bad. When he talked to me yesterday I **hardly understood** anything.*

    g Sam: Can you understand what Mark is saying?

    *h Lucy: No, this place is so noisy that I **can hardly hear** anything he's saying.*

2 Look at *f* and *h*. Is *hardly* before or after the main verbs (*understood* and *hear*)? Is *hardly* before or after *can*?

▶ adverbs, adverb clauses, adverb phrases and more, part 1

   i *John:* *Who came to your party?*

   j *Mary:* **Hardly anybody.** *I invited more than 100 people, but only 10 came.*

 3 Does *hardly anybody* mean the same as *almost nobody*?

   k *Larry:* *How often do you wear a suit and tie?*

   l *Sarah:* *I* **hardly ever** *wear a suit and tie—maybe once or twice a year.*

 4 Does *hardly ever* mean the same as *almost never*?

LEARN

▶ In present perfect and past perfect questions and negative sentences, *lately* is often used instead of *recently*. They have the same meaning.

  Have you seen Alex **lately**?

  = *Have you seen Alex* **recently**?

▶ *Hardly* is sometimes used with verbs and also with the modals *can* and *could* to mean *almost not*.

  I **hardly** *know Michael. I met him only one time.*

  Please turn up the volume. I **can hardly** *hear anything.*

▶ *Hardly* is sometimes used with *any, anyone, anybody, anything* and *anywhere*. The meaning is the same as *almost no, almost no one, almost nobody, almost nothing* and *almost nowhere*.

  He has **hardly any** *money.*

  = *He has* **almost no** *money.*

  I talked to **hardly anyone** *at the meeting.*

  = *I talked to* **almost no one** *at the meeting.*

  We ate **hardly anything** *at the party.*

  = *We ate* **almost nothing** *at the party.*

▶ *Hardly ever* has the same meaning as *almost never*.

  I **hardly ever** *watch TV.*

  = *I* **almost never** *watch TV.*

Practice 9 Complete the sentences using the words in parentheses and *hardly*.

 Example: My homework is very confusing. (understand) I _____*hardly understand*_____ anything.

 1 None of my friends is at this party. I (know) _____ anyone here.

 2 My mother's eyes are very bad. She (can, see) _____ anything without her glasses.

 3 Tom: John almost never drinks coffee.

   Sam: What did you say?

   Tom: I said that John (ever, drink) _____ coffee.

 4 I was very lazy yesterday. I (do) _____ anything all day except watch TV.

 5 I'm very tired this morning. I (could, sleep) _____ last night.

 6 My husband is useless. He (ever, get off) _____ the sofa.

 7 It's been 35 years since I studied French. I (remember) _____ anything.

 8 The music at the party was so loud that I (hear) _____ anything that anyone said.

 9 He is a very bad student. He (ever, do) _____ his homework.

Practice 10 Rewrite the sentences with *hardly*.

 Example: I have almost no money.

    I have hardly any money.

 1 Almost nobody goes there.

 2 Noura did almost nothing yesterday.

 3 I went almost nowhere last weekend.

 4 There's almost no time left.

5   Paul almost never calls his mother.

6   Almost nothing was done about the problem.

7   I talked to almost no one.

8   We almost never eat meat.

Continue to Unit 16/advanced ↓ or go to Unit 17 →

16.9/a ▶ adverb clauses about time with *be* reduced to adverb phrases
DISCOVER
      a   *While **we were studying**, we listened to music.*
      b   *While **studying**, we listened to music.*
1   How are *a* and *b* different? Do they have the same meaning?
      c   *I always listen to music when **I am exercising**.*
      d   *I always listen to music when **exercising**.*
2   How are *c* and *d* different? Do they have the same meaning?
      e   *While **he was in London**, he stayed with his sister.*
      f   *While **in London**, he stayed with his sister.*
3   How are *e* and *f* different? Do they have the same meaning?

LEARN
▶ Adverb clauses about time with *be* can be *reduced* (changed so they are shorter) to *adverb phrases*. This is possible only if the subject of main clause and the subject of the adverb clause are the same.
    *When **you**'re in Barcelona, will **you** visit your sister?*
    *= When in Barcelona, will **you** visit your sister?*

REMEMBER
▶ The subject of the main clause and the subject of the adverb clause must be the same. If they are not the same, the sentence will not make sense or will be misunderstood.
    right →   *He drove all night while **his wife** was sleeping in the back seat of his car.*
    wrong → *He drove all night while sleeping in the back seat of his car.*

▶ Sometimes *when* has the same meaning as *while*.
    *I always listen to the radio **while** driving.*
    *= I always listen to the radio **when** driving.*

Practice 11/a If it is possible, change the adverb clauses to adverb phrases.
Examples: When I am taking a shower, I like to sing.

         When taking a shower, I like to sing.

         I cooked dinner while Mary was taking a shower.

         not possible

1   I thought about the football game while I was listening to my wife.

2   While I was in college, I worked as a waiter.

3   When you are taking a bath, you should not use a hair dryer.

4   Larry read the newspaper while I was working in the garden.

5   You should never smoke when you are putting gas in your car.

6   While I am doing my homework, I like to listen to music.

7   While I was sitting in my English class, I thought about what to have for lunch.

8   Carlos washed his car while I was cutting the grass.

9   Ali had an accident while he was driving to work.

10   We always watch TV while we are eating dinner.

▶ adverbs, adverb clauses, adverb phrases and more, part 1   *169*

16.10/a ▶ adverb clauses about time with other verbs reduced to adverb phrases

DISCOVER

    a   *Before **I eat** dinner, I always wash my hands.*
    b   *Before **eating** dinner, I always wash my hands.*

1   How are *a* and *b* different? Do they have the same meaning?

    c   *Mary has been unhappy since **she lost** her job.*
    d   *Mary has been unhappy since **losing** her job.*

2   How are *c* and *d* different? Do they have the same meaning?

LEARN

▶ Adverb clauses about time with verbs other than *be* can also be reduced to adverb phrases. This is possible <u>only</u> if the subject of main clause and the subject of the adverb clause are the same.

    *After **I** graduated from college, **I** couldn't find a job.*
    = *After graduating from college, **I** couldn't find a job.*

REMEMBER

▶ The subject of the main clause and the subject of the adverb clause must be the same. If they are not the same, the sentence will not make sense or will be misunderstood.

    right →   ***Francesca** did her homework while **her brother** was swimming.*
    wrong → ***Francesca** did her homework while swimming.*

▶ What is the subject of this sentence?

    Before going to bed, lock the doors and windows.

The subject is *you*, but do you see *you*? No, you don't. Why? Because *lock the doors and windows* is *imperative*. That means it is a *command* or an *order*. The subject of an imperative sentence is always understood to be *you* even though *you* is not said.

    *Before **you go** to bed, **(you) lock** the doors and windows.*
    = *Before **you go** to bed, **lock** the doors and windows.*
    = *Before **going** to bed, **lock** the doors and windows.*

Practice 12/a If it is possible, change the adverb clauses to adverb phrases.

Examples: Since Maria got sick, she hasn't been able to work.

            Since getting sick, Maria hasn't been able to work.

            My brother has been helping me financially since I lost my job.

            not possible

1   Before you take the test, you ought to review.

2   When you drive, don't forget to wear your seat belt.

3   My brother has slept on the sofa since his wife had a baby.

4   I lived in New Zealand before I moved to Australia.

5   Since Maria got married, she has gained 20 kilograms.

6   You should always think twice before you send an angry email.

7   Since I went to Peru, I have been interested in South America.

8   Before my mother visited, I cleaned the house.

9   You have to take the plastic off before you put it in the microwave.

10 While I studied in the library, Michael finished his project in the lab.

16.11/a ▶ adverb clauses about time with *after*

DISCOVER

    a   *After **you have finished** your homework, you can go out with your friends.*
    b   *After **finishing** your homework, you can go out with your friends.*
    c   *After **having finished** your homework, you can go out with your friends.*

1   How are *a*, *b* and *c* different? Do they have the same meaning?

d   Mark finally saw the doctor after **he had waited** for two hours.

e   Mark finally saw the doctor after **waiting** for two hours.

f   Mark finally saw the doctor after **having waited** for two hours.

2   How are *d, e* and *f* different? Do they have the same meaning?

LEARN

▶ Present perfect and past perfect adverb clauses about time with *after* can be reduced to adverb phrases in two ways: with a gerund (for example, *waiting*) or with a present perfect gerund (for example, *having waited*). This is possible <u>only</u> if the subject of main clause and the subject of the adverb clause are the same. (See Unit 18 and Unit 19 for information about gerunds.)

After **he** has spoken to his lawyer, **he** will speak to the reporters.

= After speaking to his lawyer, **he** will speak to the reporters.

= After having spoken to his lawyer, **he** will speak to the reporters.

REMEMBER

▶ The present perfect gerund form in *c* and *f* above is more formal and less common than the form in *b* and *e*.

▶ The subject of the main clause and the subject of the adverb clause must be the same. If they are not the same, the sentence will not make sense or will be misunderstood.

right →   After **my children** had gone to school, **I** took a bath.

wrong → After *going to school,* **I** took a bath.

wrong → After *having gone to school,* **I** took a bath.

Practice 13/a If it is possible, change the adverb clauses to adverb phrases. Write both possible forms.

Examples: You can leave after you have done your work.

You can leave after doing your work.

You can leave after having done your work.

After Michael had died, I was very sad.

not possible

1   After you've been married as long as I have, you'll understand what I'm saying.

2   After Alex had eaten seven hot dogs, he got sick.

3   My father got angry after I had failed math.

4   Sarah will graduate after she's taken her exams.

5   After we had lived there for two years, we finally met our neighbors.

6   After John had been sick for several weeks, he died.

7   The ambulance came after somebody called 911.

8   I finally went home after I'd waited for Maria for one hour.

16.12/a ▶ adverb clauses about reasons reduced to adverb phrases

DISCOVER

a   Because **I worked** all day, I was able to finish my report.

▶ adverbs, adverb clauses, adverb phrases and more, part 1

    b   ***Working*** *all day, I was able to finish my book report.*

1   How are *a* and *b* different? Do they have the same meaning?

    c   *Because **we don't live** near a big city, we go shopping only once a month.*
    d   ***Not living*** *near a big city, we go shopping only once a month.*

2   How are *c* and *d* different? Do they have the same meaning?

    e   *Because **I am** sick, I'm going to stay home tomorrow.*
    f   ***Being*** *sick, I'm going to stay home tomorrow.*

3   How are *e* and *f* different? Do they have the same meaning?

    g   *Because **Maria isn't** a citizen of this country, she cannot get a job here.*
    h   ***Not being*** *a citizen of this country, Maria cannot get a job here.*

4   How are *g* and *h* different? Do they have the same meaning? Why is it necessary to change *she* in *g* to *Maria* in *h*?

    i   *Because **I have lived** in this city all my life, I never get lost when I am driving.*
    j   ***Having lived*** *in this city all my life, I never get lost when I am driving.*

5   How are *i* and *j* different? Do they have the same meaning?

    k   *Because **Carlos had not studied** for the test, he failed it.*
    l   ***Not having studied*** *for the test, Carlos failed it.*

6   How are *k* and *l* different? Do they have the same meaning? Why is it necessary to change *he* in *k* to *Carlos* in *l*?

    m   *Because **Alex had never traveled** outside the USA, he didn't have a passport.*
    n   ***Never having traveled*** *outside the USA, Alex didn't have a passport.*
    o   ***Not having traveled*** *outside the USA before, Alex didn't have a passport.*

7   How are *m*, *n* and *o* different? Do they have the same meaning? Why is it necessary to change *he* in *m* to *Alex* in *n* and *o*?

LEARN

▶ Adverb clauses about reasons can be reduced to adverb phrases. This is possible <u>only</u> if the subject of main clause and the subject of the adverb clause are the same.

    *Because **Larry** had studied Arabic in college, **he** understood what Noura and Ali were talking about.*
    *= Having studied Arabic in college, **Larry** understood what Noura and Ali were talking about.*

REMEMBER

▶ The subject of the main clause and the subject of the adverb clause must be the same. If they are not the same, the sentence will not make sense or will be misunderstood.

    right →   *Because **a dog** had bitten her leg, **she** had to go to the hospital.*
    wrong → *Having bitten her leg, **she** had to go to the hospital.*

▶ Adverb clauses about reasons usually begin with *because*, but *since* and *as* can also have the same meaning.

    Because *I didn't have any cash, I had to use my credit card.*
    *= **Since** I didn't have any cash, I had to use my credit card.*
    *= **As** I didn't have any cash, I had to use my credit card.*
    = Not having any cash, I had to use my credit card.

Practice 14/a Change the adverb clauses to adverb phrases.

Examples: Because I know what John thinks, I wasn't surprised by what he said.

         Knowing what John thinks, I wasn't surprised by what he said.

         Since I didn't know the answer, I guessed.

         Not knowing the answer, I guessed.

1   Because Sarah didn't know who the man was, she didn't unlock the door.

2   Because I didn't want my wife to be angry, I didn't tell her what happened.

3   Since you lack experience, it will be difficult for you to get a job.

4   Because Carlos speaks Spanish, he understood everything Maria said.

5   As I didn't have a car, I had to walk to work every day.

6   Since Mary and John have eight children, they need a larger house.

7   Because I live 50 miles from where I work, I have to leave at 5:00 in the morning to get to work on time.

Practice 15/a Change the adverb clauses to adverb phrases.

Examples: Because Mary is very tall, she doesn't like to wear high heels.

Being very tall, Mary doesn't like to wear high heels.

Since I wasn't hungry, I didn't eat anything.

Not being hungry, I didn't eat anything.

1   Since I'm overweight, it's hard to find clothes that fit.

2   Because he was on a diet, he didn't want a piece of cake.

3   As I'm not a smoker, I don't have any ashtrays in my house.

4   Since you are pregnant, you don't have to wait in line with the other people.

5   Because Carl is an English teacher, he works long hours for low pay.

6   Since he isn't a member of the club, he can't come in.

7   Because I'm from Canada, I'm used to cold weather.

8   Since I'm not married and don't have children, I don't need a big house.

Practice 16/a Change the adverb clauses to adverb phrases.

Examples: Because Carlos had grown up in Mexico, he could speak Spanish perfectly.

Having grown up in Mexico, Carlos could speak Spanish perfectly.

Because I had never been to England before, I was very excited about going to London.

Never having been to England before, I was very excited about going to London.

1   Because I've been to Italy many times before, I decided to go somewhere else for my vacation.

2   Because Michael had broken his leg, he had to cancel his trip to Puerto Rico.

3   Since Sofia has been lied to before, she's very careful about trusting people.

4   Since I've never been to Los Angeles, I'm really looking forward to going there next week.

5   Because I had had dinner only an hour earlier, I didn't want to go out for dinner with my friends.

6   Since I'd already seen that movie, I didn't want to see it again.

7   Because Francesca had never been to Egypt, she didn't know what to expect.

8   As I have had that disease before, I cannot get it again.

Unit 17 ▶ adverbs, adverb clauses, adverb phrases and more, part 2

17.1 ▶ coordinating conjunctions

DISCOVER

  a   *I went to the store, **and** I bought some eggs and milk.*
  b   *Alex looked for his lost keys, **but** he didn't find them.*
  c   *I might go to London, **or** I might go to Paris.*
  d   *Carlos has not read this book, **nor** does he want to.*
  e   *I couldn't unlock the door, **for** I had forgotten my key.*
  f   *She was lost, **so** she looked at a map.*
  g   *Ali studied hard for the test, **yet** his score was very low.*

1   What do the words in **bold** tell you about the relationship of the two clauses that they connect? Can you *paraphrase* (say the same information in different words) the sentences?

LEARN

▶ *And, but, or, nor, for, so* and *yet* are *coordinating conjunctions*. That means that they can connect independent clauses. They tell you something about how the clauses are related to each other.

▶ When coordinating conjunctions connect independent clauses, a comma must be used after the first clause. However, when the subject of both clauses is the same, it is not necessary to repeat the subject. When the subject is not repeated, no comma is necessary.
  ***Larry** called Mary, and **he** invited her to his party.*
  *= **Larry** called Mary and invited her to his party.*

When a verb is repeated in the second clause, the modal verb is sometimes canceled in addition to the subject.
  ***Larry will** call Mary, and **he will** invite her to his party.*
  *= **Larry will** call Mary and **will** invite her to his party.*
  *= **Larry will** call Mary and invite her to his party.*

▶ *Nor* connects two negative independent clauses.
  *Carlos **has not** read this book. **He does not** want to.*
  *= Carlos **has not** read this book, **nor does he** want to.*

It is common to use ellipsis with *nor*.
  *The students **won't** stop talking, **nor [will they]** start working.*

▶ *Yet* has the same meaning as *but*, but it is much less common.

REMEMBER

▶ In modern English, it is not common to use *for* as a coordinating conjunction.
▶ Notice the grammar of sentences with *nor*.
  *Rosa was not working. **Sofia was not** working.*
  *= Rosa was not working, **nor was Sofia**.*

  *Lucy doesn't have a car. **Sam does not** have a car.*
  *= Lucy doesn't have a car, **nor does Sam**.*

  *Alex will not help me. **Carlos will not** help me.*
  *= Alex will not help me, **nor will Carlos**.*

Practice 1 Use *and, but, or, nor* or *so* to complete the sentences.

Example: I don't like cold weather, _____*so*_____ I moved from Toronto to Miami.

1   We can eat dinner at home, _____ we can go to a restaurant.

2   I don't want to talk to him, _____ do I want to see him.

3   Maria did her math homework before she left school, _____ she doesn't need to do it after dinner.

4   He's been studying English for many years, _____ he can hardly speak any English at all.

5   Rosa graduated from college in June, _____ she got a good job right away.

6   We might get married in June, _____ we might get married in July.

7   I wanted to lose 10 kilograms before my high school reunion, _____ I lost only 3 kilograms.

8   Noura didn't have any money, _____ I lent her $100.

Practice 2 If it is possible, rewrite the sentence as in the example. Be careful about punctuation.

Examples: I went to the store, but I didn't buy anything.

   I went to the store but didn't buy anything.

   Alex walked to the beach, but his sister rode her bicycle there.

   not possible

1   John asked me a question, but I didn't know the answer.

2   Francesca opened her book, and she began to read.

3   We can have spaghetti for dinner, or we can go to a restaurant.

4   Mark promised to help me fix my car, but he forgot all about it.

5   I explained everything to the police, and they believed me.

6   My brother doesn't have a car, but he'll buy one soon.

7   Sarah could do it tomorrow, or I could do it now.

8   I can speak Arabic, but I can't read or write it.

17.2 ▶ connecting sentences with *and* and *but*

DISCOVER

   a   Mary *is* late, and John *is too*.
   b   Sam *won't* come to the party, but I *will*.
   c   Ali *doesn't* drink coffee, and Noura *doesn't either*.
   d   Mark *hasn't* seen that movie, and *neither has* Alex.
   e   Carlos went to the beach, but Rosa *didn't*.

1   In *a, b, c* and *d*, what is repeated in both clauses?
2   How is *e* different from the other examples?

LEARN (See Table 17a.)

▶ Sentences with equal meanings can be combined with *and*, and sentences with opposite meanings can be combined with *but*. Be or a modal verb is repeated in the second clause, but a main verb is usually not repeated.
   Francesca *was* sick, and Carlos *was* too.
   I *can* speak French, but Sarah *can't*.

When there is no form of *be* or a modal verb in the first clause, a form of *do* is used in the second clause.
   The children watched the movie, but we *didn't*.

REMEMBER

▶ When a modal is used with *be*, it is common, but not necessary, to repeat *be*.
   I *won't be* in class tomorrow, but Alex *will*.
   = I *won't be* in class tomorrow, but Alex *will be*.

▶ Questions and negative sentences with the main verb *have* can be formed in two ways.
   modern →   Tom: *Do* you *have* a pen?
                  Lucy: I *don't have* a pen, but Sam *does*.

   old-fashioned → Tom: *Have* you a pen?
                       Lucy: I *haven't* a pen, but Sam *has*.

Both ways to use *have* are correct, but most native speakers today use the modern way.

Practice 3 Complete the sentences. If the verb in the sentence is *have*, use the modern way. If there are two possible answers, write both answers.

Examples: He won't help her, but (I) _____ *I will* _____.

   Mary has a book, and (Tom) _____ *Tom does too / so does Tom* _____.

▶ **adverbs, adverb clauses, adverb phrases and more, part 2**   **175**

	combining sentences with *and* and *but*		
sentences with *be*	**−** Paul **isn't** hungry, **+** Paul **is** hungry, **+** Paul **is** hungry, Paul **is** hungry, **−** Paul **isn't** hungry, Paul **isn't** hungry,	but but and and and and	**+** Lucy **is**. **−** Lucy **isn't**. **+** Lucy **is** too. so **is** Lucy. **−** Lucy **isn't** either. neither **is** Lucy.
sentences with modal verbs	**−** Paul **can't** swim, **+** Paul **can** swim, **+** Paul **can** swim, Paul **can** swim, **−** Paul **can't** swim, Paul **can't** swim,	but but and and and and	**+** Lucy **can**. **−** Lucy **can't**. **+** Lucy **can** too. so **can** Lucy. **−** Lucy **can't** either. neither **can** Lucy.
sentences with main verbs only and no modal verb	**−** Paul **doesn't** speak English, **+** Paul speaks English, **+** Paul speaks English, Paul speaks English, **−** Paul **doesn't** speak English, Paul **doesn't** speak English,	but but and and and and	**+** Lucy **does**. **−** Lucy **doesn't**. **+** Lucy **does** too. so **does** Lucy. **−** Lucy **doesn't** either. neither **does** Lucy.
sentences with the main verb *have* (The <u>underlined</u> forms are old-fashioned and less common.)	**−** Paul **doesn't** have/**<u>hasn't</u>** a car, **+** Paul has a car, **+** Paul has a car, Paul has a car, **−** Paul **doesn't** have/**<u>hasn't</u>** a car, Paul **doesn't** have/**<u>hasn't</u>** a car,	but but and and and and	**+** Lucy **does**/**<u>has</u>**. **−** Lucy **doesn't**/**<u>hasn't</u>**. **+** Lucy **does**/**<u>has</u>** too. so **does**/**<u>has</u>** Lucy. **−** Lucy **doesn't**/**<u>hasn't</u>** either. neither **does**/**<u>has</u>** Lucy.
sentences with present perfect verbs	**−** Paul **hasn't** eaten, **+** Paul **has** eaten, **+** Paul **has** eaten, Paul **has** eaten, **−** Paul **hasn't** eaten, Paul **hasn't** eaten,	but but and and and and	**+** Lucy **has**. **−** Lucy **hasn't**. **+** Lucy **has** too. so **has** Lucy. **−** Lucy **hasn't** either. neither **has** Lucy.

1   Rosa went to the mall, and (John) _____.

2   Carlos doesn't know the answer, but (Alex) _____.

3   We're going to watch TV, and (they) _____.

4   Michael should study harder, and (you) _____.

5   I'm not happy, and (Mark) _____.

6   Larry can't speak French, and (I) _____.

7   Sam didn't have any money, and (Sarah) _____.

8   The children have gone to bed, and (their parents) _____.

9   We have air conditioning, but (they) _____.

10 Noura had gone camping many times, but (Linda) _____.

11 My father would say yes, but (my mother) _____.

12 Bill has a cat, and (his brother) _____.

13 Bill doesn't want to eat, and (I) _____.

14 Rosa hasn't gotten here yet, and (her friends) _____.

Practice 4 Complete the conversations with answers which agree with the question. If the verb in the sentence is *have*, use the modern way. Write both possible answers.

Examples: A: John didn't do his homework. Did you?

              B1: — *I didn't either.*

              B2: — *Neither did I.*

              A: Francesca can type. What about Michael?

              B1: + *He can too.*

              B2: + *So can he.*

1   A: Lucy was in the lab. Was Maria?

    B1: +

    B2: +

2   A: Noura would like to leave work early. How about you?

    B1: +

    B2: +

3   A: Mark doesn't work on Saturday. Does his wife?

    B1: —

    B2: —

4   A: Alex doesn't have a soccer ball. What about his friends?

    B1: —

    B2: —

5   A: I've already been to that restaurant. How about you?

    B1: +

    B2: +

6   A: The children aren't going to the carnival. What about Larry?

    B1: —

    B2: —

7   A: I couldn't sleep last night. Could you?

    B1: +

    B2: +

8   A: Rosa doesn't speak Russian. Does Carlos?

    B1: +

    B2: +

9   A: She has red hair. Does her sister?

    B1: +

    B2: +

10 A: I haven't eaten lunch yet. What about you?

    B1: −

    B2: −

17.3 ▶ conjunctive adverbs

DISCOVER

 a *My daughter didn't study for the final exam. **Therefore**, she failed.*
 b *After dinner, my husband will wash the dishes. **Meanwhile**, I'll help the children with their homework.*
 c *I don't like going to the beach, and I don't want to go. **Furthermore**, it's too cold to go the beach today.*
 d *I was supposed to go to work today. **However**, I told my boss I was sick and went to a baseball game.*

1 What do the **bold** words in *a, b, c* and *d* tell you about the relationship of the two independent clauses that they connect? Can you paraphrase the sentences?

LEARN

▶ *Conjunctive adverbs* show a relationship between two independent clauses.

▶ Conjunctive adverbs can be used to talk about the reason for something—that something is the reason, or cause, of something else.

 as a result (= *because of that*)
  *I hurt my ankle. **As a result**, I cannot play basketball for two months.*

 consequently (= *because of that* Consequently is usually used to talk about negative results.)
  *Jack cheated on the test. **Consequently**, he was expelled from college.*

 therefore (= *because of that*)
  *I forgot to pay my telephone bill. **Therefore**, my telephone was disconnected.*

 thus (= *because of that* Thus is very formal and more common in writing than in speaking.)
  *The bank manager stole money from the bank. **Thus**, she lost her job and went to jail.*

▶ Conjunctive adverbs can be used to talk about the time relationship between two things—something happened before, at the same time or after something else.

 in the meantime (= *at the same time*)
  *You call 911. **In the meantime**, I'll try to help the injured driver.*

 meanwhile (= *at the same time*)
  *My wife will clean the kitchen. **Meanwhile**, I will do the laundry.*

 subsequently (= *later*)
  *At first, the police believed that the man had been killed in an accident. **Subsequently**, they learned that he had been murdered.*

▶ Conjunctive adverbs can be used to talk about things that happen in a different place.

 elsewhere (= *in another place/= in other places*)
  *This part of the city is very safe. **Elsewhere**, that's not true.*

▶ Conjunctive adverbs can be used to help explain how we feel about something.

 after all (= *you need to understand/= the truth is*)
  *I was very upset when my dog died. **After all**, he was my only friend.*

▶ Conjunctive adverbs can be used to help explain something.

in other words (*In other words* introduces simpler language that helps to explain what was said before.)

*Jack has difficulty telling the truth. **In other words**, he's a liar.*

▶ Conjunctive adverbs can be used to give additional information that supports (makes stronger) what was just said.

besides (= *also*)

*I don't want to go to that restaurant. Their food is terrible and **besides**, I'm not hungry.*

furthermore (= *also*)

*We don't have time to take a vacation. **Furthermore**, we need to save money.*

in addition (= *also*)

*John works 60 hours a week at his job. **In addition**, he works at a second job on the weekend.*

moreover (= *also*)

*That hotel is too expensive. **Moreover**, it's too far away from everything that we want to see.*

▶ Conjunctive adverbs can be used to give additional information that does not support (makes weaker) something that was just said.

on the contrary (= *the opposite is true*)

*I wasn't upset when he didn't like my plan. **On the contrary**, I was glad to get his advice about how to improve it.*

▶ Conjunctive adverbs can be used to give additional information that is opposite or different from what people expect.

however (= *even though that is true*)

*I eat only salads, and I run five kilometers every day. **However**, I cannot lose weight.*

nevertheless (= *even though that is true*)

*Michael is not a good teacher. **Nevertheless**, he is very popular with his students.*

nonetheless (= *even though that is true* *Nevertheless* is more common than *nonetheless*.)

*The city hired 1,000 new police officers to fight crime last year. **Nonetheless**, crime is worse than before.*

on the other hand (= *but it is true that*)

*I can't afford to buy a new computer. **On the other hand**, I really would like to have a new one.*

▶ Conjunctive adverbs can be used to predict a different result.

otherwise (= *if this is not done/*= *if this does not happen*)

*You need to buy your ticket before Friday. **Otherwise**, the price will go up.*

REMEMBER

▶ In modern English, the most common way to punctuate the sentence which comes before a sentence which begins with a conjunctive adverb is with a period. Notice that the conjunctive adverb begins with a capital letter.

*My cell phone battery was dead. **T**herefore, I couldn't call you.*

However, some people prefer to use a semi-colon (;). Notice that the conjunctive adverb begins with a small letter.

*My cell phone battery was dead; **t**herefore, I couldn't call you.*

Both ways are correct.

Practice 5 Underline the best conjunctive adverb to finish the sentences.

Example: I don't want to go to the party. I'm tired. (Consequently / <u>Besides</u> / Nonetheless), Jack is going to be there, and I don't want to see him.

1 I looked everywhere for my lost keys. (Therefore / After all / However), I didn't find them.

2 It's 8:40 already? I need to be at work at 9:00. I have to leave now. (Meanwhile / Furthermore / Otherwise), I'll be late.

3 My wife wants to live in a small town. (In other words / On the other hand / Nevertheless), I want to live in a big city.

4 Linda loves to play tennis. (Subsequently / In addition / On the contrary), she also likes to play basketball and baseball.

5 The tornado destroyed the west side of town. (Elsewhere / Moreover / Nevertheless), there was very little damage.

6 I wasn't surprised when my son changed jobs. (Therefore / After all / Furthermore), the salary at his new job will be much higher than the salary at his old job.

7 Smoking is bad for your health. (Furthermore / However / Otherwise), cigarettes are expensive.

8 My car's at the mechanic. (After all / In the meantime / On the other hand), I have to take the bus to work until my car is fixed.

9 The airplane had mechanical problems. (Therefore / Nevertheless / Furthermore), it was able to land safely.

10   We need to leave for the cinema now. (Thus / Furthermore / Otherwise), we might miss the beginning of the movie.

17.4 ▶ other conjunctive adverb sentence patterns: *be* and other verbs

DISCOVER
    a   *Switzerland is a wonderful place to live.* **However**, *it is very expensive.*
    b   *Switzerland is a wonderful place to live. It is,* **however**, *very expensive.*
    c   *Switzerland is a wonderful place to live. It is very expensive,* **however**.
    d   *I don't want to live in Los Angeles.* **On the other hand**, *I would like to live in San Francisco.*
    e   *I don't want to live in Los Angeles. I would,* **on the other hand**, *like to live in San Francisco.*
    f   *I don't want to live in Los Angeles. I would like to live in San Francisco,* **on the other hand**.
1   Look at *b* and *c*. Look at *e* and *f*. Do conjunctive adverbs always begin a sentence?

LEARN
▶ Conjunctive adverbs do not always begin a sentence. It is common to put them in the middle and sometimes at the end of a sentence. When they are in the middle of a sentence, they usually go after *be* (as in *b*) and before other verbs (as in *e*).

Practice 6 Rewrite the second sentences with the conjunctive adverb in the middle and at the end of the sentence.
  Examples: I don't think your plan is a good idea. In other words, the answer is no.

       The answer, in other words, is no.
       The answer is no, in other words.

       Your office is having new carpeting put in. Meanwhile, you can use my office.

       You can, meanwhile, use my office.
       You can use my office, meanwhile.

1   Ali couldn't play in the game because he was injured. Nevertheless, he was happy that his team won the game.

2   You won't need sunscreen when you go to England. However, you will need an umbrella.

3   I guess I'll accept John's offer of $10,000 to buy my car. After all, it is the only offer I've gotten.

4   We cannot sell our house. Therefore, we are probably going to rent it.

5   Our new house was very expensive. On the other hand, it is a lot bigger than our old house.

6   Larry failed two of his final exams. Consequently, he was not able to graduate with the other students.

17.5 ▶ expressing reason with *such (that)* and *so (that)*

DISCOVER
    a   *I was sick,* **so** *I went to the doctor.*
    b   *I was sick.* **Therefore**, *I went to the doctor.*
    c   **Because** *I was sick, I went to the doctor.*
    d   *I was* **so** *sick* **(that)** *I went to the doctor.*
1   Do *a*, *b*, *c* and *d* have the same meaning?
2   Look at *d*. What kind of word is *sick*? Is it an adjective?
    e   *The computer was expensive,* **so** *I didn't buy it.*
    f   *The computer was expensive.* **Therefore**, *I didn't buy it.*
    g   **Because** *it was* **such** *an expensive computer, I didn't buy it.*
    h   *It was* **such** *an expensive computer* **(that)** *I didn't buy it.*

3   Do e, f, g and h have the same meaning?

4   Look at g and h. What kind of words are *an expensive computer*? Are they a noun phrase?

    *i   Carlos talks softly, **so** I can't understand him sometimes.*

    *j   Carlos talks softly. **Therefore**, I can't understand him sometimes.*

    *k   **Because** Carlos talks softly, I can't understand him sometimes.*

    *l   Carlos talks **so** softly **(that)** I can't understand him sometimes.*

5   Look at *i, j, k* and *l*. Do they have the same meaning?

6   Look at *k* and *l*. What kind of word is *softly*? Is it an adverb?

LEARN

▶ *So (that)* or *such (that)* are used to talk about reasons.

▶ *So (that)* is used with adjectives.

    *This box is **so** heavy **(that)** I cannot lift it.*

▶ *Such (that)* is used with nouns and nouns modified by adjectives.

    *The information was **such** a surprise **(that)** I didn't know what to say.*

    *This is **such** a big piece of cake **(that)** I cannot finish it.*

▶ *So (that)* is used with adverbs.

    *Bill drives **so** fast **(that)** I'm afraid to drive with him.*

REMEMBER

▶ In informal speech and writing, it is common to cancel *that*.

    *This coffee is **so** hot **that** I can't drink it.*

    *= This coffee is **so** hot I can't drink it.*

▶ It is correct but not common to use the adjective *much* in this way.

    not common → *I have **much** work to do.*   **common** → *I have **a lot of** work to do.*

▶ It is common to use *much* with *so (that)*.

    *I have **so much** work to do, **that** I will need a week to finish it all.*

Practice 7 **Write sentences using either** *so (that)* **or** *such (that)*. **Do not cancel** *that*.

Examples: This math problem is difficult. I can't figure it out.

    This math problem is so difficult that I can't figure it out.

    It's a long book. It will take a month to finish it.

    It's such a long book that it will take a month to finish it.

    Maria sings well. She could be a professional singer.

    Maria sings so well that she could be a professional singer.

1   It was a boring movie. I couldn't stay awake.

2   We have little time. We might get there too late.

3   He writes quickly. He finished his book in only two months.

4   I was very sick. I had to go to the hospital.

5   John has many problems. He doesn't know what to do.

6   It was a funny joke. I couldn't stop laughing.

7   Sarah paints well. People pay a lot of money for her paintings.

8   I have a bad headache. I'm going to lie down.

9   There are few students in our school. It might be closed.

10   My grandfather has many grandchildren. He can't remember their names.

11   It's a difficult problem. We may never solve it.

12   We were careful. I'm sure we didn't make any mistakes.

17.6/a ▶ correlative conjunctions

DISCOVER

　　a　He ate **not only** <u>three pieces of cake</u> **but** <u>four pieces of pie</u>.

　　b　I can **neither** <u>read</u> **nor** <u>write</u> German.

　　c　**Either** <u>I get a raise in salary</u> **or** <u>I quit my job</u>.

　　d　**Both** <u>my mother</u> **and** <u>my father</u> are doctors.

　　e　I would **rather** <u>go to the party</u> **than** <u>go to the library</u>.

　　f　I can't decide **whether** <u>to go on vacation</u> **or** <u>(to) stay home</u> and save money.

1　Which sentence is about what somebody prefers to do?

2　Which sentence is about two possibilities, but only one can happen?

3　Which sentence is about two negative things?

4　Which sentence is about one thing that will happen only if another thing happens?

5　Which sentence is about one thing that is a surprise and another thing that is even more of a surprise?

6　Which sentence is about two things that are the same?

7　What do you notice about the two groups of underlined words in each sentence? Are they the same (each is a noun, each is a verb, each is an independent clauses, etc.)?

LEARN

▶ *Correlative conjunctions* are pairs of words that work together to show a relationship between two words, phrases or clauses (or two groups of words, phrases or clauses). The words, phrases and clauses must be equal—each is a noun, each is a verb, each is an adjective, each is a prepositional phrases, etc.

not only/but

This correlative conjunction is similar to *in addition*—one piece of interesting or surprising information is given, and then another piece of information that is more interesting or more surprising is given. It is used in a number of ways, and there are many variations. It is common but not necessary to use *also, too, as well* and *either* with *not only/but*. Sometimes *but* is canceled. Sometimes grammar similar to question grammar is used. These variations are shown in the examples below. <u>Words in parentheses are optional and are shown as examples.</u> Remember that *too* and *as well* have the same meaning when they are at the end of a sentence.

subjects

Not only <u>the police</u> **but (also)** <u>the fire department</u> came when I called 911.

objects

She cooked **not only** <u>breakfast</u> **but** <u>lunch and dinner</u> **(too)**.

Not only did she cook <u>breakfast</u> **but (also)** <u>lunch and dinner</u>.

verbs

I **not only** <u>saw a ghost</u> **but** <u>took a picture of it</u>.

Not only did I <u>see a ghost</u> **but** <u>took a picture of it</u>.

nouns

Mark is **not only** <u>a doctor</u> **but (also)** <u>a lawyer</u>.

Not only is Mark <u>a doctor</u> **but** <u>a lawyer</u> **(as well)**.

adjectives

Jack is **not only** <u>lazy</u> **but** <u>crazy</u> **(too)**.

Not only is Jack <u>lazy</u> **but** <u>crazy</u>.

adverbs

You should drive **not only** <u>slowly</u> **but (also)** <u>carefully</u>.

Not only should you drive <u>slowly</u> **but** <u>carefully</u> **(as well)**.

prepositional phrases

I looked for my lost keys **not only** <u>in the bedroom</u> **but** <u>under the desk</u> and <u>behind the sofa</u>.

Not only did I look for my lost keys <u>in the bedroom</u> **but (also)** <u>under the desk</u> and <u>behind the sofa</u>.

independent clauses

<u>I</u> **not only** <u>don't have a TV</u>, **but** <u>I don't have a radio</u> **(either)**.

<u>Mary</u> **not only** <u>has have five cats</u>, **but** <u>she has seven dogs</u> **(too)**.

Not only <u>does Mary have five cats</u>, **but** <u>she</u> **(also)** <u>has seven dogs</u>.

Notice the punctuation in the independent clause examples. A comma is necessary only with independent clauses. Because the verb is the same in both clauses (*have*), it would also be possible to write this sentence as a single independent clause with two objects (and no comma).

> <u>Mary</u> **not only** <u>has five cats</u> **but** <u>seven dogs</u> **(too)**.
> **Not only** <u>does Mary have five cats</u> **but (also)** <u>seven dogs</u>.

When two independent clause are joined with *not only/but,* it is common to cancel *but* and use a semi-colon.

> <u>Mary</u> **not only** <u>has five cats</u>; <u>she</u> **(also)** <u>has seven dogs</u>.
> **Not only** <u>does Mary have five cats</u>; <u>she</u> **(also)** <u>has seven dogs</u>.

Sometimes, when the first item of information has already been stated in a separate independent clause, it is replaced with *that* in a second independent clause.

> *Carlos* <u>lived in Korea for many years</u>. **Not only** <u>that</u>, <u>he</u> **(also)** <u>married a Korean woman</u>.

Practice 8/a Use *not only/but* (or one of the variations) to write sentences with the same meaning. There is more than one good answer for each.

Examples: Michael saw the president. He shook his hand.

> Not only did Michael see the president, but he also shook his hand.

> The bus was late. It was full.

> Not only was the bus late, it was also full.

1   Francesca is beautiful. She is very intelligent.

2   Mark doesn't have a car. He doesn't know how to drive.

3   Sofia is a good singer. She's a really good dancer.

4   I went to China last year. I went to Mongolia last year.

5   The book was good. The movie was fantastic.

6   He bought 10 kilos of tomatoes. He bought 20 kilos of potatoes.

7   Alex washed the dishes. He cleaned the bathroom and did the laundry.

8   They will probably lose the battle. They might lose the war.

9   We had to sell our car. We had to sell our house.

10   It's more expensive. It's not as good.

LEARN

neither/nor

Neither/nor is used to connect two negative pieces of information. When *neither/nor* is used to join two subjects, the verb agrees with the subject directly before *nor.*

> **wrong** → *Neither* <u>my sister</u> *nor* <u>my brother</u> **have** *children.*
> **right** → *Neither* <u>my sister</u> *nor* <u>my brother</u> **has** *children.*

subjects
> **Neither** <u>my grandmother</u> **nor** <u>my grandfather</u> *is alive.*

objects
> *I have* **neither** <u>the time</u> **nor** <u>the right tools</u> *to fix your car.*

verbs
> *I* **neither** <u>know</u> **nor** <u>care</u> *what he thinks.*

nouns
> *Jack is* **neither** <u>a good man</u> **nor** <u>an honest man</u>.

adjectives
> *He is* **neither** <u>rich</u> **nor** <u>handsome</u>.

adverbs
> *Michael works* **neither** <u>hard</u> **nor** <u>well</u>.

prepositional phrases
> *My cell phone is* **neither** <u>in my pocket</u> **nor** <u>on my desk</u>.

independent clauses

*I will **neither** <u>write to him</u>, **nor** <u>will I speak to him</u>.*

Practice 9/a Use *neither/nor* to write sentences with the same meaning. There may be more than one good answer for some.

Example: I don't have the time to do it. I don't have the desire to do it.

I have neither the time nor the desire to do it.

1   The movie wasn't funny. It wasn't interesting.

2   He cannot see. He cannot speak.

3   I would not eat them in a box. I would not eat them with a fox.

4   Larry wasn't a good singer. He wasn't a good dancer.

5   Mark doesn't like to exercise. Mark doesn't want to exercise.

6   My brother doesn't have a job. My sister doesn't have a job.

7   I didn't see Tom last night. I didn't see his brother last night.

8   My computer isn't working. Mary's computer isn't working.

LEARN

either/or

Either/or is used to connect two pieces of information which are options—only one is possible. When *either/or* is used to join two subjects, the verb agrees with the subject directly before *or*.

wrong → ***Either*** <u>Tom</u> ***or*** <u>Ali</u> **are** *going to do it.*

right →   ***Either*** <u>Tom</u> ***or*** <u>Ali</u> **is** *going to do it.*

subjects

Either <u>Mary</u> ***or*** <u>John</u> *will be the new manager.*

objects

*You can have **either** <u>coffee</u> **or** <u>tea</u>.*

verbs

*I'll **either** <u>fix my old car</u> **or** <u>buy a new one</u>.*

nouns

*All of the people at the party were **either** <u>doctors</u> **or** <u>nurses</u>.*

adjectives

*Seven students in my class were **either** <u>late</u> **or** <u>absent</u> today.*

adverbs

*You can do it **either** <u>quickly</u> **or** <u>carefully</u> but not both.*

prepositional phrases

*I'm going to hang this picture **either** <u>next to the window</u> **or** <u>over the sofa</u>.*

independent clauses

Either <u>stop making so much noise</u>, ***or*** <u>I will call the police</u>!

Practice 10/a Use *either/or* to write sentences with the same meaning. There may be more than one good answer for some.

Example: I should call my mother. I should write to my mother.

I should either call or write to my mother.

1   I'm going to stay home today. I'm going to go to the beach today.

2   John will give me a ride downtown. Mary will give me a ride downtown.

3   You can have beef. You can have chicken.

4   The children can play outside. The children can play upstairs.

5   We will play tennis. We will go swimming.

6   This table is made of pine. This table is made of oak.

7   The cat is under the bed. The cat is in the closet.

8   Do the work right. I will find someone else who can do it right!

LEARN

both/and

Both/and is used to connect two pieces of information.

subjects

Both <u>you</u> and <u>he</u> have to be at the meeting.

objects

I went to **both** <u>Manchester</u> **and** <u>Liverpool</u> last year.

verbs

You need to **both** <u>clean</u> **and** <u>paint</u> you house.

nouns

I am **both** <u>a husband</u> **and** <u>a father</u>.

adjectives

Jack is **both** <u>cruel</u> **and** <u>dishonest</u>.

adverbs

You have to do it **both** <u>slowly</u> **and** <u>carefully</u>.

prepositional phrases

There were birds **both** <u>on the ground</u> **and** <u>in the air</u>.

REMEMBER

▶ When you use *both/and* for subjects, be sure the verb is correct for a plural subject.

Both Larry and I **are** hungry.

Both my sister and her husband **work** in the same office.

Practice 11/a Use *both/and* to write sentences with the same meaning.

Example: She spoke to you. She spoke to me.

She spoke to both you and [to] me.

1   Mark is married. I am married.

2   John wrote the book. John wrote the screenplay for the movie.

3   It's a printer. It's a scanner.

4   Linda lives in that building. Mary lives in that building.

5   It's a sofa. It's a bed.

6   There are dead leaves on the lawn. There are dead leaves in the pool.

7   My house has an indoor pool. My house has an outdoor pool.

8   I went to Florence. I went to Siena.

9   We have mice in the attic. We have mice in the basement.

10   He speaks German. His wife speaks German.

LEARN

would rather/than

Would rather/than is used to talk about preferences.

objects

I **would rather** have <u>pizza</u> for dinner **than** <u>tacos</u>.

verbs

I**'d rather** <u>watch TV</u> **than** <u>go shopping with my wife</u>.

independent clauses

I**'d rather** <u>you do this work</u> **than** <u>I do this work</u>.

▶ adverbs, adverb clauses, adverb phrases and more, part 2

Practice 12/a Use *would rather/than* to write sentences with the same meaning.

Example: I like to listen to classical music more than I like to listen to rock music.

I'd rather listen to classical music than [listen to] rock music.

1   I like to read books more than I like to watch TV.

2   Alex wants to have coffee more than he wants to have tea.

3   I prefer that you give this presentation than I give it.

4   He likes to work outside more than he likes to work in an office.

5   We like to camp more than we like to stay in a hotel.

6   Do you want to stay home more than you want to go to the gym?

7   The boss prefers that I handle the project more than you handle it.

8   Does your father want to play golf more than he wants to go bowling?

LEARN

whether/or (not)

Whether/or (not) is used to talk about decisions.

objects

   I cannot decide **whether** to buy <u>chocolate ice cream</u> **or** <u>vanilla ice cream</u>.

verbs

   Have you decided **whether** <u>to rent an apartment</u> **or** <u>[to] buy a house</u>?

In the two examples above, there were two options—*chocolate* or *vanilla, rent* or *buy*. But when there is only one option—choose it or do not choose it—it is very common to say simply *or not*. The rest of the clause is ellipted. This is possible only when the verb in both clauses is the same.

   I don't know **whether** <u>to quit my job</u> **or not** to [quit my job].

Often sentences such as these are written as

   I don't know **whether or not** <u>to quit my job</u>.

or

   I don't know **whether** <u>to quit my job</u> **or not**.

Practice 13/a Use *whether/or (not)* to write sentences with the same meaning.

Example: I can't decide/to buy a truck/to buy a car

I can't decide whether to buy a truck or [to buy] a car.

1   I'm not sure/to tell her what I think/to keep my mouth shut

2   Carlos can't decide/to study French/to study Spanish

3   she isn't sure/to accept the job offer/not to accept the job offer

4   I don't know/to say yes/to say no

5   to get married/not to get married/is a big decision

6   do you know/Linda said she was going to come to the party/Linda said she was not going to come to the party

7   Sarah wasn't sure/to do something/not to do something

8   Maria isn't sure/sell her house/not sell her house

9   he has to make up his mind/to major in finance/to major in accounting

Unit 18 ▶ gerunds, gerund phrases and infinitives, part 1

18.1 ▶ gerunds and gerund phrases as subjects

DISCOVER

    a   **This party** *is fun.*
    b   **Dancing** *is fun.*

1   What is the subject of *a*? Is the subject a noun?
2   What is the subject of *b*? Is the subject a noun, or is it a verb?

    c   **My homework** *was difficult.*
    d   **Learning to speak Chinese** *was difficult.*

3   What is the subject of *c*? Is the subject a noun?
4   What is the subject of *d*? Is the subject a single word, or is it a group of words?

LEARN

▶ Sometimes it is possible to change a verb to a noun. A verb which is changed to a noun is called a *gerund*. Gerunds are always verbs in the *-ing* form. It is important to understand that a gerund is <u>not</u> a continuous verb. There is no form of *be* before the gerund. A gerund is a <u>noun</u>.
    Geometry *is boring.* (*Geometry* is a noun.)
    Studying *is boring.* (*Studying* is a gerund, and a gerund is a noun.)

▶ Sometimes a gerund is part of a group of words called a *gerund phrase*. Like regular nouns, gerunds and gerund phrases can be the subject of a sentence.
    Tennis *is fun.* (noun subject)
    Dancing *is fun.* (gerund subject)
    Dancing at the club *is fun.* (gerund phrase subject)

▶ Gerunds can be negative.
    Not studying *for the test was a big mistake.*

REMEMBER

▶ A gerund must be in the *-ing* form.
    wrong → **Ride** *motorcycles is dangerous.*
    right →   **Riding** *motorcycles is dangerous.*

Practice 1 Complete the sentences with gerunds. Some are negative.

Example: Alex loves to play soccer. _____*playing*_____ soccer is his favorite sport.

1   I have to wake up at 4:00 every morning. _____ at 4:00 every morning is very difficult.

2   I watched a show about Italian food. _____ a show about Italian food made me hungry.

3   I don't speak Spanish, and that was a problem when I lived in Mexico. _____ Spanish was a problem when I lived in Mexico.

4   It's important to be on time for class. _____ on time for class is important.

5   It's important not to be late for class. _____ late for class is important.

6   Carlos loves to travel in South America. _____ in South America is his favorite thing to do.

7   John is not able to see, and that makes life more difficult for him. _____ able to see makes life more difficult for John.

8   I have to give a speech today. _____ speeches makes me really nervous.

Practice 2 Complete the sentences with gerund phrases. Some are negative.

Example: Francesca loves to play tennis. _____*Playing tennis*_____ is her favorite sport.

1   Gary lives in Los Angeles, but he doesn't have a car. _____ is a problem when you live in Los Angeles.

2 It was wonderful to see Larry again. _____ was wonderful.

3 We live in Las Vegas, which is very exciting. _____ is very exciting.

4 My wife wants to go to Hawaii, but I think _____ would be too expensive.

5 I have never flown in an airplane before, so I'm going to be very nervous when I fly in an airplane next week.
_____ next week is going to make me nervous.

6 You shouldn't talk on your cell phone while driving. _____ while driving is dangerous.

7 My boss thinks we should do nothing, but I think _____ would be a big mistake.

8 My boss thinks we shouldn't do anything, but I think _____ would be a big mistake.

18.2 ▶ gerunds and gerund phrases as objects

DISCOVER

    a   Mary likes **chocolate**.

    b   Mary likes **singing**.

1 Look at a. What is the object of the verb *likes*? Is the object a noun?

2 Look at b. What is the object of the verb *likes*? Is the object a noun, or is it a verb?

    c   I like **pizza**.

    d   I like **reading history books**.

3 Look at c. What is the object of the verb *like*? Is the object a noun?

4 Look at d. What is the object of the verb *like*? Is the object a single word, or is it a group of words?

LEARN

▶ Like regular nouns, gerunds and gerund phrases can be the object of a sentence.

    *I like **basketball**.* (noun object)

    *I like **swimming**.* (gerund object)

    *I like **swimming in the sea**.* (gerund phrase object)

REMEMBER

▶ Gerunds can be negative.

    *I enjoy **not waking up** early on the weekend.*

▶ A gerund can be the object of a continuous verb.

    *Tom and his wife are **discussing buying** a new car.*

Practice 3 Complete the sentences with the verb in parentheses. Some are negative.

    Example: Noura finished (do) _____*doing*_____ her homework.

1 Larry quit (smoke) _____.

2 I told him to be quiet, but he kept (talk) _____.

3 I need to lose weight, so my wife suggested (exercise) _____ more and (not, eat) _____ so much cake and ice cream.

4 Jack admitted (cheat) _____ on the test.

5 Sarah stopped (speak) _____ to me after I lied to her.

6 My wife and I need to save money, so we discussed (not, take) _____ a vacation this year.

7 I am very sick, and I'm considering (go) _____ to the hospital.

8 I'm trying to study, so would you mind (not, make) _____ so much noise?

Practice 4 Complete the sentences with gerund phrases. Some are negative.

    Example: I have to wake up a 4:30 every morning. I hate _*having to wake up at 4:30*_ every morning.

1 We often try new restaurants. We love _____.

2 Alex plays soccer a lot. He enjoys _____.

3   Carlos has to go shopping for clothes with his mother. He hates _____.

4   My wife has to work on Sundays. She doesn't like _____.

5   He asked me to go to the funeral. I don't like funerals, and I considered _____

    _____, but I finally said I would.

6   We were talking about where to go for lunch, and I suggested a Greek restaurant. I suggested _____

    _____ for lunch.

18.3 ▶ patterns of gerund use: verb + preposition + gerund / gerund phrase

DISCOVER

    a   I **_apologized for_** breaking the window.
1   Does a match this pattern: verb + preposition + gerund / gerund phrase?

LEARN

▶ Many verbs must be used with a certain preposition. Gerunds and gerund phrases, like regular nouns, can be the object of prepositions.

    Gary **_thought about_** going, but he changed my mind.
        verb + preposition + gerund / gerund phrase
    The children **_complained about_** having to go to bed early.
        verb + preposition + gerund / gerund phrase

REMEMBER

▶ There is no rule that you can learn so that you will always know which preposition to use after a verb.

▶ Sometimes apologize for is used with two prepositions.
    I apologized **to** my sister **for** forgetting to pick her up at the airport.

Practice 5 Use the correct form of the verb and a gerund to complete the sentences. Some must be continuous.

    Example: My grandfather (talk about, fight) _____ _talked about fighting_ _____ in the war when he
               was in the army.

1   Carlos loves animals. He doesn't (believe in, hunt) _____.

2   Sarah doesn't like school. She's not (plan on, go) _____ to college.

3   Tom's computer is old. Last night he (talk about, buy) _____ a new one.

4   I've never been to China. I'm (think about, go) _____ there next year.

5   Tom and Sarah were (think about, sell) _____ their house, but now

    they're (think about, not, sell) _____ it and renting it instead.

6   My father always checks my homework after I finish it. He (insist on, see) _____

    _____ it every night.

7   Oh no! Yesterday was my wife's birthday. I need to (apologize to, her, for, forget) _____

    _____ her birthday.

8   I was (think about, make) _____ hamburgers for dinner, but I (decide

    against, have) _____ hamburgers and made pizza instead.

18.4 ▶ patterns of gerund use: *have* + noun / noun phrase + gerund / gerund phrase

DISCOVER

    a   Jack has lied to me in the past, so I **_have trouble_** believing his story.
1   Does a match this pattern: have + noun / noun phrase + gerund / gerund phrase?

LEARN

▶ Many common expressions follow the have + noun / noun phrase + gerund / gerund phrase pattern.

    He hurt his leg. He **_has difficulty_** walking.
        have + noun / noun phrase + gerund / gerund phrase

▶ gerunds, gerund phrases and infinitives, part 1

*I **had a great time** singing at the party.*
   have + noun/noun phrase + gerund/gerund phrase

Practice 6 Use the correct form of *had* and a gerund to complete the sentences.

Example: I (have a hard time, believe) _____*have a hard time believing*_____ his crazy story.

1   I don't know what to think about his story. I (have no way of, know) _____
    whether he's telling me the truth.

2   I had never been to Boston before, so I (have a hard time, find) _____
    my sister's house without a map when I visited her last year.

3   Maria is (have fun, dance) _____ at this party, and she doesn't want to
    go now.

4   I was in California when the diamonds were stolen in Florida, so the police (have no reason for, think) _____
    _____ that I stole them.

5   My brother (have trouble, believe) _____ in ghosts until he saw one.

6   You were supposed to be here an hour ago! Do you (have an excuse for, be) _____
    _____ so late?

7   We're going to (have a good time, play) _____ softball at the barbecue.

8   John (have a way of, say) _____ things that makes other people angry.

9   Why are you (have difficulty, believe) _____ me? I've never lied to you before.

10 You'll (have a difficult time, make) _____ this recipe. It's very complicated.

11 I'm really sorry. I (have no excuse for, say) _____ those terrible things.

12 My son lives in Miami, so I (have a reason for, want) _____ to move there.

18.5 ▶ patterns of gerund use: verb + noun/noun phrase + gerund/gerund phrase

DISCOVER
   a   I told my son to do his homework, but later I **caught him** watching TV.
   1   Does *a* match this pattern: verb + noun/noun phrase + gerund/gerund phrase?

LEARN
   ▶ Some verbs follow the verb + noun/noun phrase + gerund/gerund phrase pattern.
   *I **heard a bird** singing.*
      verb + noun/noun phrase + gerund/gerund phrase
   *The police **found the robber** hiding in a garbage can.*
      verb + noun/noun phrase + gerund/gerund phrase

Practice 7 Use the correct form of the verb and a gerund to complete the sentences.

Example: I was driving too fast. The police saw me. The police _____*saw me driving*_____ too fast.

1   Jack cheated on the test, and his teacher noticed. Jack's teacher _____
    on the test.

2   I saw a bear at the circus. It was riding a bicycle. I _____ a bicycle at
    the circus.

3   Sarah saw a hawk. It was flying in the sky. Sarah _____ in the sky.

4   When I was in bed I heard a noise. Someone was opening the window. Last night, I _____
    _____ the window.

5   My mother told me not to eat any cookies before dinner, but I took a cookie, and my mother caught me. My mother
    _____ a cookie.

6   Carlos couldn't find his cat. Finally he found him. His cat was sleeping under the bed. Carlos _____

_____ under the bed.

7   The FBI agent observed a man at the airport. He was taking pictures. The FBI agent _____

_____ pictures at the airport.

18.6 ▶ patterns of gerund use: verb + noun/noun phrase + preposition + gerund/gerund phrase

DISCOVER
   *a   After Mary's surgery, she **thanked the doctors and nurses for** saving her life.*
1   Does *a* match this pattern: verb + noun/noun phrase + preposition + gerund/gerund phrase?

LEARN
   ▶ A group of verbs follow the verb + noun/noun phrase + preposition + gerund/gerund phrase pattern. Some require the preposition *for* and some require the preposition *from*.

blame someone for	*criticize someone for*	*forgive someone for*
keep someone from	*prevent someone from*	*prohibit someone from*
stop someone from	*thank someone for*	

   *I **thanked Lucy for** helping me.*
   verb + noun/noun phrase + preposition + gerund/gerund phrase
   *My back problem **keeps me from** playing golf.*
   verb + noun/noun phrase + preposition + gerund/gerund phrase

REMEMBER
   ▶ In British English, a preposition is not used with *stop* and *prevent*.
   USA → *I **stopped** Larry **from** making a big mistake.*
   UK → *I **stopped** Larry making a big mistake.*

   ▶ *Not blame someone for* has two meanings. The basic meaning is to say that you do not think that someone is guilty of doing something wrong.
   *After the accident, the police said that it was the other driver's fault. They did **not blame me for** causing the accident.*

   ▶ Another common meaning of *not blame someone for* is to say that you understand the reason why someone thinks something or does something.
   *I hate public speaking too, so I do **not blame you for** being nervous about your speech tomorrow.*

Practice 8 Use the best verb from the list above and a gerund to complete the sentences. There may be more than one good answer for some. You can use a verb more than once.

   Example: Jack lied to me, and I will never forgive him. I will never _____ *forgive him for lying* _____ to me.

1   After I broke my arm, I couldn't play tennis. My broken arm _____ tennis.

2   It was very nice of Francesca to give me a ride to the airport. I _____ me
   a ride to the airport.

3   My wife is very angry because I lost all our money in Las Vegas. I think she will never _____

_____ all our money in Las Vegas.

4   He called you a big stupid idiot? I don't _____ angry with him. I'd be angry too.

5   The snow was very deep, so I couldn't go to work. The snow _____ to work.

6   My sister broke our father's favorite coffee mug, but she _____ it, so I got
   in trouble and not my sister.

7   My parents told me I'm not allowed to see my boyfriend. They _____ him.

8   When I was a boy, I was lazy. My father often _____ lazy.

18.7 ▶ patterns of gerund use: *be* + adjective + preposition + gerund/gerund phrase

DISCOVER
   *a   Alex **is proud of** getting an A in his algebra class.*
1   Does *a* match this pattern: *be* + adjective + preposition + gerund/gerund phrase?

LEARN

▶ Many adjectives + preposition combinations are used with gerunds and gerund phrases.

afraid of	angry about	bad at	excited about
good at	happy about	interested in	nervous about
proud of	responsible for	scared of	sick of
tired of	upset about	used to	worried about

He **isn't happy about** having to go to his mother-in-law's house for dinner.
> be + adjective + preposition + gerund / gerund phrase

I **was sick of** studying.
> be + adjective + preposition + gerund / gerund phrase

REMEMBER

▶ There is no rule that you can learn so that you will always know which preposition to use after an adjective.

Practice 9 Use the best adjective + preposition combination from the list above, the verb in parentheses and a gerund to complete the sentences. There may be more than one answer for some. You can use an adjective + preposition combination more than once. Be ready to explain your answer.

Examples: I hate this job. I am (work) _____ *sick of working* _____ here.

Francesca has to be at her new job at 6:00 in the morning. It's going to be difficult for her because she's

not (wake up) _____ *used to waking up* _____ so early.

1   Gary is very (go) _____ to Europe tomorrow. He has wanted to go there all his life.

2   Carlos is an excellent artist. He is very (draw) _____ pictures.

3   I love to study history. I am (learn) _____ more about ancient Rome.

4   The other team cheated, so our coach was very (lose) _____ the game.

5   My wife makes Mexican food for dinner every day. I'm (eat) _____ it every day.

6   I've had this boring job for 10 years, so I'm (work) _____ here.

7   I am afraid of flying, so I'm (fly) _____ to Tokyo next week.

8   Alex always does whatever he wants to do. He's (follow) _____ instructions.

9   I was very (see) _____ my ex-wife with her new husband.

10 John is the manager. He is (make) _____ sure everything is done properly.

11 Our town is very (have) _____ the best football team in the state.

12 I was married for 35 years. It feels strange to be single again. I'm not (be) _____ _____ single.

13 Mark is very angry with me, so I'm (run into) _____ him at the party tonight.

14 Francesca was not (have) _____ to stay home Saturday night instead of going to the party with her friends.

15 My boss is crazy. She gets angry about everything, so I'm (make) _____ even one mistake on this project.

16 I'm going to use my mother's fancy dishes tonight. They're very valuable, and I'm (break) _____ _____ one of them.

18.8 ▶ patterns of gerund use: verb + time or money expression + gerund / gerund phrase

DISCOVER

a   I **spent $900** getting my car fixed.
b   John **wasted two hours** waiting in the doctor's office.

1   Do *a* and *b* match this pattern: verb + time or money expression + gerund / gerund phrase?

LEARN

▶ Some verbs can be used with gerunds to talk about using time or money. The two most common verbs are *spend* and *waste*, but there are others. For example, *blow* (informal) has a meaning similar to *waste*. Do you know how *spend* and *waste* are different? *Spend* is neutral. It is about using time or money, but it does not mean in a good or a bad way. *Waste* and *blow* always have the meaning of using time or money in a bad, unproductive or foolish way.

spend   waste   blow

She **spent three hours** *studying for her test*.
verb + time or money expression + gerund / gerund phrase

Henry **blew a million dollars** *trying to build a flying bicycle*.
verb + time or money expression + gerund / gerund phrase

REMEMBER

▶ *Waste* and *blow* have similar meanings. *Waste* is more common. *Blow* is very informal.

Practice 10 Use *spend, waste* or *blow* and a gerund to complete the sentences. There may be more than one good answer for some. Be ready to explain your answer.

Example: I went to the airport to pick up Mark. I waited two hours, but he didn't come. Later I learned that his flight had been canceled. I _____*wasted two hours waiting*_____ for Mark at the airport.

1 It cost $225 dollars to get my computer fixed, and it still doesn't work. I _____ my computer fixed, and it still doesn't work.

2 Alex studied for three hours because he had a math test. He got an A on the test. Alex _____ _____ for the test.

3 Henry searched for ten years for a lost city in the jungle, and he didn't find it. Henry _____ _____ for a lost city in the jungle, and he didn't find it.

4 I had to get my roof repaired. It cost £3,000. I _____ my roof repaired.

5 My wife's mother is coming to visit us, so I needed to clean my house. My house was very dirty, so it took all day to clean it. I _____ my house.

18.9 ▶ patterns of gerund use: verb + place and / or time expression + gerund / gerund phrase

DISCOVER

a Jack is lazy. He **sits around the house all day** *doing nothing*.
1 Does *a* match this pattern: verb + place and / or time expression + gerund / gerund phrase?

LEARN

▶ Some verbs can be used with gerunds to talk about doing something in a place. Sometimes an expression of time is also used.

drive around	*hang around*	*lie*	*lie around*	*run around*
sit	*sit around*	*stand*	*stand around*	

We **drove around the block** *looking for a parking space*.
verb + place and / or time expression + gerund / gerund phrase

I **lay on the sofa all afternoon** *reading*.
verb + place and / or time expression + gerund / gerund phrase

REMEMBER

▶ The verbs in the list above which include *around* are phrasal verbs. *About* has the same meaning as *around*.
Mary and Larry **stood around** watching me while I did all the work.
= Mary and Larry **stood about** watching me while I did all the work.

▶ Gerunds can be negative.
After Michael told me the truth, I stood there **not knowing** what to say.

Practice 11 Use the best verb from the list above, a time expression and a gerund or gerund phrase to complete the sentences.

Example: I sat at my desk for two hours. I did my math homework. I ____*sat at my desk for two hours*____ _____*doing*_____ my math homework.

▶ gerunds, gerund phrases and infinitives, part 1

1   The police drove around the city. They looked for the escaped prisoner. The police _____ _____ for the escaped prisoner.

2   Maria stood by the window. She listened to a bird sing. Maria _____ to a bird sing.

3   My lazy son-in-law hangs around the house all day. He does nothing. My lazy son-in-law _____ _____ nothing.

4   I ran around the house. I tried to find my keys. I _____ to find my keys.

5   I'm feeling sick, so I'm just going to lie around the house all day. I'm not going to do anything. I'm feeling sick, so I'm just going to _____ anything.

6   When I was in Florida, I lay on the beach all week. I did nothing. When I was in Florida, I _____ _____ nothing.

7   Our boss was angry because she saw us standing around. We weren't doing anything. Our boss was angry because she saw us _____ anything.

8   My son just sat there, listened to me and didn't say anything. He just _____ _____ anything.

9   Are you going to sit around all night? Do you hope that she'll call you? Are you going to _____ _____ that she'll call you?

18.10 ▶ patterns of gerund use: *go* + gerund/gerund phrase

DISCOVER

   a   My wife and my mother __went__ shopping at the mall.

1   Does *a* match this pattern: *go* + gerund/gerund phrase?

LEARN

▶ Many verbs which describe activities—mostly sports or other enjoyable activities—follow the pattern *go* + gerund/ gerund phrase.

   bowl   camp   dance   fish   hike   sail   shop   ski   swim   surf

   My wife __went__ shopping.   *I'm going to __go__ bowling with my friends tonight.*
   go + gerund/gerund phrase   go + gerund/gerund phrase

Practice 12 Use *go*, the best verb from the list above and a gerund to complete the sentences.

   Example: My wife and I love to dance. We _____*go dancing*_____ every weekend.

1   Alex often swims at the club. He _____ at the club last weekend.

2   My father and I love to fish. We used to _____ a lot when we lived in Minnesota.

3   Hiking in the mountains can be dangerous. Be careful of mountain lions when you _____.

4   Rosa is a good dancer. She _____ last night.

5   Tom and Jerry are at the bowling alley right now. They _____ every Saturday night.

6   Sarah and her friends ski in Colorado every winter. They're going to _____ there next January.

7   I don't like to go camping, so I haven't _____ for a long time.

8   Michael and his wife needed some new clothes, so they _____ last night.

9   I love to surf, and I'm _____ in Australia next week.

10 We're _____ next Sunday on my brother's sailboat.

18.11 ▶ patterns of gerund use: other words and expressions used with gerunds

DISCOVER

a   I hate hot weather, so I can't **get used to** living in Arizona.
b   **In addition to speaking** Danish, I also speak Dutch.
c   **Instead of** going to a movie last night, we decided to go to a restaurant.
d   I have never been to Peru, so I'm **looking forward to going** there next month.
e   You should **take advantage of** living in Mexico to practice speaking Spanish every day.
f   I'm going to **take care of fixing** my car on Saturday.

LEARN

▶ Several other expressions are used with gerunds.

get used to (See Section 10.8 for more about this use of *get*.)

When I started to work as a breakfast cook in a restaurant, it was difficult to **get used to waking up** at 4:00 in the morning, but now I'm used to it.

Mary has been a vegetarian for 10 years, so she **has gotten used to not eating** meat.

in addition to

In addition to having a car, I have a motorcycle.

In addition to not doing his work well, he also sleeps at his desk.

instead of

I watched TV all night **instead of studying**.

Instead of being angry, you should say you're sorry.

look forward to

I don't like Jack, so I'm not **looking forward to seeing** him at the conference tonight.

My father's going to retire soon, and he's **looking forward to not having** to go to his office every day.

take advantage of

Noura **took advantage of having** a day off from work to visit her mother.

There are many great museums in Washington DC. You should **take advantage of being** here to visit them.

take care of

I **took care or returning** some books to the library this morning.

If you **take care of buying** the drinks for the party, I'll **take care of cooking** the food.

Practice 13 Use one of the expressions from the list above and the verb in parentheses to complete the sentences with a gerund.

Example: Francesca is studying Italian. She has an Italian neighbor. She should (have) _____ *take advantage* _____ _____ *of having* _____ an Italian neighbor to practice speaking Italian.

1   I haven't seen my daughter for five years. She's coming to visit tomorrow. I'm (see) _____

    _____ her tomorrow.

2   Michael thought about buying a new car, but he decided to keep his old car. (buy) _____

    _____ a new car, Michael decided to keep his old car.

3   Sofia has a dog and a cat. (have) _____ a dog, Sofia also has a cat.

4   I don't have to work for a few days. I'm going to use the time to finish my project. I'm going to (not, have) _____

    _____ to work for a few days to finish my project.

5   I never pay bills. My wife does it. My wife (pay) _____ the bills.

6   After I moved downtown, I sold my car. At first it was difficult, but after a few weeks, I (not, have) _____

    _____ a car.

7   (complain) _____, why don't you do something about your problems?

18.12 ▶ gerunds and infinitives with the same meaning

DISCOVER

a   I **hate waking up** early.

▶ gerunds, gerund phrases and infinitives, part 1

b I **hate to wake up** early.

1 Do *a* and *b* have the same meaning?

LEARN

▶ There is no difference in meaning between *a* and *b*. A small group of verbs are used with gerunds and infinitives (*to* + the base form of a verb) with no difference in meaning.

begin	can't stand	continue	hate
like	love	start	

I **like watching** old movies.
= I **like to watch** old movies.

REMEMBER

▶ *Can't stand* = hate
I **can't stand** waking up early. = I **hate** waking up early.

▶ When the main verb is continuous, a gerund is not possible.
wrong → Michael is beginning **doing** his homework.
right → Michael is beginning **to do** his homework.

Practice 14 Complete the sentences with gerunds and infinitives.

Example: Alex loves (play) _____*playing / to play*_____ soccer.

1 It started (snow) _____ about an hour ago.

2 I'm going to begin (study) _____ as soon as I get home.

3 Nobody likes (pay) _____ taxes.

4 When Ali was a boy, he hated (go) _____ to school.

5 I'm going to continue (work) _____ until I finish.

6 Mark and his wife love (travel) _____.

7 Larry can't stand (listen) _____ his noisy neighbors all night.

8 Carlos sat down at the piano and began (play) _____.

18.13 ▶ gerunds and infinitives with a different meaning

DISCOVER

a Please **remember to pay** the telephone bill tomorrow.
b I **remember paying** the water bill. I paid it three days ago.

1 Which sentence is about something that needs to be done? Which sentence is about something that was already done? How are the sentences different?

LEARN

▶ The meaning of the infinitive form and the gerund form of a small group of verbs have different meanings.
remember and **forget**
A gerund is used for actions that have already happened.
Francesca **remembers going** to the White House when she was a girl.
She will never **forget seeing** the ghost of Abraham Lincoln when she was at the White House.
An infinitive is used to talk about needing to do something.
Did you **remember to turn off** the stove before you went to work?
I often **forget to lock** the door when I come home.

regret
A gerund is used for actions that the speaker feels sorry about doing.
I **regret buying** this car. It's a piece of junk.
An infinitive is used when the speaker must inform another person of bad news.
I **regret to inform** you that there has been a tragic accident.

try
A gerund is used to describe a way of doing something with the hope that it will be successful.
My computer wasn't working, so I **tried restarting** it, and it was OK after that.

An infinitive is used to describe an attempt to do something.
*I **tried to quit** smoking, but I couldn't do it.*

Practice 15 Use the verb in parentheses to complete the sentences with gerunds or infinitives.

Example: Have you tried (change) ____changing____ the batteries? Maybe that's the problem.

1 Larry wasn't at the meeting because I forgot (tell) _____ him that we changed it from 10:00 to 9:00.

2 Larry tried (push) _____ the door instead of (pull) _____ it, and then it opened.

3 The traffic was terrible on Highway 130 this morning, so I tried (take) _____ Highway 47, and it was a lot faster.

4 Sometimes I forget (feed) _____ our dog.

5 Who is that guy? I don't remember (meet) _____ him before.

6 I regret (major) _____ in history when I was in college. It was a big mistake.

7 Did you remember (tell) _____ your boss that you would be late tomorrow?

8 I regret (inform) _____ you that your parrot has died.

Continue to Unit 18/advanced ↓ or go to Unit 19 →

18.14/a ▶ subject gerund / gerund phrases = *it* + infinitives

DISCOVER

> a ***Dancing** is fun.*
> b ***It** is fun **to dance***.

1 Do *a* and *b* have the same meaning?

> c ***Learning to speak Chinese** was difficult.*
> d ***It** was difficult **to learn to speak Chinese***.

2 Do *c* and *d* have the same meaning?

LEARN

▶ It is very common to use *it* as the subject of a sentence and to use the infinitive form of the verb.
> ***Quitting smoking** is not easy.*
> = ***It** is not easy **to quit smoking***.

REMEMBER

▶ Negative infinitives do not use *do, does* or *did*.
> **wrong** → *It is important **don't be** late.*
> **right** → *It is important **not to be** late.*

Practice 16/a Change the sentences as in the example.

Example: Growing up without a father was difficult.

> *It was difficult to grow up without a father.*

1 Getting my car fixed is going to cost $450.

2 Not studying for the test was stupid.

3 Helping your sister would be very nice of you.

4 Not forgetting your passport is important.

5 Learning the truth was shocking.

6 Being big or tall isn't necessary to be a good soccer player.

7 Hearing all the bad news was depressing.

8 Correcting my boss's mistake during the meeting wasn't very smart.

9 Being honest is important.

▶ **gerunds, gerund phrases and infinitives, part 1**

18.15/a ▶ possessives used with gerunds

DISCOVER

    a   *Sam was worried about **being** sick.*

    b   *Sam was worried about **your being** sick.*

1   Look at *a* and *b*. In which sentence is Sam worried about being sick himself? In which sentence is Sam worried about another person?

    c   ***Getting to** work late every day made the boss angry.*

    d   ***His getting to** work late every day made the boss angry.*

2   Look at *c* and *d*. In one sentence, it is not clear whether the speaker is talking about him- or herself or another person? In which sentence is it clear that the speaker is talking about another person?

LEARN

▶ Possessive adjectives and possessive nouns are used to modify gerunds. Usually this is not necessary, but sometimes we want to be very clear about the connection between a gerund and a person.

    *The manager is unfair. She got angry about **my being** late, but she didn't say anything about **Sofia's being** late.*

    ***My son's crashing** our car into a tree is the reason for **my having** to take the bus to and from work every day.*

REMEMBER

▶ Many native speakers of English do not understand or do not care about using possessive adjectives and possessive nouns with gerunds. It is very common to hear these informal forms.

    formal →   *Michael was worried about **your being** sick.*

    informal → *Michael was worried about **you being** sick.*

    formal →   ***His leaving** the class early upset the teacher.*

    informal → ***Him leaving** the class early upset the teacher.*

    formal →   *The manager got angry about **my being** late, but she didn't say anything about **Sofia's being** late.*

    informal → *The manager got angry about **me being** late, but she didn't say anything about **Sofia being** late.*

▶ Gerunds can be negative.

    *The teacher wasn't happy about **my not being** in class yesterday.*

Practice 17/a Complete the sentences with gerunds and possessive adjectives or possessive nouns.

Example: We have ten cats. Some people think _____*our having*_____ ten cats is crazy.

1   You lied to your father. _____ to your father is a very serious matter.

2   Michael and Tom played the drums last night until 2:00 in the morning. Our neighbors were not happy about

    _____ the drums so late at night.

3   John has to go to the doctor tomorrow morning. Did you know about _____ to go to the doctor tomorrow morning?

4   They moved to California. My sister and I were surprised by _____ to California.

5   You helped me. I appreciate _____ me.

6   Linda laughed at my idea. I was very angry about _____ at my idea.

7   I didn't stop at the red light. _____ at the red light is why I had an accident.

8   He's very sick. _____ very sick is why he was in the hospital last week.

Unit 19 ▶ gerunds, gerund phrases and infinitives, part 2

19.1 ▶ infinitives used to show purpose

DISCOVER

    a   Tom: *Why are you saving money?*

    b   John: *I'm saving money **in order to buy** a new car.*

    c   Tom: *What did you say?*

    d   John: *I'm saving money **to buy** a new car.*

1   Look at *b* and *d*. Do *in order to buy* and *to buy* have the same meaning?

LEARN

▶ Infinitives are sometimes used to give the reason for doing something. Sometimes people say *in order to,* and sometimes people say only *to*. They have the same meaning.

    *Maria got to the cinema early **in order to get** a good seat.*

    *= Maria got to the cinema early **to get** a good seat.*

REMEMBER

▶ *To* is more common than *in order to.*

▶ It is not correct to use *for* or *for to.*

    wrong → *I went to the store **for** buy some milk.*

    wrong → *I went to the store **for to** buy some milk.*

    right →   *I went to the store **to** buy some milk.*

    right →   *I went to the store **in order to** buy some milk.*

▶ *For* is used with nouns.

    *I went to the store **for** some milk.*

Practice 1 Answer the questions with *in order to* as in the example. Use pronouns.

    Example: Why did Alex go to the bank? (get some money)

                  He went there in order to get some money.

1   Why are you calling Lucy? (ask her a question)

2   Why are you going downtown tomorrow? (go to a museum)

3   Why did Mark go to the pharmacy? (get some medicine)

4   Why do you take this medicine? (control my high blood pressure)

5   Why did your sister go to Argentina? (visit her friends)

6   Why did your friends go to the concert early? (get good seats)

Practice 2 Some of the sentences contain mistakes. Find the incorrect sentences and correct them.

1   Did you go to Larry's office to ask him a question or for another reason?

2   I turned on the TV for watch the news.

3   I exercise every day in order to lose weight.

4   Sofia went to the shoe store for to get some new shoes.

5   John went to the gas station for buy a bottle of water.

6   Rosa went to the library for a book about computers.

19.2 ▶ *so (that)* used to show purpose

DISCOVER

    a   Tom: *Why are you saving money?*

    b   John: *I'm saving money **in order to buy** a new car.*

    c   Tom: *What did you say?*

*d John: I'm saving money **so (that) I can buy** a new car.*

1 Look at *b* and *d*. Do *in order to buy* and *so (that) I can buy* have the same meaning?

LEARN

▶ Sometimes we use *so* or *so that* to give the reason for doing something.

*I went to the restaurant **so I could meet** my friends for lunch.*

*Mary's buying a lot of food **so that she'll have** enough for the party.*

REMEMBER

▶ *That* is optional. It is common to cancel *that* in informal speech and writing.

*I called Sam **so that** I could ask him a question.*

*= I called Sam **so** I could ask him a question.*

Practice 3 Rewrite the sentences using *so (that)*. Use the word in parentheses.

Examples: Lucy is looking for John in order to return her calculator. (can)

Lucy is looking for John so that she can return his calculator.

I'm setting my alarm clock in order not to oversleep. (don't)

I'm setting my alarm clock so I don't oversleep.

1 We are hurrying in order not to miss the bus. (don't)

2 Alex is studying in order to get a good grade on his exam. (will)

3 He's buying a map in order not to get lost when he goes to Rome. (doesn't)

4 Mary woke up at 4:30 this morning in order to get to work early. (could)

5 I didn't go to the party in order not to see Michael. (wouldn't)

6 We waited for three hours in order to get tickets for the game. (could)

19.3 ▶ causative verbs: *make, have, let* and *get*

DISCOVER

*a I **made** my son **do** his homework.*

*b John **had** a mechanic **fix** his car.*

*c Sarah **let** her daughter **watch** TV.*

*d My son **got** Sofia **to do** his homework for him.*

1 Which sentence is about giving permission?
2 Which sentence is about using power or authority?
3 Which sentence is about arranging for someone else to do something?
4 Which sentence is about persuading someone to do something?
5 Which sentence is different from the others?

LEARN

▶ *Causative verbs* are verbs which describe causing things to happen or causing people to do things.

Make means to use power or authority to cause people to do things.

*The robber **made** me **give** him my money.*

*Sometimes my boss **makes** me **work** on Saturday.*

Have means to arrange for someone to do something or to pay someone to do something.

*I **had** my secretary **make** a doctor's appointment for me.*

*Carlos **had** a tailor **shorten** his new pants.*

Let means to give someone permission for something or to allow something to happen.

*I **let** my daughter **go** to the party.*

*John **lets** his clothes **get** really dirty before he washes them.*

***Get** (someone to)* means to persuade someone to do something. Notice that *to* must be used with the verb after *get*.

*The price for the computer was $900, but I **got** the sales guy **to lower** the price to $800.*

*Mary wanted to stay home and watch TV, but I **got** her **to give** me a ride to the store.*

Have and ***get*** are often passive. In the passive, *have* and *get* have the same meaning. *Get* is more common.

*I talked to a dentist about **having** my teeth whitened.*

*= I talked to a dentist about **getting** my teeth whitened.*

*Carlos **had** his hair cut.*
*= Carlos **got** his hair cut.*

REMEMBER

▶ The sound of *make* is sometimes too strong, so sometimes, even when people have the power or authority to make other people do things, they use *have* for a softer and more polite sound.

*The teacher **had** his students write a three-page essay.*
*My daughter made a lot of mistakes in her homework, so I **had** her do it again.*

Practice 4 Use *make, have, let* or *get* to complete the sentences. There may be more than one good answer for some. Be sure to use the correct verb tense and form.

Example: My sister's car is at the mechanic, so I _____ let _____ her use mine.

1 I wasn't going to pay more that $25,000 for this car, but the salesperson _____ me to pay $29,000.

2 When I was a teenager, my father would never _____ me ride a motorcycle.

3 I don't want to do it, and there is no way you can _____ me do it!

4 My boss wasn't happy with my work. I think she's going to _____ me do it over.

5 Whenever I hear that song, it _____ me think of my first girlfriend.

6 My students are lazy. How can I _____ them to work harder?

7 I said I was sorry. Now will you please unlock the door and _____ me come inside?

8 My soup was cold. I _____ the waiter bring me another bowl.

9 This coffee is too hot. I need to _____ it cool off a little before I drink it.

Practice 5 Change the sentences to passive.

Example: Gary had somebody fix his flat tire.

Gary had his flat tire fixed.

1 I can't afford to have somebody do my taxes.

2 Why did you have somebody cut your hair so short?

3 I need to have somebody take a passport picture.

4 Do you know where I can get somebody to cash a check?

5 You have to get somebody to dry clean this sweater.

6 I'm going to get somebody to repair this watch.

19.4 ▶ *very, too* and *enough* used with infinitives

DISCOVER

    a   *This diamond ring is **very** expensive, but I **have enough** money **to buy** it.*
    b   *This diamond ring is **too** expensive. I **don't have enough** money **to buy** it.*

1 What is the difference between *very* and *too*. What is the meaning of *enough*? Does *enough* come after a verb or an adjective?

    c   *This sofa is **very** heavy, but I'm **strong enough to lift** it.*
    d   *This sofa is **too** heavy. I'm **not strong enough to lift** it.*

2 Think again about the difference between *very* and *too*. Look at *enough*. Does *enough* come after a verb or an adjective? Look at the verb *lift*. Is it a gerund or an infinitive?

    e   *This sofa is **too** heavy **to lift**.*
    f   *This sofa is **too** heavy **for me to lift**.*

3 Do *e* and *f* have the same meaning as *d*? In *e*, is it clear who I am talking about? Is it clear in *f*?

LEARN

▶ It is common to use *too* and *enough* with infinitives. It is also common for students to confuse *very* and *too*. *Very* is neutral. That means it is not good or bad. *Too* is <u>always</u> bad, so do not use *too* with things that cannot be bad—*too happy, too beautiful, too rich*, etc.

▶ gerunds, gerund phrases and infinitives, part 2

▶ *Too* and infinitives are used in these patterns:

be + *too* + adjective + (*for* someone) + infinitive
*He **is too short to play** basketball.*
*This book **is too difficult for me to understand**.*

verb + *too* + adverb + (*for* someone) + infinitive
*I **drove too slowly to get away** from the police.*
*She **speaks too fast for me to understand**.*

▶ *Enough* and infinitives are used in these patterns:

verb + *enough* + noun + infinitive
*I **saved enough money to buy** a car.*
*She **didn't have enough gas to drive** to the beach.*

be + adjective + *enough* + infinitive
*She **is tall enough to touch** the ceiling.*
*The suitcase **wasn't big enough to hold** all my stuff.*

verb + adverb + *enough* + (*for* someone) + infinitive
*Did Henry **run fast enough to get away** from the tiger?*
*Carlos **doesn't speak loudly enough for me to understand**.*

Practice 6 Some of the sentences contain mistakes. Find the incorrect sentences and correct them.

1 This coffee is too hot, but I like hot coffee, so no problem.

2 I don't make money enough to buy a house.

3 She arrived too late to hear the beginning of the speech.

4 This TV is too expensive for Alex buy.

5 Does Francesca write enough well to be a professional writer?

6 Lucy isn't old enough to drive.

7 Do you have enough chocolate to make a cake?

8 Put on a coat. It's very cold to go outside without a coat on.

Practice 7 Use the words in parentheses, *enough* and an infinitive to complete the sentences.

Example: (sick/stay) Sarah wasn't _____*sick enough to stay*_____ home from work.

1 (have/money/buy) Are you sure you _____ this watch? It costs $2,000.

2 (work/hard/graduate) Do you think Mary will _____ from college?

3 (early/say) I didn't get to the airport _____ goodbye to her before she left.

4 (big/for everyone/have) The wedding cake wasn't _____ a piece.

5 (tall/be) Rosa isn't _____ a model.

Practice 8 Use the words in parentheses, *too* and an infinitive to complete the sentences.

Example: (tired/keep) Let's take a break. I'm _____*too tired to keep*_____ working.

1 (busy/talk) Please call me later. I'm _____ to you right now.

2 (badly/stay) The coach told me that I play football _____ on the team.

3 (hot/drink) Be careful. That tea is _____.

4 (long/read) The novel *War and Peace* is _____ in one week.

5 (tough/cut) This cheap steak is _____.

19.5 ▶ *by* + gerund/gerund phrase used for explaining how to do something

DISCOVER
a   *I lost weight **by eating only salads and running three miles ever day**.*

1 Does *by eating only salads and running three miles ever day* explain how *I lost weight?*

   b **By saving 25% or your salary every month,** you'll have $50,000 in five years.

2 Does *by saving 25% or your salary every month* explain how *you'll have $50,000 in five years?*

LEARN

▶ *By* + gerund/gerund phrase can be used to explain how to do something.

   By working hard, you will succeed.

   I got there fast **by taking Washington Street to avoid traffic.**

Practice 9 Answer the questions by using *by* + gerund and the appropriate verb.

     cook   do   eat   sit   take   talk   ~~wash~~

Example: You might be able to get that ketchup stain out of your shirt _____*by washing*_____ it with bleach.

1 You can get to Maple Street _____ bus 42.

2 _____ this in water instead of oil, it will have fewer calories.

3 You'll save a lot of money _____ at home instead of in restaurants.

4 _____ behind Carlos and looking at his test, I was able to get an A on my test.

5 You won't solve your problems _____ about what you should do but

_____ something about them!

Continue to Unit 19/advanced ↓ or go to Unit 20 →

19.6/a ▶ past forms of gerunds

DISCOVER

   a *I talked to Larry about* **going to** *Amsterdam.*

   b *I talked to Larry about* **having gone to** *Amsterdam.*

1 Look at *a* and *b*. Is there a difference in meaning?

2 In *a*, is it clear whether I talked to Larry about going to Amsterdam in the past or about going to Amsterdam in the future?

3 In *b*, is it clear that I am talking about going to Amsterdam in the past?

LEARN

▶ When it is necessary to be clear that a gerund is about an action that happened in the past, or when people want to use very formal English, it is possible to use a gerund form of the present perfect.

   John was upset about **having lost** *the game.*

   = John was upset about **losing** *the game.*

   Having learned *Spanish helped Mark when he went to Bolivia.*

   = **Learning** *Spanish helped Mark when he went to Bolivia.*

REMEMBER

▶ Remember what we saw in Section 18.15/a—possessive adjectives and possessive nouns are possible with gerunds.

   John was upset about **his** *having lost the game.*

   Mark's *having learned Spanish in college helped him a lot when he went to Bolivia.*

Practice 10/a Complete the sentences with present perfect gerunds. Some are negative.

Example: I didn't see Mary when she visited. I am sorry about _____*not having seen*_____ Mary when she visited.

1 That was a terrible thing I did. I'm not proud of _____ that.

2 Linda saw the burglars. Linda told the police about her _____ the burglars.

3 I didn't return your phone call. I'm sorry about _____ your phone call.

4 Michael forgot to invite me. Michael apologized for his _____ to invite me.

5 Michael didn't invite me. Michael apologized for his _____ me.

▶ **gerunds, gerund phrases and infinitives, part 2**

6 I met with the president of the company. I told everyone in the office about my _____ the president of the company.

7 Sarah passed the exam. Sarah is happy about _____ the final exam.

8 I made a mistake. I was very embarrassed about my _____ a mistake.

9 I couldn't be at my son's wedding. I apologized for _____ at his wedding.

Practice 11/a Complete the sentences with present perfect gerunds. Use possessive adjectives and possessive nouns. Some are negative.

Example: I told the woman who interviewed me for the job that I had worked for the XYZ Company for several years.

She was impressed by _____ *my having worked* _____ for the XYZ Company for several years.

1 I didn't know that she had been fired. I was surprised to hear about _____ fired.

2 Bill told Tom that Larry had quit his job. Bill told Tom about _____ his job.

3 You have a big mouth! You told everyone what happened. I'm really mad about _____ everyone what happened.

4 Sam and Mary were absent. I don't care about Sam, but _____ absent was a problem.

5 We didn't finish high school. We never tell anyone about _____ high school.

6 I didn't know that they had been transferred. Did you know about _____ transferred?

7 Because of _____ it before, it will be easy for you to do it again.

19.7/a ▶ past forms of infinitives used with adjectives

DISCOVER
    a   Sarah **is proud to have graduated from** Purdue University.
1 Think about *be proud* and *graduate from*. Was Sarah proud before or after she graduated?

LEARN
▶ Some adjectives are used with past perfect infinitives.

embarrassed	glad	happy	lucky
proud	sad	sorry	surprised

He **is lucky to have been** offered the job.
I **am sorry to have hurt** your feelings.

REMEMBER
▶ Infinitives can be negative.
    Henry was lucky **not to have been killed** when he fell into the shark tank at the aquarium.

Practice 12/a Use the adjectives in parentheses and a present perfect infinitive to complete the sentences. Some are negative.

Examples: I forgot his name. I was _____ *embarrassed to have forgotten* _____ his name. (embarrassed)

He didn't get the job. He was _____ *sorry not to have gotten* _____ the job. (sorry)

1 You hurt my feelings. Are you _____ my feelings? (sorry)

2 I didn't get there on time. I am _____ there on time. (sorry)

3 John served his country. John is _____ his country. (proud)

4 She learned the truth. She's _____ the truth. (sad)

5 I saw my teacher at the party. I was _____ my teacher at the party. (surprised)

6 You were in prison. Are you _____ in prison? (embarrassed)

7 I was able to help you. I'm _____ able to help you. (glad)

8 I wasn't hurt in the accident. I'm _____ in the accident. (lucky)

Unit 20 ▶ conditional sentences

INTRODUCTION

▶ *Conditional sentences* are about a *condition*—something that must happen or must be true before something else can happen or can be true.

> *If I* **have enough time**, *I will* **help you with your homework**.

In this sentence, *have enough time* must be true before *help you with your homework* can happen. *Have enough time* is a condition—something which must be true or must happen before something else can be true or can happen.

> *have enough time* = yes → *help you with your homework* = yes
>
> *have enough time* = no → *help you with your homework* = no

There are several ways to use conditional sentences, but two ideas are important to remember:

▶ One is about time—conditional sentences can be about the past, present or future, but the grammar of present and future conditional sentences is <u>the same</u>. How can they be the same? Think of it this way: the future starts <u>right now</u>.

> **now**
>
> Larry: Can you help me fix this printer?
> Mark: OK, let me see it. *If I* **know** what is wrong, *I* **will fix** it.
>
> **future**
>
> Tom: Can you help me fix my car tomorrow?
> Alex: OK, I'll look at it tomorrow. *If I* **know** what is wrong, *I* **will fix** it.

▶ The other important idea is that with conditional sentences, there is an important difference between <u>what is true, what is real or what is possible</u> and <u>what is not true, what is not real, what is not possible or what is only imaginary</u>. Understanding this will help you to understand conditional sentences.

> Larry: Can you help me fix this printer?
> Mark: OK, let me see it. *If I* **know** what is wrong, *I* **will fix** it. (Mark thinks it is possible that he can fix it.)
> Larry: Look here at this error message.
> Mark: Sorry, I don't understand the error message. I want to help you, but I can't. *If I* **knew** what is wrong, *I* **would fix** it, but I don't know. (Mark knows that it is not possible for him to fix it.)

▶ A basic conditional sentence has two parts, an *if-clause* (the condition) and a *result clause* (what happens if the condition exists or happens). Notice that when the *if*-clause is first, a comma comes after it, but when the result clause is first, no comma is used.

> *If I* **see Michael,** *I will invite him to my party.*
>   *if*-clause   result clause
>
> *I will invite Michael to my party* **if I see him**.
>   result clause   *if*-clause

20.1 ▶ zero conditional: always true

DISCOVER

> a   **If** I **have** a question, I **ask** my teacher.
> b   Sarah **gets** sleepy **whenever** she **eats** a big lunch.
> c   **When** my wife **drinks** coffee, she **has** trouble sleeping.

1   Are these sentences about *always* or about *only one time* (maybe one time now or maybe one time in the future)?
2   What is the tense of the verbs in these sentences? Are the tenses the same in both clauses?

LEARN

▶ *A, b* and *c* are examples of what is sometimes called the *zero conditional*. They are about something that is <u>always true</u>. In fact, it is common to use *always* in zero conditional sentences.

> Sarah **always** gets sleepy whenever she eats a big lunch.

▶ Zero conditional sentences are used with *if, when* and *whenever*. There is no difference in meaning.

> **If** I eat shrimp, I get sick.
>
> = **When** I eat shrimp, I get sick.
>
> = **Whenever** I eat shrimp, I get sick.

In zero conditional sentences, the tense of <u>both</u> verbs is present.

> *If I* **eat** shrimp, *I* **get** sick.
>   present tense   present tense

REMEMBER

▶ The *if-clause* and the *result clause* can be reversed.
If I have a question, I ask my teacher.
= *I ask my teacher if I have a question.*

Practice 1 Make zero conditional sentences with the word in parentheses. Be careful about punctuation.

Examples: I have a car problem. I call my brother-in-law. (if)

If I have a car problem, I call my brother-in-law.

Her boss gets mad. She is late for work. (when)

Her boss gets mad when she is late for work.

1 My brother visits. He sleeps on the sofa. (whenever)

2 I feel awful the next day. I don't get enough sleep. (when)

3 You return a library book late. You have to pay a fine. (if)

4 She gets upset. You talk about the big mistake that she made. (whenever)

5 I don't drink coffee in the morning. I get a headache. (if)

6 My neighbors get mad. I make a lot of noise. (if)

7 The phone rings. The baby wakes up. (whenever)

8 Milk goes bad. You don't put it back in the refrigerator. (when)

9 My knee hurts. It gets cold outside. (if)

10 You leave the window open. Mosquitoes get in the house. (if)

20.2 ▶ first conditional: true in the present or in the future

DISCOVER

a *If you **give** me a 10% discount, I **will buy** it.*
b *You **might not pass** your English test if you **don't study**.*

1 Are *a* and *b* about something that might really happen? Are they about something that might always happen or about something that might happen only one time in the present or future?
2 What is the tense of the verbs in the *if*-clauses? Are the result clauses the same? Is there a modal in the result clauses?

LEARN

▶ *A* and *b* are examples of what is sometimes called the *first conditional*. First conditional sentences are about something <u>that is true, that is real or that is possible at this moment or one time in the future</u>.

▶ First conditional sentences are used only with *if*. *When* and *whenever* are not possible. In first conditional sentences, the tense of the *if*-clause is present and the result clause contains a modal. The modal is usually *will*, but *should, ought to, must, may, might, can, have to, have got to* and *be going to* are also possible.
*If he **needs** help with his homework, my sister **will help** him.*
    present tense   modal + verb

▶ The result clause of first conditional sentences can be imperative. That means there is no modal and no subject because we know that the subject is *you*. (See Section 16.10/a for more about imperative sentences.)
*I'm going to take a shower, so if the telephone **rings**, **answer** it.*

REMEMBER

▶ Zero conditionals are about something that is <u>always</u> true.
*Mary is always happy to help me. If Mary **has** time, she **helps** me.*

▶ First conditionals are about something that is true, real or possible <u>one time</u> in the present or in the future.
*You look confused. If you **don't understand** the plan, I **can explain** it again.*
*I asked Mary for help with my homework. If Mary **has** time, she **will help** me tonight.*

▶ Conditional sentences can be negative.
*When I **don't get** enough sleep, I **can't stay** awake in class.*
*If he **doesn't pass** the chemistry final exam, he **won't graduate** from high school.*

Practice 2 Make first conditional sentences with *will* and the words in parentheses.

Examples: Michael (visit) _____ will visit _____ his sister if he (go) _____ goes _____ to Chicago.

If he (not, apologize) _doesn't apologize_, I (not, speak) _____ won't speak _____ to him again.

I (not, be) _____ won't be _____ happy if you (be) _____ are late _____.

1 If I (have) _____ $10.00, I (lend) _____ it to you.

2 My neighbor (be) _____ angry, if I (not, return) _____ his lawn mower.

3 If you (not, give) _____ me a ride to work today, I (take) _____ a taxi.

4 Paris (be) _____ very crowded if you (go) _____ there in July.

5 I (not, buy) _____ the house, if they (not, lower) _____ the price.

6 If I (have) _____ time, I (help) _____ you after dinner.

7 I (not, make) _____ a cake tonight if I (not, have) _____ enough eggs.

8 If she (not, be) _____ here tomorrow, we (cancel) _____ the meeting.

Practice 3 Make first conditional sentences with the words in parentheses.

Examples: If my boss (tell) _____ tells _____ me to work late, I (might, be) _____ might be _____ late for dinner.

This is a very small project. It (should, not, take) _____ shouldn't take _____ too long if you (not, make) _____ don't make _____ any mistakes.

1 If my father (say) _____ it's OK, I (can, go) _____ to the party.

2 Francesca (ought to, finish) _____ all of her math homework in the afternoon if she (want)

_____ to go to the mall with her friends tonight.

3 If you (visit) _____ New York City, you (should, not, miss) _____ the Metropolitan Museum of Art.

4 If I (be) _____ too busy, I (may, not, be) _____ able to come to your party.

5 I feel sick. I (might, not, go) _____ to work tomorrow if I (not, feel) _____ better.

6 Mark's house (should, be) _____ right around the next corner if I (be) _____ reading this map correctly.

7 If your brother (not, need) _____ his car tonight, you (ought to, ask) _____ him if you can borrow it.

20.3 ▶ second conditional: not true in the present or in the future

DISCOVER

  a I **could buy** a new car **if** I **had** enough money.
  b **If** I **were** the president of this country, I **would make** a lot of changes.

1 In *a*, do I have enough money to buy a new car? In *b*, am I the president of this country? Are *a* and *b* about something that might really happen or might really be true or are they about something that is not true, that is not real, that is not possible or that is only imaginary?

2 What is the tense of the verbs in the *if*-clauses? Are the sentence about the past? Is it correct to say *If I were...*?

3 Are the result clauses the same as the *if*-clauses? Is there a modal in the result clauses?

LEARN

▶ *A* and *b* are examples of what is sometimes called the *second conditional*. Second conditional sentences are about something <u>that is not true, that is not real, that is (probably) not possible or that is only imaginary</u>.

▶ Second conditional sentences are used with *if*. The tense of the *if*-clause is past, and the result clause contains a modal—usually *would* or *could*. (But you will see in Section 20.5 that there are exceptions to this pattern.) Although the *if*-clause of second conditional sentences is in the past, it is important to understand that second conditional sentences are <u>not about the past</u>. Think of it as a different way to use <u>the form of the past</u>.

*If I **knew** the answer, I **would tell** you.*
<u>past tense</u>   <u>modal + verb</u>

▶ In the very best English, *were* is used in the *if*-clause for singular and plural subjects.

*If I **were** rich, I'd buy a big house.*

*He'd have more money in the bank if he **weren't** married.*

But not all native speakers of English speak the very best English, so it is very common to hear *was* instead of *were* in first conditional sentences. This is OK, but if you can remember to use *were*, you will be speaking the very best English!

OK →   *If I **was** a doctor and not an English teacher, I would make more money.*

better → *If I **were** a doctor and not an English teacher, I would make more money.*

REMEMBER

▶ Usually in speaking and very often in writing, native speakers use contractions of *would*. Although it is never necessary to use contractions, it is necessary to understand them.

*He **would** help me if he weren't so busy.*

*= He**'d** help me if he weren't so busy.*

Practice 4 Make second conditional sentences with the words in parentheses. Decide which is better—*would* or *could*. Sometimes both *would* and *could* are possible. Be ready to explain your answer.

Examples: I want to answer your question, but I don't know the answer. If I (know) _____*knew*_____ the

answer, I (tell) _____*would tell*_____ you.

He speaks English. If he (not, speak) _____*didn't speak*_____ English, he (not, be)

_____*couldn't be*_____ an English teacher.

1   I don't have a car. I (get to) _____ work faster if I (have) _____ one.

2   I don't live in Montana. If I (live) _____ in Montana, I (go) _____ hiking in the mountains.

3   Alex isn't here. I (ask) _____ him to help me if he (be) _____ here.

4   I want to go to the picnic with you, but I have to work today. If I (not, have) _____ to work today, I (go) _____ with you to the picnic.

5   I'm really busy. If I (not, be) _____ so busy, I (help) _____ you.

6   Sarah and Mary have visas. If Sarah and Mary (not, have) _____ visas, they (not, enter) _____ this country.

7   Francesca wants to go to the concert, but she has a headache. Francesca (go) _____ to the concert if she (not, have) _____ a headache.

8   Rosa is very tired. If she (not, be) _____ so tired, I'm sure she (be) _____ happy to help you.

Practice 5 Make zero, first or second conditional sentences with the words in parentheses and modal verbs that you think are correct.

1   My best friend lives in Los Angeles, and I visit her every time I travel there. If I (be) _____ in L.A., I always (visit) _____ her.

2   I want to buy some new shoes, but the shoe store is closed, so I can't. I (buy) _____ some new shoes if the shoe store (not, be) _____ closed now.

3   Sam might come for dinner tonight. If he (come) _____, we (have) _____ fried chicken for dinner.

4   Francesca usually doesn't have any problem with her homework, but when she (have) _____

a problem, she (ask) _____ her father for help.

5 I like to play tennis, but I can't play tennis anymore because I have a bad leg. I (play) _____

tennis if I (not, have) _____ a bad leg.

6 Sarah has a lot of homework. She says she (stay) _____ home tonight if she (not, finish)

_____ it.

7 John is tall, so he can reach the books on the top shelf of the bookcase. He (not, reach) _____

them if he (not, be) _____ so tall.

8 You are not rich, so you have to work, but if you (be) _____ rich and (not, have)

_____ to work, what (do) _____ you _____ with
your time?

20.4 ▶ third conditional: not true in the past

DISCOVER

  a **yesterday**
  Mary: Hi, Sarah. Can I borrow $100?
  Sarah: I'm sorry Mary. I want to help you, but I don't have $100. **If I had** $100, I **would give** it to you.
  today
  Sarah: Mary asked me for $100 yesterday.
  Lucy: Did you give it to her?
  Sarah: I wanted to help her, but I didn't have $100. **If I had had** $100, I **would have given** it to her.

1 Did Sarah want to give Mary $100? Did Sarah give Mary $100?
2 How did the conditional sentence change when Sarah was talking about the past?

  b **three years ago**
  Mark: I'm getting bad grades in my college classes.
  John: Well Mark, you **could get** better grades **if** you **didn't spend** all your time watching TV.
  today
  John: Mark got bad grades in his college classes.
  Alex: Did he work hard?
  John: No, he didn't. He **could have gotten** better grades **if** he **hadn't spent** all his time watching TV.

3 Did John think it was possible for Mark to get good grades when he was in college? Did Mark get good grades?
4 How did the conditional sentence change when John was talking about the past?

LEARN

▶ Conversations a and b are examples of what is sometimes called the *third conditional*. Third conditional sentences are about something <u>that was not true, that was not real, that was not possible or that was only imaginary in the past</u>.

▶ Third conditional sentences are used with *if*. In third conditional sentences, the *if*-clause is formed with *had* + past participle. The result clause is often formed with *would* or *could* + *have* + past participle. (But you will see in Section 20.6 that there are exceptions to this pattern.)

  If I had known you were going to visit, I **would have cleaned** the house.
  had + past participle   would + have + past participle

  He **could have gotten** to the cinema before the movie started **if** he **had left** his house 15 minutes earlier.
  could + have + past participle   had + past participle

REMEMBER

▶ Many native speakers make a grammatical error when forming third conditional *if*-clauses. They say *would have* instead of *had*. This is common, but it is not correct.

  wrong → If you **would have** left earlier, you **wouldn't have been** late for class.

  right → If you **had** left earlier, you **wouldn't have been** late for class.

▶ The following contractions are common in third conditional sentences.

  If **she had**..., etc.

  = If **she'd**..., etc.

  I **would have**..., etc.

  = I **would've**..., etc.

*You **would have**..., etc.*

*= You'**d have**..., etc.*

▶ In informal pronunciation, *would've* and *could've* often sound like *woulda* and *coulda*.

▶ Remember that you do not need to use contractions and informal pronunciation, but you must understand them.

Practice 6 Change the second conditional sentences to third conditional sentences.

Examples: If my sister were here, I would show her my new car.

If my sister had been here, I would have shown her my new car.

We couldn't figure out these math problems if we didn't have this calculator.

We couldn't have figured out these math problems if we hadn't had this calculator.

1   If we went to Beijing, we would go to the Forbidden City.

2   Sarah could make cookies if she had enough chocolate.

3   I would help her if she asked me.

4   If I saw another student cheating on the test, I wouldn't tell the teacher.

5   I couldn't see anything if I didn't have my glasses.

6   If you were sick, would you stay home from work?

7   What would you say to Maria if she were here?

8   If it were raining, the children wouldn't be playing outside.

9   I wouldn't be surprised if I were fired for making such a big mistake.

10   What would you do if you didn't have any money?

Practice 7 Make first, second or third conditional sentences with the words in parentheses and modal verbs that you think are correct.

Examples: If the supermarket (not, be) _____*hadn't been*_____ closed when we got there, we could have gotten something to make for dinner tonight.

I can't ask Rosa because she isn't here. If she were here, I (ask) _____*could ask*_____ her.

1   If I (need) _____ a ride to the mall, I'd ask my neighbor.

2   If you (not, waste) _____ your time goofing around, you could have gotten all your work done.

3   You (not, be) _____ late to the meeting yesterday if you'd left earlier.

4   Noura might come over tonight if she (have) _____ enough time.

5   If your car (be) _____ stolen, would your insurance company pay for a new one?

6   I'd go with you to the soccer game tomorrow if I (not, have) _____ to work.

7   Carlos wouldn't have burned dinner if he (not, fall) _____ asleep on the sofa after he put it in the oven.

8   Ali might visit tomorrow. If he (be) _____ here, ask him for some advice about your problem.

9   I can't tell you. If your father were here, he (tell) _____ you the whole story.

10   The movie we saw last night was terrible. You (not, like) _____ it if you had gone with us.

20.5 ▶ second conditional with past result clauses

DISCOVER

*a   My Russian neighbors are talking now. **If I spoke** Russian, I **could understand** them.*

1   What is the tense of the verb in the result clause?

*b   My German neighbors were talking yesterday. **If I spoke** German, I **could have understood** them.*

2   What is the tense of the verb in the result clause?

▶ In Section 20.3, second conditional sentences similar to *a* were discussed. The result clauses were about the present or the future. In *b* you can see that sometimes second conditional result clauses can be about the past.

*If I **liked** country music, I **would have gone** with them to the concert last weekend.*

*She **would not have said** those crazy things **if** she **didn't have** mental problems.*

Practice 8 Complete the sentences with the verbs in parentheses. Use the modals *would, could* and *might*. There may be more than one good answer for some. Be ready to explain your answer.

Example: If I didn't have financial problems myself, I (give) ___would have given___ you enough money to pay your medical bills last year, and I (give) ___would give___ Linda the money she needs now.

1 If I were you, I (not, be) _____ happy about getting an F in English last semester, and I (not, be) _____ happy about the D you got on the exam today.

2 You (not, have) _____ so much work to do yesterday and (not, have) _____ so much work to do now if you worked harder.

3 Noura (visit) _____ her brother in Australia last year if she weren't afraid of flying, and she (visit) _____ her sister in New Zealand this year too.

4 We (go) _____ to our daughter's wedding last month if it weren't so expensive to fly to South Africa from here.

5 Mark (not, be) _____ able to communicate so easily with people in China last year if he didn't speak Chinese so well.

6 If Lucy weren't a doctor, _____ she (know) _____ what to do when her husband had a heart attack?

7 I already told you I really want to have dinner at your mother's house. If I didn't want to have dinner at your mother's, I (not, say) _____ that I do.

8 I really love to go dancing, so if I didn't have so much work to do, I definitely (go) _____ dancing with you last night, and for sure I (go) _____ dancing with you tonight too.

20.6 ▶ third conditional with present result clauses

DISCOVER

    a   *Mark didn't finish high school. **If** he **had finished** high school, he **could have gotten** a better job.*

1 What is the tense of the verb in the result clause?

    b   *Mark didn't finish high school. **If** he **had finished** high school, he **could get** a better job now.*

2 What is the tense of the verb in the result clause?

LEARN

▶ In Section 20.4, third conditional sentences similar to *a* were discussed. The result clauses were about the past. In *b* you can see that sometimes third conditional result clauses can be about the present.

*If you **hadn't spent** all your money yesterday, you **would have** enough money now.*

*She **might believe** you if you **hadn't lied** to her before.*

Practice 9 Complete the sentences with the verbs in parentheses. Use the modals *would, could* and *might*. There may be more than one good answer for some. Be ready to explain your answer.

Example: If Sarah hadn't gone to Canada last week, she (be) ___would have been___ at the meeting yesterday, and she (be) ___would be___ at the meeting tomorrow.

1 If you hadn't crashed your car last week, you (not, need) _____ to ride your bicycle to work yesterday, and (not, need) _____ to ride your bicycle tomorrow.

2 If Maria could speak English better, she (understand) _____ what everybody at the party was saying last night, and she (understand) _____ what we are talking about now.

3   If I'd studied more last week, I (know) _____ the answers to yesterday's quiz, and I (know) _____ the answers to the homework I'm doing now.

4   If Sam had read my email last week, he (not, done) _____ everything wrong, and the boss (not, be) _____ angry now.

5   Ali wanted to be here. He (come) _____ if he didn't have to pick up Noura at the airport today.

6   If you had gotten gas yesterday as I suggested, you (not, run out of) _____ gas, and we (not, be) _____ sitting here now in this car on the side of the road.

7   If Linda had been paying attention yesterday, she (understand) _____ what we were talking about at the meeting, and she (not, be) _____ totally confused about what to do now.

8   Somebody stole my car. If I hadn't left it unlocked, it (not, be) _____ stolen, and I (not, be) _____ standing here on the corner right now waiting for the bus.

20.7 ▶ implied conditional

DISCOVER

a   Sam: *Was Mark at the game yesterday?*
    Dave: *Mark would have been there, but he had to work.*

b   John: *I'm thinking about quitting my job.*
    Alex: *Are you crazy? That's not a good idea. I wouldn't do that.*

c   Sarah: *Let's go the beach.*
    Noura: *What a great idea! I'd love to go to the beach.*

d   Ali: *Do you understand now?*
    Lucy: *Thanks, I couldn't have done it without you.*

e   Waiter: *May I take your order?*
    Tom: *Yes, I'd like a cheeseburger and a cup of coffee.*

f   Rosa: *Mary was at my house yesterday, and now I can't find my gold necklace. I think she stole it.*
    Larry: *That's impossible. I know Mary. She would never have done that.*

1   Each conversation contains a conditional. Do you see it?

LEARN

▶ Very often, conditionals are *implied*. Implied means that they are understood but not actually said or written. Below are the same conversations with the conditional ideas in **bold**.

a   Sam: *Was Mark at the game yesterday?*
    Dave: *Mark would have been there, but he had to work.*
            *= Mark would have been there **if he hadn't had to work**.*

b   John: *I'm thinking about quitting my job.*
    Alex: *Are you crazy? That's not a good idea. I wouldn't do that.*
            *= Are you crazy? That's not a good idea. I wouldn't do that **if I were you**.*

c   Sarah: *Let's go the beach.*
    Noura: *What a great idea! I'd love to go to the beach.*
            *= What a great idea! I'd love to go to the beach **if we went to the beach**.*

d   Ali: *OK, do you understand now?*
    Lucy: *Thanks, I couldn't have done it without you.*
            *= Thanks, I couldn't have done it without you **if you hadn't helped me**.*

e   Waiter: *May I take your order?*
    Tom: *Yes, I'd like a cheeseburger and a cup of coffee.*
            *= Yes, I'd like a cheeseburger and a cup of coffee **if I had a cheeseburger and a cup of coffee**.*

f   Rosa: *Mary was at my house yesterday, and now I can't find my gold necklace. I think Mary stole it.*
    Larry: *That's impossible. I know Mary. She would never have done that.*
            *= That's impossible. I know Mary. She would never have done that **if she had had the chance to do that**.*

Practice 10 Rewrite the sentences to complete the *if*-clauses. In addition to implied conditionals in the answers, there are examples of ellipsis. Do you see them?

Example: Mary: Can I borrow some money?

            Sofia: I'd be happy to, but I'm totally broke.

              = I'd be happy to, if _____ *I weren't totally broke* _____.

1   Mark: Larry's not here. He was a little sick yesterday. Do you think he's going to stay home?

     Sarah: No, he'd have called by now. He should be here soon.

          = No, he'd have called by now if _____. He should be here soon.

2   Alex: Is Sofia going to the movie?

     Ali: Sofia would go, but she has a lot of homework to do.

          = Sofia would if _____.

3   Tom: Have you called Carlos?

     Dave: I would have called him, but my cell phone battery's dead.

          = I would have if _____.

4   John: I have to go to school now, but Sarah might come while I'm gone. She forgot her book here last night.

     Lucy: No problem. I'll give it to her.

          = I will if _____.

5   Tom: We're going camping next week. Do you want to come with us?

     Sam: I would, but I promised my mother I'd visit her.

          = I would if _____.

6   Sam: You could have seen Michael, but you weren't here. What happened?

     Noura: Yes, I know. I could have, but I forgot he was coming.

          = Yes, I know. I could have if _____.

7   Larry: Are you going to have lunch with us?

     Mary: I would, but I have a doctor's appointment.

          = I would if _____.

8   Rosa: Mary wanted to go to the movie with you and Tom yesterday. Did you take her?

     Maria: No, but I would have if I had known.

          = No, but I would have if I had known _____.

20.8 ▶ conditional sentence pattern practice

DISCOVER

    a   If I **hadn't been taking** a shower when you called, I could have heard the telephone ring.

    b   If my husband made more money, we **wouldn't be living** in this old house.

1   Can conditional sentence *if*-clauses be continuous? Can conditional sentence result clauses be continuous?

    c   If I **were chosen** to be the new manager, I would have to work longer hours.

    d   If you leave your keys in your car, it **might be stolen**.

2   Can conditional sentence *if*-clauses be passive? Can conditional sentence result clauses be passive?

    e   If I asked you to lend me $5,000, **would you give it to me**?

    f   If you were rich, **what would you buy**?

3   Can conditional sentence result clauses be *yes/no* questions? Can conditional sentence result clauses be information questions?

    g   If you go out, **don't forget** to close the door.

    h   If you need help, **tell** me.

4   Can conditional sentence result clauses be imperative?

LEARN
▶ Conditional sentences do not always follow the basic patterns taught in Sections 20.1, 20.2, 20.3 and 20.4. It is a good idea for students to practice a variety of sentence patterns.

Practice 11 Complete the sentences.

Example: You were not listening. You don't know what's going on.

            If you _____*had been listening*_____, you'd _____*know what's going on*_____.

1   You might see Mary today. I want you to give her this bag of cookies.

    If you _____, _____.

2   Because I was studying, I wasn't listening to the radio.

    If I _____, I _____.

3   You might go to Mexico City. Go to the museum there.

    If you _____, _____.

4   We don't have to be quiet because the baby isn't sleeping.

    If the baby _____, we _____.

5   Sarah might be fired. She can easily find another job.

    If Sarah _____, she _____.

6   It didn't snow a lot yesterday. School wasn't canceled.

    If it _____, school _____.

Practice 12 Complete the questions.

Example: A: If you could live anywhere in the world, _____*where would you live*_____?

         B: I would live in Paris.

1   A: If you knew the answer, _____?

      B: Yes, I would tell you.

2   A: If Mary had accepted the job offer, _____?

      B: Her salary would have been $70,000.

3   A: If Lucy had been looking out the window, _____?

      B: No, she couldn't have seen the accident.

4   A: If you get married someday, _____?

      B: I'd like to have three children.

5   A: If you had had a problem, _____, right?

      B: Yes, you're right. I wouldn't have known what to do.

20.9 ▶ negative conditional sentence practice

LEARN
▶ Conditional sentences are always more difficult for students when they are negative. For that reason, it is a good idea to get more practice with negative conditional sentences. Conditional sentences usually contain an *if*-clause and a result clause. It is very common for one or both of these clauses to be negative.

▶ Negative zero conditional sentences often follow these patterns.

    *Whenever our father **isn't** in a good mood, we **don't talk** to him.*

    *When my boss **doesn't let** me leave at 2:30, **I'm not** home when my kids get home from school.*

▶ Negative first conditional sentences often follow these patterns.

    *If she **isn't** there when I get there, I **won't wait** for her.*

    *If you **don't hurry**, you **won't be** there when your class starts.*

▶ Negative second conditional sentences often follow these patterns.
   *If he **weren't** so sick, he **wouldn't take** so much medicine.*
   *If I **didn't speak** Swedish, I **wouldn't be** able to talk to Uncle Erik.*

▶ Negative third conditional sentences often follow these patterns.
   *If Jack **hadn't been** driving so fast, he **wouldn't have run into** a tree.*
   *If Rosa **hadn't forgotten** her keys, she **wouldn't have been** locked out of her house.*

Practice 13 Complete the zero conditional sentences with the words in parentheses.

Example: If Daniela's favorite stylist (not, be) _____*isn't*_____ working when she goes to the salon,

she (not, let) _____*doesn't let*_____ anyone else cut her hair.

1 When the kids (not, have) _____ a lot of homework, they play in the backyard or watch TV.

2 If Mary (not, be) _____ studying, we (not, have to) _____ worry about making noise.

3 Whenever Alex (not, call) _____ his mother to tell her where he is, she gets worried.

4 If people (not, be) _____ on the guest list, we (not, allow) _____ them to enter the club.

5 If my car (not, start) _____, there (not, be) _____ any other way for me to get to work.

Practice 14 Complete the first conditional sentences with the words in parentheses. Use *will* if it is necessary.

Example: If you (not, follow) _____*don't follow*_____ my instructions, I (not, be) _____*won't be*_____ responsible if you are hurt.

1 If you (not, be) _____ careful, you'll make a mistake.

2 If Larry's at the party, I (not, talk) _____ to him.

3 If they (not, have) _____ enough money, I'll lend it to them.

4 If it (not, be) _____ warm tomorrow, we (not, go) _____ to the beach.

5 If you (not, buy) _____ at least 10 pizzas, there (not, be) _____ enough for everybody.

Practice 15 Complete the second conditional sentences with the words in parentheses. Use *would* if it is necessary.

Example: If Jack (not, cheat on) _____*didn't cheat on*_____ his exams, he (not, be)

_____*wouldn't be*_____ able to pass any of his college classes.

1 If you (not, be) _____ a teacher, what would you like to be?

2 If I were you, I (not, do) _____ that.

3 If you (not, eat) _____ so much, you (not, be) _____ overweight.

4 If he teacher (not, be) _____ so boring, the students (not, fall) _____ asleep in class.

5 If she (not, stay out) _____ all night partying, she (not, be) _____ so sleepy at work.

Practice 16 Complete the third conditional sentences with the words in parentheses. Use *would have* if necessary.

Example: If Jack (not, cheat on) _____*hadn't cheated on*_____ his exams, he (not, be)

_____*wouldn't have been*_____ able to pass any of his high school classes.

1 If I (not, be) _____ hiding in the closet, her husband would have found me.

2 If she'd been more polite, I (not, get) _____ so angry.

3 If my car (not, be) _____ at the mechanic, I (not, be) _____ driving my wife's car.

4   If Francesca (not, be) _____ looking up at just the right moment, she (not, see) _____ the supernova.

5   If Sam (not, goof around) _____ all semester, he (not, have to) _____ do his final project in one day.

20.10 ▶ *wish*

DISCOVER

a   *I'm having a lot of problems with my new car.* **I wish I hadn't bought** *it.*

b   *I failed the test. I didn't study, but* **I wish I had.**

1   Are *a* and *b* conditional sentences? Where is the *if*-clause? Is the speaker wishing for something in the past, present or future?

c   *I don't speak Japanese, but* **I wish I did.**

d   *I need to ask Ali a question, but he's not here.* **I wish he were** *here.*

2   Are *c* and *d* conditional sentences? Where is the *if*-clause? Is the speaker wishing for something in the past, present or future?

e   *It hasn't rained in a long time.* **I wish it would rain.**

f   *My sister is going to Hawaii. I've always wanted to go to there.* **I wish I could go** *with her.*

3   Are *e* and *f* conditional sentences? Where is the *if*-clause? Is the speaker wishing for something in the past, present or future?

4   In all the sentences, is the speaker wishing for something that is real or possible, or is he or she wishing for something that is not real or (probably) not possible?

LEARN

▶ Sentences with *wish* are a form of conditional sentence. Why? Because when we wish for something, we are wishing for it <u>because it is not true, because it is not real, because it is (probably) not possible or because it is only imaginary</u>.

▶ We can wish for something in the past that did not happen.

That math exam was really hard. I **didn't study***, and that was a mistake.* **I wish I had studied** *for the exam.*

Our teacher reviewed for the exam yesterday, and I **was** *absent.* **I wish I hadn't been absent.**

My friends went to a nice restaurant for lunch yesterday, but I **couldn't go***.* **I wish I could have gone** *with them.*

▶ We can wish for something in the present.

I can't go bike riding with my friends because I **don't have** *a bicycle.* **I wish I had** *a bicycle.*

We can't go shopping because today **is** *a holiday, and all the stores are closed.* **I wish today weren't** *a holiday.*

I'm sorry. I want to help you, but I **don't know** *the answer.* **I wish I knew** *the answer, but I don't.*

▶ We can wish for something in the future.

I'm trying to sleep, and my neighbors keep making noise. **I wish they would shut up.**

Sarah **can't come** *with us to the movie tonight.* **I wish she could come** *with us.*

Mary and Tom **are going to bring** *their dog to our wedding.* **I wish they weren't going to bring** *their dog.*

REMEMBER

▶ It is common to use ellipsis with *wish*.

I'm not married, but **I wish I were [married]***.*

I don't have a car, but **I wish I did [have a car]***.*

▶ It is common to say *I wish you would..., I wish he would...,* etc., to say that we want something to happen, that we want something to be true or that we want somebody to do something.

I wish you would be *quiet. I'm trying to study.*

I hate this hot weather. **I wish it would cool off.**

I wish you wouldn't smoke in the house.

▶ It is common to use *stop* and *quit* with *wish*.

I wish you would stop making *so much noise. I'm trying to study.*

What you're doing is really bothering me. **I wish you would quit doing** *that.*

Practice 17 Complete the sentences with the correct form of the verb. There may be more than one good answer for some.

Examples: I get angry every time she says that. I wish she _____*wouldn't say*_____ that.

You shouldn't have bought that car. I wish you _____*had bought*_____ a different car.

1   Mary never stops calling me. I don't have time to talk to her sometimes, so I wish she _____ me so much.

2   We live in a small house. I wish we _____ a bigger house.

3   Are you ever going to quit asking me? You keep asking me and asking me, and the answer is still no. I wish you _____ me.

4   Alex isn't helping me fix my car. I wish he _____ me.

5   I told my daughter not to quit school, but she did it anyway. I wish she _____ school.

6   My plane leaves at 5:25 a.m. tomorrow morning. I wish it _____ so early.

7   It's raining, and I didn't bring my umbrella. I wish I _____ my umbrella.

8   I'm really hungry, and we're not eating until 8:00. I wish we _____ sooner.

9   I'm worried about my son. When he drives, he doesn't wear his seat belt. I wish he _____ his seat belt.

10   Sarah isn't going to make my favorite cookies for my birthday. I wish she _____ them.

11   My sister has a big mouth. I told her a secret, and now everyone knows. I wish she _____ such a big mouth.

12   It's too bad you aren't going to be at my graduation next week. I wish you _____ there.

13   I wasn't there when Francesca visited. I wish I _____ there. I haven't seen her in a long time.

14   Carlos goes to a school far away. I wish he _____ to a school that was closer to home.

15   It's too bad you couldn't go with us last night. I wish you _____ with us.

16   My house is so dirty. I didn't know you were coming. I wish I _____ you were coming.

Continue to Unit 20/advanced ↓

20.11/a ▶ canceling *if* in conditional sentences

DISCOVER

   a   **If you had** studied, you would have passed the test.
   b   **Had you** studied, you would have passed the test.

1   Do a and b have the same meaning? How is b different from a?

   c   **If she were here**, we could ask her.
   d   **Were she here**, we could ask her.

2   Do c and d have the same meaning? How is d different from c?

   e   **If Mary comes** while I am at work, please give her this book.
   f   **If Mary should come** while I am at work, please give her this book.
   g   **Should Mary come** while I am work, please give her this book.

3   Do e, f and g have the same meaning? How are f and g different from e?

LEARN

▶ Sometimes in formal writing and speaking, the *if*-clause is canceled.

   had

   If is canceled, and *had* is put in front of the subject.

   If I had known you were coming, I would have baked a cake.
   = **Had I known** you were coming, I would have baked a cake.

   were

   If is canceled, and *were* is put in front of the subject.

   If I were you, I would go to a doctor.
   = **Were I** you, I would go to a doctor.

▶ conditional sentences

should

There are two ways that first conditional sentences can be made with *should*. One of them also cancels *if*. Both of them are formal and not common. In one way, *should* can be put before the verb in the *if*-clause (notice how *has* changes to *have*).

If he has a problem, I will help him.
= **If he should have** a problem, I will help him.

In another way, *should* can be put before the subject, and *if* canceled.

If he has a problem, I will help him.
= **Should he have** a problem, I will help him.

REMEMBER

▶ *If* is canceled in these ways only in formal speaking and writing. They are not common in more relaxed speaking and writing. It is never necessary to do this, but it is a good idea to understand it.

Practice 18/a Complete the sentences without using *if*.

Examples: If you had put on sunscreen as I suggested, you would not be sunburned now.

_____Had you put on_____ sunscreen as I suggested, you would not be sunburned now.

I would have flown to Madrid if I hadn't taken the train.

I would have flown to Madrid _____*had I not taken*_____ the train.

1   I would have visited you if I had known you were in the hospital.

I would have visited you _____ you were in the hospital.

2   If you had gotten up earlier, you wouldn't have been late for class.

_____ earlier, you wouldn't have been late for class.

3   I would never have believed it if I hadn't seen it with my own eyes.

I would never have believed it _____ it with my own eyes.

4   If she had been caught by the police, she might have been put in jail.

_____ by the police, she might have been put in jail.

5   If it hadn't started raining, the fire would have continued burning for a long time.

_____ raining, the fire would have continued burning for a long time.

6   How would things be different today if your country had lost the war?

How would things be different today _____ lost the war?

Practice 19/a Complete the sentences without using *if*.

Examples: If Sarah were here, what would you say to her?

_____*Were Sarah*_____ here, what would you say to her?

We would already be there if the traffic weren't so bad.

We would already be there _____*were the traffic not*_____ so bad.

1   If Carlos were here, he might know what to do.

_____ here, he might know what to do.

2   If today were Sunday, the library would be closed.

_____ Sunday, the library would be closed.

3   If I weren't a teacher, I'd like to be an engineer.

_____ a teacher, I'd like to be an engineer.

4   If you were rich, where would you live?

_____ rich, where would you live?

5   Do you think he would still be vice-president of the company if he weren't the boss's son?

Do you think he would still be vice-president of the company _____ the boss's son?

6   We could go to the beach today if it weren't so cold.

We could go to the beach today _____ so cold.

Practice 20/a Complete the sentences without using *if*.

Examples: You might miss your connecting flight if the plane arrives late.

You might miss your connecting flight if the plane _____*should arrive*_____ late.

You might miss your connecting flight _____*should the plane arrive*_____ late.

If he's not given a raise in salary, will he look for another job?

If he _____*should not be given*_____ a raise in salary, will he look for another job?

_____*Should he not be given*_____ a raise in salary, will he look for another job?

1   Can he exchange this shirt for a larger one if this one is too small?

Can he exchange this shirt for a larger one if this one _____ too small?

Can he exchange this shirt for a larger one _____ too small?

2   If anyone is looking for me, say that I'm not here.

If anyone _____ looking for me, say that I'm not here.

_____ looking for me, say that I'm not here.

3   You can see me after class if you have any questions.

You can see me after class if you _____ any questions.

You can see me after class _____ any questions.

4   Will you cancel the barbecue if it rains tomorrow?

Will you cancel the barbecue if it _____ tomorrow?

Will you cancel the barbecue _____ tomorrow?

5   If they aren't home when we get to their house, do you want to wait for them?

If they _____ home when we get to their house, do you want to wait for them?

_____ home when we get to their house, do you want to wait for them?

6   If Mary needs some advice, I'd be happy to talk to her.

If Mary _____ some advice, I'd be happy to talk to her.

_____ some advice, I'd be happy to talk to her.

20.12/a ▶ *would rather* in conditional sentences

DISCOVER
a   Alex **wasn't** at the meeting. I'd rather he **had been**.
b   Maria **told** everybody what happened. Would you rather she **had kept** her mouth shut?
c   Maria **told** everybody what happened. Would you rather **she hadn't [told everybody what happened]**?

1   Are *a, b* and *c* conditional sentences? Where is the *if*-clause? Are they about the past, present or future? Do you see examples of ellipsis?

d   You father **is** very strict. Would you rather he **weren't**?
e   My daughter **works** in a circus. I'd rather she **worked** in an office.
f   My daughter **works** in a circus. I'd rather she **didn't [work in a circus]**.

2   Are *d, e* and *f* conditional sentences? Where is the *if*-clause? Are they about the past, present or future? Do you see examples of ellipsis?

g   Michael **isn't going to be** there. I'd rather he **were**.
h   The game**'s starting** at 7:00 in the morning. I'd rather it **were starting** later.
i   The game**'s starting** at 7:00 in the morning. I'd rather it **weren't [starting at 7:00 in the morning]**.

3   Are g, h and i conditional sentences? Where is the *if*-clause? Are they about the past, present or future? Do you see examples of ellipsis?

LEARN

▶ *Would rather* is used in conditional sentences to talk about something that is different from reality that the speaker prefers. The speaker is talking about something that is not real or (probably) not possible. G, h and i are about the future. *H* and *i* are an examples of present continuous used for future plans. (See Section 4.2/a for more about present continuous used for future plans.)

I love the theater, museums and the opera, but **we live** *in a small town. I'd rather* **we lived** *in a big city.*

Practice 21/a Complete the sentences.

Examples: My son goes to a college far away. I'd rather he _____went_____ to a college that was closer.

Our neighbor has 12 dogs. I'd rather she __*didn't have*__ so many dogs.

1   Mary lives in a dangerous neighborhood. I'd rather she _____ in a safe neighborhood.

2   Mary lives in a dangerous neighborhood. I'd rather she _____ in a dangerous neighborhood.

3   Sam is taking the bus downtown. I think this is a bad idea. I'd rather he _____ a taxi.

4   Don't do it that way. I'd rather you _____ it this way.

5   We're leaving at 10:00. Would you rather we _____ leaving later?

6   I'm not happy that you're going to do it. I'd rather you _____.

Practice 22/a Complete the sentences with the verb in parentheses.

Examples: Alex is a teacher. I'd rather he (be) ____*were a doctor*____.

My daughter got married when she was very young. I'd rather she (wait) ____*had waited*____.

1   We bought a new car last month. What a mistake. I'd rather we (keep) _____ our old car.

2   We rent an apartment. I'd rather we (own) _____ a house.

3   My husband wants to paint our house green, but I'd rather he (leave) _____ it the color it is now.

4   We went out last night, and today I'm really tired. I'd rather we (stay) _____ home.

5   You want to walk all the way to the mall? It's two miles! I'd rather you (drive) _____.

6   Larry loves fried chicken and pizza. I'd rather he (eat) _____ more fruit and vegetables.

20.13/a ▶ *would you mind* in conditional sentences

DISCOVER

a   My car won't start. **Would you mind if I borrowed** yours?
b   Teacher, **would you mind if I were** late for class tomorrow?
c   I don't think we need to borrow any money, but **would you mind if we did**?
d   I might not be at the meeting tomorrow. **Would you mind if I weren't**?
e   Larry went to his sister's wedding. **Would she have minded if he hadn't**?

1   Are these conditional sentences? Why? Do you see examples of ellipsis?

LEARN

▶ *Would you mind* can be used in conditional sentences. The sentences are conditional because they are about a possibility that is or was not real (or is not real yet) that the speaker is imagining.

My house is being painted. **Would you mind** *if I* **stayed** *with you for a few days?*

Practice 23/a Complete the sentences with the words in parentheses.

Examples: I don't want to see that movie. Would you mind if we (go) _____*went*_____ to a different movie?

Would you mind if I (not, help) __*didn't help*__ you with your homework tonight? I'm very busy.

1   I'd rather stay home and relax, so would you mind if I (not, go) _____ shopping with you?

2　I'd like to get there earlier, but it's so far away. Would you mind if I (not, get) _____ there until later?

3　I don't feel like cooking tonight, so would you mind if we (go) _____ out for dinner?

4　Would you mind if I (listen) _____ to the radio while you are studying?

5　We need to save money. Would you mind if we (not, take) _____ a vacation this summer?

6　That taxi last night cost me $75! Would you have minded if we (walk) _____ there?

Practice 24/a Use *would you mind* to make conditional sentences. Change only the second sentence.

Example:　I have a doctor's appointment. I want to leave early today.

　　　　　Would you mind if I left early today?

1　It's cold. I want to close the window.

2　We have something important to do. We want to go home at 3:30.

3　I had a lot of work to do last night. I didn't want to go shopping with you.

4　We have to stop at the bank on the way. We want to be late to your party.

5　I don't have time to do it today. I want to do it tomorrow.

6　We don't have enough money to fly to Germany. We can't go to your wedding.

20.14/a ▶ *it's (about) time* in conditional sentences

DISCOVER

　　a　Sarah's been sick for a week. ***It's time*** she ***went*** to a doctor.
　　b　You haven't taken out the garbage yet? Well, ***it's about time*** you ***did***.

1　Are *a* and *b* conditional sentences? Why? Do you see an example of ellipsis?

LEARN

▶ *It's time* and *it's about time* can be used in conditional sentences. The sentences are conditional because the speaker is suggesting or demanding a possibility that is the opposite of what is real.

*Our son is 34 years old, and he still lives with us. **It's about time** he **moved out**.*

Practice 25/a Complete the sentences with the words in parentheses.

Example:　You've been screwing around all night! It's time you (do) _____*did*_____ your homework.

1　We need to be there in 15 minutes. It's time we (get) _____ moving.

2　What I told you before was a lie. It's about time you (know) _____ the truth.

3　Look at our ugly old sofa. It's time we (buy) _____ a new one.

4　My in-laws have been living in our basement for three months. It's about time they (leave) _____.

5　It's 3:00 in the morning, and my son hasn't come home yet. It's time he (come) _____ home.

6　You're 40 years old. It's about time you (get) _____ married.

7　I haven't been to the dentist in ten years. It's about time I (go) _____.

20.15/a ▶ ellipsis examples and practice (See Section 1.9/a for an explanation of ellipsis.)

DISCOVER

　　a　Rosa:　When your husband isn't working, what does he do?
　　　　Lucy:　He loves to go fishing. Whenever he ***can***, he ***does***.
　　　　　　　　= He loves to go fishing. Whenever he ***can [go fishing]***, he ***[goes fishing]***.

　　b　Mary:　Are you going to ***figure out what's wrong with the car***?
　　　　Sofia:　I ***will*** if I ***can***.
　　　　　　　　= I ***will [figure out what's wrong with the car]*** if I ***can [figure out what's wrong with the car]***.

　　c　Ali:　You should ***leave now*** if you want to ***get there on time***.
　　　　Bill:　You're right. If I ***don't***, I ***won't***.
　　　　　　　= You're right. If I ***don't [leave now]***, I ***won't [get there on time]***.

▶ conditional sentences

d John: Do you **have a swimming pool**? Swimming is great exercise. You should **do it**.
   Mark: No, but if I **did**, I **would**.
            = No, but if I **[had a swimming pool]**, I **would [swim]**.

e Noura: Are you going to **buy a new car**?
   Sarah: I **would** if I **could**, but I **can't**, so I **won't**.
            = I **would [buy a new car]** if I **could [buy a new car]**, but I **can't [buy a new car]**, so I **won't [buy a new car]**.

f Alex: Are you **the manager of this office**?
   Paul: I wish I **were**, but I'**m not**.
            = I wish I **were [the manager of this office]**, but I'**m not [the manager of this office]**.

g Joe: Are you sure you **want to go shopping**? You don't **have to** if you **don't want to**.
            = Are you sure you **want to go [shopping]**? You don't **have to [go]** if you **don't want to [go]**.
   Rosa: Yes, I **want to**. If I **didn't**, I **wouldn't**.
            = Yes, I **want to [go shopping]**. If I **didn't [want to go shopping]**, I **wouldn't [go shopping]**.

h Lucy: Why didn't you **call the fire department**? Didn't you **smell the smoke**?
   Sofia: No, but if I **had**, I **would have**.
            = No, but if I **had [smelled smoke]**, I **would have [called the fire department]**.

i Joe: Were you **invited to Linda's wedding**?
   Gary: No, and even if I **had been**, I still **wouldn't go**.
            = No, and even if I **had been [invited to Linda's wedding]**, I still **wouldn't go [to Linda's wedding]**.

j Mary: Hi, Sarah.
   Sarah: Mary! What a surprise. I didn't **know you were coming**. If I **had**, I would have cleaned the house.
            = Mary! What a surprise. I didn't **know you were coming**. If I **had [known you were coming]**, I would have cleaned the house.

k Ali: Did you **visit your son last summer**.
   Mark: No, he **lives very far away**. If he **didn't**, I **might have**.
            = No, he **lives very far away**. If he **didn't [live very far away]**, I **might have [visited my son last summer]**.

Practice 26/a Underline the correct words.

Example: A: I'm sure you know the answer to this homework question. Will you please tell me?

            B: Sorry, but I don't know the answer. I can't tell you. If I (do/<u>did</u>), I (<u>would</u>/will), but I (<u>don't</u>/didn't).

1 A: Is the mechanic going to finish your car today?

   B: I hope so. If she (won't/doesn't), I'm going to have a problem getting to work tomorrow.

2 A: If you have to work on Saturday, will you still be able to come to our picnic?

   B: I want to come, but I may have to work Saturday. If I (didn't/don't), I (will/would).

3 A: If your company transferred you to Arizona, would you go?

   B: I hate hot weather, but I (will/would) if I had to.

4 A: Are you going to go to the museum exhibit tomorrow?

   B: I don't want to go alone, but Linda might go. If she (did/does), I (will/would) too.

5 A: Is your husband going with you on your trip to China?

   B: No, he isn't. He (will/would) if he (could/can), but he (can't/couldn't) because he has to stay here and work.

6 A: Do you really believe me?

   B: I already said I believe you. If I (don't/didn't), I wouldn't say I do.

7 A: Do you know how to fly a plane?

   B: I sure do. I'm a pilot, so if I (don't/didn't), it would be difficult for me to do my job.

8 A: Why are you wearing a tie?

   B: I'm wearing a tie because I'm going to a job interview. I (won't be/wouldn't be) if I (weren't/am not).

9   A: You should have studied for the exam. You failed it.

    B: Yes, I (should have/should), but I (don't/didn't). If I (hadn't/had), I (wouldn't/wouldn't have).

10 A: Is it true that Henry was eaten by a dragon?

    B: Yes, it's true. I wish he (hadn't been/wouldn't have been) because it certainly ruined our vacation.

Practice 27/a Complete the conditional sentences using ellipsis. There may be more than one good answer for some.

Examples: A: Do you want to go to a Japanese restaurant with us?

              B: I'm not hungry, and even if I _____*were*_____, I don't like Japanese food.

              A: How did you finish that big project so fast?

              B: By working all night. If I _____*hadn't*_____, I _*couldn't have*_ .

1   A: Can you translate this letter in Spanish for me?

    B: Sorry, I can't speak Spanish, but if I _____, I would.

2   A: Did Sofia go to the doctor yesterday?

    B: No, she didn't because if she _____, she would have been late for work.

3   A: Can you give me a ride to the airport tomorrow?

    B: I want to help you, but I have to work. I _____ if I _____, but I _____.

4   A: Does John have a car?

    B: Yes, he does. If he _____, he would have to take the bus to work every day.

5   A: Do you always eat breakfast?

    B: Yes, I do. If I _____, I get really hungry at work.

6   A: Are you married?

    B: Yes, I am. If I _____, why would I be wearing this wedding ring?

7   A: Does Mary smoke?

    B: I'm not sure. If she _____, I have never seen her.

8   A: Wow! How did you get such a good grade on the calculus exam?

    B: I studied like crazy. If I _____, I couldn't have done so well.

9   A: Francesca wanted to go to the party. Did she go with you?

    B: Francesca wanted to go, but she doesn't have a car, so she couldn't go without me, and I didn't go. If I _____, she _____ too.

10 A: You lost your keys? How did you get inside your house?

    B: I got in through a window that was open. I don't know how else I _____ if it _____.

Practice 28/a Complete the sentences so that the speaker is wishing for the opposite for what is real or true. Use ellipsis.

Examples: I don't know the answer. I wish I _____*did*_____, but I don't.

              Gary started smoking when he was in high school, but he wishes he _____*hadn't*_____.

1   John bothers me. He's here now, but I wish he _____.

2   Sam bothers me too. He was here yesterday, but I wish he _____.

3   Larry found out what happened. I wish he _____, but he did.

4   I couldn't go to the concert last night, but I wish I _____.

5   I'm not taking a vacation next summer. I wish I _____, but I'm not.

6   Rosa can't help me. I wish she _____, but she can't.

7   Michael isn't going to be there. I wish he _____, but he isn't.

8   Noura won't go with us, but I wish she _____.

9   I don't live in Canada. I wish I _____, but I don't.

10   My husband doesn't know how to dance, but I wish he _____.

Practice 29/a Complete the sentences. Use ellipsis.

Examples: Sam talks too much. I'd rather he _____*didn't*_____.

Are you going to paint the house purple? I'd rather you _____*weren't*_____.

1   You have a gun? They're dangerous. I'd rather you _____.

2   My wife got her hair cut really short. I'd rather she _____.

3   Larry isn't going to be there, but I'd rather he _____.

4   Linda didn't follow the plan. I'd rather she _____.

5   John won't take my advice. I'd rather he _____.

6   Why did you do that? I'd rather you _____.

7   My son doesn't have a job. I'd rather he _____.

8   Michael is planning to go skydiving, but I'd rather he _____.

9   He didn't listen to me. I'd rather he _____.

10   I don't exercise. My wife would rather I _____.

Appendix ▶ irregular verbs

infinitive	past simple	past participle
be	was, were	been
bear	bore	borne/born
beat	beat	beat/beaten
begin	began	begun
bend	bent	bent
bet	bet	bet
bid	bid	bid
bind	bound	bound
bite	bit	bitten
bleed	bled	bled
blow	blew	blown
break	broke	broken
bring	brought	brought
build	built	built
burn	burned/burnt	burned/burnt
buy	bought	bought
catch	caught	caught
choose	chose	chosen
come	came	come
cost	cost	cost
creep	crept	crept
cut	cut	cut
deal	dealt	dealt
dig	dug	dug
dive	dived/dove	dived/dove
do	did	done
draw	drew	drawn
dream	dreamed/dreamt	dreamed/dreamt
drink	drank	drunk
drive	drove	driven
eat	ate	eaten
fall	fell	fallen
feed	fed	fed
feel	felt	felt
fight	fought	fought
find	found	found
fit	fit/fitted	fit/fitted
flee	fled	fled
fly	flew	flown
forbid	forbade	forbidden
forget	forgot	forgotten
forgive	forgave	forgiven
freeze	froze	frozen
get	got	gotten/got[1]
give	gave	given
go	went	gone
grow	grew	grown
hang	hung/hanged[2]	hung/hanged[2]
have	had	had
hear	heard	heard
hide	hid	hidden
hit	hit	hit
hold	held	held
hurt	hurt	hurt
keep	kept	kept
know	knew	knew
lay	laid	laid
lead	led	led
learn	learned/learnt	learned/learnt
leave	left	left
lend	lent	lent
lie	lay	lain
light	lighted/lit	lighted/lit
lose	lost	lost
make	made	made
mean	meant	meant
meet	met	met
mistake	mistook	mistaken
pay	paid	paid
put	put	put
quit	quit	quit
read	read	read
rid	rid	rid

infinitive	past simple	past participle
ride	rode	ridden
ring	rang	rung
rise	rose	risen
run	ran	run
say	said	said
see	saw	seen
seek	sought	sought
sell	sold	sold
send	sent	sent
set	set	set
shake	shook	shaken
shine	shone/shined	shone/shined
shoot	shot	shot
show	showed	shown/showed
shrink	shrank	shrunk
shut	shut	shut
sing	sang	sung
sink	sank	sunk
sit	sit	sit
sleep	slept	slept
slide	slid	slid
smell	smelled/smelt	smelled/smelt
speak	spoke	spoken
speed	sped/speeded	sped/speeded
spell	spelled/spelt	spelled/spelt
spit	spit/spat	spit/spat
split	split	split
spoil	spoiled/spoilt	spoiled/spoilt
spread	spread	spread
spring	sprang/sprung	sprang/sprung
stand	stood	stood
steal	stole	stolen
stick	stuck	stuck
sting	stung	stung
stink	stank/stunk	stank/stunk
strike	struck	struck/stricken
string	strung	strung
swear	swore	sworn
sweep	swept	swept
swim	swam	swum
swing	swung	swung
take	took	taken
teach	taught	taught
tear	tore	torn
tell	told	told
think	thought	thought
throw	threw	thrown
understand	understood	understood
undertake	undertook	undertaken
upset	upset	upset
wake	woke	woken
wear	wore	worn
weave	wove	woven
weep	wept	wept
win	won	won
wind	wound	wound
withdraw	withdrew	withdrawn
write	wrote	written

In English, the infinitive form (also called the base form or simple form) and the present form of all verbs (except *be*) are always the same. Only the *-s* form (also called third person singular) is different. For example, *go*. The infinitive form is *go*, and the present form is also *go*. Only *goes* is different. See Section 3.1 for more about this.

[1]*Gotten* is used in America English. *Got* is used in British English.

[2]*Hung* is used for pictures, clothes, etc. *Hanged* is used for criminals.
   He **hung** his coat in the closet.
   The criminal was sentenced to death and **hanged** the next day.

# Answer Key

UNIT 1

Practice 1, page 1
1. am
2. are
3. are
4. is
5. are
6. is
7. are
8. are
9. are
10. is
11. is
12. am

Practice 2, page 2
1. She's angry.
2. I'm on the phone.
3. They're watching TV.
4. The door's open.
5. We're here.
6. Her mother's a pilot.
7. Michael's in the library.
8. They're there.
9. Arabic's spoken in Egypt.
10. We're teachers.

Practice 3, page 2
1. The children are playing in the park.
2. Francesca's doing her homework.
3. Dinner's served at 7:00.
4. I'm listening to the radio.
5. The students are studying.
6. Tom and Jerry are in the kitchen.
7. Larry's here.
8. The girl's tall.
9. The boys are short.
10. My children and I are at the beach.

Practice 4, page 3
1. They're not outside.
   They aren't outside.
2. The doctor's not at the clinic.
   The doctor isn't at the clinic.
3. You and I aren't playing.
4. The windows aren't washed every day.
5. She's not listening.
   She isn't listening.
6. He's not an engineer.
   He isn't an engineer.
7. I'm not hungry.
8. She's not from Holland.
   She isn't from Holland.
9. Tobacco's not sold to people under 18.
   Tobacco isn't sold to people under 18.

Practice 5, page 3
1. The pencil's not on the table.
   The pencil isn't on the table.
2. John's not a student.
   John isn't a student.
3. We're not in front of the supermarket.
   We aren't in front of the supermarket.
4. The men aren't singing.
5. Michael's not here.
   Michael isn't here.
6. I'm not finished.
7. He's not in bed.
   He isn't in bed.
8. They're not here.
   They aren't here.
9. It's not cold outside.
   It isn't cold outside.
10. We're not next.
    We aren't next.

Practice 6, page 4
1. I'm not eating breakfast.
2. Mark's not reading a book.
   Mark isn't reading a book.
3. The projects aren't finished.
4. She's not here.
   She isn't here.
5. The book's not under the magazine.
   The book isn't under the magazine.
6. He and I aren't mechanics.
7. Carlos and Alex aren't going to school.
8. English isn't spoken in France.
9. You're not washing the car.
   You aren't washing the car.
10. He and Sofia aren't married.

Practice 7, page 5
1. the pilot's sleeping
2. Ali's not in the library
   or Ali isn't in the library
3. the soldiers are fighting
4. Toyotas are made in Japan
5. her sister's not here
   or her sister isn't here
6. Sarah's an artist
7. Larry's not tired
   or Larry isn't tired
8. the truck's not driven by Sam
   or the truck isn't driven by Sam
9. John and Alex are hungry
10. the kids aren't in the car

Practice 8, page 6
1. Are the cats under the sofa?
2. Is Carlos tired?
3. Are Tom and his wife in the gym?
4. Are you and John working hard?
5. Is the house dirty?
6. Are they cheap?
7. Is Larry a sailor?
8. Is the restaurant near the park?
9. Are Mark and Sarah at work?
10. Is she correct?
11. Is the pizza in the oven?

Practice 9, page 6
1. was
2. were
3. was
4. were
5. was
6. were
7. was
8. was
9. was
10. was
11. were

Practice 10, page 7
1. Noura was dancing.
2. The coffee was hot.
3. The men were truck drivers.
4. The house was sold.
5. My parents were there.
6. Francesca was drawing a picture.
7. They were sick.
8. Michael was on the corner.
9. Your wife was cleaning.
10. The people were outside.

Practice 11, page 7
1. I wasn't upstairs.
2. The women weren't at the party.
3. She and I weren't angry.
4. My house wasn't clean.
5. Maria wasn't a secretary.
6. The sick man wasn't taken to the hospital.
7. The boys weren't playing basketball.

8 We weren't shopping.
9 The cat wasn't behind the sofa.
10 The guy wasn't there.
11 We weren't swimming in the lake.
12 The salad wasn't eaten.

Practice 12, page 8
1 John and Mark weren't in the bank.
2 The keys weren't in my pocket.
3 I wasn't talking on the telephone.
4 Her car wasn't stolen.
5 Our father wasn't cutting the grass.
6 We weren't cooking dinner.
7 The book wasn't on the desk.
8 She wasn't a good student.
9 The window wasn't broken.
10 Alex wasn't downstairs.
11 She wasn't with her friends.

Practice 13, page 8
1 My friends weren't at the game.
2 John wasn't taking a test.
3 The letters weren't sent yesterday.
4 I wasn't happy.
5 Gary wasn't riding a horse.
6 The door wasn't locked.
7 The cake wasn't made with flour.
8 Carlos wasn't ready.
9 I wasn't doing my homework.
10 The pens weren't in the desk.
11 The show wasn't over.
12 We weren't done.

Practice 14, page 9
1 the party was fun
2 John and Michael weren't at the meeting
3 the students were listening to the teacher
4 the doctor wasn't in the clinic
5 the movie wasn't good
6 Mary and her friend were playing outside
7 Linda wasn't riding her bicycle
8 the women weren't there
9 Larry was drinking milk
10 the sandwiches were made by me

Practice 15, page 9
1 Were Sofia and her sister sleeping?
2 Was the calculator on the table?
3 Was his father a police officer?
4 Were the men late?
5 Were the cookies eaten by the children?
6 Were they running?
7 Was the baby crying?
8 Was the mechanic fixing the car?
9 Was John speaking Chinese?
10 Was Ali reading a book?
11 Was the criminal caught by the police?

Practice 16, page 10
1 Michael was washing the dishes.
2 It wasn't here.
3 We were angry.
4 Were the girls in the classroom?
5 Was Tom riding his bicycle?
6 They weren't there.
7 Sarah wasn't in the house.
8 I wasn't doing my homework.
9 They weren't eating lunch.
10 Was Noura talking to her friend?

Practice 17, page 10
1 Are you at the beach?
2 Maria's not in the hospital.
   or Maria isn't in the hospital.
3 Three boys are outside.
4 Is the bird flying?
5 Are Tom and Lucy married?
6 She's not reading in the library.
   or She isn't reading in the library.
7 Is the boy swimming?
8 The car is parked in the garage.
9 Larry's not at work.
   or Larry isn't at work.
10 My classes are boring.
11 She's mopping the floor.

Practice 18, page 11
1 I am
2 we weren't
3 it was
4 she wasn't
5 they are
6 she's not
   or she isn't
7 it is
8 they weren't
9 we're not
   or we aren't
10 he was

Practice 19/a, page 12
2 d
3 f
4 c
5 e
6 a
7 b
8 c
9 e
10 f
11 b
12 f
13 a or f (See Section 10.6 and Section 10.9.)

Practice 20/a, page 13
1 My house is big, but your house isn't ~~big~~.
2 John wasn't there, but I was ~~there~~.
3 Rosa's working hard. Is her sister ~~working hard~~ too?
4 The doctor is in the lab, but the nurse isn't ~~in the lab~~.
5 The chocolate cake is good. Is the apple pie ~~good~~ too?
6 Mark is a taxi driver, but Linda isn't ~~a taxi driver~~.
7 My car was stolen, and my motorcycle was ~~stolen~~ too.
8 You were listening to the teacher, but I wasn't ~~listening to the teacher~~.
9 Alex was home, but I wasn't ~~home~~.
10 Your car is in the garage, and my car is ~~in the garage~~ too.
11 Sarah is learning to drive, but Sofia isn't ~~learning to drive~~.

Practice 21/a, page 13
1 riding his bicycle
2 wrong
3 in the lab
4 done
5 sick
6 studying
7 broken
8 ready to go
9 working hard
10 married

Practice 22/a, page 14
1 My house isn't big, but your house is.
2 John was there, and I was too.
3 He's in the basement, but Francesca isn't.
4 The cow is in the field, and the horse is too.
5 Mexican food is spicy, but Swedish food isn't.
6 John is playing football, but Michael isn't.
7 Larry is rich, but I'm not.
8 My mother wasn't home, but my father was.
9 Lucy is on the plane, but her husband isn't.
10 Henry was eaten by a dinosaur, but I wasn't.

UNIT 2
Practice 1, page 15
1 The birds are flying.
2 I'm reading a book.
3 Michael's dancing.
4 Tom and Jerry are fighting.
5 Ali's playing cricket.
6 The pilot's sleeping.
7 Mark's using his computer.
8 The teachers are talking.

Practice 2, page 16
1 The printer's not working.
   The printer isn't working.
2 He's not doing his homework.
   He isn't doing his homework.
3 Ali's not listening to the radio.
   Ali isn't listening to the radio.
4 The children aren't being bad.

Answer Key

5 Mark's not helping his mother.
   Mark isn't helping his mother.
6 His sister's not shopping.
   His sister isn't shopping.
7 John and his brother aren't talking to their friends.
8 The manager's not driving to work.
   The manager isn't driving to work.
9 I'm not eating dinner.
10 Sofia and Rosa aren't studying.

Practice 3, page 16
1 Is the cat looking out the window?
2 Is Noura talking on the phone?
3 Is the mechanic fixing the truck?
4 Is Gary swimming in the pool?
5 Is Francesca sitting on the sofa?
6 Are Mary and Sarah playing a game?
7 Is the soldier exercising?
8 Is your father cooking dinner?
9 Are the children being noisy?
10 Am I doing this the right way?
11 Is the wolf eating Henry?

Practice 4, page 17
1 John's not working now.
   or John isn't working now.
2 The baby's sleeping.
3 Is Mark studying?
4 The horse's running.
5 Is Sarah sleeping now?
   or Sarah is sleeping now.
6 The doctor is working.
7 I'm not listening to you now.
8 He's reading.
9 Are you listening?
10 Michael's eating breakfast.

Practice 5, page 17
1 The nurse was helping the doctor.
2 I was driving my car.
3 Maria was cleaning the kitchen.
4 Alex and I were talking.
5 Carlos was reading a book.
6 They were trying to answer the question.
7 The students were doing their homework.
8 My mother was writing a letter.
9 Linda was downloading a song.
10 The cook was frying a hamburger.
11 Lucy was taking a test.

Practice 6, page 18
1 Maria and her son weren't washing the dishes.
2 The pilot wasn't talking on the radio.
3 I wasn't flying to Poland.
4 Tom wasn't making dinner.
5 Her husband wasn't looking for a job.
6 The truck drivers weren't eating lunch.
7 Mary and Larry weren't doing their homework.
8 The secretary wasn't finishing her work.
9 Michael wasn't taking a shower.
10 We weren't waiting for the bus.

Practice 7, page 18
1 Were your children waiting for you?
2 Was John drinking coffee?
3 Were the managers having a meeting?
4 Was Mary working in a bank?
5 Was Rosa planting flowers?
6 Were Alex and his friends going to the mall?
7 Was Sarah buying fruit?
8 Were you lying on the sofa?
9 Was the airplane landing?
10 Was the sun shining?

Practice 8, page 19
1 I was not working.
2 We were going to the beach.
3 Were they doing their homework?
4 She was not listening.
5 My sister wasn't playing tennis.
6 The bird was not singing.
7 They were not working.
8 John wasn't sleeping.
9 Were you studying?
10 Were you riding a horse?
   or You were riding a horse.

Practice 9/a, page 19
1 was sleeping / is watching
2 are fighting
3 was working
4 isn't doing
5 Were / listening
6 were making
7 is sleeping
8 was exercising / is taking
9 weren't playing
10 are eating
11 is being
12 weren't being

Practice 10/a, page 20
1 was reading
2 was watching / am doing
3 are sleeping
4 Were / playing
5 is driving
6 am trying / are being
7 was raining / is shining
8 was looking / was teaching
9 is being
10 is ringing

UNIT 3
Practice 1, page 21
1 goes
2 am talking
3 drinks
4 eat
5 comes
6 is fixing
7 fly
8 is flying
9 watch
10 is being

Practice 2, page 22
1 speak
2 lives
3 drinks
4 play
5 eats
6 eat
7 listen
8 wants
9 have
10 work
11 has

Practice 3, page 22
1 You don't have a car.
2 The dog doesn't eat potato chips.
3 Sarah doesn't have a computer.
4 Our father doesn't go to work at 7:30.
5 My mother doesn't like ice cream.
6 She and I don't know the answer.
7 Mary doesn't get up at 7:00.
8 I don't work on Saturdays.
9 He and I don't work together.
10 Carlos doesn't watch TV.

Practice 4, page 23
1 Does Maria swim in the lake?
2 Do they want to move to Canada?
3 Does Ali go to work at 8:00?
4 Do you and John watch TV?
5 Do his friends like to dance?
6 Does Carlos read a lot?
7 Does Mary have blue eyes?
8 Do you live in a big house?
9 Does Larry sleep all day?
10 Do Susan and her sister ride horses on the weekend?

Practice 5, page 24
1 Yes, he does.
2 No, he doesn't.
3 Yes, he does.
4 No, they don't.
5 Yes, they do.
6 No, he doesn't.
7 Yes, they do.

8 Yes, they do.
9 No, he doesn't.
10 Yes, he does.

Practice 6, page 25
1 They lived in Spain.
2 We cooked dinner.
3 You walked to school.
4 She rode her bicycle.
5 Mary and I drove to California.
6 I saw it.
7 You went to the beach.
8 He had a book.
9 John looked at the pictures.
10 Carlos bought chocolate.

Practice 7, page 25
1 He didn't work yesterday.
2 John didn't go to the mall.
3 Michael didn't talk to his sister.
4 We didn't have a red truck.
5 Your dog didn't eat my dinner.
6 Sarah and her friend didn't take the bus.
7 Alex didn't think about the answer.
8 Bill didn't fly to Lima.
9 My father didn't call me.
10 Mary didn't put the baby on the bed.

Practice 8, page 26
1 Did Ali finish his homework?
2 Did she fly to Russia?
3 Did you and John watch TV?
4 Did Linda see Larry?
5 Did he write a letter?
6 Did Carlos sleep late?
7 Did the students read their books?
8 Did Jack lie to you?
9 Did he cut the pizza?
10 Did Sofia know the answer?

Practice 9, page 27
1 Yes, he is.
2 Yes, he does.
3 No, he isn't.
  or No, he's not.
4 No, he isn't.
  or No, he's not.
5 Yes, he does.
6 Yes, he does.
7 Yes, she was.
8 No, she didn't.
9 Yes, she does.
10 No, she doesn't.
11 No, she isn't.
  or No, she's not.

Practice 10/a, page 27
1 don't
2 didn't
3 didn't
4 Do
5 doesn't
6 don't
7 don't
8 doesn't
9 doesn't
10 didn't
11 didn't
12 Did
13 did
14 Do

Practice 11/a, page 28
1 I don't do a lot of work.
2 Lucy doesn't do everything well.
3 We don't do all our shopping on Saturday.
4 I don't do my homework in the library.
5 She doesn't do it carefully.
6 Mark doesn't do the dishes after dinner.
7 They don't do it every day.
8 Carlos and I don't do our work in the morning.
9 We don't do the laundry on Sunday.

Practice 12/a, page 28
1 Does he do his work slowly?
2 Do they do the dishes after dinner?

3 Do they always do it the wrong way?
4 Does Sarah do her homework at school?
5 Do they do their exercises before dinner?
6 Does Michael do his work well?
7 Does he do his work in his office?
8 Do Francesca and Alex do the shopping?
9 Does he do the ironing badly?

Practice 13/a, page 28
1 She didn't do her work badly.
2 I didn't do it.
3 He didn't do the laundry.
4 He didn't do his homework last night.
5 You didn't do the right thing.
6 Tom didn't do everything wrong.
7 Larry didn't do a lot of work.
8 Maria didn't do her exercises in the afternoon.

Practice 14/a, page 29
1 Did Larry do his exercises?
2 Did you do the laundry this morning?
3 Did she do the best she could?
4 Did Carlos do a good job?
5 Did he do his homework after dinner?
6 Did they do the wrong thing?
7 Did he do it yesterday?
8 Did she do it right?

Practice 15/a, page 29
1 My horse does have five legs.
2 I did sleep for 18 hours.
3 Carlos does put coffee on his cereal.
4 I did see a pink elephant.
5 Alex and Carlos do live in a tree house.
6 I did go to Mars in a UFO.
7 My dog did eat my homework.
8 I do believe you.
9 I did do my homework yesterday.
10 I do do my homework every day.

Practice 16/a, page 30
1 Mary followed the plan, but Michael didn't ~~follow the plan~~.
2 I feel sick. Does he ~~feel sick~~ too?
3 My mother likes to eat fish, but my father doesn't ~~like to eat fish~~.
4 We agree with you, but they don't ~~agree with you~~.
5 Sarah went to college. Did her brother ~~go to college~~?
6 He has a job, but she doesn't ~~have a job~~.
7 My son sent me a birthday card, but my daughter didn't ~~send me a birthday card~~.
8 Cheese and butter have a lot of calories, but vegetables don't ~~have a lot of calories~~.
9 One of the students did her homework, but the other one didn't ~~do her homework~~.
10 We went to the concert last night. Did you ~~go to the concert last night~~?

Practice 17/a, page 31
1 like to play pool
2 go to the library
3 do it
4 want to eat
5 drink coffee
6 do it
7 stay open late
8 eat breakfast in the morning

Practice 18/a, page 31
1 The library closes at 8:30, and the supermarket does too.
2 Susan bought a TV last week, and I did too.
3 Mary read that book, and Michael did too.
4 I know how to swim, and my brother does too.
5 John thinks it's a good idea, and Sam does too.
6 I like to dance, and Linda does too.
7 Ali passed the test, and I did too.
8 I know the answer, and you do too.

UNIT 4
Practice 1, page 33
1 I'll make you a sandwich.
2 They'll get a good grade.
3 He'll write a book.
4 Larry and Carlos will go to the mall.
5 He'll be angry.
6 Sarah will go to the beach.
7 Noura and Ali will be at the mall.
8 I'll be late.

Answer Key

9 We'll be at the food court.
10 She'll be doing her homework.

Practice 2, page 33
1 They won't help her.
2 I won't go.
3 He won't change his mind.
4 Alex won't be there.
5 She won't do it.
6 We won't buy it.
7 The engineer won't finish the plan.
8 I won't go to the party.
9 She won't be at the museum.
10 We won't wait for him.

Practice 3, page 33
1 Will they come after dinner?
2 Will he lend Mark $1,000?
3 Will you help me?
4 Will Carlos be at the party?
5 Will the girls draw pictures?
6 Will she do her homework?
7 Will Mary, Larry, Gary and their parents be at the graduation?
8 Will they be camping in the desert?
9 Will the medicine be given to the sick children?
10 Will a killer whale be eating Henry?

Practice 4, page 34
1 My mother's going to go to Alaska.
2 The doctor's going to call me.
3 John's going to have a pizza.
4 They're going to buy a new car.
5 Larry's going to be late.
6 They're going to be early.
7 She's going to work hard.
8 I'm going to go to the supermarket.
9 The class is going to be taught in the fall semester.
10 I'm going to wait for you in the lobby.

Practice 5, page 34
1 He's not going to be here later.
  or He isn't going to be here later.
2 I'm not going to do it.
3 We're not going to eat in that restaurant again.
  or We aren't going to eat in that restaurant again.
4 He's not going to read this book.
  or He isn't going to read this book.
5 They're not going to have dinner after the movie.
  or They aren't going to have dinner after the movie.
6 Larry's not going to fly to Iceland.
  or Larry isn't going to fly to Iceland.
7 The test's not going to be difficult.
  or The test isn't going to be difficult.
8 She's not going to look for a new job.
  or She isn't going to look for a new job.
9 You're not going to be sorry.
  or You aren't going to be sorry.
10 I'm not going to be there.

Practice 6, page 34
1 Is Sofia going to have chicken for dinner?
2 Are you going to wash your car?
3 Are your friends going to go to Taiwan?
4 Are they going to work in the garden?
5 Are you and she going to be here next Sunday?
6 Are the children going to go to a movie?
7 Is her sister going to get married?
8 Is it going to be cold tomorrow?
9 Is the team going to be driven to the stadium?
10 Is he going to be studying?

Practice 7/a, page 35
1 Mary is calling me at 8:00.
2 When are we eating dinner?
3 We're eating dinner in a few minutes. We're having hamburgers.
4 When are you doing your homework?
5 I'm doing it in an hour.
6 How many people are coming to the party?
7 Around 25 people are coming to the party.
8 Is Carlos cooking dinner?
9 When are you going to Ottawa?
10 Why are you going there?

Practice 8/a, page 36
1 The show starts at 8:00.
2 When does the game begin?

3 It begins at 2:00.
4 What time does the store open?
5 The store opens at 10:00.
6 My English class begins at 8:20.
7 His flight arrives at 1840.
8 The meeting is at 10:30.
9 When is the test?
10 The test is next Tuesday.

Practice 9/a, page 37
1 I will tell Linda the news when I see her.
2 After Alex leaves the gym, he is going to go home.
3 Carlos is going to eat dinner before he does his homework.
4 When we are in Rome, we will go to the Vatican.
5 Maria will go to her hotel as soon as she arrives in Athens.
6 When I get there, I'll call you.
7 Will you help me with the laundry after we get home?
8 After John gets married, he's not going to have time to play golf.
9 When she is here, I'll be happy.
10 Bill will return this book to the library after he finishes it.

Practice 10/a, page 37
1 I will tell Linda the news <u>when I see her</u>.
2 <u>After Alex leaves the gym</u>, he is going to go home.
3 Carlos is going to eat dinner <u>before he does his homework</u>.
4 <u>When we are in Rome</u>, we will go to the Vatican.
5 Maria will go to her hotel <u>as soon as she arrives in Athens</u>.
6 <u>When I get there</u>, I'll call you.
7 Will you help me with the laundry <u>after we get home</u>?
8 <u>After John gets married</u>, he's not going to have time to play golf.
9 <u>When she is here</u>, I'll be happy.
10 Bill will return this book to the library <u>after he finishes it</u>.

Practice 11/a, page 37
1 <u>When I ~~will~~ arrive in Madrid</u>, I will call you.
2 She's going to wash the dishes <u>after she ~~is going to~~ eats dinner</u>.
3 Is the teacher going to return our tests <u>after she grades them</u>?
4 <u>Before I go to the beach</u>, I'll stop to buy gas.
5 We won't eat dinner <u>until Daddy ~~will~~ gets home from work</u>.
6 Are you going to do your homework <u>after you ~~will~~ get home</u>?
7 <u>As soon as I ~~will~~ get home</u>, I will start to cook dinner.
8 I'll meet you at the gym <u>after I change my clothes</u>.
9 <u>After I ~~will~~ leave my office</u>, I'll get a taxi to the airport.
10 <u>When you get to work</u>, come to my office with the sales report.
11 <u>When you ~~will~~ go to Paris</u>, will you see the Eiffel Tower?

Practice 12/a, page 38
1 He's about to answer the phone.
2 She was about to turn on the TV.
3 I was about to take a shower.
4 He was about to leave.
5 I'm about to close the window.
6 It's about to rain.

Practice 13/a, page 39
1 Rosa isn't going to be here today, but she is going to be ~~here~~ tomorrow.
  Rosa isn't going to be here today, but she is ~~going to be here~~ tomorrow.
2 I'm not going to ride my bike before dinner, but I am going to ~~ride my bike~~ after dinner.
  I'm not going to ride my bike before dinner, but I am ~~going to ride my bike~~ after dinner.
3 Paul is going to speak at the conference. Is Sam going to ~~speak at the conference~~?
  Paul is going to speak at the conference. Is Sam ~~going to speak at the conference~~?
4 They're going to go, and I am going to ~~go~~ too.
  They're going to go, and I am ~~going to go~~ too.
5 I'm going to leave early today. Are you going to ~~leave early today~~ too?
  I'm going to leave early today. Are you ~~going to leave early today~~ too?

Practice 14/a, page 39
1 I didn't say anything, but I was about to ~~say something~~.
2 We'll get to the meeting around 9:00, but Carlos won't ~~get to the meeting~~ until later.
3 I'm not going to be on time for the meeting, but Gary is going to be ~~on time for the meeting~~.
  I'm not going to be on time for the meeting, but Gary is ~~going to be on time for the meeting~~.
4 Francesca won't be working when we get there, but Sofia will be ~~working when we get there~~.
  Francesca won't be working when we get there, but Sofia will ~~be working when we get there~~.
5 I won't be at work tomorrow. Will you be ~~at work tomorrow~~?
  I won't be at work tomorrow. Will you ~~be at work tomorrow~~?

Practice 15/a, page 40

1 B1 'm not going to
   B2 'm not
2 B will
3 B1 's not going to
      or isn't going to
   B2 's not
      or isn't
4 B1 'm going to
   B2 am
5 B was about to
6 B 're about to

UNIT 5
Practice 1, page 41

1 I/them
2 He/us
3 She/me
4 They/her
5 We/him
6 They/us
7 She/us
8 I/her

Practice 2, page 41

1 He/her
2 We/them
3 He/us
4 They/them
5 They/us
6 He/it
7 You/them
8 They/you
   *(Confused about 7 and 8? Remember
   that* you *is singular and plural in English.)*

Practice 3, page 42

1 Our/yours
2 mine/yours
3 ours/theirs
4 my
5 My/hers
6 Your/ours
7 my/yours
8 hers/mine
9 Ours
10 theirs/yours

Practice 4, page 43

1 Sarah's
2 boys'/girls'
3 Larry's
4 company's
5 babies'
6 children's
7 women's
8 men's
9 friend's/parents'

Practice 5, page 44

1 a a
   b the
   c the
   d the
   e a
2 a A
   b The
   c the
   d a
   e The
   f the
3 a an
   b a
   c the
   d a
   e the
   f The
   g an
   h the
   i the

Practice 6, page 45

1 Ø
2 The

3 Ø
4 Ø
5 The
6 The
7 Ø
8 Ø
9 Ø

Practice 7, page 45

1 any *or* some
2 any
3 some
4 any *or* some
5 some
6 any
7 any/some
8 any *or* some
9 any
10 any *or* some

Practice 8, page 46

1 Nobody went to the meeting.
2 I don't have anything.
   or I have nothing.
3 Not every man likes sports.
4 Is everyone here?
5 Everyone in the office hates the new manager.
6 If everybody is ready, we will start the test.
7 I didn't see anybody.
   or I saw nobody.
8 No student understands the homework.
9 Someone took my dictionary.
10 Every cat likes to eat meat.

Practice 9, page 47

1 Michael spoke to nobody.
   or Michael spoke to no one.
2 She didn't say anything.
3 Don't let anyone in this room.
   or Don't let anybody in this room.
4 Tell no one what happened.
   or Tell nobody what happened.
5 John knows nothing about computers.
6 He has no money.
7 I don't have any idea.
8 Mary doesn't want anything.
9 She went nowhere.
10 Don't say anything to anybody.
   or Don't say anything to anyone.

Practice 10, page 47

1 I bought a lot of food yesterday.
   or I bought lots of food yesterday.
   or I bought a great deal of food yesterday.
2 correct
3 correct
4 Our teacher gave us a lot of homework today.
   or Our teacher gave us lots of homework today.
   or Our teacher gave us a great deal of homework today.
5 This book has a lot of interesting information in it.
6 I was late for work because there was a lot of traffic.
7 correct
8 Many of the students failed the test.
   or A number of the students failed the test.
   or A lot of the students failed the test.
   or Lots of the students failed the test.
9 I need the right equipment to do this job correctly.
10 The history of my country is very interesting.
11 correct

Practice 11, page 49

1 The hunter shot himself in the foot.
2 Sam and Dave did the work themselves.
3 My wife and I own a house in Florida.
4 I looked at myself in the mirror.
5 We did all the work ourselves. Nobody helped us.
6 Larry and I will meet with you tomorrow at 10:00.
7 Ali lives by himself.
8 The boss asked Sarah and me to come to her office.
9 The girls did all of the work themselves.
10 Michael and I will meet with you tomorrow.

Practice 12, page 49

1 himself
2 myself

Answer Key

3 yourselves
4 myself
5 herself
6 themselves
7 myself
8 ourselves
9 herself
10 yourself

Practice 13/a, page 50
1 each of
2 All
3 Many of
4 several of
5 Some of
6 most of
7 few of
8 a few of
9 hardly any of
10 some of
11 a little
12 little

Practice 14/a, page 55
1 a his
  b his
  c his
  d him
  e He
2 a him or her
  b he or she
3 a their
  b them
  c them
4 a him/her
    or him or her
  b his/her
    or his or her
  c his/her
    or his or her
  d He/She
    or He or She
  e his/her
    or his or her
5 a them
  b they
  c their
  d they

UNIT 6
Practice 1, page 57
1 Are they happy?
2 Is the nurse in the lab?
3 Is she a teacher?
4 Was his mother sleeping?
5 Is it finished?
6 Are you sure?
7 Is it written in pencil?
8 Is it time to eat?
9 Are we leaving soon?
10 Is Linda being helped by the police officer?

Practice 2, page 57
1 Can she speak Italian?
2 Should Noura take her medicine?
3 Will the girls go to the picnic?
4 Can Carlos ride a bicycle?
5 Will you help me later?
6 Would Maria like to help?
7 Should we be going?
8 Can Alex change the oil?
9 Should the books be returned to the library?
10 Will we be there soon?

Practice 3, page 57
1 Does Mary want to eat?
2 Does her sister live in San Francisco?
3 Do her brothers live in Los Angeles?
4 Do you play basketball?
5 Do you and he play basketball?
6 Does the secretary have three children?
7 Does Sarah go to work at 5:30?
8 Do you go to work at 6:00?
9 Does Alex run fast?
10 Does our teacher have a big nose?

Practice 4, page 58
1 Is he in the lab?
2 Are they doctors?
3 Was Lucy driving?
4 Will Mary go to Japan?
5 Should Paul be here?
6 Can Larry swim?
7 Does Sam have three children?
  (*Did you answer* Has Sam three children? *This is correct, but it is old-fashioned. See Section 17.2 for an explanation.*)
8 Did Tom go to Ireland?
9 Do they work in a bank?
10 Does Sarah take the 7:30 train every day?
11 Did Ali have fun at the party?

Practice 5, page 59
1 Where was John?
2 What did Carlos buy?
3 Who will she talk to?
4 When did Alex call Sarah?
5 Why does Mary walk to work?
6 What can Jim play?
7 Why is the student absent?
8 Who does Tom work with?
9 What is John making?
10 What is Ali going to buy?

Practice 6, page 60
1 Whose
2 What kind of
3 Which
4 What time
5 What kind of
6 Whose
7 Which
8 Which
9 Whose
10 When
11 Which

Practice 7, page 60
1 What time does the class start?
2 Which one did you buy?
  or Which did you buy?
3 What kind of music does the radio station play?
4 Whose pen is it?
5 When will she come?
6 Which one do you want?
  or Which do you want?
7 Whose dog is that?
8 Who are you going to stay with?
9 What kind of books does he like?
10 When does Francesca get home?
11 Which one is yours?
  or Which is yours?

Practice 8, page 61
1 How far
2 How much
3 How far
4 How often
5 How many
6 How much
7 How often
8 How many
9 How much
10 How many
11 How far

Practice 9, page 62
1 How far is it to the park?
2 How often do you go shopping?
3 How many children does she have?
  (*Did you answer* How many children has she? *This is correct, but it is old-fashioned. See Section 17.2 for an explanation.*)
4 How much money is there in your bank account?
5 How far is it from your house to your job?
6 How often do you go there?
7 How much orange juice is there in the refrigerator?
8 How many cookies did they eat?
9 How often do you eat Japanese food?
10 How far is it to the beach?

      Answer Key

Practice 10, page 63
1. How
2. How deep
3. How soon
4. How tall
5. How long
6. How
7. How big
8. How hard
9. How well
10. How old

Practice 11, page 63
1. How long does it take to drive to work?
2. How long did it take you to do your homework?
3. How long will it take you to drive to Toronto?
4. How long should it take to install this program?
   (See Section 12.4 for an explanation of this way to use should.*)*
5. How long did it take to get there?

Practice 12, page 64
1. What did you do last night?
2. What are you doing?
3. What will he do on Saturday?
4. What's she going to do tomorrow morning?
5. What are you doing tonight?
   (Why doing *in 5? See Section 4.2/a.)*

Practice 13, page 65
1. Who did Sarah dance with?
2. Who danced with Michael?
3. What did the car hit?
4. What hit the tree?

Practice 14/a, page 65
1. Aren't you listening to me?
2. Didn't you do your homework?
3. Didn't you get my message to bring potato chips to my party?
4. Isn't the test on Monday?
5. Isn't this painting beautiful?
6. Don't you know anything?
7. Isn't your name John?
8. Don't you care that I got fired?
9. Shouldn't you be studying?

Practice 15/a, page 67
1. shouldn't we
2. didn't you
3. had she
4. didn't he
5. aren't there
6. would he
7. did she
8. is it
9. was there
10. am I not
11. would you
12. is she

UNIT 7
Practice 1, page 68
1. a I made up a story.
   b I made a story up.
   c I made it up.
2. a Carlos put away his shoes.
   b Carlos put his shoes away.
   c Carlos put them away.
3. a The teacher will call off the test.
   b The teacher will call the test off.
   c The teacher will call it off.
4. a The bank turned down Sarah.
   b The bank turned Sarah down.
   c The bank turned her down.
5. a He called back his friend.
   b He called his friend back.
   c He called him back.
6. a Please clean up this mess.
   b Please clean this mess up.
   c Please clean it up.
7. a They're tearing down the building.
   b They're tearing the building down.
   c They're tearing it down.
8. a Paul let down his father.
   b Paul let his father down.
   c Paul let him down.

Practice 2, page 69
1. a Jack cheats on the tests.
   b Jack cheats on them.
2. a She looked for her son.
   b She looked for him.
3. a The nurse is caring for Lucy.
   b The nurse is caring for her.
4. a I'll get on the horse.
   b I'll get on it.
5. a I'm counting on John.
   b I'm counting on him.
6. a Don't fall for his lie.
   b Don't fall for it.
7. a I dealt with the problem.
   b I dealt with it.
8. a Alex stepped on a banana.
   b Alex stepped on it.

Practice 3, page 70
1. shakeup
2. break up
3. follow-up
4. back up
5. breakdown
6. lay off
7. hand out
8. get-together

Practice 4, page 71
1. adj
2. v
3. adj
4. v
5. adj
6. adj
7. adj
8. adj

UNIT 8
Practice 1, page 72
1. I've got brown hair.
2. He's got brown hair too.
3. We've got a small house.
4. Paul's got a broken arm.
5. Michael's got three dogs.
6. Elephants have got big ears.
7. Mark's got an old book.
8. My car's got a flat tire.
9. The boys have got a new soccer ball.
10. I've got a headache.
11. You've got a big mouth.

Practice 2, page 73
1. Our house hasn't got a garage.
2. We haven't got enough time.
3. Tom and Linda haven't got any children.
4. Jack hasn't got a job.
5. My mother and father haven't got a TV.
6. I haven't got your dictionary.
7. The children haven't got their homework.
8. Carlos hasn't got a calculator.
9. Snakes haven't got legs.
10. Noura hasn't got a car.

Practice 3, page 73
1. Has Francesca got a box of rocks?
2. Have you got enough money?
3. Has Lucy got a problem?
4. Has the hotel room got a balcony?
5. Have your sisters got tickets?
6. Has her house got a basement?
7. Have I got food in my teeth?
8. Has Mark got brown hair?
9. Have you got time to help me with my math homework?

Practice 4, page 74
1. I've got to take my son to soccer practice.
2. We've got to take our cat to the vet.
3. Rosa's got to do her homework.
4. The pilot's got to fly to Norway.
5. The students have got to take a test.
6. Michael's got to clean his house.
7. I've got to get to work early tomorrow.
8. You've got to be quiet.

Answer Key

9 My father's got to work on Sunday.
10 We've got to wake up at 6:15.
11 Linda's got to have an operation.

Practice 5, page 75
1 She hasn't got to wake up early on Saturday.
2 I haven't got to go to the meeting.
3 Carlos hasn't got to go to school on Thursday.
4 You haven't got to do it.
5 The store hasn't got to return your money.
6 Susan and Noura haven't got to go to the doctor.
7 Rosa hasn't got to work on July 4th.
8 They haven't got to get there until 11:00.
9 John hasn't got to go shopping with his mother.
10 You haven't got to be here until 10:00.

Practice 6, page 75
1 Has he got to pay his tuition?
2 Have they got to fly to Moscow?
3 Has she got to be here early tomorrow?
4 Have the children got to brush their teeth?
5 Has the car got to be in the garage?
6 Have I got to wear a suit?
7 Has Mary got to pick up her friend at the airport?
8 Has Alex got to wash the car?
9 Have Francesca and Sofia got to go to school?
10 Has the milk got to be in the refrigerator?
11 Has she got to make a reservation?

Practice 7/a, page 76
1 No, she doesn't.
 No, she hasn't
2 Yes, it does.
 Yes, it has.
3 I don't, but my wife does.
 I haven't, but my wife has.
4 I do, but he doesn't.
 I have, but he hasn't.

Practice 8/a, page 76
1 Yes, I do.
 Yes, I've got to.
2 No, he doesn't.
 No, he hasn't got to.
3 Carlos and Alex do, but John doesn't.
 Carlos and Alex have got to, but John hasn't got to.
4 Yes, he does.
 Yes, he's got to.

UNIT 9
Practice 1, page 78
1 She's thrown the ball.
2 Sofia's written a letter.
3 We've done our work.
4 Mary's read the book.
5 The plant's died.
6 Michael's left.
7 Larry's seen the movie.
8 The show's begun.
9 John's taken a taxi.
10 I've cut my finger.

Practice 2, page 78
1 Have you ridden a camel?
2 Have they gone home?
3 Has she fallen asleep?
4 Have Sarah and her sister seen that movie?
5 Has Francesca painted her room pink?
6 Have we been here before?
7 Has she put her coat in the closet?
8 Has John gotten a new dog?
9 Has Mary done her work?
10 Have you read this book?

Practice 3, page 78
1 They haven't been there before.
2 She hasn't met him.
3 Jim hasn't worn his new shoes.
4 We haven't had dinner.
5 I haven't taught this class.
6 Michael hasn't done his work.
7 The store hasn't closed.
8 I haven't talked to her.
9 She hasn't flown to France.
10 They haven't lost their dog.

Practice 4, page 79
1 Have...seen
2 has fallen
3 have ridden
4 has taken
5 haven't told
6 haven't done
7 hasn't seen
8 haven't eaten
9 has...been
10 has...done

Practice 5, page 79
1 for
2 since
3 since
4 for
5 since
6 for
7 for
8 for

Practice 6, page 80
1 have eaten
2 ate
3 have been
4 has been
5 was
6 has known
7 have been
8 left

Practice 7, page 80
1 's sleeping / 's been sleeping
2 are studying / 've been studying
3 'm driving / 've been driving
4 's watching / 's been watching
5 're looking / 've been looking
6 'm reading / 've been reading
7 're working / 've been working
8 's riding / 's been riding

Practice 8, page 81
1 B already
2 A yet
3 B just
4 A yet
 B yet
 A already
 or just
5 B just
6 A yet
 B yet / just / yet
 A yet
 B already
 or just

Practice 9, page 82
1 Has John ever written a book?
2 Has your father ever driven a truck?
3 Have you ever been to Australia?
4 Have you ever eaten sushi?
5 Has Carlos ever read this book?
6 Has Mark ever spoken to you?
7 Have you ever had a broken heart?
8 Has she ever been in the hospital?
9 Has Larry ever ridden a motorcycle?
10 Has she ever flown in a hot air balloon?

Practice 10, page 82
3 am
4 reading
5 Have
6 been
7 have
8 did
9 go
10 went
11 Have
12 been
13 have
14 been

Practice 11, page 83
2 am studying
3 am doing
4 told
5 am writing
6 Have
7 been
8 moved
9 was
10 am
11 have lived
12 have been
13 went
14 was
15 saw
16 Have
17 seen
18 is waiting
19 have been using
20 is

Practice 12, page 84
1 They'd done their work.
2 She hadn't left yet.
3 We'd been working for three hours.
4 He'd lived in Chicago since 1985.
5 They'd already had dinner.
6 I'd never been to Timbuktu before.
7 We'd never driven on that road.
8 Noura and Alex had just eaten.
9 I'd never gone skiing before.
10 We'd never watched that channel before.

Practice 13, page 84
1 Had Michael finished?
2 Had Carlos taken a shower?
3 Had they had breakfast?
4 Had she been there all day?
5 Had he given her some money?
6 Had you been reading?
7 Had Tom already arrived?
8 Had Sofia just gone to bed?
9 Had they already done it?
10 Had she been waiting a long time?

Practice 14, page 84
1 She hadn't flown to Tibet.
2 The movie hadn't begun.
3 Maria hadn't spoken with her sister.
4 Carlos hadn't been to Oman.
5 I hadn't told her the answer.
6 They hadn't been watching TV.
7 We hadn't taken the bus.
8 She hadn't thought of the answer.
9 They hadn't already done it.
10 The train hadn't left the station.

Practice 15, page 85
1 Larry was late for work because his car had broken down.
2 I didn't talk to Sofia when I called because she'd gone to bed.
3 Bill failed the test because he hadn't studied for it.
4 I was hungry all day because I'd forgotten to bring my lunch to work.
5 I didn't know what to do because I hadn't paid attention to the teacher.
6 I couldn't call Sarah because I'd forgotten her telephone number.
7 Sam was locked out of his house because he'd lost his keys.
8 Tom did it all wrong because he hadn't listened to me.
9 I didn't know where to go because I hadn't brought a map.

Practice 16, page 85
1 She said that she'd gotten married.
2 He said that he'd never read that book.
3 He told her that he'd lost his watch.
4 He said that his sister had moved to Canada.
5 She told him that she'd looked at his X-ray.
6 She told him that she'd already washed the dishes.
7 She said that Maria hadn't been to Africa.

Practice 17, page 86
2 a hadn't
   b seen
   c has
   d lost
3 a had
   b forgotten
4 a had

b just
c had
5 a hadn't
   b finished
6 a haven't
   b gotten
   c yet
   d had
   e planned
   f have
   g looked
   h haven't
   i found

Practice 18/a, page 87
1 will have been
2 will have been
3 will not have finished
4 will have been driving
5 will not have saved
6 will have arrived
7 will have been waiting
8 will have gotten
9 will have been working

Practice 19/a, page 87
1 there
2 been there
3 finished dinner
4 left
5 gotten there on time
6 lived in this town all your life
7 studying all day
8 been studying all day
9 had dinner
10 heard about the change

Practice 20/a, page 88
1 Francesca has gone to school, and Sofia has too.
2 Tom had been sleeping, but Jerry hadn't been.
   Tom had been sleeping, but Jerry hadn't.
3 Paul's flown to Paris, and Sam has too.
4 Sam's flight has arrived, but Tom's flight hasn't.
   Sam's flight has arrived, but Tom's hasn't.
5 We'd finished, and he had too.
6 You've been to Italy, but I haven't been.
   You've been to Italy, but I haven't.
7 Tom had done his work, and I had too.
8 Maria and Sofia have flown in a hot air balloon, and Larry has too.

UNIT 10
Practice 1, page 89
1 nice perfume
2 sick student
3 comfortable shoes
4 good idea
5 wrong answer
6 fantastic house
7 salty soup
8 angry man

Practice 2, page 90
1 He seems upset.
2 It feels soft.
3 It looks beautiful.
4 They smell stinky.
5 It tastes terrible.
6 It sounds interesting.
7 He's sick.
8 He got fat.

Practice 3, page 90
1 taller
2 more dangerous
3 easier
4 angrier
5 better
6 farther
   or further
7 quieter
8 nicer

Practice 4, page 91
1 Your house is small. My house is bigger.
2 Is Beijing smaller than Shanghai?

Answer Key

3   BMWs are more expensive than Toyotas.
4   The book was better than the movie.
5   Spanish is easier to learn than Portuguese.
6   I got a bad grade on the English test, but Mary's grade was worse.
7   Mark is lazy, but Larry is lazier.
8   I play tennis better than Michael.

Practice 5, page 92
1   smallest
2   most modern
3   loveliest
4   simplest
5   most expensive
6   farthest
    or furthest
7   worst
8   most common
9   best

Practice 6, page 92
1   Is the Amazon River the longest river in the world?
2   Sam is the craziest guy I know.
3   I got a 99 on my quiz. That was the best grade in my class.
4   Mount Everest is the highest mountain in the world.
5   Michael has the messiest desk in our office.
6   My youngest child is eight years old.
7   Yesterday was the worst day of my life.
8   Alex is taller than Carlos.

Practice 7, page 93
1   b
2   a
3   b
4   d
5   b
6   a
7   b
8   d

Practice 8, page 95
1   hardest
2   prettiest
3   hardest
4   stupidest
5   most beautiful
6   most expensive
7   largest
8   least interesting

Practice 9, page 96
1   worried / adj
2   invited / v
3   married / adj
4   hidden / v
5   done / adj
6   lost / v
7   forbidden / adj
8   mistaken / adj
9   confused / adj

Practice 10, page 97
1   absent from
2   wrong about
    or mistaken about
    or confused about
3   ready to
4   interested in
    or curious about
5   mad at
    or angry with
6   made of
7   sure about
8   used to
9   mad at / about
    or angry with / about
10 ready for

Practice 11, page 98
1   getting
2   got
3   getting
4   got
5   get
6   get
7   get
8   getting

Practice 12, page 98
1   used to
2   get used to / getting used to
3   get used to
4   get used to
5   used to
6   get used to

Practice 13, page 99
1   confusing
2   annoying
3   challenging
4   relaxed
5   embarrassed
6   embarrassing
7   exciting / excited
8   frightening / frightened
9   irritated
10 fascinating

Practice 14, page 100
1   baseball stadium
2   cigarette lighter
3   apple juice
4   TV show
5   magazine article
6   can opener
7   tree house
8   school teacher
9   bird cage
10 school bus
11 bus driver *or* school bus driver

Practice 15, page 101
1   50,000-a-year
2   two-hour
3   four-bedroom
4   black-and-white
5   100-meter
6   20-minute
7   four-day-a-week
8   well-known
9   three-hour

Practice 16, page 102
1   My house is the same as my sister's house.
2   Is this watch similar to your watch?
3   Carlos and Alex are different from each other.
4   Austria and Australia are different countries.
5   Spain and Mexico have the same language.
6   North Korea and South Korea are very different.
7   This book is different from that book.
8   My house and your house are not the same.
9   Paul's bicycle is similar to my bicycle.
10 These shoes are like those shoes.

Practice 17, page 102
1   New York City and Los Angeles are different.
    New York City is different from Los Angeles.
2   My tie and your tie are alike.
    My tie is like your tie.
3   Larry and his twin brother are the same.
    Larry is the same as his twin brother.
4   My car and your car are similar.
    My car is similar to your car.
5   Spanish and Italian are similar.
    Spanish is similar to Italian.
6   These shoes and those shoes are the same.
    These shoes are the same as those shoes.
7   Canada and the USA are different.
    Canada is different from the USA.
8   Your idea and his idea are alike.
    Your idea is like his idea.

Practice 18/a, page 103
1   kind of
2   absolutely
3   very
4   pretty
5   a bit
6   terribly
7   extremely
8   very
9   a little
10 totally

UNIT 11
Practice 1, page 106
1 May I open the window?
   or Could I open the window?
   or Can I open the window?
2 May my sister use your car?
   or Could my sister use your car?
   or Can my sister use your car?
3 May we go home early?
   or Could we go home early?
   or Can we go home early?
4 May I use your camera?
   or Could I use your camera?
   or Can I use your camera?
5 May I have another piece of cake?
   or Could I have another piece of cake?
   or Can I have another piece of cake?
6 May I use your dictionary?
   or Could I use your dictionary?
   or Can I use your dictionary?
7 May I have a glass of water?
   or Could I have a glass of water?
   or Can I have a glass of water?
8 May I have more time to finish my project?
   or Could I have more time to finish my project?
   or Can I have more time to finish my project?
9 May we smoke?
   or Could we smoke?
   or Can we smoke?
10 May I ask you a personal question?
   or Could I ask you a personal question?
   or Can I ask you a personal question?

Practice 2, page 106
1 Would you mind if I used your calculator?
2 Would you mind if I closed the door?
3 Would you mind if my son swam in your pool?
4 Would you mind if I were late for class tomorrow?
   (Why were *and not* was? *See Section 20.3.)*
5 Would you mind if we watched the game at your house?
6 Would you mind if I turned up the heat?
7 Would you mind if I used your phone?
8 Would you mind if I spoke with your manager?
9 Would you mind if I didn't go shopping with you tonight?
10 Would you mind if I weren't the best man at your wedding?
   (Why weren't *and not* wasn't? *See Section 20.3.)*

Practice 3, page 107
1 Would you fix my bicycle?
   or Could you fix my bicycle?
   or Will you fix my bicycle?
   or Can you fix my bicycle?
2 Would you help me with my homework?
   or Could you help me with my homework?
   or Will you help me with my homework?
   or Can you help me with my homework?
3 Would you talk to my son after class?
   or Could you talk to my son after class?
   or Will you talk to my son after class?
   or Can you talk to my son after class?
4 Would you close the window?
   or Could you close the window?
   or Will you close the window?
   or Can you close the window?
5 Would you get me a cup of coffee?
   or Could you get me a cup of coffee?
   or Will you get me a cup of coffee?
   or Can you get me a cup of coffee?
6 Would you turn off the TV?
   or Could you turn off the TV?
   or Will you turn off the TV?
   or Can you turn off the TV?
7 Would you be quiet?
   or Could you be quiet?
   or Will you be quiet?
   or Can you be quiet?
8 Would you pick me up at the train station?
   or Could you pick me up at the train station?
   or Will you pick me up at the train station?
   or Can you pick me up at the train station?
9 Would you feed the dog?
   or Could you feed the dog?
   or Will you feed the dog?
   or Can you feed the dog?
10 Would you help me?
   or Could you help me?
   or Will you help me?
   or Can you help me?

Practice 4, page 108
1 Would you mind moving this sofa for me?
2 Would you mind taking us to the library?
3 Would you mind going shopping with me tomorrow?
4 Would you mind being here at 7:00?
5 Would you mind giving me a ride to work?
6 Would you mind saying that again?
7 Would you mind calling me back?
8 Would you mind being quiet?
9 Would you mind not walking so fast?

Practice 5, page 109
1 c
2 a
3 b
4 d
5 c

Practice 6, page 109
1 Can I borrow your bicycle?
   Would you mind lending me your bicycle?
2 Would you lend me your football?
   May I borrow your football?
3 Would you mind if I borrowed your dictionary?
   Will you lend me your dictionary?
4 Could I borrow your snow shovel?
   Will you lend me your snow shovel?
5 Would you mind if I borrowed your grill?
   Would you mind lending me your grill?

Practice 7, page 110
1 Mark had to do his homework.
2 I had to go to the airport.
3 He had to help his father.
4 Did you have to wake up early?
5 Did you have to make dinner?
6 Did she have to go shopping?
7 I didn't have to practice the piano.
8 We didn't have to turn in our homework.
9 Did it have to be typed?

Practice 8, page 111
1 NN
2 NA
3 NN
4 NA
5 NA
6 NN
7 NA
8 NN

Practice 9, page 111
1 had better
2 should
   or ought to
3 had better
4 should
5 had better
6 should
   or ought to
7 had better
8 had better
9 should
   or ought to
10 had better

Practice 10, page 112
1 You should have eaten breakfast.
2 You shouldn't have exercised for two hours.
   or You shouldn't have exercised so much.
   or You should have exercised less.
3 She should have kept her big mouth shut.
4 He should have called his father.
5 You shouldn't have eaten six pieces of chocolate cake.
   or You shouldn't have eaten so much chocolate cake.
   or You should have eaten less chocolate cake.
6 He shouldn't have forgotten to bring his glasses to the movie theater.
   or He should have brought his glasses to the movie theater.
7 You should have bought coffee yesterday.

Answer Key

8 You shouldn't have tried to start a fire with gasoline.
9 He shouldn't have jumped off the roof.
10 You shouldn't have said, "yes."
   or You should have said, "no."

Practice 11, page 113
1 couldn't sleep
2 could walk
3 Could...understand
4 Can...tell / can't read
5 Can...reach
6 can't open / Can...do
7 can't come
8 Can...figure out
9 can do / couldn't do
10 couldn't call

Practice 12, page 113
1 Are you able to walk with that broken leg?
2 I'm not able to sleep on airplanes.
3 Gary wasn't able to see the play from the back row of the theater.
4 Was the tech guy able to figure out what was wrong with your computer?
5 Linda is able to speak several languages.
6 I am able to see a lot better with my new glasses.
7 We weren't able to make any sense out of the instructions.
8 The doctors weren't able to save him.
9 I wasn't able to get my car started.
10 Are you able to walk and chew gum at the same time?

Practice 13, page 114
1 used to
2 used to / both
3 used to / both
4 both
5 used to
6 both
7 both
8 both

Practice 14, page 114
1 won't be able to come
2 may not have to pay / might be able to get
3 will have to rewrite
4 should be able to pass
5 might be able to see
6 will have to leave
7 shouldn't have to explain
8 might not be able to fly
9 should be able to speak
10 will have to take
11 may not be able to enter
12 wouldn't be able to

Practice 15/a, page 116
1 would you rather do—stay home or go to the library
2 you rather go to the beach than go shopping
3 would you rather leave—today or tomorrow
4 he rather drive all night or stop at a hotel
5 would he rather go—to Munich or [to] Berlin
6 she rather be married than be single
7 would she rather have—onion rings or potato chips
8 they rather live in a small town or [live in] a big city

Practice 16/a, page 116
1 rather go to London than [go to] Paris
  rather go to London
2 rather play tennis than go swimming
  rather play tennis
3 rather walk to the beach than drive [to the beach]
  rather walk to the beach
4 rather buy a new TV than get this one fixed
  rather buy a new TV
5 rather take a taxi than go in your car
  rather take a taxi
6 rather not go out for dinner
  rather not
7 rather not eat at 6:00 than wait until 7:00
  rather not
8 rather live in Chicago than [live] in New York
  or rather live in Chicago than [live in] New York
  rather live in Chicago
9 rather not go shopping with his mother
  rather not
10 rather have chicken [for dinner] than [have] beef [for dinner]
   rather have chicken

11 rather be watching TV than [be] doing my homework
   rather be watching TV
12 rather be eaten by a tiger than [be eaten by] a shark
   rather be eaten by a tiger

Practice 17/a, page 118
1 John had to, but Carlos didn't.
  or John had to, but Carlos didn't have to.
  or John did, but Carlos didn't.
2 No, I won't.
  or No, I won't able to.
3 I know I should. I want to, but I can't.
  or I know I should quit. I want to quit, but I can't quit.
4 You're right. I'd better.
5 No, you can't. I'm going to be using it.
6 Yes, I shouldn't have, but I did.
7 No, I can't. Nobody can.
8 I'd better. My mother is coming to visit tonight.
9 No, I shouldn't have. It was a big mistake.
10 No, I'd better not. If I do, I might get robbed.

UNIT 12
Practice 1, page 121
1 might be
2 may have
3 could be
4 must smoke
5 has to be
6 must not know
7 may be
8 must be
9 might be
10 must not like
11 can't be / have got to be
12 must have

Practice 2, page 121
1 may have gone
2 must have gone
3 must have arrived
4 might have arrived
5 cannot have arrived
6 may not have gotten
7 must have finished
8 must have seen
9 must have been
10 might have been
11 must not have been
12 may not have seen
13 might not have heard
14 didn't see

Practice 3, page 123
1 will
  or is going to
2 might
  or may
  or could
3 may not
  or might not
4 will (probably) not
  or am (probably) not going to
5 may not
  or might not
6 will (probably)
  or am (probably) going to
7 (probably) will not
  or (probably) am not going to
8 may not
  or might not
  or (probably) will not
  or (probably) are not going to
9 will (probably)
  or is (probably) going to
10 (probably) will not
  or (probably) am not going to
11 may not
  or might not
12 may not
  or might not
13 will not
  or am not going to

Practice 4, page 125

1 should come
   or ought to come
2 shouldn't have taken
3 shouldn't have cost
4 shouldn't take
5 shouldn't take
6 should have come
7 should be
   or ought to be
8 shouldn't be
9 should be
   or ought to be
10 shouldn't have
11 shouldn't have been
12 should be
   or ought to be
13 should love
   or ought to love

Practice 5, page 127

1 B were going to
2 A were going to
   B wasn't going to / was going to
3 A were...going to
   B was going to
4 A were going to
   B was going to
5 B were...going to
   A was going to / were going to

Practice 6, page 128

1 I am supposed to finish this work before I go home.
2 You're not supposed to talk in a library.
3 John is supposed to give a presentation next week.
4 Are we supposed to read Chapter 5 or Chapter 6 for our homework?
5 The show is supposed to start at 9:00.
6 I have to go home. I am not supposed to stay out after midnight.
7 You are supposed to take your hat off inside a building.
8 I don't understand. What am I supposed to do?

Practice 7, page 128

1 B is supposed to
2 B was supposed to
3 B are supposed to
4 B aren't supposed to
5 A are...supposed to
   B are supposed to
6 A Were...supposed to
7 A am...supposed to
   B are supposed to
8 B aren't supposed to
9 B was supposed to

Practice 8/a, page 129

1 are to
2 are to
3 are not to
4 was to have / is to
5 are to
6 were to have
7 was to have
8 is to / are to / was to have

Practice 9/a, page 130

1 Medford is only 15 kilometers from here. He must have by now.
2 It's got to be. It looks exactly like his car.
3 I don't know. They might have.
4 They ought to be, but they're not.
5 It's after 5:00, so he should have by now, but I don't know if he has yet.
6 I wanted to, I was going to, and I should have, but I didn't.
7 I was going to, but I was busy, so I didn't.
8 I was supposed to, but I didn't.
9 Yes, she was to have, but she didn't.
10 She should be. She never goes anywhere in the evening.
11 He may. He's not sure.
12 Yes, the judges were to have, but they postponed their decision..
13 He must have.

UNIT 13
Practice 1, page 132

1 ~~He~~ works in my office.
2 ~~It~~ cost $25,000.
3 ~~They~~ live next to me.

4 ~~He~~ called you.
5 ~~She~~ is from Russia.
6 ~~They~~ live in that house.
7 ~~She~~ fell out of a tree.
8 ~~It~~ is on Maple Street.

Practice 2, page 133

1 (who / that live near me)
2 (which / that was 450 pages long)
3 (which / that was really funny)
4 (who / that waited on us)
5 (which / that didn't make any sense at all)
6 (who / that works in Office 307)
7 (who / that were killed in the plane crash)
8 (who / that lives in the big house next to the library)
9 (which / that was very interesting)

Practice 3, page 133

1 A woman who lives in my building speaks French.
2 She told me a story that was interesting.
3 My wife bought some shoes that cost $50.
4 People who ride motorcycles should wear helmets.
5 The man who sold me his car is a liar.
6 A person who speaks two languages is bilingual.
7 The people who sat behind us at the movie theater talked a lot.
8 How many people who live in Florida speak Spanish?
9 The teacher asked me a question that was very difficult.
10 Did the searchers find the woman who was lost in the forest?

Practice 4, page 134

1 We ate ~~it~~ at the picnic.
2 I live next to ~~him~~.
3 I had never met ~~her~~ before.
4 You were talking to ~~them~~.
5 I bought ~~them~~ yesterday.
6 Your sister took ~~it~~ out of the library this morning.
7 I know ~~him~~.
8 We saw ~~them~~ last night.
9 You saw ~~it~~ at the museum.

Practice 5, page 134

1 (which / that we had last night)
2 (which / that she wore to the party)
3 (who(m) / that I talked to)
4 (which / that he made)
5 (who(m) / that I sat next to on the plane)
6 (who(m) / that you told me about)
7 (which / that I was using before)
8 (who(m) / that you don't know)
9 (which / that she gave to the police)

Practice 6, page 135

1 The mechanic whom I talked to said it would cost $1,000 to fix my car.
   The mechanic who I talked to said it would cost $1,000 to fix my car.
   The mechanic that I talked to said it would cost $1,000 to fix my car.
   The mechanic I talked to said it would cost $1,000 to fix my car.
2 We don't understand the language which she speaks.
   We don't understand the language that she speaks.
   We don't understand the language she speaks.
3 Some people whom I know never take a bath.
   Some people who I know never take a bath.
   Some people that I know never take a bath.
   Some people I know never take a bath.
4 The guy whom I live next to is interesting.
   The guy who I live next to is interesting.
   The guy that I live next to is interesting.
   The guy I live next to is interesting.
5 The man whom I saw was very tall.
   The man who I saw was very tall.
   The man that I saw was very tall.
   The man I saw was very tall.
6 The questions which Gary asked were difficult.
   The questions that Gary asked were difficult.
   The questions Gary asked were difficult.
7 The bread which my wife baked was delicious.
   The bread that my wife baked was delicious.
   The bread my wife baked was delicious.
8 Nobody whom I talked to believed me.
   Nobody who I talked to believed me.
   Nobody that I talked to believed me.
   Nobody I talked to believed me.
9 The book which I took with me to read on the plane was very boring.
   The book that I took with me to read on the plane was very boring.
   The book I took with me to read on the plane was very boring.

Answer Key

Practice 7, page 136
1 I talked to a man whose wife is a heart surgeon.
2 Did the woman whose arm was broken go to the doctor?
3 The airplane whose wing fell off crashed.
4 I know a girl whose father is a naval officer.
5 People whose native language is Spanish can learn Italian easily.
6 The guy whose hair was on fire was taken to the hospital.
7 Where is the man whose wallet was stolen?
8 I sat next to a woman whose daughter is a violinist.
9 The actor whose show was canceled was working as a waiter.
10 The woman whose husband was hurt in the accident was very upset.

Practice 8, page 137
1 January is the month when we always go to Florida.
2 That's the park where we play soccer sometimes.
3 I can't remember the place where I took this picture.
4 Do you know a store where I can buy extra large shoes?
5 I still remember the day when my son was born.
6 Is there a day when I can meet with you?
7 August 4th is the day when I will fly back to Chicago.
8 Is this the place where the crime happened?
9 Did he tell you where he went?
10 The day when my parachute didn't open was the worst day of my life.

Practice 9/a, page 137
1 The cat ~~which is~~ sleeping on the sofa is 14 years old.
2 The people ~~who are~~ coming to our dinner party are really boring.
3 A man ~~who was~~ riding a bicycle on the highway was run over by a bus.
4 Don't use the dishes ~~which are~~ on the top shelf.
5 The woman ~~who was~~ interviewed on TV was from England.
6 The guys ~~who were~~ not chosen for the show were disappointed.
7 Cars ~~which are~~ made in Germany are usually expensive.
8 I like the song ~~which is~~ on the radio now.
9 Many of the buildings ~~which were~~ destroyed in the earthquake were never rebuilt.
10 Applications ~~which are~~ not submitted before the deadline will not be accepted.

Practice 10/a, page 138
1 The family living next to us has a swimming pool.
2 Drivers not wearing seat belts are risking their lives.
3 Anyone doing that is crazy.
4 Students wanting to try out for the soccer team should talk to the coach.
5 I have a lot of friends working in that factory.
6 Anyone smoking in the theater will be kicked out.
7 Kids going to that school have to wear uniforms.
8 Any student not turning in his or her project by Friday will get an F.
9 Anybody not having identification cannot enter the building.
10 There were so many kids making noise outside that I couldn't sleep.

Practice 11/a, page 139
1 no change
2 Professor Grant, who is my history teacher, has written several books.
3 Elephants, which are native to Africa and India, are very intelligent.
4 My boss, whom I met with yesterday, told me that she is planning to retire next year.
5 Mary Johnson, whose husband is the mayor of this city, was my college roommate.
6 no change
7 My house, which was built in 1685, is the oldest building in our town.
8 Coffee, which originally came from the Middle East, is now grown in many countries.
9 Abraham Lincoln, who was born in 1809, was the 16th president of the United States.
10 no change
11 Riverwoods, where I grew up, is a small town.
12 no change

Practice 12/a, page 140
1 The boy behind whom I sat in grammar school is a lawyer now.
2 Blue Lake, near which we live, flooded last summer.
3 I didn't get the job for which I applied.
4 The woman with whom I work is from Lebanon.
5 The guy for whom I voted lost.
6 Peter Martin, with whom I used to work, speaks Chinese.
7 The subject about which she gave a presentation was interesting.
8 The opera during which I slept was by Wagner.

Practice 13/a, page 140
1 I don't know the man to whom you were talking.
2 Main Street, on which I live, is a very busy street.
3 The car for which the police are looking is blue.
4 The student in front of whom I sit is from Germany.
5 The man about whom I was talking is not here.
6 John, from whom I got a letter, lives in Rome.

7 The boys with whom I was playing football live next to me.
8 I saw a movie with some friends with whom I work.
9 The woman under whom we live plays loud music all night.
10 Lucy, for whom we bought a birthday gift yesterday, will be 9 years old.
11 It is an amazing story about which many books have been written.
12 The people with whom I have to work on this project are idiots.

Practice 14/a, page 141
1 A man helped me fix my bicycle, which was very nice of him.
2 Francesca got an A on her final exam, which didn't surprise me.
3 Sarah is very sick, which makes me worry.
4 Michael crashed his car, which didn't surprise me because he always drives too fast.
5 I forgot to bring my homework to class yesterday, which wasn't very smart and made my teacher angry.
6 The doctor said my friend doesn't have cancer anymore, which was great news.
7 It will cost $3,000 to fix my car, which is more than the car is worth.
8 Our team won a game, which was a miracle.
9 The men in our office make more than the women, which, if you ask me, is very unfair and illegal.
10 Last year we went to Venice, which, in my opinion, is the most beautiful city in the world.

Practice 15/a, page 141
1 Our neighbors have a big dog, which I don't like at all.
2 My daughter dropped out of high school, which I was, of course, very angry about.
3 We spent last summer traveling in Italy, which we really enjoyed.
4 I wear the same socks every day for a week, which my wife thinks is disgusting.
5 My husband wants to buy a horse, which I think is a crazy idea.
6 The guy who works next to me never stops talking, which I find very annoying.
7 Ali spent three hours helping me with my homework, which I really appreciated.
8 My son got in trouble at school, which I'm not happy about.
9 Larry told his boss that her idea wasn't very good, which I think was a pretty dumb thing to do.
10 He believed me when no one else did, which I will never forget.

UNIT 14
Practice 1, page 142
1 A1
2 A2
3 A1
4 A2
5 A2
6 A1
7 A1
8 A2

Practice 2, page 143
1 it is
2 he has
3 he's going
4 the teacher said
5 the game starts
6 he was late
7 Noura lives
8 she's got to work
9 I'm supposed to do

Practice 3, page 144
1 what time it is
2 where he went
3 what it is
4 when it starts
5 when we're going to eat dinner
  or when we're going to eat
6 Why he was angry
7 when it began
8 where he has gone
9 when it begins
10 What it said
11 who he went to the library with
  or who he went there with
  or who he went with

Practice 4, page 144
1 I asked Ali what he wants for dinner.
2 Do you know what his name is?
3 correct
4 Ask Carlos how much money he has.

5 I'm not sure when Maria will get here.
6 correct
7 Please tell me how much money he needs.
8 I did not understand what he was talking about.
9 correct
10 Do you know whose car that is?

Practice 5, page 145
1 if she is going to work tomorrow
   or if she is going to work tomorrow or not
   or whether she is going to work tomorrow
   or whether or not she is going to work tomorrow
   or whether she is going to work tomorrow or not
2 if he has a car
   or if he has a car or not
   or whether he has a car
   or whether or not he has a car
   or whether he has a car or not
3 if she believes me
   or if she believes me or not
   or whether she believes me
   or whether or not she believes me
   or whether she believes me or not
4 if she still thinks about me
   or if she still thinks about me or not
   or whether she still thinks about me
   or whether or not she still thinks about me
   or whether she still thinks about me or not
5 if cats are smarter than dogs
   or if cats are smarter than dogs or not
   or whether cats are smarter than dogs
   or whether or not cats are smarter than dogs
   or whether cats are smarter than dogs or not
6 Whether I should call her
   or Whether or not I should call her
   or Whether I should call her or not
7 if she has done her homework
   or if she has done her homework or not
   or whether she has done her homework
   or whether or not she has done her homework
   or whether she has done her homework or not
8 if they were talking about me
   or if they were talking about me or not
   or whether they were talking about me
   or whether or not they were talking about me
   or whether they were talking about me or not
9 if the show starts at 9:00
   or if the show starts at 9:00 or not
   or whether the show starts at 9:00
   or whether or not the show starts at 9:00
   or whether the show starts at 9:00 or not
10 Whether she's got a boyfriend
   or Whether or not she's got a boyfriend
   or Whether she's got a boyfriend or not
11 if he's the new teacher
   or if he's the new teacher or not
   or whether he's the new teacher
   or whether or not he's the new teacher
   or whether he's the new teacher or not
12 if he'd like to go to the beach with us
   or if he'd like to go to the beach with us or not
   or whether he'd like to go to the beach with us
   or whether or not he'd like to go to the beach with us
   or whether he'd like to go to the beach with us or not

Practice 6, page 146
1 I want to know if he will come to the party.
   or I want to know if he will come to the party or not.
   or I want to know whether he will come to the party.
   or I want to know whether or not he will come to the party.
   or I want to know whether he will come to the party or not.
2 Can you tell me if Paul is going to be here tomorrow?
   or Can you tell me if Paul is going to be here tomorrow or not?
   or Can you tell me whether Paul is going to be here tomorrow?
   or Can you tell me whether or not Paul is going to be here tomorrow?
   or Can you tell me whether Paul is going to be here tomorrow or not?
3 correct
4 I don't remember if we are supposed to read this book or that book.
   or I don't remember if we are supposed to read this book or that book or not.
   or I don't remember whether we are supposed to read this book or that book.

or I don't remember whether or not we are supposed to read this book or that book.
   or I don't remember whether we are supposed to read this book or that book or not.
5 Whether Michael speaks French is not something I know.
   Whether or not Michael speaks French is not something I know.
   Whether Michael speaks French or not is not something I know.
6 correct
7 I wonder if they know the answer.
   or I wonder if they know the answer or not.
   or I wonder whether they know the answer.
   or I wonder whether or not they know the answer.
   or I wonder whether they know the answer or not.

Practice 7, page 146
1 Mark told me what to do.
2 Can you tell me where to get my car fixed?
3 I've told you everything I know. I don't know what else to say.
4 The recipe doesn't say how long to cook it.
5 I've been thinking about what to do about this problem for many days.
6 I told Carlos where to cash a check.

Practice 8, page 147
(possible answers)
1 to eat, to order, to have
2 to solve, to fix
3 to buy, to rent, to lease, to get / [to] keep, [to] hold on to, [to] hang on to
4 to get to, to go to
5 to buy, to read, to get
6 to come, to get there

Practice 9, page 147
(answers will vary)

Practice 10, page 148
(answers will vary)

Practice 11, page 149
1 he would be the next head of the sales department
   or he will be the next head of the sales department
2 she had nine children
   or she has nine children
3 he was going to work harder
   or he is going to work harder
4 he had bought a new car
   or he has bought a new car
5 her father had lost his wallet
   or her father has lost his wallet
6 she might call me tomorrow
   or she may call me tomorrow
7 he had to read 100 pages tonight
   or he has to read 100 pages tonight
8 his father would not let him use his car next weekend
   or his father will not let him use his car next weekend
9 her grandfather had called her this morning
   or her grandfather called her this morning
10 he didn't have time to help me
   or he doesn't have time to help me

Practice 12, page 150
1 Tom would cook dinner
2 she would arrive at 3:15
3 Larry would take out the garbage
4 he would meet me at the library at 7:30
5 she would call me later
6 he would do his homework after dinner
7 his sister would be there
8 they would be there at 9:00

Practice 13, page 151
1 Whenever you want to eat dinner is OK with me.
2 Bob tells the same joke to whomever he meets.
3 Whoever comes to the party needs to bring something to eat or drink.
4 I hate this city, so wherever I move to would be better than this place.
5 You can sit in whatever chair you like.
6 My daughter cannot do whatever she wants. She's only 14.
7 These are all the same. You can use whichever one you want.
8 However you drive to Chicago, the traffic is going to be very slow.
9 Jack is a liar. You can be sure whatever he says is not true.
10 However you want to do it is fine. Just get the job done.

UNIT 15
Practice 1, page 152
1 is
2 wasn't
3 is being

Answer Key

4　will be
5　have been
6　was being
7　is going to be
8　had been

Practice 2, page 153
1　English is taught by me.
2　My request wasn't approved by the boss.
3　The bus is taken by many people.
4　Milk isn't drunk by us.
5　Many books are read by Francesca.
6　Pictures are drawn by Carlos.
7　This computer isn't used by him.
8　The store is managed by Noura.

Practice 3, page 153
1　The money is being hidden by John.
2　The toys are being put away by the children.
3　It's not being done by me.
4　Players are being chosen by the coach.
5　The letters are being sent by them.
6　The report isn't being written by her.
7　Nothing is being done by Larry.
8　The train isn't being taken by us.

Practice 4, page 154
1　The cookies have been eaten by the kids.
2　A new company has been started by us.
3　The letter hasn't been read by Michael.
4　We have been helped by Professor Flagg.
5　I've been bitten by a dog.
6　That movie hasn't been seen by me.
7　Our rooms haven't been cleaned by us.
8　The window has been broken by her.

Practice 5, page 154
1　My car was stolen by Jack last week.
　or My car was stolen last week by Jack.
2　The sandwiches weren't made by her.
3　A criminal was caught by the police.
4　Rosa was taken by me to the hospital.
　or Rosa was taken to the hospital by me.
5　The airplane was flown by the pilot.
6　It wasn't done by them.
7　The correct answer wasn't given by him.
8　Henry was eaten by an octopus.

Practice 6, page 154
1　A bicycle was being ridden by Francesca.
2　The car wasn't being driven by him.
3　A lot of noise was being made by the people at the party.
4　The tests weren't being graded by the teacher.
5　The broken window was being fixed by my father.
6　A movie was being watched by you.
7　The dishes weren't being done by Noura and me.
8　The winner was being chosen by the judges.

Practice 7, page 155
1　The news had already been heard by everyone.
2　A meeting hadn't been set up by Linda.
3　The work had been done by me.
4　A zebra had never been seen by them.
5　The workers hadn't been paid by the company.
6　Indian food had never been eaten by John and me.
7　The exam had already been finished by Ali.
8　The motorcycle had already been ridden by us.

Practice 8, page 155
1　The new plan will be explained by the manager at the meeting.
　or The new plan will be explained at the meeting by the manager.
2　Dinner won't be cooked by her.
3　The light bulb will be changed by him.
4　A speech will be given by John and him.
5　The report won't be written by me.
6　Your money won't be stolen by him.
7　He'll be spoken to by me later.
　or He'll be spoken to later by me.
8　The patient will be seen by the doctor at 11:00.
　or The patient will be seen at 11:00 by the doctor.

Practice 9, page 155
1　A conference is going to be organized by Paul.
2　A test isn't going to be taken by the students today.
　or A test isn't going to be taken today by the students.
3　You're going to be surprised by the news.

4　The hot dogs are going to be brought by me.
5　Their wedding isn't going to be paid for by us.
6　The bus is going to be taken by them.
7　The car was going to be driven by him.
8　The helicopter was going to be flown by Carlos.

Practice 10, page 156
1　Gunpowder was invented in China.
2　Dinner will be cooked by Michael.
3　Spanish is taught in my high school.
4　The photocopier was broken.
5　A package was delivered this morning.
6　The bank was robbed.
7　The bank was robbed by a man with red hair.
8　My education was paid for by my grandfather.
9　A new restaurant is going to be opened on Main Street.
10　The treasure was buried by pirates.

Practice 11, page, 157
1　A taxi might be taken by Mary.
2　The hot water heater was supposed to be fixed by the plumber.
3　A better job may already have been found by Paul.
4　The fuel level had better be checked by the pilot.
5　You should already have been contacted by the manager.
6　My note must not have been seen by her.
7　Your leg has got to be looked at by a doctor.
8　Her diary should not have been read by you.
9　This could have been done by anyone.
10　The project will not have been finished by him.

Practice 12, page 157
1　must have been borrowed
2　may be transferred
3　are supposed to be put on
4　might have been bitten
5　has got to be finished
6　should have been done
7　can't be used
8　had better be turned in
9　may have been sent
10　has got to be paid
11　is going to be built
12　have got to be replaced
13　might be sold
14　ought to be taken
15　won't be delivered

Practice 13, page 159
1　Michael got hurt in a rugby game.
2　I got fired.
3　The police said two guys got killed last night.
4　Paul got hit by a truck.
5　I forgot to lock up my motorcycle, and it got stolen.
6　Mark got hurt in a fight.
7　I got shot.
8　He got arrested.
9　He got kicked out of the party.
10　Henry got eaten by a monster.

UNIT 16
Practice 1, page 160
1　Although I was very angry, I didn't say anything.
2　You can go home when you are finished.
3　As soon as I saw the fire, I called the fire department.
4　I've taught French since I graduated from college.
5　In case my ATM card doesn't work, I always take cash when I travel.
6　I'm going to watch TV now that I've finished my homework.
7　Every time I think about what Sam said about me, I get angry.
8　I took a shower before I jumped into the swimming pool.
9　Until you have completed the first level, you can't go on to the second.
10　The next time we go to that restaurant, we should try the sushi tacos.

Practice 2, page 162
1　While
2　every time
3　as soon as
4　by the time
5　Once
6　As
7　since
8　As long as
9　After
10　Whenever
11　until

12 before
13 when
14 The last time

Practice 3, page 162

1 When your mother is ready, we can go.
   We can go when your mother is ready.
2 Every time she says that, it makes me angry.
   It makes me angry every time she says that.
3 Before you take the test, you should review.
   You should review before you take the test.
4 As long as you live in my house, you will follow my rules.
   You will follow my rules as long as you live in my house.
5 After I got to work, I started to feel sick.
   I started to feel sick after I got to work.
6 Whenever you need my car, you can borrow it.
   You can borrow my car whenever you need it.
7 While Noura was finishing her homework, I went to the store.
   I went to the store while Noura was finishing her homework.
8 Since we bought this printer, we have been having problems with it.
   We have been having problems with this printer since we bought it.

Practice 4, page 163

1 Now that you are married, you had better get life insurance.
   You had better get life insurance now that you are married.
2 Since you asked me, I will tell you the truth.
   I will tell you the truth since you asked me.
3 Because I wasn't careful, I cut my hand.
   I cut my hand because I wasn't careful.
4 As it was raining, the picnic was canceled.
   The picnic was canceled as it was raining.
5 Since you have failed the final exam, you cannot pass the class.
   You cannot pass the class since you have failed the final exam.
6 As the war has ended, it's now safe to travel in that country.
   It's now safe to travel in that country as the war has ended.
7 Now that the party is over, we have to clean up the house.
   We have to clean up the house now that the party is over.
8 As he is 21 years old, he can do whatever he wants.
   He can do whatever he wants as he is 21 years old.
9 Because Carl is an English teacher, he doesn't make a lot of money.
   Carl doesn't make a lot of money because he is an English teacher.

Practice 5, page 164

1 Even though we looked everywhere for our dog, we couldn't find her.
   We couldn't find our dog even though we looked everywhere for her.
2 Although I had a map, I still got lost.
   I still got lost although I had a map.
3 Even though I left for the airport three hours before my flight, I still missed my plane.
   I still missed my plane even though I left for the airport three hours before my flight.
4 Even though she makes a lot of money, she's always broke.
   She's always broke even though she makes a lot of money.
5 Although I hate basketball, I promised to go to a game with my husband.
   I promised to go to a game with my husband although I hate basketball.
6 Even though you have a headache, do you still want to go to the movie?
   Do you still want to go to the movie even though you have a headache?
7 Although he offered to pay me $75,000 for my car, I said no.
   I said no although he offered to pay me $75,000 for my car.
8 Though the doctors did everything they could, she didn't get better.
   She didn't get better though the doctors did everything they could.

Practice 6, page 165

1 in case
2 Unless
3 Whether or not
4 In case
5 if
6 even if
7 In case
8 unless
9 even if
10 unless

Practice 7, page 166

1 Mary drives well.
2 Carlos plays chess badly.
   Carlos doesn't play chess well.
3 Tom and Jerry sing well.
4 Larry taught badly.
   Larry didn't teach well.
5 They think Sofia dances well.
6 You write badly.
   You don't write well.

7 Jim swam well.
8 Michael cooks badly.
   Michael doesn't cook well.

Practice 8, page 167

1 adv
2 adj
3 adv
4 adj
5 adj
6 adv
7 adj
8 adv
9 adv

Practice 9, page 168

1 hardly know
2 can hardly see
3 hardly ever drinks
4 hardly did
5 could hardly sleep
6 hardly ever gets off
7 hardly remember
8 hardly heard
9 hardly ever does

Practice 10, page 168

1 Hardly anybody goes there.
2 Noura did hardly anything yesterday.
3 I went hardly anywhere last weekend.
4 There's hardly any time left.
5 Paul hardly ever calls his mother.
6 Hardly anything was done about the problem.
7 I talked to hardly anyone.
8 We hardly ever eat meat.

Practice 11/a, page 169

1 I thought about the football game while listening to my wife.
2 While in college, I worked as a waiter.
3 When taking a bath, you should not use a hair dryer.
4 not possible
5 You should never smoke when putting gas in your car.
6 While doing my homework, I like to listen to music.
7 While sitting in my English class, I thought about what to have for lunch.
8 not possible
9 Ali had an accident while driving to work.
10 We always watch TV while eating dinner.

Practice 12/a, page 170

1 Before taking the test, you ought to review.
2 When driving, don't forget to wear your seat belt.
3 not possible
4 I lived in New Zealand before moving to Australia.
5 Since getting married, Maria has gained 20 kilograms.
6 You should always think twice before sending an angry email.
7 Since going to Peru, I have been interested in South America.
8 not possible
9 You have to take the plastic off before putting it in the microwave.
10 not possible

Practice 13/a, page 171

1 After being married as long as I have, you'll understand what I'm saying.
   After having been married as long as I have, you'll understand what I'm saying.
2 After eating seven hot dogs, Alex got sick.
   After having eaten seven hot dogs, Alex got sick.
3 not possible
4 Sarah will graduate after taking her exams.
   Sarah will graduate after having taken her exams.
5 After living there for two years, we finally met our neighbors.
   After having lived there for two years, we finally met our neighbors.
6 After being sick for several weeks, John died.
   After having been sick for several weeks, John died.
7 not possible
8 I finally went home after waiting for Maria for one hour.
   I finally went home after having waited for Maria for one hour.

Practice 14/a, page 172

1 Not knowing who the man was, Sarah didn't unlock the door.
2 Not wanting my wife to be angry, I didn't tell her what happened.
3 Lacking experience, it will be difficult for you to get a job.
4 Speaking Spanish, Carlos understood everything Maria said.
5 Not having a car, I had to walk to work every day.
6 Having eight children, Mary and John need a larger house.
7 Living 50 miles from where I work, I have to leave at 5:00 in the morning to get to work on time.

Answer Key

Practice 15/a, page 173

1. Being overweight, it's hard to find clothes that fit.
2. Being on a diet, he didn't want a piece of cake.
3. Not being a smoker, I don't have any ashtrays in my house.
4. Being pregnant, you don't have to wait in line with the other people.
5. Being an English teacher, Carl works long hours for low pay.
6. Not being a member of the club, he can't come in.
7. Being from Canada, I'm used to cold weather.
8. Not being married and not having children, I don't need a big house.

Practice 16/a, page 173

1. Having been to Italy many times before, I decided to go somewhere else for my vacation.
2. Having broken his leg, Michael had to cancel his trip to Puerto Rico.
3. Having been lied to before, Sofia's very careful about trusting people.
4. Never having been to Los Angeles, I'm really looking forward to going there next week.
   or Not having been to Los Angeles before, I'm really looking forward to going there next week.
5. Having had dinner only an hour earlier, I didn't want to go out for dinner with my friends.
6. Having already seen that movie, I didn't want to see it again.
7. Never having been to Egypt, Francesca didn't know what to expect.
   or Not having been to Egypt before, Francesca didn't know what to expect.
8. Having had that disease before, I cannot get it again.

UNIT 17
Practice 1, page 174

1. or
2. nor
3. so
4. but
5. and
6. or
7. but
8. so

Practice 2, page 175

1. not possible
2. Francesca opened her book and began to read.
3. We can have spaghetti for dinner or go to a restaurant.
4. Mark promised to help me fix my car but forgot all about it.
5. not possible
6. My brother doesn't have a car but will buy one soon.
7. not possible
8. I can speak Arabic but can't read or write it.
   or I can speak Arabic but not read or write it.

Practice 3, page 175

1. John did too / so did John
2. Alex does
3. they are too / so are they
4. you should too / so should you
5. Mark isn't either / neither is Mark
6. I can't either / neither can I
7. Sarah didn't either / neither did Sarah
8. their parents have too / so have their parents
9. they don't
10. Linda hadn't
11. my mother wouldn't
12. his brother does too / so does his brother
13. I don't either / neither do I
14. her friends haven't either / neither have her friends

Practice 4, page 177

1. She was too.
   So was she.
2. I would too.
   So would I.
3. She doesn't either.
   Neither does she.
4. They don't either.
   Neither do they.
5. I have too.
   So have I.
6. He isn't either.
   Neither is he.
7. I couldn't either.
   Neither could I.
8. He doesn't either.
   Neither does he.
9. She does too.
   So does she.
10. I haven't either.
    Neither have I.

Practice 5, page 179

1. However
2. Otherwise
3. On the other hand
4. In addition
5. Elsewhere
6. After all
7. Furthermore
8. In the meantime
9. Nevertheless
10. Otherwise

Practice 6, page 180

1. He was happy, nevertheless, that his team won the game.
   He was happy that his team won the game, nevertheless.
2. You will, however, need an umbrella.
   You will need an umbrella, however.
3. It is, after all, the only offer I've gotten.
   It is the only offer I've gotten, after all.
4. We are, therefore, probably going to rent it.
   We are probably going to rent it, therefore.
5. It is a lot bigger, on the other hand, than our old house.
   It is a lot bigger than our old house, on the other hand.
6. He was not, consequently, able to graduate with the other students.
   He was not able to graduate with the other students, consequently.

Practice 7, page 181

1. It was such a boring movie that I couldn't stay awake.
2. We have so little time that we might get there too late.
3. He writes so quickly that he finished his book in only two months.
4. I was so sick that I had to go to the hospital.
5. John has so many problems that he doesn't know what to do.
6. It was such a funny joke that I couldn't stop laughing.
7. Sarah paints so well that people pay a lot of money for her paintings.
8. I have such a bad headache that I'm going to lie down.
9. There are so few students in our school that it might be closed.
10. My grandfather has so many grandchildren that he can't remember their names.
11. It's such a difficult problem that we may never solve it.
12. We were so careful that I'm sure we didn't make any mistakes.

Practice 8/a, page 183

(Answers may vary. More than one possible answer is given for each, and there are other possible correct answers. Words in parentheses are optional and are shown as examples. Words that would probably be ellipted by native speakers are shown in brackets.)

1. Francesca is not only beautiful, but she is (also) very intelligent.
   or Not only is Francesca beautiful; she is very intelligent (too).
   or Francesca is not only beautiful but (also) very intelligent.
   or Not only is Francesca beautiful but very intelligent (too).
2. Mark not only doesn't have a car; he doesn't know how to drive (either).
   or Mark not only doesn't have a car but doesn't know how to drive (either).
   or Not only does Mark not have a car, but he (also) doesn't know how to drive.
3. Not only is Sofia a good singer; she's a really good dancer (too).
   or Sofia is not only a good singer, but she is (also) a really good dancer.
   or Sofia is not only a good singer but a really good dancer (as well).
4. I not only went to China last year, but I went to Mongolia (as well).
   or I not only went to China last year but [to] Mongolia (as well).
   or Not only did I go to China last year, but I went to Mongolia (too).
5. Not only was the book good, but the movie was fantastic.
   or Not only was the book good; the movie was fantastic.
   or The book was good. Not only that, the movie was fantastic.
6. He bought not only 10 kilos of tomatoes but (also) 20 kilos of potatoes.
   or Not only did he buy 10 kilos of potatoes; he bought 20 kilos of potatoes (too).
   or He bought 10 kilos of tomatoes. Not only that, he bought 20 kilos of potatoes (too).
7. Alex not only washed the dishes, but he cleaned the bathroom and did the laundry (as well).
   or Alex not only washed the dishes but (also) cleaned the bathroom and did the laundry.
   or Not only did Alex wash the dishes, he cleaned the bathroom and did the laundry (too).
8. They will not only probably lose the battle but might lose the war (too).
   or They will not only probably lose the battle, but they might lose the war (as well).
   or They will probably lose the battle, and not only that, they might lose the war (too).
   or Not only will they probably lose the battle; they might lose the war (too).

9 We not only had to sell our car; we (also) had to sell our house.
  or We not only had to sell our car but also our house (as well).
  or Not only did we have to sell our car, but we had to sell our house (too).
10 Not only is it more expensive; it's not as good.
  or Not only is it more expensive, but it's not as good.
  or It's not only more expensive, but it's not as good.

Practice 9/a, page 184
(Answers may vary. More than one possible answer is given for some, and there may be other possible correct answers. Words that would probably be ellipted by native speakers are shown in brackets.)
1 The movie was neither funny nor interesting.
  or The movie was neither funny, nor was it interesting.
2 He can neither see nor speak.
  or He can neither see, nor can he speak.
3 I would neither eat them in a box nor with a fox.
  or I would neither eat them in a box, nor would I eat them with a fox.
4 Larry was neither a good singer nor a good dancer.
  or Larry was neither a good singer, nor was he a good dancer.
5 Mark neither likes to exercise nor wants to [exercise].
  or Mark neither likes to exercise, nor does he want to [exercise].
6 Neither my brother nor my sister has a job.
7 I saw neither Tom nor his brother last night.
8 Neither my computer nor Mary's [computer] is working.

Practice 10/a, page 184
(Answers may vary. More than one possible answer is given for some, and there may be other possible correct answers. Words that would probably be ellipted by native speakers are shown in brackets.)
1 I'm going to either stay home today or go to the beach.
  or I'm either going to stay home today, or I'm going to go to the beach.
2 Either John or Mary will give me a ride downtown.
  or Either John will give me a ride downtown, or Mary will [give me a ride downtown].
3 You can either have beef or [have] chicken.
  or You can have either beef or chicken.
  or You can have either beef, or you can have chicken.
4 The children can either play outside or [can play] upstairs.
  or The children can play either outside or upstairs.
  or The children can either play outside, or they can play upstairs.
5 We will either play tennis, or we will go swimming.
  or We will either play tennis or [will] go swimming.
6 This table is made of either pine or [of] oak.
  or This table is either made of pine or [is made of] oak.
  or This table is either made of pine, or it is made of oak.
7 The cat is either under the bed or in the closet.
  or The cat is either under the bed, or it is in the closet.
  or Either the cat is under the bed or in the closet.
  or Either the cat is under the bed, or it is in the closet.
8 Either do the work right, or I will find someone who can [do it right]!

Practice 11/a, page 185
(Words that would probably be ellipted by native speakers are shown in brackets.)
1 Both Mark and I are married.
2 John wrote both the book and [the] screenplay for the movie.
3 It's both a printer and [a] scanner.
4 Both Linda and Mary live in that building.
5 It's both a sofa and [a] bed.
6 There are dead leaves both on the lawn and in the pool.
7 My house has both an indoor [pool] and outdoor pool.
8 I went to both Florence and [to] Siena.
9 We have mice in both the attic and [in the] basement.
  or We have mice in both the attic and [in] the basement.
10 Both he and his wife speak German.

Practice 12/a, page 185
(Words that would probably be ellipted by native speakers are shown in brackets.)
1 I'd rather read books than watch TV.
2 Alex would rather have coffee than [have] tea.
3 I'd rather you give this presentation than I [give it].
4 He'd rather work outside than [work] in an office.
5 We'd rather camp than stay in a hotel.
6 Would you rather stay home than go to the gym?
7 The boss would rather that I handle the project than you [handle it].
8 Would your father rather play golf than go bowling?

Practice 13/a, page 186
(Answers may vary. More than one possible answer is given for some, but there may be other possible correct answers. Words that would probably be ellipted by native speakers are shown in brackets.)
1 I'm not sure whether to tell her what I think or [to] keep my mouth shut.
2 Carlos can't decide whether to study French or [to] study Spanish.

  or Carlos can't decide whether to study French or [to study] Spanish.
3 She isn't sure whether (or not) to accept the job offer.
  or She isn't sure whether to accept the job offer or not.
4 I don't know whether to say yes or [to] say no.
  or I don't know whether to say yes or [to say] no.
5 Whether to get married or not [to get married] is a big decision.
  or Whether to get married or not [to] get married is a big decision.
  or Whether (or not) to get married is a big decision.
6 Do you know whether (or not) Linda said she was going to come to the party?
  or Do you know whether Linda said she was going to come or not [come to the party]?
7 Sarah wasn't sure whether to do something or not [to do something].
  or Sarah wasn't sure whether to do something or not to [do something].
  or Sarah wasn't sure whether or not to do something.
8 Maria isn't sure whether to sell her house or not [to sell her house].
  or Maria isn't sure whether to sell her house or not to [sell her house].
  or Maria isn't sure whether (or not) to sell her house.
9 He has to make up his mind whether to major in finance or [to major in] accounting.
  or He has to make up his mind whether to major in finance or [to major]in accounting.
  or He has to make up his mind whether to major in finance or [to] major in accounting.

UNIT 18
Practice 1, page 187
1 Waking up
2 Watching
3 Not speaking
4 Being
5 Not being
6 Traveling
7 Not being
8 Giving

Practice 2, page 187
1 Not having a car
2 Seeing Larry again
3 Living in Las Vegas
4 going to Hawaii
5 Flying in an airplane
6 Talking on your cell phone
7 doing nothing
8 not doing anything

Practice 3, page 188
1 smoking
2 talking
3 exercising/not eating
4 cheating
5 speaking
6 not taking
7 going
8 not making

Practice 4, page 188
1 trying new restaurants
2 playing soccer
3 going shopping for clothes with his mother
4 having to work on Sundays
5 not going [to the funeral]
6 going to a Greek restaurant

Practice 5, page 189
1 believe in hunting
2 planning on going
3 talked about buying
4 thinking about going
5 thinking about selling/thinking about not selling
6 insists on seeing
7 apologize to her for forgetting
8 thinking about making/decided against having

Practice 6, page 190
1 have no way of knowing
2 had a hard time finding
3 having fun dancing
4 have no reason for thinking
5 had trouble believing
6 have an excuse for being
7 have a good time playing
8 has a way of saying
9 having difficulty believing

Answer Key

10 have a difficult time making
11 have no excuse for saying
12 have a reason for wanting

Practice 7, page 190
1 noticed Jack cheating
2 saw a bear riding
3 saw a hawk flying
4 heard someone opening
5 caught me taking
6 found his cat sleeping
7 observed a man taking

Practice 8, page 191
1 stopped me from playing
 or prevented me from playing
 or kept me from playing
2 thanked her for giving
3 forgive me for losing
4 blame you for being
5 stopped me from going
 or prevented me from going
 or kept me from going
6 blamed me for breaking
7 prohibited me from seeing
8 criticized me for being

Practice 9, page 192
1 excited about going
 or happy about going
2 good at drawing
3 interested in learning
4 angry about losing
 or upset about losing
5 sick of eating
 or tired of eating
6 sick of working
 or tired of working
7 nervous about flying
 or scared of flying
8 bad at following
9 angry about seeing
 or upset about seeing
10 responsible for making
11 happy about having
 or proud of having
12 used to being
13 afraid of running into
 or nervous about running into
 or scared of running into
 or worried about running into
14 happy about having
15 afraid of making
 or nervous about making
 or scared of making
 or worried about making
16 afraid of breaking
 or nervous about breaking
 or scared of breaking
 or worried about breaking

Practice 10, page 193
1 spent $225 getting
 or wasted $225 getting
 or blew $225 getting
2 spent three hours studying
3 spent ten years searching
 or wasted ten years searching
 or blew ten years searching
4 spent £3,000 getting
5 spent all day cleaning

Practice 11, page 193
1 drove around the city looking
2 stood by the window listening
3 hangs around the house all day doing
4 ran around the house trying
5 lie around the house all day not doing
6 lay on the beach all week doing
7 standing around not doing
8 sat there listening to me [and] not saying
9 sit around all night hoping

Practice 12, page 194
1 went swimming
2 go fishing
3 go hiking
4 went dancing
5 go bowling
6 go skiing
7 gone camping
8 went shopping
9 going surfing
10 going sailing
 (*Why* going *in 9 and 10? See Section 4.2/a.*)

Practice 13, page 195
1 looking forward to seeing
2 Instead of buying
3 In addition to having
4 take advantage of not having
5 takes care of paying
6 got used to not having
7 Instead of complaining

Practice 14, page 196
1 snowing/to snow
2 studying/to study
3 paying/to pay
4 going/to go
5 working/to work
6 traveling/to travel
7 listening/to listen
8 playing/to play

Practice 15, page 197
1 to tell
2 pushing/pulling
3 taking
4 to feed
5 meeting
6 majoring
7 to tell
8 to inform

Practice 16/a, page 197
1 It's going to cost $450 to get my car fixed.
2 It was stupid not to study for the test.
3 It would be very nice of you to help your sister.
4 It's important not to forget your passport.
5 It was shocking to learn the truth.
6 It isn't necessary to be big or tall to be a good soccer player.
7 It was depressing to hear all the bad news.
8 It wasn't very smart to correct my boss's mistake during the meeting.
9 It's important to be honest.

Practice 17/a, page 198
1 Your lying
2 their playing
 or Michael and Tom's playing
3 his having
 or John's having
4 their moving
5 your helping
6 her laughing
 or Linda's laughing
7 My not stopping
8 His being

UNIT 19
Practice 1, page 199
1 I'm calling her in order to ask her a question.
2 I'm going there in order to go to a museum.
3 He went there in order to get some medicine.
4 I take it in order to control my high blood pressure.
5 She went there in order to visit her friends.
6 They went there early in order to get good seats.

Practice 2, page 199
1 correct
2 I turned on the TV to watch the news.
 or I turned on the TV in order to watch the news.
3 correct
4 Sofia went to the shoe store to get some new shoes.
 or Sofia went to the shoe store in order to get some new shoes.
5 John went to the gas station to buy a bottle of water.
 or John went to the gas station in order to buy a bottle of water.
6 correct

Practice 3, page 200

1. We are hurrying so (that) we don't miss the bus.
2. Alex is studying so (that) he will get a good grade on his exam.
3. He's buying a map so (that) he doesn't get lost when he goes to Rome.
4. Mary woke up at 4:30 this morning so (that) she could get to work early.
5. I didn't go to the party so (that) I wouldn't see Michael.
6. We waited for three hours so that we could get tickets for the game.

Practice 4, page 201

1. got
2. let
3. make
4. have
   or make
5. makes
6. get
7. let
8. had
   or made
9. let

Practice 5, page 201

1. I can't afford to have my taxes done.
2. Why did you have your hair cut so short?
3. I need to have a passport picture taken.
4. Do you know where I can get a check cashed?
5. You have to get this sweater dry cleaned.
6. I'm going to get this watch repaired.

Practice 6, page 202

1. This coffee is very hot, but I like hot coffee, so no problem.
2. I don't make enough money to buy a house.
3. correct
4. This TV is too expensive for Alex to buy.
5. Does Francesca write well enough to be a professional writer?
6. correct
7. correct
8. Put on a coat. It's too cold to go outside without a coat on.

Practice 7, page 202

1. have enough money to buy
2. work hard enough to graduate
3. early enough to say
4. big enough for everyone to have
5. tall enough to be

Practice 8, page 202

1. too busy to talk
2. too badly to stay
3. too hot to drink
4. too long to read
5. too tough to cut

Practice 9, page 203

1. by taking
2. By cooking
3. by eating
4. By sitting
5. by talking / by doing

Practice 10/a, page 203

1. having done
2. having seen
3. not having returned
4. having forgotten
5. not having invited
6. having met
7. having passed
8. having made
9. not having been

Practice 11/a, page 204

1. her having been
2. Larry's having quit
3. your having told
4. Mary's having been
5. our not having finished
6. their having been
7. your having done

Practice 12/a, page 204

1. sorry to have hurt
2. sorry not to have gotten
3. proud to have served
4. sad to have learned
5. surprised to have seen
6. embarrassed to have been

7. glad to have been
8. lucky not have been hurt

UNIT 20

Practice 1, page 206

1. Whenever my brother visits, he sleeps on the sofa.
2. I feel awful the next day when I don't get enough sleep.
3. If you return a library book late, you have to pay a fine.
4. She gets upset whenever you talk about the big mistake that she made.
5. If I don't drink coffee in the morning, I get a headache.
6. My neighbors get mad if I make a lot of noise.
7. Whenever the phone rings, the baby wakes up.
8. Milk goes bad when you don't put it back in the refrigerator.
9. My knee hurts if it gets cold outside.
10. If you leave the window open, mosquitoes get in the house.

Practice 2, page 207

1. have / will lend
2. will be / don't return
3. don't give / will take
4. will be / go
5. won't buy / don't lower
6. have / will help
7. won't make / don't have
8. isn't / will cancel

Practice 3, page 207

1. says / can go
2. ought to finish / wants
3. visit / shouldn't miss
4. am / may not be
5. might not go / don't feel
6. should be / am
7. doesn't need / ought to ask

Practice 4, page 208

1. would get to / had
   or could get to / had
2. lived / would go
   or lived / could go
3. would ask / were
   or could ask / were
4. didn't have / would go
5. weren't / would help
   or weren't / could help
6. didn't have / couldn't enter
7. would go / didn't have
8. weren't / would be

Practice 5, page 208

1. am / visit
2. would buy / weren't
3. comes / will
4. has / asks
5. would play / didn't have
6. will stay / doesn't finish
7. couldn't reach / weren't
8. were / didn't have / would...do

Practice 6, page 210

1. If we had gone to Beijing, we would have gone to the Forbidden City.
2. Sarah could have made cookies if she had had enough chocolate.
3. I would have helped her if she had asked me.
4. If I had seen another student cheating on the test, I wouldn't have told the teacher.
5. I couldn't have seen anything if I hadn't had my glasses.
6. If you had been sick, would you have stayed home from work?
7. What would you have said to Maria if she had been here?
8. If it had been raining, the children wouldn't have been playing outside.
9. I wouldn't have been surprised if I had been fired for making such a big mistake.
10. What would you have done if you hadn't had any money?

Practice 7, page 210

1. needed
2. hadn't wasted
3. wouldn't have been
4. has
5. were
6. didn't have
7. hadn't fallen
8. is
9. could tell
10. wouldn't have liked

Answer Key

247

Practice 8, page 211

1. wouldn't have been/wouldn't be
2. wouldn't have had/wouldn't have
   or wouldn't have had/might not have
   or might not have had/wouldn't have
   or might not have had/might not have
3. would have visited/would visit
   or would have visited/might visit
   or might have visited/would visit
   or might have visited/might visit
4. would have gone
   or could have gone
   or might have gone
5. wouldn't have been
6. would...have known
7. wouldn't have said
8. would have gone/would go

Practice 9, page 211

1. wouldn't have needed/wouldn't need
2. would have understood/would understand
   or could have understood/could understand
   or might have understood/might understand
3. would have known/would know
   or would have known/might know
   or might have known/would know
   or might have known/might know
4. wouldn't have done/wouldn't be
   or might not have done/wouldn't be
5. would have come
6. wouldn't have run out of/wouldn't be
7. would have understood/wouldn't be
   or might have understood/might not be
8. wouldn't have been/wouldn't be

Practice 10, page 213

1. he were going to stay home
2. she didn't have so much work to do
3. my cell phone battery weren't dead
4. she comes
5. I hadn't promised my mother I'd visit her
6. I hadn't forgotten he was coming
7. I didn't have a doctor's appointment
8. (that) she wanted to go to the movie with us yesterday

Practice 11, page 214

1. see Mary today/give her this bag of cookies
2. hadn't been studying/would have been listening to the radio
3. go to Mexico City/go to the museum there
4. were sleeping/would have to be quiet
5. is fired/can easily find another job
6. had snowed a lot yesterday/would have been canceled

Practice 12, page 214

1. would you tell me
2. what would her salary have been
   or how much would her salary have been
3. could she have seen the accident
4. how many children would you like to have
5. you wouldn't have known what to do

Practice 13, page 215

1. don't have
2. isn't/don't have to
3. doesn't call
4. aren't/don't allow
5. doesn't start/isn't

Practice 14, page 215

1. aren't
2. won't talk
3. don't have
4. isn't/won't go
5. don't buy/won't be

Practice 15, page 215

1. weren't
2. wouldn't do
3. didn't eat/wouldn't be
4. weren't/wouldn't fall
5. didn't stay out/wouldn't be

Practice 16, page 215

1. hadn't been
2. wouldn't have gotten
3. hadn't been/wouldn't have been

4. hadn't been/wouldn't have seen
5. hadn't goofed around/wouldn't have had to

Practice 17, page 216

1. would stop calling
2. lived in
3. would quit asking
4. were helping
5. hadn't quit
6. didn't leave
   (*Why* didn't leave? *See Section 4.3/a.*)
7. had brought
8. were eating
   (*Why* were eating? *See Section 4.2/a.*)
9. would wear
10. were going to make
11. didn't have
12. were going to be
13. had been
14. went
15. could have gone
16. had known

Practice 18/a, page 218

1. had I known
2. Had you gotten up
3. had I not seen
4. Had she been caught
5. Had it not started
6. had your country

Practice 19/a, page 218

1. Were Carlos
2. Were today
3. Were I not
4. Were you
5. were he not
6. were it not

Practice 20/a, page 219

1. should be
   should this one be
2. should be
   Should anyone be
3. should have
   should you have
4. should rain
   should it rain
5. shouldn't be
   Should they not
6. should need
   Should Mary need

Practice 21/a, page 220

1. lived
2. didn't live
3. were taking
4. did
5. were
6. weren't

Practice 22/a, page 220

1. had kept
2. owned
3. left
4. had stayed
5. drove
6. ate

Practice 23/a, page 220

1. didn't go
2. didn't get
3. went
4. listened
5. didn't take
6. had walked

Practice 24/a, page 221

1. Would you mind if I closed the window?
2. Would you mind if we went home at 3:30?
3. Would you mind if I came in late tomorrow?
4. Would you have minded if I hadn't gone shopping with you?
5. Would you mind if I did it tomorrow?
6. Would you mind if we couldn't go to your wedding?

Answer Key

Practice 25/a, page 221

1 got
2 knew
3 bought
4 left
5 came
6 got
7 went

Practice 26/a, page 222

1 doesn't
2 don't/will
3 would
4 does/will
5 would/could/can't
6 didn't
7 didn't
8 wouldn't be/weren't
9 should have/didn't/had/wouldn't have
10 hadn't been

Practice 27/a, page 222

1 could
2 had
   or had gone
3 would/could/can't
4 didn't
5 don't
6 weren't
7 does
8 hadn't
9 had/would have
   or had gone/would have gone
   or had/would have gone
   or had gone/would have
10 would have/hadn't been
    or could have/hadn't been

Practice 28/a, page 223

1 weren't
2 hadn't been
3 hadn't
4 had
   or could have
5 were
6 could
7 were
8 would
9 did
10 did

Practice 29/a, page 224

1 didn't
2 hadn't
3 were
4 had
5 would
6 hadn't
7 did
8 weren't
9 had
10 did

Index

Index

Index

R

S

T

U

V

Index

Index